Austria's International Position after the End of the Cold War

Günter Bischof, Ferdinand Karlhofer (Eds.)

CONTEMPORARY AUSTRIAN STUDIES | VOLUME 22

UNO PRESS *innsbruck* university press

Copyright © 2013 by University of New Orleans Press, New Orleans, Louisiana, USA

All rights reserved under International and Pan-American Copyright Conventions. No part of this book may be reproduced or transmitted in any form, or by any means, electronic or mechanical, including photocopy, recording, or any information storage nd retrieval system, without prior permission in writing from the publisher. All inquiries should be addressed to UNO Press, University of New Orleans, LA 138, 2000 Lakeshore Drive. New Orleans, LA, 70119, USA. www.unopress.org.

Library of Congress Cataloging-in-Publication Data

Austria's international position after the end of the Cold War / Günter Bischof, Ferdinand Karlhofer (Eds.).
    pages cm. -- (Contemporary Austrian studies ; volume 22)
    Includes bibliographical references and index.
    ISBN 978-1-60801-116-2 (alk. paper)
    1. Austria--Foreign relations--1955- 2. National security--Austria. 3. Austria--Strategic aspects. 4. World politics--1989- I. Bischof, Günter, 1953- editor of compilation. II. Karlhofer, Ferdinand, 1956- editor of compilation.
    DB47.A88 2013
    943.605'3--dc23
                                        2013027576

Printed in the United States of America

Design by Lauren Capone

Cover photo credit: Hopi Media

Published in the United States by
University of New Orleans Press:
ISBN: 9781608011162
UNO PRESS

Published and distributed in Europe
by Innsbruck University Press
ISBN: 9783902936011
iup

Contemporary Austrian Studies

Sponsored by the University of New Orleans
and Universität Innsbruck

Editors
Günter Bischof, CenterAustria, University of New Orleans
Ferdinand Karlhofer, Universität Innsbruck

Assistant Editor	Production and Copy Editor
Dominik Hofmann-Wellenhof	Lauren Capone
	University of New Orleans

Executive Editors
Christina Antenhofer, Universität Innsbruck
Kevin Graves, University of New Orleans

Advisory Board

Siegfried Beer
Universität Graz
Peter Berger
Wirtschaftsuniversität Wien
John Boyer
University of Chicago
Gary Cohen
University of Minnesota
Christine Day
University of New Orleans
Oscar Gabriel
Universität Stuttgart
Malachi Hacohen
Duke University
Reinhard Heinisch
Universität Salzburg
Pieter Judson
Swarthmore College
Wilhelm Kohler
Universität Tübingen
Helmut Konrad
Universität Graz

Sándor Kurtán
Corvinus University Budapest
Günther Pallaver
Universität Innsbruck
Joseph Patrouch (ex officio)
Wirth Institute for Austrain and
Central European Studies,
University of Alberta
Peter Pulzer
University of Oxford
Oliver Rathkolb
Universität Wien
Sieglinde Rosenberger
Universität Wien
Alan Scott
Universität Innsbruck
Heidemarie Uhl
Austrian Academy of Sciences
Ruth Wodak
University of Lancaster

Publication of this volume has been made possible through generous grants from the Austrian Ministry of European and International Affairs through the Austrian Cultural Forum in New York as well as the Austrian Ministry of Science and Research. The Austrian Marshall Plan Anniversary Foundation in Vienna has been very generous in supporting CenterAustria at the University of New Orleans and its publications series. The College of Liberal Arts at the University of New Orleans and the *Auslandsamt* of the University of Innsbruck provided additional financial support.

Table of Contents

PREFACE ix

INTRODUCTION

Günter Bischof: *Of Dwarfs and Giants: From Cold War Mediator to Bad Boy of Europe Austria and the U.S. in the Transatlantic Arena (1990-2013)* 13

AUSTRIAN FOREIGN AND SECURITY POLICY

Ursula Plassnik: *On the Road to a Modern Identity: Austria's Foreign Policy Agenda from the Cold War to the European Union* 55

Emil Brix: *Austrian Cultural and Public Diplomacy after the Cold War* 95

Erwin A. Schmidl: *Austrian Security Policy after the End of the Cold War* 108

James Sheehan: *What Does it Mean to be Neutral? Postwar Austria from a Comparative Perspective* 121

EASTERN EUROPE AND THE BALKANS

Arnold Suppan: *Austria and Eastern Europe in the Post-Cold War Context: Between the Opening of the Iron Curtain and a New Nation-Building Process in Eastern Europe* 143

Hanspeter Neuhold: *The Return of History in the Balkans after the Cold War: International Efforts at Conflict Resolution*   167

Andreas Resch: *Austrian Foreign Trade and Austrian Companies' Economic Engagement in Eastern Europe (CEE) since 1989*   198

FOREIGN POLICY AND MEMORY

Norman Naimark: *Historical Memory and the Debate about the* Vertreibung *Museum*   227

NONTOPICAL ESSAYS

Ferdinand Karlhofer: *The Rise and Decline and Rise of Austria's Radical Right*   245

BOOK REVIEWS

Harold James: Dieter Stiefel, *Camillo Castiglioni oder die Metaphysik der Haifische*   271

Gerhard Weinberg: Birgitte Kepplinger and Irene Leitner, eds., worked on by Andrea Kammerhofer, *Dameron Report: Bericht des War Crimes Investigating Teams No. 6824 der U.S. Army vom 17.7 1945 über die Tötungsanstalt Hartheim*   274

Berndt Ostendorf: Thomas König, *Die Frühgeschichte des Fulbright Program in Österreich: Transatlantische "Fühlungnahme auf dem Gebiete der Erziehung"*   277

David Schriffl: Adrian von Arburg and Tomáš Staněk, eds.,
*The Expulsion of the Sudenten Germans
from Postwar Czechoslovakia*   282

Anton Pelinka: Heinz Kienzl and Herbert Starke, eds.,
Anton Benya und der Austrosozialismus   290

Günter Bischof: Margit Reiter and Helga Embacher, eds.,
Europa und der 11, September 2011   292

ANNUAL REVIEW

Reinhold Gärtner: *Austria 2012*   299

LIST OF AUTHORS   304

Preface

Günter Bischof

In the historical profession today diplomatic history and foreign relations are not considered sexy and fashionable topics. Many colleagues think this is a hidebound field. Young colleagues engage in cultural studies, the history of emotions, and continue to show great interest in social history and the history of minorities. Political history does not attract young scholars much either. Yet the need to assess a nation's foreign relations persists. In the past quarter century we have moved from the Cold War to the Post-Cold War era in Austria, Europe and the world at large. Yet relatively little assessment is available what the change from the Cold War to the Post-Cold War era signaled for Austria's position in the world. Austrian foreign policy went through sea changes. The country lost its exposed Cold War geopolitical location on the margins of Western Europe along the iron curtain. With the removal of the iron curtain Austria moved back into its central location in Europe and rebuilt her long-standing traditional relations with neighbors to the East and South. Austria joined the European Union in 1995 and thus further "Westernized." Its policy of neutrality—so central to its foreign policy during the Cold War—largely eroded during the past quarter century, even though *pro forma* and reasons of identity, the country holds on to its neutral position. Austrian failed to join NATO and gained the reputation of a "security free rider."

From these basic post-1989 foreign policy reorientations many subsequent political, social and mental departures followed. As a result of the country's opening to East and South, Austrian business and banking invested big time in the formerly communist Soviet satellites—since 1989 newly independent countries. Austrian businesses wreaked tremendous profits from helping to rebuild prosperity and thus "Westernizing" (not necessarily "Americanizing") the region. Austria continued to act as a "cultural superpower" and established a whole host of highly visible cultural representations in Eastern and Southern Europe. While Austria's relations with its traditional neighbors to the East and South and Western Europe flourished, and strong diplomatic representations were built in Asia and

China, relations with the United States wilted. In 2007 the Austrian Foreign Ministry was renamed Ministry of European and International Affairs, reflecting these new priorities in the world. Even the ancient locus of the center of foreign policy formulation has changed. Austrian diplomacy is no longer conducted from the *Ballhausplatz* but from *Albertinaplatz* and *Herrengasse* in Vienna's first district. Austrian diplomats, building on an old and distinguished tradition, managed to be appointed to many important assignments as mediators, particularly in the post-Yugoslav conflict region in the Western Balkans, by the European Union and the international community. Also, the face of the Austrian foreign service changed dramatically; it is no longer a preserve of male dominance—women increasingly have seized the reins of power in Austrian diplomacy. In the past quarter century Austria distanced itself from its postwar politics of history of claiming to be a "victim of Hitlerite Germany." Austrian governments concede now that many of their co-nationals had been perpetrators of war crimes during World War II and Austria took responsibility of paying restitution to those truly victimized during World War II. So, an assessment of Austria's foreign relations and international position in the years since the end of the Cold War is needed.

A core portion of the papers in this volume (Arnold Suppan, Erwin Schmidl, Hanspeter Neuhild, James, Sheehan, Norman Naimark) were first delivered in a conference organized by the "European Forum" at Stanford University and the University of Vienna in March 2009 (for the program see http://iis-db.stanford.edu/evnts/5377/Stanford-University_of_Vienna _Conference-March_5-6-2009-Conference_Schedule_-_FINAL.pdf). We would like to thank the Stanford European Forum's Roland Hsu und Amir Eshel for the conference arrangements and Sean McIntyre for a first round of editing the Stanford papers. Wolfgang Mueller and Arnold Suppan were among the Austrian participants of the workshop and kind enough to suggest these papers be published in *Contemporary Austrian Studies*. While I was a guest scholar at Vienna's *Institut für die Wissenschaften vom Menschen* in June 2012, Mueller engaged me in mapping out a CAS volume built on the Stanford papers. At this point the rest of the authors were invited to contribute essays to flesh out the range of themes in this volume (Ursula Plassnik, Emil Brix, Andreas Resch). We are very grateful to Wolfgang Mueller for his vital contribution in helping us put together the core portion of the volume—the essays dealing with the foreign and security policy issues. Ferdinand Karlhofer's non-topical essay provides an update on the state of the post-Haider Austrian Freedom Party FPÖ, the ups and downs of an Austrian policy field that CAS has been covering for the past twenty years. As always, book reviews and the Annual Review of Austrian

Politics complete the volume. We are grateful to all the contributors of the volume for their cooperative spirit in completing the editing process of their essays.

Apart from Wolfgang Mueller and the colleagues at Stanford, a number of people have been instrumental in making the completion of this collection possible. Dominik Hofmann-Wellenhof, the 2012/13 Austrian Ministry of Science Dissertation Fellow at UNO and PhD student in German Studies at the University of Graz, worked hard on tracking every manuscript through copy-editing and proof-reading and towards final publication. Lauren Capone at UNO Publishing put her customary skills into copy-editing the individual manuscripts and type-setting the final pdf of the volume. At CenterAustria Gertraud Griessner and Christian Riml conducted the Center's daily business with superb efficiency to allow the co-editor to work on his essay and manage the completion of the volume. Without the CenterAustria-UNO Publishing Team there would be no CAS series. At *innsbruck university press* Birgit Holzner was helpful with the final round of proof-reading and then producing the volume for the European market. Cooperating with her has become a big bonus in the production of these volumes. Günther Haller of the photo archives of *Die Presse* in Vienna was most helpful in helping us find the pictures to illustrate this volume. *Die Presse, Hopi Media*, and the *Austrian Press Agency* granted us rights to publish these pictures. We are grateful to them all.

As always, we are grateful to our sponsors for making the publication of the CAS series possible at all: at the Universities of Innsbruck and New Orleans our thanks got to Matthias Schennach of the *Büro für Internationale Beziehungen* as well as Klaus Frantz and Christina Sturn of the UNO Office as well as Kevin Graves, the Acting Dean of the College of Liberal Arts. We are also grateful to *Rektor* Tilmann Märk and President Peter Fos for their support of the UNO – Innsbruck partnership agenda, including its publications. At the Austrian Cultural Forum in New York Andreas Stadler and Hannah Liko have supported our work as has Martin Eichtinger, the chief of the Cultural Division of the Austrian Ministry of European and International Affairs. In the Ministry of Science and Research and its student exchange office Österreichischer Auslandsdienst (ÖAD), we are grateful to Barbara Weitgruber, Christoph Ramoser, Josef Leidenfrost, and Florian Gerhardus. Eugen Stark and the board members of the Austrian Marshall Plan Foundation have been our strongest supporters for more than a decade now. It is a great pleasure and privilege to work with them all and acknowledge their unerring support of CenterAustria and its activities.

New Orleans, April 2013

Of Dwarfs and Giants
From Cold War Mediator to Bad Boy of Europe—
Austria and the U.S. in the Transatlantic Arena
(1990-2013)

Günter Bischof[1]

Introduction

During the Cold War Austria was the superpowers' "darling" of sorts and saw itself playing a "special role" between East and West. As a Cold War neutral it played a crucial role as a mediator and "bridge builder" between East and West. Vienna was the site of important summit meetings (Kennedy-Khrushchev in 1961, Carter – Brezhnev in 1979), and long-running arms control conferences (Conventional Force Reduction Talks), as well as becoming the third host (with New York and Geneva) of important United Nations agencies like the International Atomic Energy Agency (IAEA). Austria was an important player among the Neutral & Non-Aligned states in the preparation and execution of the Conference of Security and Cooperation in Europe, culminating in the Helsinki meeting in 1975 and cementing détente in Europe, and its follow-up meetings. After the end of the four-power postwar occupation (1945-1955), U.S. – Austrian relations "normalized." Politically, Washington respected Austrian neutrality since Foreign Minister and then Chancellor Bruno Kreisky defined his "active neutrality" policy as very pro-Western. Economically, Austria continued to profit from the counterpart funds left over by the Marshall Plan. In 1961, the American government handed over the entire counterpart account to the government of Julius Raab, who initiated the *"ERP-Fonds"* as an important permanent long-term, low-interest investment vehicle for the Austrian economy.[2] Austrians' perceived their

---

1. I would like to thank both Judeh Maher for his online research in American newspapers and Christian Riml for his help with researching Austrian newspapers. For their suggestions, critiques and keen advice I am very grateful to Alexander Smith, Berthold Molden, Peter Moser, Emil Brix and Anton Pelinka. Hanspeter Neuhold graciously saved me from some embarrassing formulations relating to international law. Mistakes and ill-advised interpretations continue to remain my own.
2. Günter Bischof/Anton Pelinka/Michael Gehler, eds., *Austrian Foreign Policy in Historical*

"special case" during four-power occupation (1945-55) and then as a Cold War neutral as a "*Sonderfall*" – call it "Austro exceptionalism."

The U.S. tolerated the Austria's growing trading relationship with Eastern Europe in the 1970s but looked askance at Austrian high-tech export to the Communist Bloc during the Reagan 1980s. Culturally, like the rest of Western Europe growing "Americanized" defined Austrian youth and acted on its part as a quasi-"cultural superpower" in its representations in the U.S.[3] Austria made up its failure to integrate into the European Economic Community by closely aligning with the West German economy; while serving as a "secret ally" of the West during the occupation decade and beyond, it kept its defense expenditures to a minimum, never amounting to a credible level to defend its neutrality. Austria's neutral status was incompatible with joining NATO and the transatlantic structures and networks emanating from it.[4]

The end of the Cold War (1989-1991) dramatically changed both the U.S.'s and Austria's international positions. The United States transmuted into a hegemonic giant (what the French Foreign Minister Hubert Védrine termed "hyperpower")[5], while Austria joined the European Union and became a dwarf of sorts (in the EU and in the world at large). Since the Presidency of George H.W. Bush, Austria—with its absorption into the EU and its failure to join NATO—figured less significantly in the U.S.' geopolitics. The Bush administration virtually ignored Austria during the dramatic events of 1989/90.[6] On the mental map of American policy makers

---

Context (Contemporary Austrian Studies [CAS] 14) (New Brunswick: Transaction, 2006), 113-169.

3. Günter Bischof/Anton Pelinka, eds., *The Americanization/Westernization of Austria* (CAS 12) (New Brusnwick; Transaction, 2004).

4. Günter Bischof/Anton Pelinka/Ruth Wodak, eds., *Neutrality in Austria* (CAS 9) (New Brunswick: Transaction, 2000): Manfried Rauchensteiner, ed., *Zwischen den Blöcken: NATO, Warschauer Pakt und Österreich (*Vienna: Böhlau Verlag, 2010); Oliver Rathkolb, *Internationalisierung Österreichs seit 1945* (Österreich – Zweite Republik 15) (Innsbruck: StudienVerlag, 2006). On transatlanticism see Mary Nolan, *The Transatlantic Century: Europe and America, 1890-1920* (Cambridge: Cambridge University Press, 2012); Jussi M. Hanhimäki/Benedikt Schoenborn/Barbara Zanchetta, *Transatlantic Relations since 1945* (London: Routledge, 2012).

5. Andrew J. Bacevich, *American Empire: The Realities and Consequences of U.S. Diplomacy* (Cambridge: Harvard University Press, 2004); Günter Bischof, "Das amerikanische Jahrhundert: Europas Niedergang - Amerikas Aufstieg," *Zeitgeschichte* , vol. 28 (March-April 2001), 75-95.

6. This is the impression one is left with after reading the hitherto opened National Security Council files in the Bush Library in College Station, TX. While the Bush White House views the reform process in Poland and Hungary with baited breath (Bush even visits these countries in July 1989), the opening of the iron curtain along the Austro-Hungarian border is hardly noticed, see also George H.W. Bush/Brent Scowcroft, *A World* Transformed (New

Austria moved from Central to Western Europe (the European Economic Communities, NATO), while formerly communist "Eastern Europe" became "Central Europe," namely the new post-Communist countries of East Central Europe that were rushing towards NATO and the EU.[7]

In 1989, when the Iron Curtain came down, Austria redirected her foreign policy both towards Central and Western Europe as Ursula Plassnik explains in considerable detail in her contribution to this volume. It rebuilt traditional ties with her East Central European and Western Balkans neighbors, building stronger trading and banking ties and investing enormously in the new markets of formerly communist Eastern Europe, while completing its economic integration into the European Economic Communities. In 1995 Austria joined the European Union and both its developing "Common Foreign and Security Policy" and (later under the Lisbon Treaty) "European Security and Defence Policy."[8] Becoming part and parcel of the ever deepening European political, military and economic integration processes, Vienna realigned its foreign policy with Brussels, abandoning Washington's formerly tight embrace, which had been loosening since the Reagan years anyway.[9] Austria moved towards full political and economic integration with Western Europe but never fully aligned its security policy with the Atlantic community—thusly it never fully arrived in the West. Meanwhile, Austria's investments and trade grew with her newly democratic neighbors in Central and Eastern Europe, as Andreas Resch's essay shows, as did Austria's cultural activities in the region and her public diplomacy position as Emil Brix's essay deeply documents in this collection.

York: Vintage, 1998).
7. The State Department's changing postwar geographic assignments of Austria were always politically motivated. The State Department's official documentation *Foreign Relations of the United States* (FRUS) assigned Austria a "Central European" position along with West Germany in the volumes covering the years 1945 to 1960. In the 1961-63 volume Austria was moved eastward and grouped with Eastern Europe and, from Washington's perspective, and presumably continues to be part of "Eastern Europe" until the end of the Cold War (the FRUS volumes are now being published for the first half of the 1970s). See Günter Bischof, "Verliert Österreich seinen guten Ruf? Österreichs Image in den USA nach der Bildung der neuen ÖVP/FPÖ-Regierung," in: Heinrich Neisser/Sonja Puntscher-Riekmann, eds., *Europäisierung der österreichischen Politik: Konsequenzen der EU-Mitgliedschaft* (Vienna: WUV, 2002), 377-63 (here 39). In 1994, Clinton's State Department elevated formerly communist Eastern Europe to "Central Europe" (see below).
8. Gunther Hauser, "ESDP and Austria: Security Policy Between Engagement and Neutrality," in Bischof/Pelinka/Gehler, eds., *Austrian Foreign Policy*, 207-45.
9. Alexander Schröck, "Die US-Perzeption Österreichs in der Détente und Post-Détente-Ära," in: Oliver Rathkolb/Otto Machke/Stefan August Lütgenau, eds., *Mit anderen Augen gesehen: Internationale Perzeptionen Österreichs 1955-1990* (Österreichische Nationalgeschichte nach 1945 2) (Vienna: Böhlau 2002), 35-86.

Foreign Minister Mock is celebrated by the Austrian delegation on the occasion of Austrian accession to the European Union. Photo credit: Austrian Press Agency.

On March 1, 2007, the Austrian Foreign Ministry was renamed "Federal Ministry for European and International Affairs." This name change reflected the growing importance of "*EUropean* affairs" and the relative decline of all other foreign policy priorities. It also reflected a fear of the conservative People's Party to lose EU competencies to the Social Democratic Chancellor. Yet after 1995 Austrian foreign policy alignment with EU foreign policy made Austria part and parcel of the *transatlantic structures-sans* NATO membership, including the dramatic ups and downs during the Clinton and Bush II years.[10] With the close embrace of EU integration, Austria lost its "special" Cold War international status; one might argue it marked the end of Austrian exceptionalism.

During the Cold War the Austrian embassies in Washington and Moscow served as the most important missions abroad, after 1995 the

---

10. For three insider perspectives on the changing parameters of Austrian diplomacy and foreign policy and its "Western EUropeanization" and globalization, see Eva Nowotny, "Diplomats: Symbols of Sovereignty become Managers of Interdependence: The Transformation of the Austrian Diplomatic Service," in: Bischof/Pelinka/Gehler, eds., *Austrian Foreign Policy*, 25-38; Peter Moser, *Bewegte Zeiten: 40 Jahre im auswärtigen Dienst* (TRANSATLANTICA vol. 5) (Innsbruck: StudienVerlag, 2011), 167-74; Thomas Nowotny, *Diplomacy and Global Governance: The Diplomatic Service in an Age of Worldwide Interdependence* (New Brunswick: Transaction, 2011).

Brussels Representation received highest priority on the Ballhausplatz. Moreover, the Lisbon Treaty (2009) established the "European External Action Service"—the beginning of a EUropean diplomatic service that is bound to further absorb Austrian foreign policy with the common EUropean foreign policy agenda. Austria's relations with the United States experienced downgrading and lost its former Cold War pride of place. Vis-à-vis the U.S., Austria increasingly has been acting within this common EUdiplomatic framework since 1995. Since the end of the Cold War, Austria has become an even smaller and less significant player from Washington's perspective, especially since it failed to join NATO. As Austria's neighbors in – what Washington now calls—"Central Europe" became part of NATO enlargement, their stature in Washington grew. On their stopovers in Europe these days, American presidents visit Prague and Warsaw rather than Vienna. While bilateral economic and cultural relations are holding their own, political relations are weakening between Austria and the U.S..

During the first half of the Cold War, Washington regularly posted top-notch *professional* career foreign service officers such as Llewelyn "Tommy" Thompson as ambassadors to Vienna.[11] As Austria's importance was waning on Washington's foreign policy agenda, presidents since Richard Nixon have dispatched political appointees to Vienna. After the end of the Cold War, all U.S. ambassadors to Austria have been wealthy *political appointees*, long and strong on big campaign contributors and as "bundlers" to successful presidential campaigns but not always richly endowed with Austrian expertise.[12] Ambassadorial appointments were an important indicator of Austria's relative standing on the Washington totem pole of global significance as a country. Meanwhile, the Austrian governments consistently has been posting top diplomats as ambassadors to Washington, signaling the continued importance of the Washington as the imperial center of the world for the Ballhausplatz.[13]

Frauen-Power began to prevail both on the Ballhausplatz/Minoritenplatz in Vienna and Foggy Bottom in Washington. For the first time in history, women became principal diplomatic actors on both

---

11. In 1951 the legation in Vienna was upgraded to an Embassy; John G. Erhardt (1946-1950), Walter J. Donnelly (1950-1952), Llewelyn E. Thompson, Jr. (1952-1957), H. Freeman Matthews (1957-1962), James G. Riddleberger (1962-1967), Douglas MacArthur II (1967-1969).
12. Roy M. Huffington (1990-1993), Swanee Grace Hunt (1993-1997), Kathryn Walt Hall (1997-2001), Lyons Brown, Jr. (2001-2005), Susan Rasinski McCaw (2005-2007), David F. Girard-diCarlo (2007-2009), William Eacho (2009-)
13. Fredrich Höss (1987-1993), Helmut Türk (1993-1999), Peter Moser (1999-2003), Eva Nowotny (2003-2007), Christian Prosl (2007-2011), Hans Peter Manz (2011-)

sides of the U.S. – Austrian relationship. Prominent women ambassadors were appointed on both sides (Nowotny, Hunt, Walt, McCaw) as were the first female secretaries of state/foreign ministers. President Bill Clinton promoted Madeleine Albright, his U.N. ambassador (1993-97), to become the first lady Secretary of State (1997-2001). President Bush II appointed his NSC-adviser Condoleezza Rice (2001-5) as his Secretary of State (2005-9) in his second term. President Obama made his rival in the 2008 campaign Hillary Clinton his Secretary of State (2009-13). Chancellor Wolfgang Schüssel promoted two career diplomats as foreign ministers: Benita Ferrero-Waldner (2000-4)[14] and his former chief-of-staff Ursula Plassnik (2004-8). However, foreign policies did not markedly change or soften under female leadership, maybe due to the fact that the foreign ministry staffs continued to remain largely male bastions of power.[15] Particularly Albright and Rice were as militant in their conduct of U.S. foreign policy as their male counterparts, if not more so. Ferrero-Waldner and Plassnik were often overshadowed by Schüssel's dominant role in foreign policy formulation, especially vis-à-vis the EU.[16] Ursula Plassnik's essay in this volume gives a good summary of Austrian foreign policy priorities since the end of the Cold War and also provides a personal view of sorts on crucial turning points.

The U.S. – Austrian relationship, becoming a small cog in the wheels of EUropean – American relations, became part and parcel of the growing transatlantic turmoil. U.S. – European relations since the end of the Cold War were a story of "divergence, disagreement, and at times overt hostility."[17] The everyday flow of bilateral U.S. – Austrian relations during the presidencies

---

14. Ferrero Waldner ran for the office of Austrian president in 2004 and lost the race; she then received the prestigious appointments of European Commissioner for External Relations (2004-9) and European Commissioner for Trade and Neighborhood Policy (2009-10). The outside world presumably perceived her role in Brussels as "European" rather than "Austrian." Ever since the Balkans wars of the 1990s, the EU leadership often leaned on Austrian diplomatists in key diplomatic missions.
15. On "male bastions of power" see Gehler, "Vom EU-Beitritt zur EU-Osterweiterung," in: Kriechbaumer/Schausberger, eds., *Die umstrittene Wende*, 491. Marlene Streeruwitz, Austrian writer and feminist and critic of the Schüssel government, charged that Ferrero-Waldner functioned like a man in the male dominated foreign ministry – in fact "she is a man" – see *Tagebuch der Gegenwart* (Vienna 2002) 7, cited in Ernst Hanisch, "Die Vergangenheitspolitik der schwarz-blauen Regierung," in: Robert Kriechbaumer/Franz Schausberger, eds., *Die umstrittene Wende: Österreich 2000-2006* (Vienna: Böhlau, 2013), 405.
16. Reinhard Heinisch, "Unremarkably Remarkable, Remarkably Unremarkable: Schüssel as Austria's Foreign Policymaker in a Time of Transition," in: Günter Bischof/Fritz Plasser, eds., *The Schüssel Era in Austria* (CAS 18) (New Orleans-Innsbruck: UNO/iup, 2010), 147f.
17. See Nolan's chapter "Imperial America, Estranged Europe" in: *the Transatlantic Century*, 356-73, 331 (quotation).

of George H.W. Bush ("Bush I"), William Jefferson "Bill" Clinton and George W. Bush ("Bush II") were rocked by significant international crises that reoriented and redefined the Austro-American relationship.[18] As American foreign policy inclinations became more *unilateralist* after the end of the Cold War, they also became more imperial.[19] These, then, were the significant markers and turning points that rocked and tended to lead to a steady deterioration of transatlantic relations:[20] 1) the end of the Cold War and the fall of the iron curtain from 1989 to 1991; 2) the breakup of Yugoslavia and the Bosnian crisis 1991 to 1995 and the Kosovo war in 1999; 3) the formation of the Schüssel government coalition government with the right-wing FPÖ in January 2000 and the subsequent international isolation of Austria;[21] 4) the terrorist attacks of September 11, 2001, on New York and Washington and the following "wars of preemption" against Afghanistan and Iraq (in the case of the former lasting to this day). "Bush's wars" in the Middle East produced the worst transatlantic discord since the Vietnam War and split Europe into US-critical "old" and US-friendly "new" Europe and unleashed a global wave of anti-Americanism, spilling over into Austria as well.[22] While the presidency of Barack Obama aroused

---

18. There is hardly any scholarly literature concentrating on the specific U.S. – Austrian relationship after the Cold War. Michael Gehler's expansive chronicle of post-World War II Austrian foreign policy covers the post-Cold War foreign policy, but largely from the perspective of Austria's integration in the EU and with a concentration on the various crises; he largely ignores the U.S. – Austrian relationship. See *Österreichs Außenpolitik der Zweiten Republik*, 2 vols. (Innsbruck: Studienverlag, 2005); the best analytical introduction is Heinisch, "Unremarkably Remarkable," 119-58.
19. Former German foreign minister Joschka Fischer points out that Washington's "unilateralist inclinations" started with the end of the Cold War, see "Between Kosovo and Iraq: The Process of Redefining the Transatlantic Relationship," *Bulletin of the German Historical* Institute 41 (Fall 2007): 9-19 (quotation 13).
20. For a hard-nosed persuasive analysis, arguing for a steady demise of transatlantic relations since the Clinton era, long before 9/11, see Edwina S. Campbell, " From Kosovo to the War on Terror: The Collapsing Transatlantic Consensus, 1999-2002," *Strategic Studies Quarterly* vol. 1, no. 1 (Fall 2007): 36-78.
21. The domestic political, diplomatic, and international legal aspects of the "EU-14 sanctions" have received considerable scholarly attention, see Erhard Busek/Martin Schauer, eds., *Eine Europäische Erregung: Die "Sanktionen" der Vierzehn gegen Österreich im Jahr 2000. Analysen und Kommentare* (Vienna: Böhlau, 2003); Waldemar Hummer/Anton Pelinka, eds., Österreich unter *"EU-Quarantäne": Die "Maßnahmen der 14" gegen die österreichische Bundesregierung aus politikwissenschaftlicher und juristischer Sicht. Chronologie, Kommentar, Dokumentation* (Vienna: Linde, 2002).
22. The Bush II period has received the most scholarly attention, but usually from the perspective of deteriorating transatlantic relations. Apart from Margit Reiter's chapter on the Austrian response to the 9/11 terrorist attacks in Margit Reiter/Helga Embacher, eds., *Europa und der 11. September 2011* (Vienna: Böhlau Verlag, 2011), none of these works concentrate on Austria, see Waldemar Zacharasiewicz, ed., *Transatlantische Differenzen/ Transatlantic Differences* (Vienna: Böhlau, 2004); Gustav E. Gustenau/Otmar Höll/Thomas

great expectations in Austria too, the Obama administration has been paying little attention to Austria. As President Obama has been "pivoting" his foreign policy from the Atlantic to the Pacific, the entire transatlantic partnership has been losing its prior Cold War significance.

A preliminary word on sources: writing about very recent contemporary history can be treacherous terrain for historians used to digging up the primary record in archives. However, a "first draft of history" is possible by going to newspaper archives and online sources such as the homepages of Presidential Libraries and extensive Wikileaks files as well as a rare treasure trove of personal papers coming from a top Austrian diplomat who served as ambassador in Washington. American politicians and diplomats—with their big egos and strong sense of obligation in a democracy towards the attentive public—regularly explain their politics and world view in voluminous memoir volumes; Austrian politicians and diplomats rarely make the effort to explain their actions.[23] A scouring of such primary ego documents by Presidents Clinton and Bush, along with key cabinet members such as Madeleine Albright, Warren Christopher, Condoleezza Rice, Donald Rumsfeld, Richard Cheney, Richard Holbrooke and George Tenet leaves one with the impression that Austria has become a minute speck in the infinite universe of Washington's global purview. Thousands of pages of these memoirists have produced only a meager three references to "Austria" in the indexes of these voluminous memoirs.[24] There is considerable secondary literature both on Austrian and American foreign policy during the post-Cold War era in general but hardly any on U.S. - Austrian relations in particular.

Nowotny, eds., *Europe – USA: Diverging Partners* (Baden-Baden: Nomos, 2006); Michael Gehler, "From accidental disagreement to structural antagonism: the US and Europe: old and new conflicts of interest, identities, and values, 1945-2005," in: Barry Eichengreen/Michael Landesmann/Dieter Stiefel, eds., *The European Economy in an American Mirror* (London: Routledge, 2008), 458-499; Friedrich Korkisch," Die österreichische Sicherheitspolitik – Neue Aufgaben für die militärische Landesverteidigung," in: Alfred Payrleitner, ed., *Die Fesseln der Republik: Ist Österreich reformierbar?* (Vienna: Molden, 2002), 151-70, see also the essays by Michael Gehler of Austrian foreign policy, Paul Luif on neutrality, and Gunther Hauser on security policy in: Kriechbaumer/Schausberger, eds., *Die umstrittene Wende*, 461-625.

23. An exception is Franz Vranitzky, *Politische Erinnerungen* (Vienna: Paul Zsolnay, 2004).
24. Bill Clinton, *My Life* (New York: Vintage, 2005); George W. Bush, *Decision Points* (New York: Broadway, 2011); Warren Christopher, *In the Stream of History: Shaping Foreign Policy for an Era* (Stanford, Stanford University Press, 1998); Madeleine Albright with Bill Woodward, *Madame Secretary: A Memoir* (New York: Hyperion, 2002); Condoleezza Rice, *No Higher Honor* (New York: Crown, 2011); Donald Rumsfeld, *Known and Unknown: A Memoir* (New York: Sentinel, 2011); Dick Cheney with Liz Cheney, *In My Life: A Personal and Political Memoir* (New York: Threshold, 2011); George Tenet with Bill Harlow, *At the Center of the Storm: My Years at the CIA* (New York: HarperCollins, 2007).

Still Mediator? The End of the Cold War, the War against Iraq, and the Breakup of Yugoslavia 1989-1995

Austrian foreign minister Alois Mock cuts the iron curtain with Hungarian Foreign Minister Gyula Horn on June 27, 1989, on the Austro-Hungarian border in this staged photo op. Photo credit: Austrian Press Agency.

The Iron Curtain began to come down on the Austrian – Hungarian border on May 2, 1989, most spectacularly iconized on June 27, 1989, when Austrian and Hungarian foreign Ministers Alois Mock and Gyula Horn cut the barbed wire with much press in attendance. When thousands of East German "tourists" began to take advantage of this border opening in the fall of 1989, the Vranitzky government in Vienna was as surprised as the Bush administration in Washington.[25] The subsequent events leading to the collapse of the Berlin Wall and the iron curtain coming down on the Austrian-Czechoslovak border starting on December 17, 1989), as well as the fall of Communist regimes in Eastern Europe and German (re)unification by October 1990 rendered observers reeling—the implosion of the Soviet Union in 1990/91 left them speechless. No one had seen this coming—none of the Western intelligence service had been predicting

---

25. The best detailed analysis of these dramatic events is Andreas Oplatka, *Der erste Riss in der Mauer: September 1989 – Ungarn öffnet die Grenze* (Vienna: Zsolnay, 2009).

it. These sea changes in Eastern Europe were occurring during the very months when the Austrian government was debating a "letter to Brussels." After months of internal debate it sent the letter on June 17, 1989, asking for admission to the European Economic Communities (which by 1995, when Austria joined, had become the European Union [(EU]). Given Austria's neutral status, the letter received an "icy reception."[26] Austria began to move *westward* towards EU integration while the fall of the iron curtain opened up unexpected opportunities *eastward* as Eastern and Western Europe were growing together. The "Europeanization" of Austrian foreign policy and the questioning of its neutral status quickly gained traction. The Bush I administration was overwhelmed by the rapidity of these sea changes unfolding in Eastern Europe and reacted overly timid. It welcomed the fall of the Iron Curtain and the collapse of communism and encouraged the path of the bold Kohl government in West Germany when it rushed towards unification and integration of the unified Germany into NATO. Neutral Austria was dangling in these winds of change and quickly losing its Cold War bonus as mediator across the Iron Curtain separation. In the rapidly changing European security environment, Austrian neutrality seemed curiously hidebound. From Washington's perspective Austria became just another one of the many small European countries that became game for NATO enlargement.[27]

Saddam Hussein's invasion of Kuwait in the summer of 1990 intersected with the end of the Cold War and opened up a new post-Cold War front in the Near East for the Bush I administration—a front that is still active to this day. While President Bush acted overly cautious and slowly vis-à-vis the revolutions in Eastern Europe, he showed determination in the Near East and forged a powerful coalition that kicked Saddam out of Kuwait and invaded southern Iraq in the winter months of 1991. The United Nations sanctioned action against Saddam, which gave Austria the green light to open its air space and transit routes for American military transports towards the Mediterranean and the Middle East. During the 1958 Lebanon crisis

---

26. "An Icy Reception for Austria's Bid to Join European Community," *New York Times*, May 1, 1989, D-8. For a sound scholarly analysis, see Paul Luif, *On the Road to Brussels: The Political Dimension of Austria's, Finland's and Sweden's Accession to the European Union* (Vienna: Braumüller, 1995); for a useful survey see also Michael Gehler, *Österreichs Weg in die Europäische Union* (Innsbruck: StudienVerlag, 2009). Chancellor Vranitzky comments much more extensively on Austria's "letter to Brussels" in 1989 than the iron curtain coming down, see *Politische Erinnerungen*, 312-344.

27. Günter Bischof, "Die Amerikaner, die Deutsche (Wieder)Vereinigung und Österreich," in: Oliver Rathkolb/Georg Schmidt/Gernot Heiss, eds., *Österreich und Deutschlands Größe: Ein schlampiges Verhältnis* (Salzburg: Otto Müller, 1990), 224- 34.

Austria granted limited use of her air space for American military overflights from Germany to Lebanon; when the Americans abused the privilege and dispatched more flights (100) than had been approved (80), the Austrian government protested. Here was a first signal of Austrian neutrality policy becoming better defined between East and West (the American ambassador castigated it as "neutralism").[28] Demonstrating solidarity with the West and allowing such transports after the end of the Cold War initiated the process of eroding Austrian neutrality. Nevertheless, local peace initiatives in the Tyrol protested the transfer of American tanks across the Brenner route.[29] The first Gulf War (or the second if you count the Iraq-Iranian War of the 1980s as the first), as well as the eventual Eastern expansion of the post-Cold War NATO alliance began to put pressure on neutral Austria to begin rethinking its own role in the emerging new European security environment. James S. Sheehan's essay in this volume traces the changing nature of Austrian neutrality from the Cold War to the post-Cold War eras in a comparative perspective between European neutrals.

While the Soviet Empire and the Soviet Union imploded peacefully, Yugoslavia exploded with a bang, booming throughout the 1990s. When Slovenia and Croatia declared their independence from Yugoslavia in 1991, Austria (along with Germany) quickly recognized these two new states in the Balkans, thereby actively interfering as a neutral state in a civil war (in Serbia's view "fomenting separatism"[30]). The President of Yugoslavia/Serbia Slobodan Milosevic sent his army into Slovenia and Croatia to stop the breakup of Yugoslavia but failed to do so. When Bosnia-Herzegovina declared its independence in 1992, a protracted and very bloody war of "ethnic cleansing" ensued in this breakaway province between Serbs, Croats and Bosnians. During the Yugoslav wars of the 1990s Austria no longer pursued a policy of strict neutrality. This prepared the way for further erosion of Austrian neutrality in the following years when the conservative ÖVP was pushing Austrian membership in the Western European Union and NATO yet failed. With Austria's integration into the European Union in 1995 the country joined the EU's Common Foreign and Security Policy

---

28. Andrew E. Harrod, "Austrian Neutrality: The Early Years, 1955-1958," *Austrian History Yearbook* 41 (2010): 216-46 (esp. 238-45); see also David McIntosh. "In the Shadow of Giants: U.S. Policy Toward Small Nations: The Cases of Lebanon, Costa Rica, and Austria in the Eisenhower Era," in: Günter Bischof/Anton Pelinka, eds., *Austro-Corporatism: Past – Present – Future* (CAS 4) (New Brunswick: Transaction, 1996), 222-79.
29. Gehler, *Österreichs Außenpolitik*, II, 664.
30. Heinisch, "Unremarkably Remarkable," 126. Under international law though, neutrality does not prohibit political preference and does not include civil wars unless the rebels are recognized as belligerents. I thank Hanspeter Neuhold for this clarification.

continuing "the undeclared erosion of Austrian neutrality."[31]

The EU assumed that the widening and deepening European integration process would make wars on the continent impossible – they were wrong, they still needed the U.S. for military intervention. European Union negotiators (Vance-Owen Plan) and peace keepers failed to mediate and resolve a deepening conflict close to the heart of Europe, leading to genocidal actions by the Serbs against the Bosnian population in towns like Srebrenica. In the new post-Cold War environment, the U.S. initially expected EUrope to take care of its "backyard" and refused to get involved. Europe, however, was deeply divided and "marginalized" itself. No one wanted to touch the "tar baby" Yugoslavia.[32] When the EC/EU failed to show the muscle and use force to resolve this growing civil war in the Balkans, a reluctant Clinton Administration intervened, eventually including the use of force. Clinton's chief negotiator Richard Holbrooke engineered the "Dayton Agreement", setting up an independent Bosnian state protected by NATO and administered by the international community (the UN, EU, and the Organization of Security and Cooperation in Europe all being involved).[33] After the failure of European intervention, the Dayton Agreement brought "the Pax Americana."[34] William Hyland castigates Clinton's "first serious foray in great power politics" in Bosnia as "amateurish." His procrastination in intervening earlier may have cost thousands of lives.[35]

---

31. Anton Pelinka cited in Gehler, "Vom EU-Beitritt zur EU-Osterweiterung," in: Kriechbaumer/Schausberger, eds., *Die umstrittene Wende*, 473; see also Luif, "Austria's Permanent Neutrality," in: Bischof/Pelinka/Wodak, *Neutrality in Austria*, 143-48.
32. As Richard Holbrooke argues perceptively about the vicious circle of Europe and the U.S. expecting the other to take care of the problem: "In this sorry sequence, Europe and the United States proved to be equally misguided. Europe believed it could solve Yugoslavia without the United States; Washington believed that, with the Cold War over, it could leave Yugoslavia to Europe. Europe's hour had *not* dawned in Yugoslavia; Washington *had* a dog in this particular fight. It would take four years to undo these mistakes—four years before Washington belatedly and reluctantly, but decisively, stepped in and asserted leadership" [Holbrooke's emphasis]." See Holbrooke, *To End A War*, 29.
33. Ivo H. Daalder stresses these deep disagreements and the "Atlantic divide" over Bosnia, see *Getting to Dayton: The Making of America's Bosnia Policy* (Washington: Brookings, 2000); See the chapter "Horror in the Balkans" in Albright, *Madame Secretary*, pp. 224-44. The best inside view of the Bosnian crisis and the making of the Dayton Accords is the very readable memoir by Richard Holbrooke, *To End A War* (New York: Random House, 1998).
34. Anton Pelinka, *Nach der Windstille: Eine politische Autobiographie* (Vienna: Braumüller, 2009), 149.
35. William G. Hyland, *Clinton's World: Remaking American Foreign Policy* (Westport, CT: Praeger, 1999), 29-49 (quotation 38). More defensive of their policies are three of the premier actors on Clinton's foreign policy team, see the chapters "Bringing Peace to Bosnia," in: Warren Christopher, *In the Stream of History: Shaping Foreign Policy for a New Era* (Stanford: Stanford University Press, 1998), 343-71, and the chapter "Horror in the Balkans," in: Albright, *Madam Secretary*, 224-44; Holbrooke, *To End A War*.

Austrian peace keepers and key mediators such as Ambassador Wolfgang Petritsch were involved, too, in securing the Dayton agreements (and later a resolution to the Kosovo conflict).[36] Long before 9/11 and the "Bush's wars", a deep "Atlantic divide" began to open up with the disagreements over how to handle Milosevic and the genocidal Bosnian Serbs during this crisis. Both Arnold Suppan's and Hanspeter Neuhold's essays in this volume deal with the Balkans crises of the 1990s and Austria's role in greater detail – Neuhold's article from the perspective of the involvement of international organizations' approaches to the "Balkans laboratory."

Austrian policies in what now became known as the "Western Balkans" region in international parlance was being submerged in EEC/EU foreign policy ("with the EU and through the EU"[37]). In the wake of the quick German recognition of the new states of Slovenia and Croatia[38], Foreign Minister Alois Mock followed suit and helped speed up the collapse of Yugoslavia.[39] The Austrian people's enormous humanitarian aid to region and acceptance of tens of thousands of refugees contributed much to alleviate the humanitarian crisis in the Balkans. Austria's significant dispatch of peace keepers to Bosnia-Herzegovina and later on to the Kosovo region—within EU and UN missions—as Erwin Schmidl argues in his essay in this volume, further enhanced its role in the Balkans arc of crises in the 1990s. The Ballhausplatz's regular offers towards diplomatic mediation of the conflicts were accepted by the international community. All of this seemed to indicate that neutral Austria was looking for a new role in the post-Cold War environment, especially in neighboring regions such as the Balkans where the European Union (less so the Americans) welcomed Austrians' expertise[40]; these conflicts were close to home and threatened to spill over

---

36. The American memoirists are characteristically ungenerous in giving key European players such as Petritsch any credit.
37. So summarized by Austria's top-Balkans expert Ambassador Wolfgang Petritsch, see his essay "Recent Balkans Diplomacy from the Austrian Perspective," in Bischof/Pelinka/Gehler, eds., *Austrian Foreign Policy*, 264-79.
38. Steven Philip Kramer argues that in the first post-Cold War European crisis in Yugoslavia Germany was called upon to act as "'normal' nation through its unilateral recognition of Croatian independence" but it backfired, see "The Return of History in Europe," *Washington Quarterly* 34/4 (Fall 2012): 8i-91 (here 83).
39. Great tensions characterized the formulation of Austrian foreign policy during these years within the governing SPÖ-ÖVP coalition. Chancellor Vranitzky and Vice Chancellor and Foreign Miniter Mock did not see eye to eye in the alignment of foreign policy issues, see Vranitzky, *Politische Erinnerungen*, 149, 201-204 and *passim*.
40. Ex-Chancellor Franz Vranitzky served as the EU envoy in Albania; Wolfgang Petritsch as a EU special envoy and chief negotiator at the Rambouillet Conference for Kosovo, as well as EU Special High Representative in Bosnia-Herzegovina as did Valentin Inzko (the High Representative was the highest authority under the Dayton/Paris Agreement);

into her own territory. Yet apart from the Western Balkans region, Austrian diplomatic mediation was less sought after by the international community in the post-Cold War environment. While the U.S. welcomed Austria's cooperation during the Gulf War and recognized Austrian humanitarian efforts in the Balkans, it paid less attention to the good services of Viennese diplomats than during the Cold War. Moreover, when the later Kosovo reconstruction was lingering on, the George W. Bush administration was not impressed with what it uncharitably called the "washed up" diplomats European governments were sending to the Balkans.[41]

Neutrality or NATO?
Austria's Accession to the European Union
and Role in the Kosovo Conflict 1995-2000

Together with Finland and Sweden, Austria joined the European Union in 1995—from Brussels' perspective all three bearing "the stigma of neutrality."[42] While Austria's excellent economic performance allowed her to enter as a "net payer", her insistence on maintaining her neutral international status created many headaches in Brussels and Vienna. During the first years in the EU, Austrians warmly embraced the European Union, even though there were clashes over environmental policies and trans-Alpine traffic flows. During the first half of 1998, Austria successfully organized her first term in the revolving "EU Presidency." Austrian found it much harder though to hang on to their cherished neutral status while vowing to fully join in the new European security architecture. In 1997/98 there was a great national debate about the country's future security status. Were the EU's expanded "Common Foreign and Security Policy" (CFSP) and "European Security and Defense Policy" (ESDP) after the Amsterdam Treaty compatible with Austria's neutral status? Was Austria's growing involvement as a peacekeeper in the Balkans eroding its neutral status? Should Austria become a member of the Western European Union (WEU)

Stefan Lehne served as EU "foreign minister" Javier Solana's Balkan coordinator; the EU appointed former Vice Chancellor Erhard Busek as its special Stability Pact Coordinator in the Balkans as did Albert Rohan in the role of Martti Ahtisaari's number two.
41. The newly elected President Bush had visited Kosovo in 2001 and was "appalled by the lethargic UNO presence more than two years after the war had ended." Condoleezza Rice recalls that the "President had opined that Kosovo seemed to be where European government sent their washed-up diplomats rather than their best and brightest." She adds: "I couldn't disagree," see *No Higher Honor*, 191.
42. "Austria, Finland and Sweden in Europe's New Security Plans," *New York Times*, June 29, 1995. The Austrian Parliament did pass Art 23 (f) as Constitutional amendments to avoid legal problems with the Maastricht and Amsterdam Treaties of the European Union.

and/or NATO? Or should Austria hold on to her low defense spending and continue as a "free rider" of the Western security architecture and hold on to her cherished yet eroding neutral status? ÖVP Foreign Minister Alois Mock (1987-95) had a vision to fully integrate Austria in the West, including "anchoring it as much as possible in the Western alliance system."[43] The U.S. observed Austrian security debates carefully and – given Austria's vital geostrategic position between NATO's southern and northern flanks – would have welcomed Austria joining NATO.[44] In 1995 Austria joined the "Partnership for Peace" (PFP), widely seen as the first step on the path to NATO accession.[45] Yet while the SPÖ/ÖVP coalition government under Chancellor Viktor Klima debated these "options" for Austria's future security policy, deep partisan fissures emerged and no agreement was reached. The ÖVP and the FPÖ strongly supported joining the Atlantic Alliance, whereas the SPÖ—after a tortuous debate about the WEU and NATO options—decided not to join NATO. Andreas Khol, an ÖVP parliamentary leader, boldly predicted that "by 2003, we will be a member of NATO for sure."[46] The left wing of the Social Democrats and the pacifist Green Party saw NATO as a tool for strengthening America's "hegemonic" position in Europe and wanted to have nothing to do with it.[47] Given that two thirds of the population consistently insisted on maintaining Austria's neutral status, the decision not to join NATO was popular. Neutrality had become part of the Austrian identity during the Cold War and therefor was not easily abandoned; safely ensconced in their neutralist cocoon, Austrians lived in a Cold War time warp. For many pacifist Austrians on the Left in the Social Democratic and Green camps, NATO stood for war-mongering. On April 1, 1998, the SPÖ made the fateful decision not to support the "options report" that would have opened up the opportunity to join NATO. Austria nevertheless had signed the Amsterdam Treaty and continued to confess to support the EU's CFSP and ESDP, including support of the "Petersberg Tasks" (1992). The

---

43. Heinisch, "Unremarkably Remarkable," 122. On Mock see also Martin Eichtinger/ Helmuth Wohnout, "Alois Mock – Pioneer of European Unity," in: Günter Bischof/Fritz Plasser/ Eva Maltschnig, eds., *Austrian Lives* (CAS 21) (Innsbruck-New Orleans: UNO/ iup Press, 2012), 164-86, and idem *Alois Mock: Ein Politiker schreibt Geschichte* (Graz: Styria, 2008).
44. "Geography is the reason that NATO would it more convenient to have Austria in rather than out," see "Torn by NATO Debate, Coalition Parties Can't Devise a Security Policy: Neutrality Issue Deeply Divides Austria," *New York Times*, July 8, 1998.
45. "PFP provided a road map to NATO membership," see Albright, *Madam Secretary*, 212.
46. Quoted in *New York Times*, July 8, 1998.
47. A classic text of the Greens' anti-American, anti-hegemonic posture is Peter Pilz, *Mit Gott gegen Alle: Amerikas Kampf um die Weltherrschaft* (Suttgart: dva, 2003).

"Petersberg Tasks" have been part of the CFSP, envisioning humanitarian and rescue missions, peacekeeping tasks, and tasks of combat forces in crisis management; this agenda was also designed to combat terrorism.[48] Sending Austrian "peace keepers" to Bosnia, Kosovo, and Afghanistan as a commitment to these common European missions, needless to say, have been further undermining and eroding Austrian neutrality to the point where it has become an empty shell.[49] Anton Pelinka derides Austria's "rest neutrality" as "fictional." As long as the EU's Common Foreign and Security Policy remains underdeveloped, Austrians can live with this fiction.[50]

During the spring of 1999 the crises in the Balkans continued, this time over the future of the Kosovo region. Milosevic and the Serbs had been reducing the autonomy status of Kosovo and began "ethnic cleansing"; tensions grew in the region as a result of refugees flooding neighboring states. Austria sent its leading diplomats to the region to mediate the conflict between Serbs and Kosovars, meandering "between neutrality and European solidarity."[51] NATO decided to fly air attacks against Serbian targets in Belgrade and elsewhere. The NATO air campaign continued for 78 days (April – June 1999) with thousands of missions flown (three quarters of them by American planes). For the first time in its history, NATO—including Germany—engaged in a controversial "out of area" military operations. During the intervention Washington found it difficult to operate through NATO since the European allies were "operationally irrelevant, and the Americans had made and carried out operational decisions *unilaterally*" [emphasis mine].[52] Given that the UN did not support the NATO air campaign against Serbia with a formal resolution, Austria did not open its airspace for NATO overflights during the Kosovo crisis. The State Department's Ambassador Thomas Pickering met Chancellor Klima, when he visited Washington for the 50th anniversary meeting of NATO, asking for permission for NATO planes to cross Austrian air space on their missions to Serbia. Klima fended him off with a non-committal reply,

---

48. Hauser, "ESPD and Austria," in: Bischof/Pelinka/Gehler, eds., *Austrian Foreign Policy*, 207-45. For a dense and insightful discussion of the contested 1998 "options report," see Heinrich Schneider, "Der sicherheitspolitische 'Optionenbericht' der österreichischen Bundesregierung: Ein Dokument, das es nicht gibt – ein Lehrstück politischen Scheiterns," in: Erich Reiter, ed., *Jahrbuch für international Sicherheitspolitik 1999* (Hamburg: E.S. Mittler, 1998), 419-96.
49. Markus Krottmayer, *Die Neutralitätsfalle: Österreichs Sicherheitspolitik in der Sackgasse* (Vienna: LIT, 2009).
50. Pelinka, *Nach der* Windstille, 151.
51. Gehler, "Vom EU-Beitritt zur EU-Osterweiterung," in: Kriechbaumer/Schausberger, eds., *Die umstrittene Wende*, 481.
52. Campbell, "From Kosovo to the War on Terror," 42-6 (quotation 44).

making the State Department believe that permission was granted. It was not. The State and Defense Departments were upset and many American observers were very unhappy with the position of the Austrian government, failing to show solidarity with the West. Hungary had just been admitted to NATO as part of the 50th anniversary celebrations of the alliance in Washington and provided bases and its air space to the NATO bombing campaign.[53] Hungary's new NATO membership made Austria's neutral position more manageable for NATO and deepened the irrelevancy of Austria's ambiguous security position and the isolation of Foreign Minister Wolfgang Schüssel's foreign policy.[54]

Failing to join NATO hurt Austria's stature in the U.S. The U.S. defense alliance with the formerly communist Hungary, Czech Republic and Poland elevated them ahead of Austria towards trusted *transatlantic partnership* status. Austria dropped out of what Washington's new focus on post-Communist "Central Europe" (formerly Communist "Eastern Europe") – "the newly independent nations, wanting to rejoin the West quickly."[55] NATO accession became the fast track for them to join "the

---

53. Moser, *Bewegte Zeiten*, p. 102.
54. Schüssel was in charge of Austrian foreign policy, especially EU-policy, for 11 years, first as Foreign Minister (1995-2000), then as chancellor (2000-6). Unlike Mock, he was a neophyte without a vision – always giving priority to domestic affairs, he left Austrian foreign policy frequently isolated and "standing alone", see Heinisch, "Unremarkably Remarkable," 123f, 131ff, 148f, 150; for the opposite view, see the Plassnik essay in this volume.
55. When Richard Holbrooke became Assistant Secretary of State for European Affairs (EUR)in the summer of 1994, he reorganized the European Bureau's Central European division to reflect "the new emphasis we wished to place on that region." The "outdated" Office of Eastern European Affairs was abolished on Holbrooke's first day in office in September 1994 and three news offices – one of them dealing with "Central Europe"– were created "reflecting the post-Cold War realities of Europe.""Eastern Europe"was banned from the official State Department vocabulary and replaced with "Central Europe." Holbrooke laments: "Unfortunately, most people, including the media, still use the outmoded phrase." See *To End a War*, 7f.

Daniel Hamilton, who was Holbrooke's policy adviser in EUR, remembers the arcana of Washington "bureaucratics" at the time: "We created a new office of Nordic-Baltic affairs, (EUR/NB) taking the Balts out of the former Soviet orbit and the office that had previously been reporting to officials responsible for relations with Soviet Union and then the former Soviet Union. Politically speaking, that was the major change. Clinton had appointed Strobe Talbott to deal with relations with the then-crumbling Soviet Union; The intention had been to split the Bureau of European and Eurasian Affairs, a huge bureau that accounted for about half of the memos and traffic going to the Secretary's office, into two, with Strobe overseeing the Soviet bureau, which was transitioning to the New Independent States. But Congress -- particularly Jesse Helms, then head of the Senate Foreign Relations Committee -- objected to this, claiming that Clinton was accepting the notion of a Russian "sphere of influence." So the result was an awkward bureaucratic arrangement in which the New Independent States were simply placed directly in the Secretary's office (hence the bureaucratic designation S/NIS). It was thus not a separate bureau, so avoiding the

West." High U.S. officials—"fellow Slavs and natives of Central Europe"—such as Czech-born Secretary of State Madeleine Albright and the Polish-born Chairman of the Joint Chiefs of Staff John Shalikashvili became their champions in Washington.[56] Austria had no such champions in the corridors of power in Washington. In an analysis written in 2003 at the height of the Irak War, Ambassador Peter Moser observed that the US increasingly viewed Austrian neutrality in disbelief – even making fun of it like Secretary of Defense Donald Rumsfeld during the Iraq crisis in 2002. Washington did not understand how Austria so desperately hung on to neutrality in spite of the rapidly changing international security environment after the end of the Cold War. Washington looked critically at Austria professing solidarity with European defense efforts being organized through the EU's CFSP but not within the NATO alliance framework, argued Moser. With the new NATO members in Central Europe, Austria was becoming irrelevant for Washington as NATO was mutating "into a platform of discussions and coordination" with the new NATO members from which Vienna was absent. Moreover, Austrian companies were missing out on securing defense contracts from the European defense industry that was moving together. Austria was also losing out on the U.S. political good will that Austria's neighbors were richly garnering from their alliance membership, concluded Moser, as the U.S. routinely treated its NATO allies better than the non-NATO partners.[57] Austria's stock in Washington fell as a result of

---

Jesse Helms problem. But the Bureau of European and Eurasian Affairs became simply the Bureau for European Affairs, and the Assistant Secretary for that Bureau, eventually Holbrooke, did not have the NIS under his portfolio. Talbott also moved from this original posting—which was not confirmed by the Senate—to become Deputy Secretary of State, and he continued to oversee relations with Russia and NIS, including many other areas. In the Bush years the Bureau was made once again Bureau for European and Eurasian Affairs, and continues to be so under Obama."

Hamilton adds: "The office including Austria at the time was labeled AGS, standing for Austria, Germany, Switzerland, a Germanic clustering. This office did report to a Deputy Assistant Secretary in EUR whose portfolio also included an office called Western Europe (EUR/WE), with countries like Spain, Portugal, France, etc. A separate office dealt with the UK and Benelux. In recent years, however, there have been other reorganizations at office level, so that Germany is now part of EUR/WE, and Austria and Switzerland are part of EUR/CE, or Central Europe. There is also EUR/SCE, which deals with countries in Southeastern Europe. The organization usually has to do with resources as much as priority themes. It could change again under a new Secretary." Personal e-mail Daniel Hamilton to author, February 6, 2013.

56. Albright, *Madame Secretary*, 210, 211.

57. GZ. 3.42/10/03, "NATO und Österreich aus US-Sicht," E-Mail Moser to Foreign Ministry, Sept. 2, 2003, Peter Moser Private Papers, CenterAustria. Even though this report was written in September 2003, the arguments used were as relevant for the 1990s debates. This revealing document is added *in toto* as an appendix to this essay. We are grateful to

the botched NATO membership fight in Vienna. It dropped to an all-time low with the formation of the new Schüssel government.

European Pariah?
The Formation of ÖVP – FPÖ Coalition Government in 2000- 2001

Wolfgang Schüssel is sworn in as Chancellor by President Thomas Klestil who watches frostily as the Chancellor shakes hands with FPÖ party leader Jörg Haider. Photo credit: APA.

The October 1999 Austrian election produced close to a three-way tie among the SPÖ (33 percent), and the FPÖ and ÖVP both at 27 percent, with the right wing Freedom Party for the first time overtaking the conservative People's Party by a few hundred votes. When the Socialists failed to form a government, the FPÖ and ÖVP surprisingly succeeded in agreeing to form a coalition government. Even though the ÖVP's Wolfgang Schüssel became chancellor and the *enfant terrible* of Austrian politics Jörg Haider did not join the government as the vice chancellor or minister, the international community reacted with great indignation.[58] For the

---
Ambassador Moser for sharing it.
58. On Schüssel's leadership style, see David Wineroither, *Kanzlermacht – Machtkanzler?*

first time a xenophobic right wing party had entered a Western European government. The fourteen EU countries reacted strongly and issued "measures" vis-à-vis the new Austrian government by maintaining minimal bureaucratic contact with and isolating it. Israel withdrew its ambassador and the Clinton government recalled its ambassador in Vienna Kathryn Hall for consultation, but otherwise did not join the strong EUropean front bestowing a pariah status on the Schüssel government.[59] The Austrian Embassy concluded that the American reaction to the formation of the Schüssel government was "devastating" ("*verheerend*") to the image of the country in the U.S. While American newspapers first reported about the events in Vienna objectively in the front pages, after a couple of weeks the commentary slipped into the subjective "opinion" back pages. Especially Haider's multiple statements "friendly to National Socialist [...] tore open old wounds" and revived all the old clichés of Austria's failed mastering of its World War II past ("*Austria = Hitler + Waldheim + Haider*" [emphasis mine]). It would take years to recover from collapse of the Austrian image in the U.S. public.[60] Ambassador Moser (and his successor in Washington) spent enormous efforts on preserving a decent Austrian image in the U.S., containing the "campaign against Austria" ("*Österreichhatz*").[61] Eventually the EU appointed a troika of "wise men" to go to Vienna and take a close look at the policies of the Schüssel government and eventually putting relations with the "EU-14" governments back on a normal track.[62]

The U.S. quickly unfroze relations with Vienna, especially once the Schüssel government in the early days of the administration embarked on a remarkable new path of restitutions for World War II injustices committed in Nazi-occupied Austria during World War II in which the Clinton administration acted as the mediator. Chancellor Schüssel appointed special envoys both for negotiating restitution settlements with Eastern European

---

Die Regierung Schüssel im historischen und internationalen Vergleich (Vienna: LIT, 2009), and the essays in Kriechbaumer/Schausberger, eds., *Die umstrittene Wende*.
59. "Austria Coalition Sworn In as Diplomatic Fallout Rises," *New York Times*, Feb. 5, 2000, A-6.
60. GZ. 3.1/59/00, "Neue Bundesregierung; Imageschäden in den USA – Gegenstrategie," E-Mail Moser to Foreign Ministry, Mar. 1, 2000, and GZ. 1.30/45/03, Aug. 28, 2003, "Abschlussbericht: 4 Jahre USA, Rückblick," E-Mail Moser to Foreign Ministry, Aug. 28, 2033, both Peter Moser Private Papers, CenterAustria.
61. Ibid..
62. For a summary of these events see Michael Gehler, "Präventivschlag als Fehlschlag: Motive, Intentionen und Konsequenzen der EU-14 Sanktionsmaßnahmen gegen Österreich 2000," in: Busek, ed., *Eine Europäische Erregung*, pp. 19-74, and the Suppan essay in this volume. The Schüssel government and the Austrian press were quick to castigate the EU-14 "measures" as "sanctions" in order to unleash a patriotic backlash against the European Union, see Pelinka, *Nach der Windstille*, 154-58.

slave laborers working on the territory of Austria during World War II (the former governor of the National Bank Maria Schaumayr), as well as filling "gaps and deficiencies" in restitutions to Jews whose houses, apartments, businesses and assets had been seized and stolen by Austrian "aryanizers" of Jewish property after the Anschluss in March 1938 (Ambassador Ernst Sucharipa).[63] Based on its official doctrine of having been "the first victim of Hitlerite aggression," the Austrian government had been slow in admitting responsibility and procrastinating in making restitution payments for such World War II injustices.[64] In complex negotiations with the American government and numerous legal counsels who had filed class action lawsuits on behalf of Jewish organizations and victims[65], the Schüssel government managed to come to terms in record time and signed agreements with the Clinton Administration in its final days in office. Stuart Eizenstat, the Undersecretary of the Treasury and Clinton's chief negotiator dealing with Holocaust era assets, was impressed with personal Schüssel's engagement in the details of the "substantive negotiations [...] underscoring both his knowledge of the subject and its extreme political sensitivity." Eizenstat credited the Austrian chancellor with engaging him in "the most intensive negotiation with a head of government during all the years of my Holocaust pursuits."[66] During the 1990s Austria's politics of restitution had got caught up in the "Americanization of the Holocaust." Swiss banks, German and Austrian companies and their governments all bowed to the pressure from

---

63. Günter Bischof, "Watschenmann der europäischen Erinnerung"? Internationals Image und Vergangenheitspolitik der Schüssel/Riess-Passer-ÖVP/FPÖ-Koalitionsregierung," in: idem/Michael Gehler/Anton Pelinka, eds., *Österreich in der EU: Bilanz einer Mitgliedschaft* (Vienna: Böhlau, 2003), pp. 445-78; Günter Bischof/Michael S. Maier, „Reinventing Tradition and the Politics of History: Schüssel's Restitution and Commemoration Policies," in Günter Bischof/Fritz Plasser, eds., *The Schüssel Era in Austria* (CAS 18) (New Orleans-Innsbruck: uno press-iup, 2010), pp. 206-34; on Schüssel's „politics of history" and the restitution negotiations, see also the essays by Robert Kriechbaumer, Ernst Hanisch and Michael Gehler in Kriechbaumer/Schausberger, eds., *Die umstrittene Wende*, pp. 183-210, 397-416, 497-508.
64. For a tight summary of the spillover of "the Americanization of the Holocaust" ever since the "Waldheim fiasco" of the late 1980s, see Christian Thonke, *Hitlers Langer Schatten: Der mühevolle Weg zur Entschädigung der NS-Opfer* (Vienna: Böhlau, 2004). For a comparative perspective on the international politics of restitutions after totalitarian regimes, see Oliver Rathkolb, ed., *Revisiting the National Socialist Legacy: Coming to Terms with Forced Labor, Expropriation, Compensation, and Restitution* (Innsbruck: StudienVerlag, 2002).
65. One such group was the Claims Conference pressuring "the Austrian government to acknowledge complicity during the Nazi regime and to improve reparations to Jews", see "Holocaust Group to Step Up Pressure on Austria for Reparations," *New York Times*, July 20, 2000, A-5.
66. Stuart E. Eizenstat, *Imperfect Justice: Looted Assets, Slave Labor, and the Unfinished Business of World War II* (New York: Public Affairs, 2003), 298.

Washington during the late Clinton years to come clean of their failed or procrastinated restitution politics of the past.[67]

Peter Moser, the Austrian Ambassador to the U.S. (1999-2003), managed Austrian relations with the Clinton (and then Bush II) governments during these difficult years when Austria sunk to "pariah" status.[68] He travelled the country and spoke to many different audiences explaining that the Schüssel government had been formed meeting all provisions of the Austrian constitution. While Haider's FPÖ may have been obnoxious and appealing to the prejudiced and xenophobic elements in society, it was not "neo Nazi." The poisonous Governor of Carinthia Haider made life difficult for his own party and the government coalition with his two superfluous visits of Saddam Hussein in Bagdad. Vice Chancellor Susanne Riess-Passer from the FPÖ came to the opening of the Winter Olympics in Salt Lake City in February 2002. Her party "boss" Haider surprised her with a call that he had just visited Saddam on a "humanitarian mission." During her visit to Washington, the Vice Chancellor dismissed Haider's "private exploits" (*Privataktion*). The State Department spokesman noted that Haider's visit was "a punch in the face of the civilized world", then pooh-poohed Haider's visit as "Saddam Hussein and Jörg Haider—birds of the same feather stick together."[69] Next to playing fire brigade with the State Department over Haider "going off the reservation", Moser walked the halls of Congress tirelessly to prevent even harsher American reactions vis-à-vis the new governing coalition such as "freezing" relations with Austria. Appealing to the Jewish electorate, Tom Lantos (D-CA) wanted the House of Representatives to pass a resolution calling Haider's party a "Neo-Nazi" party and boycotting Austrian businesses (trade with Austria, tourism, flights by Austrian Airlines etc.). Ambassador Moser managed to have the Resolution railroaded towards insignificance by the House leadership and thereby preventing the U.S. response becoming even more severe than the "EU-14 measures." During the period when Washington's relations were "frozen" with Austria, official Austrian visitors did not get appointments with their high level counterparts in the Washington government and bureaucracy. Starting in June 2000, with the visit of the Austrian Interior

---

67. On the spillover effects of the "Americanization of the Holocaust" ever since the 1980s "Waldheim fiasco", see Thonke, *Hitlers Langer Schatten*, 88-105.
68. The *Times* dedicated a story to Moser's "nightmare" days, see "Diplomat Picks Up the Pieces of Austria's Broken Image," *New York Times*, Feb. 14, 2000, 14.
69. This episode is recounted in Moser, *Bewegte Zeiten*, 145; see also "Iraq-Reise: Entsetzen über Haiders Besuch bei Saddam," *Der Spiegel*, Feb. 12, 2002 http://www.spiegel.de/politik/ausland/irak-reise-entsetzen-ueber-haiders-besuch-bei-saddam-a-182066.html (accessed February 5, 2013).

Minister, the ice was broken and meetings on the ministerial level were restarted.[70]

Since the late 1990s restitution of famous art treasures "expropriated" during the World War II era became another big issue in Austrian – American relations.[71] As soon as he arrived in the U.S., Ambassador Moser was confronted with two famous Egon Schiele pictures ("Portrait of Wally" and "*Tote Stadt* III") on loan from the Leopold Foundation Museum in Vienna for an exhibit to the Museum of Modern Art in New York; they were seized by the New York District Attorney's Office. Descendants of the former proprietors claimed the pictures as their inheritance. After a long court battle Ambassador Moser managed to snag *Tote Stadt* III from the U.S. authorities in September 2009, put it on a plane and sent it back to Austria ("*Wally*" was bought back in 2010). Moser was not so lucky with the "Portrait of Adele Bloch-Bauer I" (known as the "Golden Adele"), a famous Gustav Klimt painting that had been hanging since World War II in the Austrian Gallery in Vienna. The picture had a similarly complex history of previous ownership and ended up property of the Austrian state. "Adele I" was claimed by the legal heiress, Adele's niece Maria Altmann, a Jewish refugee from Vienna living in Los Angeles since World War II. After an even longer court battle going all the way to the U.S. Supreme Court and ending in mediation, Altmann was proclaimed the legal heir. Billionaire Ronald Lauder, an heir to a cosmetics empire and the former American ambassador in Austria, bought the picture for an alleged $137 million, at the time the highest price ever paid for a painting. Today it is a masterpiece hanging in Lauder's "Neue Gallerie" in New York. "Adele's" departure to New York is considered a significant loss to Austria's famed artistic patrimony.[72]

---

70. Peter Moser is the rare ambassador to write memoirs. These memoirs are a great source of information for historians and intimately document this period of Austrian-American relations exceptionally well, see his *Bewegte Zeiten*, pp. 101-21; see also GZ. 1.30/45/03, Aug. 28, 2003, "Abschlussbericht: 4 Jahre USA, Rückblick," E-Mail Moser to Foreign Ministry, Aug. 28, 2033, Peter Moser Private Papers, CenterAustria. Based on reports like this one and a treasure trove of personal papers, Moser wrote these memoirs while serving as the Marshall Plan Chair at UNO in 2009/2010. He donated these private papers to CenterAustria at UNO and they are utilized here for the first time.
71. A good introduction to the larger issues of Nazi art theft in Austria are the essays in Verena Pawlowsky/Harald Wendelin, eds., *Enteignete Kunst: Raub un Rückgabe – Österreich von 1938 bis heute* (Vienna: Mandelbaum, 2006); for the larger background of Nazi art politics, see Jonathan Petropoulos, *The Faustian Bargain: The Art World in Nazi Germany* (New York: Oxford University Press, 2000).
72. For a good summary of the complex legal and diplomatic issues, see Moser, *Bewegte Zeiten*, 102, 136-42; see also the documentary *Adele's Wish* by Terence Hunter, Calendar Films 2008.

Chancellor Schüssel visits President at the White House on October 31, 2001. Photo credit: APA.

During the late Clinton years Austrian relations with the United States hit some rocky patches. Austrian reactions to the contested November 2000 elections of George W. Bush, often disparagingly called "the cowboy" from Texas, were as critical as in the rest of Western Europe. Relations remained frosty during early visits. Moser suggested to Vienna to overcome the bad blood with a visit from Chancellor Schüssel. The Bush White House not only granted an appointment with the President, but also invited the Schüssel delegation to stay in "Blair House," the president's guest house for official high level visitors to Washington. Only Chancellor Kreisky had been given the honor to stay in this official U.S. government residence by President Gerald Ford, when he visited in the mid-1970s. Chancellor Schüssel visited Washington on October 31, 2001, only a few weeks after the September 11 attacks. He had lunch with a number of senators and an appointment with Bush in the White House where Iran and Iraq were prominent issues discussed. The Chancellor then went to New York and visited the 9/11 site and mayor Rudolf Giuliani. Schüssel refused to be interviewed by the famous CNN host Larry King – a great mistake in Moser's estimation to improve Austria's image in the U.S. The high level Schüssel visit, however, "normalized" relations after the rocky Clinton years.⁷³ The honeymoon did not last long.⁷⁴

A Neutral Stuck in 'Old Europe'?
Terrorism and the Bush Wars (2001-2008)

When the terrorists attacks crashed their planes into the towers of the World Trade Center in New York and into the Pentagon in Washington on September 11, 2001 ("9/11"), the American mainland was attacked from the outside for the first time in American history (the Japanese attack on Pearl Harbor on December 7, 1941, was an attack on American overseas territory—Hawaii only became a state of the union in 1958).⁷⁵ The world and international politics changed forever as a result of these brazen and bloody attacks into the hearts of American financial and military power (a fourth plane, probably directed against the Capitol, the heart of American political power, was brought down by the passengers in Pennsylvania). The Bush II administration was shocked and angered—Americans were sickened and deeply hurt.⁷⁶ European governments and publics quickly proclaimed their deep sympathy for the victims and their families and their "undivided solidarity" with Americans. The Austrian government, too, chimed in with this chorus of enormous pain and regret. Politicians

---

73. Moser, *Bewegte Zeiten*, pp. 142-44. Eva Male, the Washington correspondent of *Die Presse*, reported that the Bush administration wanted to get to know one of the few conservative chancellors in Europe, was grateful for the Austrian support in the "war on terror" (Austria had allowed overflights and cooperated in tightening the banking laws), and wanted to pay tribute to Austria's restitution legislation compensating Holocaust victims, see "Post 9/11: Zusammenarbeit zur Terrorbekämpfung/Sanktionen u. Haider kein Thema," *Die Presse*, Nov. 2, 2011.
74. The ups and downs of U.S. – Austrian relations can also be gleaned from the writings of Austrian reporters that covered the Clinton and Bush years. For a superficial book written by a television journalist in the breathless style of a diarist, see Eugen Freund, *Mein Amerika: Bestandaufnahmen, Beobachtungen, Berichte 1995-2001* (Klagenfurt: Wieser, 2001). For more thoughtful reflections by a print journalist, see Eva Male, "I feel like I have two homes, or maybe none at all ... Four years [1999-2003] in the United States as a Correspondent for the Austrian Daily *Die Presse*," in: Günter Bischof/Anton Pelinka/Hermann Denz, eds., *Religion in Austria* (CAS 13) (New Brunswick: Transaction, 2005), 165-75.
75. For a comparison of the Pearl Harbor and the 9/11 attacks within their respective historical contexts, see John W. Dower, *Cultures of War: Pearl Harbor/Hiroshima/9-11/Iraq* (New York: W. W. Norton, 2010).
76. The profound shock produced by the 9/11 attacks and deep-seated fear and paranoia about more attacks is a principal theme in the memoirs of all the members of the Bush administration, see Melvyn P. Leffler, "The Foreign Policies of the George W. Bush Administration: Memoirs, History, Legacy," *Diplomatic History* 37 (April 2013): 190-216 (esp. 199f).

and commentators joined the European community of solidarity with Americans. Yet solidarity soon turned to questioning attitudes, blaming Americans themselves and their policies in the Near East and elsewhere for the attacks; finally came naughty *Schadenfreude*—the "hegemonic" Americans have been asking for this.[77]

The "Bush revolution" and his policies of "preemption" had been long in the making. Some of his foreign policy advisers like Paul Wolfowitz and Dick Cheney—called the "Vulcans"—had been calling for a new policy of anticipating threats and preempting them with the help of "ad-hoc coalitions of the willing" since the early 1990s. Bush's determined foreign policy team detested Clinton's cautious and often indecisive engagement of the world – along with his humoring of reluctant allies like the Europeans; the "Vulcans" had only disdain for Clinton's reliance on multilateral frameworks (be it the United Nations or NATO, the Kyoto Protocol), or nuclear disarmament such as the bilateral U.S.-Soviet ABM treaty. Any close Austrian or European observer following the details of Bush presidential campaign should have discerned this.[78] The massive shock of the 9/11 attacks gave the Bush White House the cause and the wherewithal to implement what had been brewing in the "neo-conservative" foreign policy community and Republican think tanks; the Bush administration embarked on bold new policies. The relentless "war on terror" painted the world in black and white ("those that are for us and those that are against us").[79] 10 years after the Iraq invasion Cheney is still unapologetic about this disastrous war.[80] Europeans never fully appreciated Americans' dark reading of 9/11 and the new strategic realities in Washington's global war on terror, where NATO and Europe no longer were any longer on top of the U.S. foreign policy priority list.[81]

---

77. Margit Reiter, "Signaturen des 11. September, 2001 in Österreich," in idem/Embacher, eds., *Europa und der 11. September 2001*, 161-92
78. Joschka Fischer believes that the U.S. abandoned its consensual Cold War *modus operandi* within a multilateral transatlantic framework in the final Clinton years, drawing the wrong conclusions from the Kosovo air campaign, arguing that "coalition war" was too complicated and "going it alone" was easier, see "Between Kosovo and Iraq," 13.
79. Anatol Lieven, *American Right or Wrong: An Anatomy of American Nationalism* (New York: Oxford University Press, 2004), 72-80.
80. "Iraq_Krieg: Dick Cheney hat ein reines Gewissen," *Die Presse*, March 20, 2013 http://diepresse.com/home/politik/aussenpolitik/1378658/IrakKrieg_Dick-Cheney-hat-ein-reines-Gewissen?_vl_backlink=/home/politik/aussenpolitik/1377526/index.do&direct=1377526 (accessed March 22, 2013); Cheney is similarly dismissive of critics in his memoirs.
81. Campbell, "From Kosovo to the War on Terror," 46-61; Ivo H. Daalder/James M. Lindsay, *America Unbound: The Bush Revolution in Foreign Policy* (Washington: Brookings, 2003).

Between the campaign launched against Afghanistan (October 2001) and the war unleashed against Iraq (March 2003), Austria joined the "coalition of the unwilling" in Europe that produced enormous *transatlantic discord*. While most European allies and the Austrians by and large supported the intervention against Afghanistan to clean out the Al Qaeda nests and remove the Taliban regime ("non-military solidarity"), Austria was not prepared to contribute troops, if the Americans had wanted it ("military solidarity"). Austrian neutrality was not entirely obsolete.[82] Western European allies began to part ways with the Bush administration when the CIA began to round up suspected terrorists from the Afghanistan/ Pakistan/Iraq to the Balkans and detain them on the American naval base in Guantanamo, Cuba, without extending them the protections for "prisoner of war" under the Geneva Convention. Yet at the same time many European allies – among the 54 nations, Austria included – cooperated with the Bush administration in the CIA's top secret "rendition" program, as has been revealed by the Open Society Institute in a February 2013 report.[83] There may have been more collusion between the Bush and Schüssel governments in the post-9/11 era than we know today.

President Bush announced a new "strategy of preemption" in 2002 to fight terrorists worldwide (the "Bush Doctrine").[84] At this point many Europeans saw the new policy as a departure from America's foreign policy traditions and began to part ways. The Iraq war unleashed was a turning point. Bush intervened in Iraq—without the authorization to use force by a resolution of the UN Security Council—to topple the "rogue" Saddam

---

82. "Was Österreichs Neutralität alles nicht verbietet. Teilnahme an kollektiver Selbstverteidigung," *Die Presse*, Sept. 26, 2001; see the op-ed – critical of Austrian "neutralism" – by Wolfgang Streitenberger, "Solidarität: Was verstehen die Österreicher darunter? Eine beunruhigende Frage," *die Presse*, Sept. 25, 2001; see also Gehler, "Vom EU-Beitritt zur EU-Osterweiterung," in: Kriechbaumer/Schausberger, eds., *Die umstrittene Wende*, 512f..

83. "Austria permitted the use of its airspace for flights associated with CIA extraordinary rendition, and may have assisted with the apprehension of an Austrian resident extraordinary rendition victim." See Open Society Justice Initiative, *Globalizing Torture: CIA Secret Detention and Extraordinary Rendition* (New York, 2013), 67f (here 67) http://www.opensocietyfoundations.org/sites/default/files/globalizing-torture-20120205.pdf (accessed Feb. 7, 2013); see also "54 Staaten halfen CIA mit verschleppten Terrorverdächtigen, " *Der Standard*, Feb. 5, 2013, http://derstandard.at/1358305742204/Bericht-54-Staaten-halfen-CIA-mit-verschleppten-Terrorverdaechtigen (accessed Feb. 7, 2013).

84. For excellent analyses of Bush's foreign policies see Timothy Naftali's essay on the war on terror and Fredrick Logevall's essay on Bush Iraq invasion in Julian E. Zelizer, ed., *The Presidency of George W. Bush* (Princeton, 2010), 59-113. Leffler notes that the doctrine of preemption (drafted by Rice's friend Philip Zelikow) did not play as prominent a role in the White House as many of Bush's critics have it – it was designed more to be an ideological statement like the famous "NSC 68" document, see Leffler, 203.

Hussein regime. Saddam allegedly harbored terrorists and was hiding an arsenal of "weapons of mass destruction" (WMD).[85] Key European countries like Russia and allies such as Germany, France and Belgium, as well as the neutrals, did not join the "coalition of the willing" that supported Bush in the Iraq war. Secretary of Defense Donald Rumsfeld castigated these dissenters in Europe as "old Europe," while supporters of the war such as Spain, Italy and Great Britain, along with the new NATO allies Poland, Hungary and the Czech Republic, now were advertised as the "new Europe."[86] Rumsfeld's statement further aggravated the deep European divisions over American policy in Iraq. Moreover, Washington did not understand the "endless European infighting" during times of crises. The spring of 2003 is generally seen as the nadir of transatlantic relations (Austrian – American relations included).[87] National Security adviser Rice recalled that the President was "particularly shocked" about the Germans since Chancellor Schröder had led Washington to believe that he would support the U.S. action against Saddam "as long as it was quick." Rice's advice to President Bush in getting back at these recalcitrant European triumvirate was "punish France, forgive

---

85. Cheney keeps insisting that terrorists at WMD were the principal causes of the U.S. war against Iraq, see Cheney, *In My Life*, 411-20; Rice gives a more nuanced explanation, *No Higher Honor*, 194-24; Rumsfeld claims surprise, when it became clear that Saddam's alleged WMD caches were not found and the debate shifted to democracy promotion after intelligence failure—("the shift to democracy seemed to some as a way to change the subject"), Rumsfeld, *Known and Unknown*, 500; Tenet asserts that the WMD threat in Saddam's Iraq was manufactured in Washington – it was an obsession with people like Cheney. The U.S. "did no go to war in Iraq solely because of WMD, I doubt it was even the principal cause. Yet it was the public face that was put on it," see *At the Center of the Storm*, 301-39 (quotation 331). Leffler surely is correct in arguing that the Bush era memoirists like to "blame one another" when trying to "blunt the attacks of their critics," see Leffler, "Foreign Policies of Bush," 206

86. Rumsfeld insists that the comment was "unintentional" and amused that it "entered the vernacular"; he was surprised that it "touched a raw nerve", see *Known and Unknown*, 444f.

87. Günter Bischof, "American Empire and Its Discontents: The United States and Europe Today," in: idem/Michael Gehler/Volker Kühnhardt/Rolf Steininger, eds., *Towards a European Constitution: A Historical and Political Comparison with the United States* (Vienna: Böhlau 2005), pp. 185-207; Reinhard Heinisch, "Ungeliebt und unverstanden – die Beziehungen zwischen den USA und Europa aus amerikanischer Sicht," in: Reiter/Embacher, eds., *Europa und der 11. September* 2001, 193-220; William W. Boyer, "Confronting Transatlantic Discord: Major Policy Differences between the United States and Europe," in: Zacharasiewicz, ed., *Transatlantische Differenzen*, pp. 79-94; Philip Gordon, "Bridging the Atlantic Divide," *Foreign Affairs* 82/1 (January/February 2003): 70-83. This deep "transatlantic divide" was also extensively analyzed in a special report prepared by the Austrian Embassy for the Foreign Ministry, "Wie tief ist die Krise in den Transatlantischen Beziehungen? Eine Übersicht über Zustand und Zukunft der transatlantischen Beziehungen aus amerikanischer Sicht," Peter Moser Private Papers, CenterAustria.

Russia, and ignore Germany."⁸⁸ The Iraq War unleashed the worst crisis in US – EU relations since the existence of the European Communities.⁸⁹

Chancellor Schüssel explains Austria's position on the U.S. invasion of Iraq to parliament. Photo Credit: Presse.

Austria was firmly in the camp of "old Europe"; most Austrians shared in the uniformly hostile critique of the Bush policies in the Near East. After September 11, many Austrians, too, quickly moved from solidarity to *Schadenfreude*, descending into conspiracy history and blaming the Americans themselves for the 9/11 attacks.⁹⁰ Since Bush failed to get a UN Resolution to support his war against Iraq, Austria closed its air routes and roads to American overflights and transports from German bases to the Mediterranean and Near East. The Iraq war was not a NATO-campaign, but many of the new NATO members from "Central Europe" eagerly supported Bush's Iraq invasion to demonstrate their reliability as the allies of "new Europe." Neutral Austria was firmly in the camp of "old Europe" (Germany, France, Belgium) protesting against the war, distancing itself

---

88. Rice, *Ho Higher Honor*, 202, 212-15.
89. Gehler, "Vom EU-Beitritt zur EU-Osterweiterung," in: Kriechbaumer/Schausberger, eds., *Die umstrittene Wende*, 513. Gehler adds that the Iraq War was a major defeat for U.S. diplomacy and its failure in building a solid "coalition of the willing."
90. For an excellent summary of Austria's 9/11 responses, see Margit Reiter, "Signaturen des 11. September 2001 in Österreich," in idem/Embacher, eds., *Europa und der 11. September 2001*, 161-92.

even further from Bush's Washington. Almost fifty percent of the Austrian population was against the war in Iraq, the opposition Social Democratic and Green parties argued that Bush's war broke international law.[91] Peter Pilz of the Green Party, denouncing the Washington government as the "junta of the bushmen,"[92] charged the Schüssel coalition government for having secretly allowed American overflights during the Afghanistan campaign and maybe doing so again in the Iraq war without presenting evidence.[93] In Vienna and many Western European capitals there were massive anti-war demonstrations against "Bush's war." Along with many Western European publics, a major upsurge of anti-Americanism marked Austrian public opinion too.[94] Marc Trachtenberg's spirited defense of America's international law position in the Iraq War suggests how ill-intentioned many of these European critiques were and how much they hurt the future of the NATO alliance.[95]

On May 1, 2004, Poland, Hungary, the Czech Republic, Slovakia, and Slovenia as well as the three Baltic States joined the European Union. After the deep divisions over the Iraq war, this move brought "old" and "new" Europe together and anchored these former communist nations more firmly in the West. Austria had supported these nations accession to the EU with all kinds of technical help.[96] However, many Austrians did not welcome EU-Eastern expansion. Due to a feared influx of cheap labor from these new EU members, the Socialist Labor Unions and some conservatives militated against it; the populist Freedom Party kept sniping against the accession of the Czech Republic unless they rescinded the "Beneš decrees" (1943-45) that led to the deportation of some three million Germans and Hungarians from Czechoslovakia (1945-47); a broad segment of Austrian

---

91. "Umfragen; Österreicher lehnen Militärschlag gegen Irak ab," *Die Presse*, Nov. 2, 2003; "Kein Konsens in Österreich zu Iraq-Krieg," *Die Presse*, March 25, 2003.
92. Pilz, *Mit Gott gegen alle*, 260. Green Party foreign policy spokesperson Ulrike Lunacek attacked Bush Ambassador Lyons Brown in an open letter printed in *Der Standard* for using napalm bombs again in Iraq, having learned no lessons from Hiroshima/Nagasaki and Vietnam, see her collection *Zwischenrufe: Kolumnen, Kommentare, Interviews* Vienna: Milena, 2006), 219-21.
93. "Guter Glauben," *Der Standard*, Jan. 8, 2003.
94. On the long history of Austrian anti-Americanism, see Günter Bischof, "Two Sides of the Coin: The Americanization of Austria and Austrian Anti-Americanism," in: Alexander Stephan, ed., *The Americanization of Europe: Culture, Diplomacy, and Anti-Americanism after 1945* (New York: Berghahn 2006), 147-81.
95. See his article "The Iraq Crisis and the Future of the Western Alliance," in *idem*, *The Cold War and After: History, Theory, and the Logic of International Politics* (Princeton, 2012), 281-311.
96. Martin Sajdik/Michael Schwarzinger, *European Union Enlargement: Background, Developments, Facts* (New Brunswick: Transaction, 2008).

society demanded stricter controls on the Czech nuclear energy industry.[97] Washington did not consider Austria part of the "Central Europe" due to her failure to join NATO; her old neighbors—and new EU members—did not consider Austria part of their grouping as a result of Vienna's mixed record in welcoming them, in spite of the Ballhausplatz's efforts to form a "strategic partnership" with them. Schüssel failed to reign in his Freedomite coalition partners and their constant sniping against EU Eastern expansion and thus further isolated Austrian foreign policy.

In spite of the Iraq war descending into a violent slugging match with local guerillas and terrorists, George W. Bush was re-elected in November 2004. He had begun rebuilding bridges with "Old Europe" and visited Rome and Paris during his visit as part of the 60th anniversary of the Normandy invasion in June 2004.[98] He continued to "sooth tensions", visiting Brussels, Germany and Slovakia in February 2005 and Italy, the Netherlands, Latvia, Russia, Georgia, Denmark, culminating in a G-8 meeting in Scotland in April 2005. The Bush Administration clearly snubbed Austria during the May 2005 50th anniversary ceremonies in Vienna of the signing of the Austrian State Treaty in 1955 by sending retired Minnesota Senator Rudy Boschwitz to represent the U.S. in lieu of Secretary of State Condoleezza Rice (as one Vienna sage put it: "Who the hell is Rudy Boschwitz?"). Ursula Plassnik clearly suggests in her contribution to this volume that the Ballhausplatz took it as an egregious offense. For President Bush it was "pay-back time" for Austria joining "old Europe" in opposing his war in Iraq.

In the first half of 2006 Austria for the second time (after the first Presidency during January-June 1998) headed the revolving EU-Presidency and Ursula Plassnik notes how much the organization these EU presidencies was a "trial by fire" for a small EU country like Austria. In June 2006 President Bush came to Vienna for a summit—a day of consultations—with EU leaders during the Austrian EU-Presidency. Under the coordination of Eva Nowotny, Austria's ambassador to the U.S., both sides worked very hard to agree on a "Vienna Summit Declaration" (June 21, 2006) in which a transatlantic agenda was agreed on.[99] The President

---

97. Heinisch, "Unremarkably Remarkable," 137-40; Gehler, "Vom EU-Beitritt zur EU-Osterweiterung," in: Kriechbaumer/Schausberger, eds., *Die umstrittene Wende*, 514-20.
98. Günter Bischof/ Michael S. Maier, "'Sie Kommen': From Defeat to Liberation – German and Austrian Memory of the Allied "Invasion" of June 6, 1944," in: Michael Dolski, Sam Edwards, John Buckley, eds., D-Day in *History and Memory: Comparative Perspectives on the Normandy Invasion* [Denton: University of North Texas Press, forthcoming in 2013].
99. For the "Vienna Summit Declaration, see http://trade.ec.europa.eu/doclib/docs/2006/june/tradoc_129053.pdf (accessed Feb. 6, 2012); see also Eva Nowotny, "Die österreichische

then went on to Hungary and to Russia after Vienna. Many popular local protests against the Iraq war and banners reading "World's No. 1 Terrorist" marred his visit to Vienna, as did brutal press commentary about Bush being "the worst president of the past 100 years." While trying to promote transatlantic unity, he had to defend himself against attacks of the U.S. being a "bigger threat to global stability" than the rogue states North Korea and Iran. When asked about polls showing the low opinion Europeans held of him, he passionately defended his policies: "Look, people didn't agree with my decision on Iraq, and I understand that. For Europe, September 11th was a moment; for us, it was a change of thinking." Emphasizing peaceful diplomacy over military options, President Bush regained credibility with European governments, but remained highly unpopular with European people.[100] The news magazine *Profil* ran a cover story about "The crazy world of George W. Bush."[101] Bush visited the Austrian President Heinz Fischer who thanked him for postwar economic aid but raised the difficult issues of Iranian nuclear weapons and Guantanamo inmates.[102] Transatlantic relations somewhat improved in the final years of the Bush II presidency.

Conclusion

Austria got caught up in "Obamamania" like the rest of Europe and enthusiastically welcomed the election of the first African American president and the victory of the Democrats in the November 2008 election. This reflected the nostalgia of better times when the democratic world could look up to Uncle Sam and rely on his strong shoulders. "Obamamania" revived the belief in the American dream in Europe and the continent's need for the U.S. being the primus inter pares in the Western world.[103] After his electoral victory, *Profil* magazine put Obama on its cover as the "man of the year" 2008, expressing the hope that he would visit Austria soon.[104] On her almost 40 trips to Europe, Secretary of State Hillary Clinton probably

---

EU-Präsidentschaft in Washington - - sechs spannende Monate in den transatlantischen Beziehungen," in: Anton Pelinka/Fritz Plasser, eds., *Europäisches Denken und Lehren: Festschrift für Heinrich* Neisser (innsbruck: iup, 2007), 213-218 (here 215).
100. "Bush's Visit to Vienna Is Marked by Tension," *New York Times*, June 21, 2006.
101. "Die verrücke Welt des George W. Bush: Wie tickt der mächtigste Mann der Welt wirklich?," *Profil*, June 17, 2006.
102. "Bush bei Fischer: Bundespräsident sprach Guantanamo an," *Der Standard*, June 22, 2006.
103. See Ian Buruma's op-ed "Auf den Spuren einer Liebeskrankheit namens 'Obamamania'," *Der Standard*, Nov. 7, 2008.
104. "Barack Obama – Der Mann des Jahres: Wie der neue Präsident das Jahr geprägt hat," *Profil*, Jan. 1, 2009.

contributed more than anyone in the Obama administration "to negotiate, consult, and mend bridges" with Europe.[105] Yet if Washington focusses on the middle of Europe, it has its sights set on post-communist "Central Europe." Since the end of the Cold War the State Department has been defining its relations with Central Europe almost exclusively through the lens of NATO membership. "Washington and Central Europe are bound together by shared values and a common commitment to protect those values," pronounces Philip H. Gordon the Assistant Secretary of State for European and Eurasian Affairs, and adds "NATO remains the bedrock of that commitment."[106] Eastern Europe expert Charles Gati feels that it was the U.S. that "paved the way" to EU Eastern expansion by "providing security to the countries admitted to NATO" first – in spite of both the opposition of the Pentagon against NATO enlargement and the EU against eastern enlargement.[107] Austria is no longer part of this militarized NATO-*"Central Europe" imaginary* in Washington.

During the election campaign of 2012, however, the 2008 European high of "Obamamania" had been deflated.[108] In domestic politics as in transatlantic relations, the President could not deliver what he had promised during the 2007 campaign. Anti-Americanism in the Austrian left and far right are slumbering but might be revived any day over issues such as Obama's lack of interventionism in bloody crises such a Libya and the Syrian civil war and safe long-distance interventionism with deadly drone attacks.[109] His foreign policy has been pivoting to the Asia-Pacific arena and Europe

---

105. She shaped NATO consensus on Afghanistan, hammered out tighter sanctions on Iran, and a new missile defense strategy while antagonizing Russia less, see Michael O'Hanlon, "State and the Stateswoman: How Hillary Clinton Reshaped U.S. Foreign Policy – But Not the World," *Foreign Affairs*, Jan. 29, 2013 http://www.foreignaffairs.com/articles/138793/michael-e-ohanlon/state-and-the-stateswoman (accessed Feb. 2, 2013).
106. Philip S. Gordon's remarks on "U.S. Relations with Central Europe" delivered at the Center for European Policy Analysis, Sept. 20, 2012, http://www.state.gov/p/eur/rls/rm/2012/197986.htm (accessed Jan. 7, 2013).
107. Gati feels that democratization is being arrested in the region in places such as Hungary and that the U.S. should "put democracy promotion and integration promotion first on its agenda" to complement security-military concerns, see his keynote address at the U.S.-Central European Strategy Forum, Sept. 20, 2012, http://www.cepa.org/ced/view.aspx?record_id=362 (accessed Jan. 7, 2012).
108. See the Karin Krichmayr Interview with Margit Reiter, *Der Standard*, Oct. 30, 2012, http://derstandard.at/1350259872261/Obama-wurde-eingemeindet-als-einer-von-uns (accessed Dec. 15, 2012).
109. On the latency of Austrian anti-Americanism and its deep traditions in the elites, see the interviews with Andrei Markovits, "Obama ist das quintessentielle Amerika," *Der Standard*, Oct. 2, 2012, and Margit Reiter, "Obama wurde eingemeindet als einer von uns," *ibid.*, Oct. 30, 2012, and Günter Bischof, "Abrufbereiter Antiamerikanismus," *Profil*, Dec. 10, 2010, 26.

has been losing in importance on the American foreign policy agenda.[110] Due to this "Asian pivot" the Atlantic arena is losing in importance for Washington and Europe is in danger of becoming peripheral.[111] Albeit Vice President Joe Biden averred during the Munich Security Conference in early February 2013 that, "President Obama and I continue to believe that Europe is the cornerstone of our engagement with the rest of the world and is the catalyst of our global cooperation," the U.S. increasingly acts as both an Atlantic and Pacific power.[112] This further diminishes Austria's dwarfish and insignificant status in the U.S. imaginary. Meanwhile, we are moving towards a "post-American" world with many new regional powers (China, India, Japan, Indonesia, Turkey, Russia, EUrope, Brazil) in which American hegemonic influence may be more regional than global.[113]

Austria's foreign policy continues to be further absorbed into EU foreign policy and has ceased to be exceptional after the end of the Cold War.[114] Foreign Minister Michael Spindelegger (2008-) is a neophyte in the foreign policy arena, and like Schüssel is the chief of the ÖVP and more interested in domestic policy – since 2011 he also has been serving as Vice Chancellor. Austrian foreign policy continues to focus on human rights issues and is sending peace keepers abroad. Spindelegger also has developed the Black Sea region as an Austrian foreign policy focus. Bilateral relations with the United States are proper but continue to be conducted within the focus of the EU transatlantic framework. In a late January 2013 plebiscite the Austrian population opted by a large margin for the continuation of a conscript army rather than following the lead of its European NATO neighbors into building a professional army. Austrian politicians continue to "stick their head into the sand" and ignore NATO as a necessity for European and Atlantic security needs and for tying the US to European

---

110. David Milne, "Pragmatism or what? The future of US foreign policy," *International Affairs* 88 (2012): 935-51.
111. Turkey therefore is considering joining the Shanghai Group and abandoning its goal of accessing the European Union, see Burkhard Bischof, "Europa den Rücken kehren? Erdogan denkt darüber nach," *Die Presse*, Jan. 31, 2013 http://diepresse.com/home/meinung/kommentare/leitartikel/1339028/Europa-den-Ruecken-kehren-Erdogan-denkt-darueber-nach (accessed Jan 31, 2013).
112. Remarks by Vice President Joe Biden to the Munich Security Conference, Feb. 2, 2013 http://www.whitehouse.gov/the-press-office/2013/02/02/remarks-vice-president-joe-biden-munich-security-conference-hotel-bayeri (accesed Feb. 4, 2013).
113. Fareed Zakaria, *The Post-American World* (New York: W.W. Norton, 2008).
114. For the parameters of such a EUropean common foreign policies within a highly heterogeneous Union, where the U.S.'s fundamental role within NATO has changed from a supportive to a divisive one, see Werner Link, "Möglichkeiten und Grenzen einer gemeinsamen Außenpolitik," *Aus Politik und Zeitgeschichte* 63/6-7 (Feb. 4, 2013): 23-30 (for the U.S. and NATO, see p. 25).

security interests.[115] Looking at a number of the 1,700 WikiLeaks cables from the Vienna Embassy to Washington, the daily business of bilateral relations is defined by economic issues. Austria's contact with the Iranian government is of interest to Washington and Austria seems to serve as a go-between. Austrian politicians such as (former) defense minister Norbert Darabos are criticized as being "disinterested in international and security issues" – Foreign Minister Spindelegger for only being interested in advancing Austrian economic interests in regions such as the BlackSea/Caucasus. Washington was also disappointed that Austria refused to grant asylum to any of the Guantanamo prisoners. Austrian companies such as the oil multinational OMV are carefully watched in their dealings with Iran and the Nabucco pipeline project. Austrians come across as provincials in the WikiLeaks cable trove, they are disinterested in foreign affairs and among the most "eurosceptic" people on the continent.[116] Austrians gloated in *Schadenfreude* about the blow to U.S. secrecy in the WikiLeaks revelations.[117] Austrian neutrality continues to be underappreciated in Washington. Given the continued popularity of Austria's (eroded) neutrality in two thirds of the population, the conservatives People's Party never returned to its late 1990s mission to lead Austria into NATO. Austria never had an "America strategy," argues elder statesman Erhard Busek and adds: "We have become a rather unimportant country for the U.S."[118]

European and American security interests are increasingly diverging; after the provocations of the Iraq War fiasco, the NATO alliance and its transatlantic dimension may indeed be "dying."[119] The Obama

---

115. Burkhard Bischof, "Österreichs Sicherheitspolitik ist auf die Krankenwägen gekommen," *Die Presse*, Jan. 22, 2013, http://diepresse.com/home/meinung/gedankenlese/1334795/Oesterreichs-Sicherheitspolitik-ist-auf-die-Krankenwaegen-gekommen (accessed Jan. 22, 2013).
116. The cables from the U.S. Embassy in Austria represent a relatively small number in the massive 250,000 "Secret US Embassy Cables" database in Wikileaks http://wikileaks.org/cablegate.html. For a report on the Austrian cables, see Otmar Lahodynsky, "Nebenrollenspiele," *Profil*, Dec. 13, 2010, 25-27; Thomas Seifert, "Wiener WikiLeaks: Rückzug in die geistige Alpenfestung," *Die Presse*, Dec. 5, 2010; Helmar Dumbs, "Die US-Not mit den störrischen Älplern," *Die Presse*, Dec. 5, 2010; Wikileaks: Die wichtigsten Enthüllungen auf einen Blick," *Die Presse*, Dec. 3, 2010.
117. See the op-ed by Christian Ortner, "Doktor Freuds Heimat und ihr unheilbarer Amerika-Komplex," *Die Presse*, Dec. 9, 2010. Ortner saw the roots in the deep-seated anti-Americanism of Austrians in both the resentments of the older generation who never felt liberated but occupied by the Americans after World War II, and the "anti-capitalist poses" of the younger generation of lefty 1968ers.
118. Busek quoted in *ibid.*, 27.
119. With the end of the Cold War, the U.S. "is seen as getting so little benefit from its continuing commitment to the security of Europe," see Trachtenberg, *The Cold War and After*, 308f ("dying", p. 309).

administration's reluctance to intervene prompted the French to lead interventions in Libya and Mali. Obama is practicing a cautious "lean back" foreign policy in crises such as Syria. Obama is looking for a "light footprint" in the world and intervening clandestinely with drone attacks and special forces rather than with the overwhelming force of the Bush Wars (Powell Doctrine) and "boots on the ground."[120] Postwar Western European-American relations were built on common security and defense policies (neutral Austria, of course, was not part of these arrangements). Given that there are no major security threats of the past on the horizon, the Europeans are less inclined to invest in defense. Of course, both Europeans and Americans are redefining security threats of the present and future like terrorism, WMD, rogue and failed states (such as Mali), cyber warfare, etc. Only the British and the French are still willing to spend on defense in order to project power. Germany and most of the European nations "envision Europe as a big Switzerland." Given the weakening of the common security and defense ties that had governed the Cold War transatlantic relationship, the common bonds are slackening too and the U.S. no longer seems to be of "transcendent importance" to most Europeans.[121] Issues such as Syria and WMD in Iran test current transatlantic cooperation. Surveys show that both Americans and Europeans continue to back NATO "but they want out of Afghanistan, currently the joint U.S.-European military operation." Future public support for NATO may well depend on "how that disengagement" will be handled, notes Bruce Stokes, the director of the Pew's Global Economic Attitudes. While the current Euro crisis will continue to absorb the Europeans, American are turning more isolationist. 83% of Americans want their leadership pay more attention to problems at home than overseas.[122]

Yet at the heart of this growing transatlantic divide since the end of the Cold War may well be what is called the "values gap." Of course, Europe and the U.S. still share common democratic values based on human rights and rule of law. Yet one can no longer assume that European and American values are entirely congruent as they had been for much of the

---

120. John Arquilla, "America in Decline," *Foreign Policy* http://www.foreignpolicy.com/articles/2013/01/28/america_in_recline (accessed Jan 30, 2013); see also Leon Wieseltier, Washington diarist: "Welcome to the Era of the Light Footprint Obama finally finds his doctrine," *New Republic*, Jan. 29, 2013, http://www.newrepublic.com/tags/washington-diarist (accessed Jan. 30, 2013)
121. Kramer, "The Return of History in Europe," 84.
122. Bruce Stokes special to CNN, "A big year for transatlantic ties?," http://globalpublicsquare.blogs.cnn.com/2013/01/14/a-big-year-for-transatlantic-ties/ (accessed Jan. 16, 2013).

Cold War when a common enemy bound them together. The two sides of the Atlantic are divided by a number of gaps, namely "market-", "god-" war- "and social policy gaps."[123] American values constitute the "American Creed" and continue to represent the belief in American exceptionalism.[124] These "values gaps" persist as the Pew Research Center regularly documents in its "Global Attitudes Project." While the pervasive anti-Americanism of the Bush years has receded and the "Obama effect" has produced soaring favorability ratings (from 42% to 75% in France), the values gap in issues such as use of military force, religion, the death penalty and gun laws is alive and well. European models of solidarity grounded in the welfare state and social market economies are quite different from American models grounded in individualism and toleration of excessive inequality.[125] Europeans and Americans harbor very different ideas about the place and role of religion in society and politics, environmental risks and global poverty, as well as individualism. They differ widely on notions of patriotism, as Timothy Garton Ash has noted: "American-style belligerent patriotism is rare in contemporary Europe." Americans promote market capitalism, Europeans socially equalizing welfare capitalism. Americans think about international relations in martial terms, Europeans in a peace-making imaginary. The U.S. is good at war-making, Europeans spend little on defense and much on the welfare state – while "the *terribles simplificateurs*" (Timothy Garton Ash) like Robert Kagan and Samuel Huntington "babble glibly of Mars and Venus" or "clashing civilizations."[126] The U.S. prefers to act unilaterally in international politics, Europeans with their daily experience in Brussels politicking like to operate within multilateral frameworks.[127] These differences in values could be multiplied. This transatlantic divide is deepening and will make European (including Austrian) relations with the United States more difficult in the "post-American world." In Mary Nolan's estimation: "The American Century in Europe is over."

---

123. Nolan, *The Transatlantic Century*, 9, 366-373; negotiating between these differing European and American values discourses has become a big challenge in bilateral diplomacy, see Nowotny, "Die österreichische EU-Präsidentschaft in Washington - sechs spannende Monate in den transatlantischen Beziehungen," 217.
124. Lieven, *American Right or Wrong*, 48-87.
125. GZ. 1.30/40/03, "Abschlussbericht: 4 Jahre USA, Rückblick," E-Mail Moser to Foreign Ministry, Aug. 28, 2033, both Peter Moser Private Papers, CenterAustria
126. The reference here, of course, is to Robert Kagan's controversial essay *Of Paradise and Power: America and Europe in the New World Order* (New York: Knopf, 2003).
127. See Tony Judt's review essay "The Good Society: Europe vs. America," in: *Reappraisals: Reflections on the Forgotten Twentieth Century* (New York: Penguin, 2008), 393-409; see also Nolan, *Transatlantic Century*, 331-73.

Appendix

E-Mail # 3/42/10/03, Austrian Embassy Washington to Foreign Ministry, Vienna, Sept. 2, 2003[1]

NATO and Austria from a US Perspective

Besides "Mutual Assured Destruction," the balance of the Cold War rested on two alliances, the NATO and the Warsaw Pact. In a manner of speaking, Austria's neutrality was the third child of the Cold War. The Warsaw Pact dissolved after the end of the Cold War, and NATO changed from an exclusively defensive alliance to a dynamic security organization, with the term "security" extending far beyond its military meaning.

Only the neutrality of Austria—rightly taught to generations of Austrians as an advantage and a marker of their identity—has not changed much, at least on the surface or with regard to the way Austrians understand themselves. Austrians hardly noticed turning points that reach back as far as 1955 and culminated in Austria's accession to the UNO and the NATO "Partnership for Peace," a change that was marked by various exceptions in the Austrian constitution. The further development of European solidarity, with its attendant obligation to assist other European nations, will further erode the meaning of Austrian neutrality.

Many arguments support Austrian's accession to the NATO, but there are some counterarguments that need to be taken seriously, most of them of an emotional, semantic, or moral nature. Because of these emotions and convictions, it is hard to conduct logical debates because Austrian neutrality is too often used as a slogan in electoral campaigns.

The Washington Embassy would like to present a few remarks on the issue of the "permanent" debate of Austrian neutrality, remarks that view the issue from some distance and from an American perspective:
1. The USA has viewed Austrian neutrality with increasing skepticism since the end of the Cold War. Granted, one understands the origin and historical justification of neutrality. One acknowledges the constitutional importance of neutrality, and one knows the legal sanctions of endangering neutrality, but one does not understand why Austria has reacted so sluggishly to recent developments, why Austria has used the domestic difficulties to change its constitution as an excuse for not making changes at all. Americans have at times derided Austria and at times been bothered (e.g. Rumsfeld in

Congress in February), and sometimes they have suspected Austria of not wanting to change at all even though its accession to the EU has demonstrated that it can react very actively to changes in its environment.

2. The trans-Atlantic crisis has made the USA suspicious of European attempts to leave NATO. Even though Austria's military potential in the overall European security structure seems negligible, the USA is watching Austria very closely to see if it would declare its solidarity with a European defense system, with or without NATO membership. Without joining NATO, Austria would appear to be a potential dividing factor to the USA, who would like to see congruency between NATO and any European defense system.

3. In the wake of 10 new states' joining the EU and thereafter becoming members of NATO, Austria will be at a definite disadvantage with regard to the "regional partnership" which it desires to establish with its neighbors and will increase its current irrelevance within NATO and the European security structure. Regular NATO contacts, in particular, would offer opportunities for debate and coordination with our neighbors. Because NATO's influence goes far beyond military matters, Austria would isolate itself in important issues and would earn the same derision from its regional partners that it has received from the USA.

4. In the future, a pan-European security system will lead to a pan-European armament industry. EU members will fight egotistically to get their share of the pie. Austria's rivals will try to thwart Austria because of its refusal of NATO partnership. (On several previous occasions, Austria's neutrality has been used in the USA as an argument against awarding it contracts. Would not our European partners do the same?)

5. Lastly, one has to point out a non-military, but utterly political aspect of NATO membership, a side issue, so to speak, and certainly not the main reason for joining NATO: The USA takes solidarity with and responsibilities toward its allies very seriously. Non-membership is acknowledged as a fact. However, once a state is an ally, much is expected of it, but the USA is very loyal to its allies as well. As long as there are no serious conflicts with US interests, NATO members can count on American goodwill in non-military questions as well. For example, the US is more critical of Austria's Nazi past than it is of Germany's. New NATO members like

Poland, the Czech Republic, and Hungary get more deferential treatment in questions of restitution than does Austria. Austria is always in danger of getting bad press, from which the new NATO members are largely safe.

The Ambassador
Moser

Endnotes

1. This hitherto unpublished document is in the collection of Personal Papers that Ambassador Peter Moser donated to CenterAustria at the University of New Orleans and has been translated by Inge Fink (Department of English, UNO) from German into English. We would like to thank Peter Moser for providing us with the document and Inge Fink for her translation.

Austrian Foreign
and Security Policy

On the Road to a Modern Identity: Austrian Foreign Policy from the Cold War to the European Union

Ursula Plassnik[1]

If one had to identify a single **game changing year** in the recent history of Austria, it would be 1989. Within a few months, two events radically changed the very parameters of Austrian foreign policy:
- In June, Austria **applied for membership in the European Economic Community,** a move with far-reaching consequences for Austria's political and economic landscape that transformed large parts of domestic and foreign policy into European policy.
- The **fall of the Berlin Wall** on November 9 and the self-liberation of the former Eastern bloc countries from Communist oppression pushed Austria from the edge of the "Free World" into the heart of a continent in full re-calibration.

Setting a new course in domestic politics and having to respond to geopolitical change from outside—never had there been so much peaceful renewal in such a short period of time. Austria was propelled into an economic and political paradigm shift. It was induced to definitely leave behind the cherished mental comfort zone of the "Island of the Blessed" diffusely protected by some "magical hat" providing invisibility. 1989 thus marks a political Copernican revolution, whose impact on the Second Republic can only be compared to the Austrian State Treaty of 1955.

For Austria, the end of the Cold War also marked the end of its beloved self-definition as a builder of bridges and a mediator between East and West. Without East and West, no more demand for go-betweens. We had been deprived of our well established foreign policy identity. What would the future hold in store?

Next came a tedious learning process. It was devoid of "quick breeders," but enabled Austria to re-define its international identity in a new and multi-facetted way. The pleasures of **co-management and co-accountability as shareholders of the European Union** were to be discovered. A yet

---

1. Inge Fink, Department of English, University of New Orleans, translated this essay from German into English.

unfamiliar matrix had to be mastered. The aim of this article is to contribute certain facts and elements of analysis relative to this process. Inevitably, this piece meal approach in no way claims to do justice—or only even partial justice—to the complexity of the matters at stake.

However, I explicitly disagree with the wide spread opinion that the foreign policy of a mid-sized EU member state can no longer have a distinct profile. In his large-scale study on "Austrian Foreign Politics in the Second Republic," Michael Gehler seems to adopt this position: "The autonomy and independence of Austrian foreign politics, within the EU framework, is a thing of the past."[2] In my view, such a **mental surrender of sovereignty is both unjustified and inappropriate**. The range of practical options available falls in between the megalomania of some and the inferiority complex of other critical observers of Austrian foreign politics.

What Paul Lendvai, the great European, Hungarian, and Austrian, said about the politics of the Second Republic in general, applies to its foreign policy in equal measure: "Despite all mistakes and systemic weaknesses, the success story of the Second Republic was a triumph of sensible politics, of careful consideration and sober calculation of all possible consequences of important decisions, of compromise, of adaptation, of balancing. At a time of monumental change in European politics, the price for political folly could be very high: it could mean Austria's self-isolation."[3]

The Point of Departure

Today, the United Nations has 193 member states. During a period of 34 years, between Austria's UN-accession in 1955 and 1989, the **number of members** more than doubled, increasing from 76 to 159. Then, over the next four years, membership increased massively; 25 new nations joined the UN between 1989 and 1994, most of them emerging from the Soviet Union's and Yugoslavia's break-up. In Europe, the latecomer Montenegro joined the UN in 2006. Since the end of World War I, Austria had not seen any political transformation of comparable extent in its immediate vicinity.

A few months after taking over the position of Austrian foreign minister in October 2004, I happened to run into Fritz Bauer, a former political director and ambassador to the Soviet Union, the Federal Republic of Germany and the German Democratic Republic. Almost a quarter of

---

2. Michael Gehler, *Österreichs Außenpolitik der Zweiten Republik. Von der alliierten Besatzung bis zum Europa des 21. Jahrhunderts* (Innsbruck: StudienVerlag, 2005), 1021.
3. Paul Lendvai, *Reflexionen eines kritischen Europäers* (Vienna: Kremayr & Scheriau/Orac, 2005), 21.

a century before, when I had just joined the Austrian foreign service, he had been my first boss. We had kept up our trusting working and personal relationship. Would we have been able to imagine, back in 1981, how to design a sensible Austrian foreign policy with regard to Kosovo, Serbia, Montenegro, or the Ukraine? The sheer question seemed a thing of wonder to both of us.

Austria had to enter a **process of continental self-assertion**. Even those actively involved in the sea changes of 1989 were slow to understand their full significance. Before the accession to the European Union (EU), multilateral diplomacy for Austria primarily spelled as UN politics, the Conference on Security and Cooperation in Europe (CSCE), the Council of Europe, and the European Free Trade Association (EFTA). EU accession in 1995 then marked the beginning of a brand new stage as a shareholder of the dynamic project of European integration. Austria had to rapidly establish itself as an equal partner among fifteen states in this ambitious undertaking—long before the EU took on its present interior and exterior shape.

In retrospect, Austrian foreign politics, during the second half of the 1990s, went through a period of learning, adaptation and profound re-orientation: a kind of semi-voluntary crash course in "advanced globalization." A period of self-assertion. We had to unlearn thinking in terms of "UN + bilateral world" and learn thinking in terms of "EU + UN + bilateral world." This process often involved pressure from a population that felt insecure and thus openly flirted with populism.

Austria—and Austrian diplomacy in particular—had to pass a double stress test. The period of rapidly expanding options with regard to our neighbors in the East and in the South was simultaneously a period of a fundamental re-orientation brought about by our EU accession. This apparent simultaneity was, of course, no mere coincidence but a reflection of deeper change. Since the mid-1970s, Austrian foreign policy had focused on East-West relations and the policy of *détente* pursued in the CSCE-process. The tension between the Soviet Union and USA/Canada had gradually disclosed a new space for international politics in which to develop a broad array of themes, from disarmament and arms control to family reunions and working conditions for journalists. Erhard Busek perceptively connects the historical contribution of the CSCE to "perforating" physical and psychological frontiers with the EU's current Schengen-concept of abolishing internal borders.[4]

---

4. Erhard Busek, *Ein Seele für Europa* (Vienna: Kremayr & Scheriau, 2008), 41.

During the run-up to the 1986 CSCE follow-up meeting in Vienna, it became apparent that the next logical step would be nothing less than the fall of the Berlin Wall, which was logical but still completely unthinkable in terms of "Realpolitik." As a long-time member of various CSCE delegations, I was invited with others by the German government to Berlin in August 1989. A gesture of appreciation of the hard work Austria and the other "N+N" (Neutral and Non-Aligned) states had invested for many years. Even at this late point in time, none of us realized that the Wall would be history before the end of the year and that very soon we would see Germany re-unified.

In 1989 the Cold War did not end with a bang. The political forces in the East, crystallized in popular revolutions, brought about the implosion of the Soviet Union and in time led to the birth of the Russian Federation. Communism as an ideology had reached the end of its rope. This much was clear. But would the nations in Eastern Europe, so long dominated by Soviet Russia, actually be able to achieve internal and external freedom?

When asked what, in his view, had been the most amazing aspect of the world-historical upheaval of 1989, Wolfgang Schäuble answered as follows: "That an empire like the Soviet Union could implode practically without shedding a drop of blood. This was a true miracle. Nobody could have imagined it."[5] Edward Schewardnadse, the Soviet foreign minister at the time, emphasized the underlying drama of the moment when he referred to half a million Russian soldiers stationed in the German Democratic Republic (GDR), "ready to march across Europe all the way to the Atlantic. If these 500,000 soldiers had intervened during the fall of the Wall, World War III would have erupted."[6]

For Austria, the most immediate outcome of the new geopolitical realignment was that we were finally **free to regulate our relationship with the European Community** (EC), later the European Union (EU). As late as August 1989 the Soviet Union formally protested against Austria's accession to the EC. However, the historical events of the summer and fall of 1989 most likely rendered Austria's EC aspirations "negligible" even in Soviet eyes. Austria is, by the way, the only EFTA nation that applied for EC membership before the change of 1989. EFTA partners Sweden and Finland followed significantly later.[7] With a small margin, Norwegians, in a referendum, voted against EC membership in 1972 and against EU

---

5. Paul Schulmeister, *Wendezeiten* (St. Pölten: Residenz-Verlag, 2009), 198.
6. Eduard Schewardnadse, in an interview with Tessa Szsyzkowitz for *Profil*, 14 Sept. 2009.
7. Sweden in July 1991, Finland in February 1992.

membership in 1994.[8] Former Belgian foreign minister Mark Eyskens' bizarre reaction in 1989 to Austria's application for EC-accession has since become anecdotic: He suggested to the EC to negotiate Austrian neutrality with the Soviet Union.[9]

For a long time, Austria's accession to the EC was a hot topic in Austrian domestic politics. Social democrats showed considerable caution at first; under the leadership of Chancellor Franz Vranitzky and Peter Jankowitsch, the head of the Socialist Party and a leading voice in the Austrian Socialist Party regarding foreign politics, the Social Democrats gradually adopted a sustainable pro-accession position. Jörg Haider, governor of Carinthia since 1989, at that time ardently supported Austrian EC-accession. The Green Party was reluctant if not opposed; Andreas Voggenhuber, in particular, was an eloquent opponent of the European project in the Austrian parliament. It is interesting to note how the attitude toward European politics, especially among the parties of the opposition, underwent dramatic changes in the years to come. The Austrian People's Party arguably showed the greatest consistency of all, which enabled it to build a lasting reputation as Austria's "European party."

In this context, Austria's most widely read daily newspaper, the *Kronenzeitung*, was a significant factor. Having thrown in its mobilizing power in favor of Austrian EU-accession in 1994, it consequently grew more and more critical and ended up on a fierce anti-European course.[10] European foreign and domestic politics had to learn to accommodate not only to a constantly changing EC and a revamped geopolitical environment, but also considerable fluctuations in the Austrian media and political parties.

---

8. Today, Norway has close connections with the EU through the EEA (European Economic Area) and its participation in the Schengen border zone.
9. Martin Eichtinger/Helmut Wohnout, *Alois Mock: Ein Politiker schreibt Geschichte* (Graz: Styria, 2008), 245: "Eykens said in front of journalists, 'We love Austria very much, but we love Europe more!' and contemplated publicly if one should enter negotiations with the Soviet Union regarding Austrian neutrality because, in his opinion, the neutrality imposed on Austria represented an obstacle in its accession to the EC." [trans. Inge Fink]
10. Compare editor Hans Dichand's impassioned pro-Europe plea in the editorial of January 1, 1994, *Look Ahead!*: "We have to understand that we cannot remain alone without endangering ourselves. A fragmented Europe is powerless against the giant USA, Japan with parts of Asia.... Will we choose the crisis-prone existence of a dwarf or will our old pan-European desires rule the day?" Consider also the sobering analysis of many Austrian journalists after Hans Dichand's death, who had become an embittered anti-European, i.a. Alexandra Föderl-Schmid, "Die *Krone* regiert weiter" ["The *Krone* Reigns on"]), *Standard*, 7 Oct. 2010, Hubert Patterer in the *Kleinen Zeitung*, of 20 June 2010, ("Letzte Unterwerfung" ["Last Act of Submission"]), Hans Peter Lingens, ("Der Manipulator" ["The Manipulator"]), *profil*, 21 June 2010.

From the Transitory EEA Experience to EU Accession

Austria's road to full participation in European integration was a serpentine rather than a straight line. The Austrian application for membership was handed over to Roland Dumas, then the French foreign minister and president of the EC-council, on July 17, 1989. It did not meet with universal approval, serious misgivings persisted. France had a particularly hard time imagining a reunited Germany. Arguably, this had unspoken but tangible consequences for Austria's EC membership chances. Former Chancellor Franz Vranitzky reports that French president Francois Mitterand at their third direct discussion on this issue finally withdrew French opposition while lamenting that now the **"third German nation"** had to be admitted to the EC. Mitterand's former finance minister and later president of the European Commission,[11] Jacques Delors, shared his skepticism about EC enlargement during the 90s. For Delors, leading the EC towards economic and monetary union clearly took precedence. Delors' creation of the "European Economic Area" (EEA) presumably was a direct result of this order of priorities. At the time, I served as an Austrian delegate at the Council of Europe in Strasbourg. I remember the tension I felt in the Hemicycle when I watched Delors give his trailblazing speech in the European Parliament (EP) on January 17, 1989.[12] My Swiss colleague, by his Ambassador's orders, was forbidden to hear Delors' speech live because, as the Ambassador put it, there were more important issues for Switzerland.

Was membership in the EEA a welcome training camp for later admittance to the European Community or would it become an infinite loop slowing down or even preventing full accession? This question was a hot topic with Austrian diplomats and politicians. While some of them advised courageous engagement, others warned of an inescapable trap. 1989, the "year of miracles," had only just begun.

The seven EFTA nations[13] realized very soon that it would be in their

---

11. 1985-1994.
12. Delors saw the EEA as an opportunity for Eastern-European nations. Jacques Delors, *Erinnerungen eines Europäers* (Berlin: Parthas-Verlag, 2004), 425: "In a programmatic speech in front of the European Parliament in January of 1989, I suggested to these countries, which are forever looking toward the advantages of an expanded domestic market, to let Eastern-European nations participate and to work together in forming the 'European Economic Area'. The idea found much resonance. As an example, I mentioned the European countries that had been separated from us by the Iron Curtain. How to treat those who have the same rights we do to call themselves Europeans but who have not been able—institutionally and economically—to manage the accession in a short period of time?" [trans. Inge Fink]
13. Austria, Finland, Iceland, Norway, Sweden, Switzerland, and Liechtenstein.

interest to get involved in the EEA project. A structured process began to unfold. At the EFTA summit in Oslo in March 1989, Delors's EEA plan was accepted at the highest political level, followed first by the preparatory "Oslo-Bruxelles Process" at the end of April 1989, and then by proper EEA negotiations as of December 12, 1989.

In the meantime, the entire continent was undergoing profound changes, people started to move: Along a short stretch of the border between Hungary and the Czech Republic, near Bratislava, the dress rehearsal for the physical dismantling of the Iron Curtain began as early as April 18, 1989, with the razing of a completely out-dated signal station.[14] Next, the barriers along the Austro-Hungarian border were removed piece by piece, until, on June 27, 1989, Foreign Minister Alois Mock, together with his Hungarian counterpart, Gyula Horn, symbolically cut the Iron Curtain near Klingenbach with a huge set of scissors. Many citizens of the GDR were allowed to cross the border into Austria, a development that contributed significantly to the break-down of the Eastern Bloc. In August and September increasing numbers of people fled the GDR. When, on November 9, the Wall fell in Berlin and border controls on the GDR side were lifted, thousands of GDR citizens poured into the Federal Republic of Germany (FRG). At the end of November, Chancellor Helmut Kohl issued a "Ten-Point Program to Overcome the Division of Germany and Europe." Only a week later, on December 2 and 3, George Bush and Mikhail Gorbachev declared the **end** of the Cold War at the USA/Soviet summit in Malta. Europe was free. Would it also become "Europe reunited"?

In its ambition to join the EC, Austria was not detracted by the EEA. While the Austrian People's Party had already decided to support EC accession by early 1988, the considerably more skeptical Socialist Party did not join the bandwagon until April 1989. The "neutrality question" was the most controversial topic within and among Austrian political parties. Then push came to shove: on April 17, 1989, the federal government submitted a "report on the future relationship between Austria and the European Communities" to parliament; on June 19, the Austrian People's Party and the Socialist Party finally agreed on integration policy; on June 29, the Austrian Parliament (National Council) decided, by a vote of 175 against 7, to apply for membership in the European Communities;[15] on July 4, the federal government decided to apply for Austria's EC-accession; on July 17,

---
14. See the description given by Janos Székely, who, at the time, served as commander of the Hungarian border troops: "So viel Anfang vom Ende," ["Such a lot of beginning of the end"] *Die Presse-Spectrum*, 20 June 2009.
15. The seven opposing votes in the National Council came from the Green Party.

Foreign Minister Mock handed the "Letter to Brussels" to Roland Dumas, French foreign minister and chair of the EC council of ministers.

The stage was set for Austrian EC-accession, regardless of the EEA-project's future course. In retrospect, the EEA negotiations proved a clear advantage for Austria. First, multilateral cooperation inside EFTA and with the EC intensified and accelerated, a welcome added-value in Austrian diplomacy's negotiating experience. Second, thousands of pages of EEC legislation were screened with regard to their compatibility with Austrian legislation, an unprecedented legal and political process. Austria was forced to leave behind its tendency for self-complacency. Our economic and social structures were examined on the basis of concrete European rules and regulations representing the European mainstream, and adaptions where necessary.

1992 was an important moment for both sides of the EEA project: For the EU this was the year of "Maastricht." Three years before, in June of 1989, the European Council of Madrid had already adopted a three-step plan to create an economic and monetary union. This plan was integrated into the Maastricht Treaty, which, in turn, became the foundation for the common European foreign policy and cooperation in both judicial and home affairs. Jacques Delors' concept of Europe found its best expression in the "Maastricht Treaty" (signed on February 7, 1992, ratified in November 1993). Maastricht signified a quantum leap, not entirely uncontroversial to this day, in the process of European integration: The economic community had become—at least on paper—the European Union.

When the EEA-Treaty was signed in Porto on May 2, 1992, Austria's aim was, without any doubt, full EU membership. Fears of getting "stuck" in the EEA proved false. Austria had successfully completed the first step on its road to EU membership. Only a year after the entry into force of the EEA- Treaty on January 1, 1994, Austria was to change sides, along with Sweden and Finland, by becoming a full member of the European Union by January 1, 1995.[16]

By the end of 1992, the European Council of Edinburgh decided to start membership negotiations with Austria, Sweden, and Finland. Formally, negotiations with Austria opened on February 1, 1993. Alois Mock, foreign minister from 1987 to 1995 and known as the "Father of the Austrian EU accession," led the negotiations on the Austrian side. Together with Brigitte Ederer (SPÖ), then State Secretary for European affairs, he completed accession negotiations on March 1, 1994; Ministers Ferdinand

---

16. EEA partner Norway, who had handed in an application for accession in 1992, did not join the EC after a negative 1994 referendum.

Lacina, Viktor Klima, and Franz Fischler were other leading negotiators. Wolfgang Schüssel, minister of commerce since April 4, 1989, supported Alois Mock throughout the negotiations; he acted as team leader in the EEA negotiations.

On the civil service level, Austrian diplomats deserve a lot of credit for the success of these negotiations. In his capacity as director general for European integration in the ministry of foreign affairs and later as Austria's permanent representative in Brussels, Ambassador Manfred Scheich and his team were in charge of both domestic transversal coordination and the negotiation of Austrian interests in day-to-day work in Brussels.[17] It should be mentioned in this context that the tool of temporary "transitional periods" as interimistic "buffers" for the entry into force of certain parts of EU-legislation avoided the use of permanent "opt outs" by Austria. Unlike other EC members (Denmark, Sweden, the United Kingdom and Ireland), Austria thus complies to all dimensions of the EU rulebook without exception. In a national referendum on June 12, 1994, 66.6% of Austrians voted in favor of EU accession. This two-thirds majority was the result of an unprecedented social and political mobilization, in which the *Kronenzeitung* and its then editor-in-chief, Hans Dichand, played a vital part. On July 24, 1994, the act of accession was signed in Korfu. Austria became a full member of the European Union on January 1, 1995.

EU-accession confirmed that Austrian politics and diplomacy - against considerable odds - had passed a major test. Six years after the membership application and against the background of momentous changes, Austria had dropped anchor in a rapidly integrating Europe.

Neighbors Near and Far

In the new post-1989 geopolitical landscape, the term of "neighborhood policy" had to be completely re-defined at several levels. First, with regard to the immediate geographical neighbors. From now on, Austria would work as an equal partner in the Brussels institutions, alongside Germany and Italy, both EC founding members.

On its Eastern and Southern borders, Austria could finally re-define, under the conditions of liberty, the relationships with its neighbors who had "disappeared" behind the Iron Curtain for decades after the war. Half of the continent was in flux-politically, socially, and economically. Would these

---

17. Manfred, Scheich, *Tabubruch: Österreichs Entscheidung für die Europäische Union*, Schriftenreihe des Herbert-Batliner-Europainstitutes, Forschungsinstitut für Europäische Politik und Geschichte, Vol. 9 (Vienna: Böhlau, 2005).

changes come to pass without violence and bloodshed? Huge challenges faced the former Eastern-Bloc countries as well as their neighbors. At the beginning of the 90s, few people could even imagine in their dreams that by May 1, 2004, all of Austria's neighbors, from the Czech Republic to Slovenia, would be members not only of NATO but also of the European Union. As of 2007, 1,200 kilometers of Iron Curtain would be replaced by the open "Schengen border"; barbed wire and watchtowers were banned forever. And the world would have ample cause to believe that the bloody Balkan conflicts before the turn of the millennium would be the last wars fought on European soil. What a bold vision!

West of Austria the world was changing as well. Our former EFTA partners Switzerland and Liechtenstein decided to go their own ways in European integration, different from Austria. Besides, the Swiss are not likely to forget that at the European Council in Vienna in December 1998, Foreign Minister Wolfgang Schüssel, together with Chancellor Viktor Klima, brought about the breakthrough in their so-called "bilaterals" with the EU. The midnight agreement created the legal basis for our neighbor's long-desired special status in the EU, six years after the Swiss sovereign had said "no" to EEA membership in 1992. As the Vice-chancellor's chief of cabinet, I had the dubious honor to wake up the Swiss foreign minister well after midnight to give him the news. Flavio Cotti jumped on a plane the very same night and was in Vienna early next morning to sign the agreement.

Accession to the EEA and EU brought South Tyrol and Tyrol even closer yet. The tail winds of historic change brought the decades-long negotiations on "the package" of South Tyrol's autonomy to a positive end. In June 1992, Austria acknowledged the fulfillment of "the package" by Italy. The presentation of the formal dispute resolution declaration to UN-Secretary General Boutros Boutros-Ghali by the Austrian and the Italian foreign ministers on June 19, 1992, ended the 32-year dispute between Austria and Italy about the interpretation of the 1946 Treaty of Paris. Today, throughout Europe and the world, South Tyrol serves as a model for solving minority conflicts.

The Austrian population adjusted to the new conditions with some difficulty. As is often the case in times of change, feelings of unease and insecurity arose. A cartoon, which hung above my desk in those days, expressed this discomfort: the cartoon depicted Austria as a small goldfish in a glass bowl, threatened by aggressive Western rival sharks from the left and Eastern fighting fish hungry to catch up from the right. An uncomfortable situation, indeed!

Austrian foreign politics have always had a strong regional component. This is reflected in their respective regional neighborhood policies practiced by the individual provinces, almost each of which has had some tension with one or the other of its immediate neighbors. Every once in a while, such a strained relationship spilled over to the level of national foreign policy. This was the case with bilingual place-name signs in Carinthia. On the other hand, the conscious practice of good neighborhood policies often provided positive spill-over effects for the national level.

The end of the Cold War made it possible to at least start discussing among neighbors the particularly controversial topics of the Benes and Avnoij decrees, topics that had hitherto been a total taboo in Austrian foreign politics. The Austrian Freedom Party, without doubt, left an imprint on Austrian foreign policy by raising these issues. These decrees and regulations by today's standards violate human rights; they had served after World War II to justify the expropriation and expulsion of German-speaking inhabitants of the Sudetenland and Yugoslavia. An incident during the 2013 Czech presidential campaign was a recent reminder of how controversial - and thus in need of clarification - these chapters of European history still are: Miloš Zeman, a candidate for the presidency, attacked his rival foreign minister Karel Schwarzenberg by claiming that the latter had called the Benes decrees "violating human rights"; President Vaclav Klaus had voiced similar criticism in the past.

Austria's EU accession and Eastern enlargement also led to major changes in our relations with the four signatories of the Austrian State Treaty. Great Britain and France were now equal partners in the EU-framework, the relationship more "eye-to-eye" than ever before. Austria's bilateral relations with the European "P-5" states (the five permanent members of the UN Security Council) were from now on inextricably linked to our common destiny as EU-partners.

The Russian Federation was busy dealing with the economic and political effects of the downfall of Communism and the breakup of the Soviet Union. These were years of humiliation and painful insecurity for a super power still conscious of its status. The trauma of the 1990s can still be felt today. The wounded superpower had to watch passively as one country after the other joined NATO and removed itself from Russian dominance. Relations with Ukraine and Georgia remained strained for a long time. Austria continued to cultivate its bilateral relationship with the Russian Federation with great seriousness. Both sides have great interest in close economic relations. It was, however, a matter of chance, that day one of Austria's EU presidency, January 1, 2006, started with the news that the Russian Federation's supply of natural gas to the Ukraine—and thus to Europe—had been stopped altogether or dramatically reduced.

Understandably, in times of world-wide change, the US spelled out its security policy interests mostly via NATO. Political insiders in Washington thus had little sympathy for Austria's neutrality. As the supposedly last remaining superpower, the US had trouble dealing with the transformation of Europe, in particular the process of European integration. Domestic changes in the US, especially the rise of evangelical and patriotic movements, further chilled the relationship. Post-9/11 US foreign politics, especially the war in Iraq and the crisis in Guantanamo Bay, led to a real estrangement between Europeans and Americans. Both sides felt misunderstood by the other. Among Europeans, anti-American sentiment spread rapidly. Pointing out the continuing vital economic relationship between the EU and the US did not change matters. Guantanamo had dealt a severe blow to the much-touted community of values between America and Europe.

The USA's lack of interest in Austria became manifest in 2005 on the occasion of the 50-year anniversary of the Austrian State Treaty. As foreign minister, I invited the four signatory states to the festivities, which included posing for pictures on the balcony of the Belvedere palace in a re-enactment of the historical State Treaty imagery. As expected, Russian chief diplomat, Sergei Lawrow, quickly confirmed that he was coming to Vienna, his visit was prepared and staged with utmost professionalism. Foreign Minister Michel Barnier represented France. Great Britain sent the young Minister of European Affairs, Douglas Alexander. However, it took a lot of persuasion until the US sent 75-year-old former senator Rudy Boschwitz.[18]

Coming to Terms with the Past and Relations with Israel

For long periods of time, Austria's relationship with Israel had been determined by the situation in the Middle East and its impact rather than by bilateral issues. Bruno Kreisky's Middle-East policy was—and remains—not uncontroversial when it comes to specific questions. However, in the words of his long-time close associate, Peter Jankowitch, Kreisky's merit certainly is to have "provided—again and again—decisive contributions to conflict-resolution in the Middle East through dialogue and negotiations rather than violence. Kreisky's ideas and contributions have established the indispensable basis of what later, after his death in 1990, became feasible

---

18. For more information about this episode, see Paul Lendvai in Michael Gehler, *Österreichs Außenpolitik in der Zweiten Republik*, 1026.

between Israel and its Arab neighbors, and in particular with the Palestinian leadership."

For many years during the Cold War, Austria had been a vital hub for Jewish emigration from the Soviet Union. This position was not risk-free for Austria.[19] Between the 1956 Hungarian Revolution and the opening of the border in 1989, Austria passed "a historical test" by helping some 270,000 Soviet Jews emigrate.[20] Before the fall of the Iron Curtain, the CSCE process was an important channel for Soviet Jews to immigrate to Israel. Austria's efforts in the CSCE/OSCE (Organization for Security and Cooperation in Europe) process remained continuous and undisputed in domestic politics.

Did the end of the Cold War have direct implications for Austrian-Israeli relationships? I venture to say that it was no coincidence that Austria, at this very point in time, intensified efforts to come to terms with its World War II past. The great East-West antagonism had somehow put the serious and self-critical analysis of past wrongs into a deep-freeze, not only in Communist countries. The end of the conflict between the systems also released tensions on many seemingly unrelated issues, in Austria and elsewhere.

Franz Vranitzky deserves credit for being the first Austrian Chancellor who admitted the participation of Austrians in the crimes committed by the Nazi regime and who publicly criticized the still-existing myth of Austrian victimhood. In a speech delivered in Jerusalem on July 9, 1993, Vranitzky said, "We admit all the dates of our history and the deeds of all of our people, the good and the bad. And as we take credit for the good, we have to apologize for the bad." And he named the victims: "Jews, gypsies, the physically and mentally handicapped, homosexuals, members of minorities, those persecuted for political and religious reasons." Vranitzky knew that, almost half a century after the end of World War II, we still had a long way to go in terms of making amends in material matters.

The speech President Thomas Klestil gave in November 1994 to the Israeli Knesset further gave testimony to a more mature Austrian self-understanding in dealing with the past. Other important steps in the long and often stop-and-go process of restitution and reconciliation were the 1995 "National Fund of the Republic of Austria for the Victims of National Socialism," the work of the "Historians Commission," set up in 1998, and

---

19. Take, for example, the attack on a Soviet train that carried thirty-seven Jewish emigrants bound for Israel in the border town of Marchegg on September 1973 and the closing of the Schönau transit camp despite Israeli protests.
20. Lendvai, *Reflexionen*, 26.

the law concerning the restitution of art objects from Austrian national museums and collections (1998).

In 2000 and 2001, Wolfgang Schüssel's administration managed to address the still-existing deficits in the restitution of Jewish property on the one hand, and the compensation payments for forced labor victims on the other. The "General Restitution Fund" helped solve the open questions of making amends to the victims of National Socialism. Once the prerequisite of legal certainty was established in December 2005, first pay-offs were made without delay. State Secretary Hans Winkler and Ambassadors Ernst Sucharipa and Hans Peter Manz have earned lasting merit for their role in these difficult negotiations. To those interested in the larger context, I recommend reading US Chief Negotiator Stuart Eizenstat's memoir *Imperfect Justice*.[21]

In Austria, the need to compensate forced laborers did not surface on the political radar screen until very late, more than ten years after the end of Communism and the fall of the Iron Curtain.[22] The core idea was to show respect to and solidarity with the former forced laborers, who often belonged to forgotten or persecuted groups of Nazi victims in their native countries (Austria's institutional partners included the Russian Federation, Ukraine, Belarus, Poland, Hungary, and the Czech Republic).[23] The following people were instrumental in "de-fogging" this hitherto ignored segment of Austrian history: former President of the Austrian Federal Reserve Maria Schaumayer and her team under the leadership of Ambassador Martin Eichtinger, currently the director general for cultural affairs of the Federal Ministry for European and International Affairs, as well as former ambassadors Ludwig Steiner and Richard Wotava.

Austria's accession to the EU altered the parameters for its relationship with Israel. While the bilateral relations had so far been largely determined by individuals and specific subject matters, it was now part and parcel of the larger context of EU-Israel relations. The gradual development of a common EU foreign policy sharpened senses on all sides for new potential and possibilities. During Austria's EU presidency, in 1998 and 2006, we

---

21. Stuart Eizenstat, *Imperfect Justice: Looted Assets, Slave Labor, and the Unfinished Business of World War II* (New York: Public Affairs, 2003).
22. In the preface to Hubert Feichtlbauer's book, *Zwangsarbeit in Österreich 1938-1945: Fonds für Versöhnung, Frieden und Zusammenarbeit. Späte Anerkennung Geschichte, Schicksale* (Wien: Braintrust, 2005), the author states: "For 55 years, the fate of former slaves and forced laborers, which were victimized on the territory of today's Austria, was not considered an Austrian problem. Today we all agree that our country's moral obligation includes this group of victims, particularly because many Austrians were among the perpetrators."
23. There were direct proposals from other countries, among them France, Israel, USA, Serbia, Croatia, Germany, Canada, Great Britain.

devoted a lot of attention, time and political energy to the strategic EU-Israel relationship. Innovative EU-initiatives were designed: EU-BAM Rafah,[24] an initiative to support border control in and out of the Gaza strip, and EUPOL-COPPS[25], the police training initiative for Palestinians. Austrian female experts participated in both missions. The break-down in mutual trust between Austria and Israel which was a result of the formation of the coalition government by the Austrian People's Party and the Freedom Party in 2000 and the recall of the Israeli ambassador, had to be repaired in many small confidence-building steps.

In some ways, the fifty-year anniversary of the Austrian-Israeli relations in 2006 was the occasion to open a new chapter.[26] My Israeli colleague Tzipi Livni and I were jointly determined to express this new dimension visually. On December 3, 2006, we spoke side by side in front of an audience of mostly elderly gentlemen at the Hebrew University in Jerusalem. Some in the audience could only shake their heads in disbelief at the sight of two comparatively young female "chief diplomats," clearly on excellent personal and professional terms, who spoke about mastering the international challenges of the future together.

Austria's good relations with other countries and population groups in the Middle East have benefitted from the new context of Austrian-EU foreign policy as well. In June 2008, I organized a donors conference for the reconstruction of the destroyed Palestine refugee camp Nahr-el-Bared. Austria, acting as a traditional point of contact, thus contributed significantly to the stabilization of Lebanon at a crucial moment. By participating in the United Nations Disengagement Observer Force (UNDOF), the United Nations Interim Force in Lebanon (UNIFIL), and the United Nations Peacekeeping Force in Cyprus (UNFICYP), the Austrian Federal Armed Forces have helped keeping the peace in a chronically unstable region for many years, a service appreciated by all parties involved.

From High School to College: Austria as Member of the EU

For Austrian foreign policy, 1989 brought a **paradigm shift from the bilateral to the supranational**. We had to learn how to think and act as a

---

24. European Union Border Assistance Mission at the Rafah Crossing Point (EUBAM RAFAH), in operation since November 24, 2005.
25. EU Police Mission in the Palestinian Territories (EUPOL COPPS), in operation since January 1, 2006.
26. Ursula Plassnik, "Mazal tov zum fünfzigsten Jahrestag! Für eine Zukunft in Vertrauen und Gemeinsamkeit," *Das Jüdische Echo* 55 (2006): 12-16.

shareholder in a large enterprise. We had to internalize the dimension of Europe as part of our new mental framework.

The transition from the preparatory EEA phase and EU-membership negotiations to full membership was substantially more difficult than it looked from the outside. While the negotiations were structured in a linear way, following a clear goal and advancing in accordance with the tightly-knit process imposed by EU law, the first day of EU membership found the newcomer standing suddenly alone and with a surprising lack of "instructions." We no longer had a "teacher" to tell us how to proceed. Austria now had to find its own voice in the EU orchestra. It was like having to fend for oneself in college after graduating high school. Good advice, however, was never short of supply: Austria had to find partners, ally itself with kindred spirits, act more confidently, and defend its interests more vigorously.

Austria did not have an easy start as an EU member. Our marked special interests in Alpine transit traffic, our visceral opposition to nuclear power, and the very idea of neutrality made our EU apprenticeship difficult. Seen from our partners' point of view, these topics were, in essence, non-negotiable. Despite all efforts, sensible alliances proved fleeting or downright impossible. Austria was left to its own devices. Access to universities, banking secrecy, and later the EU accession of Turkey issue constituted other pressure points. In addition, the bloody conflicts on the Balkans made Austrians feel insecure. By involving our closest regional neighbors, these wars brought wave after wave of refugees and immigrants to Austria. Meanwhile, the EU itself struggled with new challenges like the BSE crisis and the opening of Eastern Europe. Austria's political leitmotif during these early formative years was the determination to participate in all segments and sectors of the EU without exceptions.

Many great EU projects were historical pilot projects. There was no precedent for introducing a common currency in twelve sovereign states or for doubling the number of members of a supranational construct in less than a decade - from twelve members in the European Community in 1994 to twenty-five in 2004. The Schengen space is a further example of such pioneering projects: internal European borders were not abolished, as some claim, but their very nature changed for each individual EU citizen. All of a sudden, borders were no longer an obstacle for living and working together. One can understand the reservations voiced by some. Today, despite all doubts, nobody could seriously imagine "Schengen reversed."

The dominant geopolitical issue before the turn of the millennium was, without doubt, the so-called **Eastern enlargement of the EU**, its planning, preparation, negotiation, and implementation. Some "backseat drivers" in their ivory towers claim that Austria under the leadership of Foreign Minister and then Chancellor Wolfgang Schüssel was not fully engaged in Eastern enlargement. Their arguments are both annoying and untrue. No other politician in Austria fought as long and hard as Schüssel did for the EU's integration of the Eastern and Southeastern European new democracies. A European through and through, Schüssel saw their EU-integration as both a personal issue of heart and a historical opportunity. Moreover, he realized early on that enlargement was in Austria's very self-interest. Faster than other politicians, the former chairman of the economic wing of the People's Party and minister of economic affairs recognized the growth potential for Austria's economy and private business and the opportunities for job creation. Like any skillful politician, he had to strike a balance between his political vision of an integrated European mission and pushing through specific Austrian national interests.

On a number of vital issues, Austria scored remarkable points. Thus, we successfully managed to involve the European Commission (Günter Verheugen), an EU-institution without any mandate for questions on nuclear safety, in our fight against nuclear power; in this context, the "Process of Melk" contributed to a certain decrease of tensions with our Czech neighbors on the subject of Temelin. Without Austria's insistence, several out-dated nuclear power plants in EU-applicant countries would never have been closed down or refurbished.[27] Another example is the inclusion of ecological provisions in the EU-directive on the cost of road traffic. No doubt, Austria considerably irritated its EU partners with these issues, but our tenacity was rewarded.[28]

We should not neglect mentioning the achievements of various Austrian top representatives in EU institutions. Long-serving EU-Commissioner for agriculture Franz Fischler designed an innovative and comprehensive common EU policy for rural areas. Without the tireless EU-Commissioner for external relations Benita Ferrero-Waldner, the EU's world-wide network with its partners would be much less efficient. In addition, many Austrian members of the European Parliament (EP) are highly appreciated by their peers for reasons of expertise and dedication to substantive issues: Hannes Swoboda (Chair of the European Social-Democratic Party), Othmar Karas

---

27. Bohunice und Mochovce (Slovakia), Kozloduy (Bulgaria), Ignalina (Lithuania).
28. Only once in the course of negotiations did Austria temporarily prevent a state from joining: The Czech Republic, because of energy concerns, in the fall of 2000. See Martin Sajdik and Michael Schwarzinger, *Die EU-Erweiterung: Hintergrund, Entwicklung, Fakten* (Vienna: Verlag Österreich, 2003), 271.

(Vice President of the EP), and Ulrike Lunacek (Foreign policy Speaker of the Green Party/EFA Fraction).

Much to the initial dismay of their bosses, the "clerks of the Republic" took advantage of the new career opportunities in Brussels, which led to a brain drain of well-educated EU-experts leaving their jobs in Austria to join the European institutions. Conditions for moving from Vienna to Brussels and vice versa have since improved a great deal. Today, we are proud of our top people when they take on important responsibilities in the European External Action Service: Dietmar Schweisgut served as the Austrian permanent representative in Brussels before he was called to the position of EU representative in Tokio. When he was political director and a member of the Armed Forces Reform Commission, Thomas Mayr-Harting was an important voice in Austrian foreign and security politics; today he represents the EU at the United Nations in New York.

Austria almost lost a head of government to the **brain drain to Brussels**. In June of 2004, Wolfgang Schüssel was talked about as a serious candidate for the presidency of the European Commission. Supposedly, France prevented his nomination because of his "coalition with neo-Nazi Jörg Haider." This account is given by a disinterested witness, Jonathan Powell, Tony Blair's former Chief of staff.[29] The long-time president of the European People's Party and former Belgian Prime Minister Wilfried Martens writes about the goings-on around the 2004 nomination of the new Commission-President in his book *Europe: I Struggle, I Overcome* (Springer, 2008). When Schüssel was still debated as a possible candidate, Nicolas Sarkozy, who finally rejected his nomination, remarked to Angela Merkel that they might as well choose a German for the job.[30]

In unprecedented ways EU-accession turned European politics into part of the daily routine in all Austrian ministries. It also led to quality-leap in broadening the basis of expertise in Austrian foreign politics. The accession negotiations were a challenging learning process for many civil servants, who had not had much contact with each other before. A new caste of experts emerged who not only worked closely with the ministry of foreign affairs but also kept close direct contact with their European counterparts. Especially during the phase of Eastern enlargement, Austria was able to coordinate its resources and employ them in a collective effort. The ministers of the interior became important partners and have remained so to this

---

29. See Jonathan Powell, *The New Machiavelli – How to Wield Power in the Modern World* (London: Bodley Head, 2010).
30. See Wolfgang Schüssel, interviewed by Michael Gehler, "Interview mit Bundeskanzler a. D. Dr. Wolfgang Schüssel," in *Die umstrittene Wende Österreichs 2000-2006*, ed. Robert Kriechbaumer and Franz Schausberger (Vienna: Böhlau, 2013), 841.

day. They and their colleagues in the justice department had acquired a wealth of practical knowledge about political and economic transformation processes in post-Communist countries. The visa liberalization, long-desired by our friends in the Balkans, would not have been possible without the cooperation of the ministries of foreign affairs, the ministries of interior and the European Commission.

Austria is considered a **cultural super power**, and rightfully so. Our heritage as well as our creativity singled us out for this position. Membership in the EU requires to hear, see, understand and never lose interest in each other. For this, culture is our number-one tool. Having Graz and Linz elected "Cultural Capitals of Europe" therefore was a smart move. During our 2006 EU presidency, we developed innovative cultural landmarks like "Café d' Europe" and "The Sound of Europe."

The Service of the EU Presidency

No state is born as an EU-member, but some are "baptized" into the EU. For Austria, its EU presidency in the second half of 1998 was such a "baptism." EU nations can be considered true members only once they understand all topics, procedures, and institutions from inside out. Outsiders cannot possibly imagine how much work is invested in the planning, preparation, and execution of an EU presidency. Only precise and committed teamwork makes this "service to the community" of all EU-members possible. Putting one's own interests and domestic priorities on the back burner and making oneself available at all times to all partners is part of the recipe for success. As a reward for these efforts, the presidency receives an abundance of information as all the other members want to make sure that the group leader actually fully understands their respective concerns. By the end of the presidency, the entire crew is exhausted but better informed than ever before. Austria served two 6-month terms chairing the EU, in 1998 and 2006, both times under Wolfgang Schüssel's creative and dynamic leadership.

At the start of the first EU presidency during the second half of 1998, the economic and political crisis in Russia took center stage and became the leading topic of the Gymnich meeting on September 5 and 6 in Salzburg. The official beginning of negotiations with six new democracies in Central and Eastern Europe was a litmus test for all involved, including the European Commission. Never before had the EU started simultaneous negotiations with so many candidates. Everybody knew that these talks would be hard and controversial over long stretches. In fact, even the act of formally starting the negotiations had to be achieved against considerable resistance from "big brothers and sisters" in the EU family.

In addition, developments in the Balkans and especially in Kosovo weighed heavily on Austrian diplomats. How could Austria as the EU presidency fulfill its role as coordinator without access to confidential NATO information and the NATO decision shaping process? During the November 1998 retreat of the Austrian People's party in Telfs/Tyrol, as the first snow quietly fell outside, Foreign Minister and Party Chief Wolfgang Schüssel fought behind closed doors for his reform of severance pay regulations, then a hot topic on the Austrian domestic policy agenda. At the same time, as EU president he was in charge of the Kosovo issue. As disturbing news about the Serbian "Operation Horseshoe" increased, he received phone calls from colleagues from all over Europe.

As his staff, we worried during those hours how the Austrian foreign minister would get the military information necessary to manage a possible crisis. We had never been more aware of how much Austrian information even about its close neighborhood depended on NATO partners. We managed by the skin of our teeth. Five months later, on March 24, 1999, during the German EU presidency, NATO launched a military intervention in Kosovo. Joschka Fischer, the first German foreign minister from the Green Party, was at the helm. He negotiated the difficult situation of a German involvement in a joint NATO military operation (without a UN mandate) in an admirably straightforward way.

The second Austrian EU presidency during the first half of 2006 was overshadowed by the EU's internal crisis of confidence following the June 2005 negative referenda in France and the Netherlands on the subject of the "EU Constitution." After the initial shock and grief period, we were at least able to restart the discussion on the European constitution and the future of Europe. Called at short notice, the informal meeting of foreign ministers in Klosterneuburg in May 2006 was dedicated to the strengthening of the European sense of togetherness. For this purpose, I ordered an oval table built: Every foreign minister had to look in the eye of his/her colleagues when he/she answered the question of the future fate of the EU-treaty. The "table trick" worked; at the EC in June, we were able to agree on a road-map. During the German EU presidency in 2007 this breakthrough became instrumental for finalizing the Treaty of Lisbon.

The EU - USA summit took place on June 21 in Vienna in a very tense atmosphere. European anti-American sentiments had been building up during the Bush presidency over the Iraq war, Abu Ghraib, Guantanamo, and the accusation of secret prisoner renditions. On the eve of the summit,

Alfred Gusenbauer, the head of the Social Democratic opposition party, a renowned Bush-critic, insisted on personally welcoming the President at the Vienna airport with great publicity, a provocative gesture widely broadcast in Austria.

Austrian and American diplomacy firmly in the hands of female leaders during the Vienna EU – USA summit: (from left to right Benita Ferrero-Waldner, EU Commissioner for External Relations and European Neighborhood Policy; Condoleezza Rice, U.S. Secretary of State; Ursula Plassnik, Austrian Foreign Minister; Hubert Gorbach (FPÖ), Vice Chancellor of Austria; Eva Nowotny, Austrian ambassador to the U.S.; Susan Razinsky-McCaw, U.S. ambassador to Austria. Photo Credit: Hopi Media (Bernhard Holzer)

By contrast, the atmosphere at the EU-Latin American summit in May was much more relaxed, although the event was an organizational nightmare. We had to provide security for sixty heads of states and governments from the EU (including accession candidates Bulgaria and Rumania), Latin America and the Caribbean, along with their respective delegations. As we were taking the "family photo," a half-naked beauty walked into the picture. She carried a Greenpeace poster in protest against the construction of paper mills on the border of Uruguay and Argentina. A smart security guard grabbed her elegantly around her waist and danced her off the scene, Samba-style.

The Near East took center stage on the foreign policy agenda. The unexpected victory of Hamas in the Palestinian legislative council elections overshadowed the first few weeks. The EU was expected to express its position, among others, on the Danish cartoons controversy, the Iranian nuclear question, on Guantanamo, the repercussions of the Iraq war, as well as on an EU strategy on Africa. For the EU presidency, this meant managing the complex and multi-faceted opinion shaping process among the members in a way that did not look like disagreement from the outside. Within six months, we painstakingly elaborated a total of 121 carefully calibrated "presidency statements" on a variety of global topics and conducted numerous interventions in human rights matters. The many third-party meetings during the Austrian EU presidency took up much of our energy in foreign relations; we participated in 16 meetings of foreign ministers of the EU troika, 11 meetings of foreign ministers in Association or Cooperation Councils with neighboring states, and two EU accession conferences. State Secretary Hans Winkler became an esteemed regular in the European Parliament, an institution increasingly powerful as a co-legislative body and an opinion leader on many issues. Ambassador Gregor Woschnagg, the permanent representative, acted as the indefatigable and circumspect Brussels "dispatcher."[31]

For me, the end of our second EU presidency is closely associated with the Middle East. By the end of June 2006, I had finally managed to take a day off, which I planned to spend in the country before going to Moscow for the G8 Foreign Ministers Meeting. However, Tzipi Livni rang me early in the morning with breaking news with the kidnapping of Gilad Shalit, a young Israeli soldier in the Gaza strip. This started a search that would last for years and received huge attention in Israeli politics and public opinion. That summer, by arrangement with Israel, I secretly met Ali Laridjani, then the Iranian chief nuclear negotiator, in Germany; an arduous "mediation attempt" that would unfortunately remain unsuccessful.

As the EU-Council chair, I was free to choose the lead topic of only one of the traditional informal meetings of ministers, the so-called "Gymnich meeting." The agenda for all other EU Foreign Ministers' Council meetings had been determined through tedious negotiations way in advance. The Salzburg Gymnich meeting on 11 March 2006 focused on the European perspective of the Western Balkans under the motto "Export stability, don't import instability." The meeting ambitiously aimed at advancing a step further on the accession track with every single Balkan partner. The meeting included all EU foreign ministers, the High Representative and

---

31. Gregor Woschnagg provides interesting insights into the Austrian EU presidency, see *Hinter den Kulissen der EU: Österreichs EU-Vorsitz und die Zukunft Europas* (Vienna: Styria, 2007).

the Commissioner for external relations and the foreign ministers of all the Balkan states and the respective representatives of the International Community. Toward the end, just before the concluding press conference, news broke that Slobodan Milosevic had died. All present held their breath. Everybody in the room had had some terrible personal experience with the Serb dictator. At the same time, we all felt that the future of the region was already present around that very table in Salzburg. We knew: Europe would remain incomplete without full membership of all the Balkan states.

The 2006 EU presidency brought Austria much international acclaim. Ironically, Wolfgang Schüssel, the Austrian head of government and head of the Austrian People's Party, lost the parliamentary elections in September of the same year.

Austria—Balkans—Europe

Alois Mock, who served as foreign minister during the years of dramatic change after 1989, had the foresight to realize that there would be no return to times past for our neighbors in the East and Southeast. A dedicated proponent of national independence of the Balkan states, he prevailed against many who hemmed and hawed, both in his own country and in the EC. In 1991, Mock urged the EC to recognize the former Yugoslav republics Slovenia, Croatia, and Bosnia and Herzegovina as sovereign states. In this way, he secured lasting gratitude both for himself and for Austrian diplomacy. His action also defined a guideline for Austrian foreign politics to this day: the re-unification of Europe in freedom will only be achieved once all Balkan states have become EU members.

Austria's engagement in support of its neighbors in the East and Southeast has garnered considerable international esteem. We owe this success to the perseverance of many individuals and groups, who, over generations, had paved the way. Their work includes the welcome extended to Hungarian refugees in 1956, the handling of the Prague Spring, Erhard Busek's Eastern politics and Alois Mock's efforts on behalf of Slovenia, Bosnia and Herzegovina, and Croatia. At the 1998 Salzburg Gymnich meeting, Wolfgang Schüssel prevailed against heavy opposition from France and Germany in starting the enlargement negotiations. In 2005, I in turn managed to start accession negotiations for Croatia, which had been delayed due to the Causa Gotovina, and consequently to decouple them from the Turkey EU negotiations. The speedy recognition of Kosovo in 2008 by the Gusenbauer/Molterer administration is part of this policy, as well.

In the quarter century since 1989, Austrian support of the Balkans has remained a priority not only for every administration but also for every government minister. Inside the EU, Austrians have established themselves as successful participants in various "twinning" projects, among them border management and the creation of sustainable democratic processes and structures. The Austrian Federal Armed Forces contributed significantly to the region's security, an accomplishment acknowledged by Austrians as well as NATO. Austrian civil society's active and generous participation in reconstruction efforts on the Balkans demonstrated our neighborliness and our humanitarian tradition. Numerous great and small relief and assistance initiatives sprang up. Doctors and farmers, church communities and universities, everybody lent a helping hand. "Neighbor in Need", this great relief effort organized by the Austrian Broadcasting Network (ORF), became a flagship of civil society humanitarian support.

Austrian diplomats took key positions in the work for peace and reconstruction on the Balkans: Wolfgang Petritsch (in Rambouillet, Dayton and Sarajewo), Erhard Busek (as indefatigable coordinator of the regional initiative Stability Pact/ RRC), Stefan Lehne (Javier Solana's right-hand man in Macedonia /Former Yugoslavian Republic of Macedonia (FYROM), Albert Rohan (as part of Matti Ahtisaari's staff), Valentin Intzko (as the High Representative of the EU and the International Community in Bosnia/Herzegovina), Jan Kickert (with Bernard Kouchner in Sarajewo und as the EU Representative's deputy in Kosovo). In addition, the numerous first-rate Austrian bilateral ambassadors in the region and their teams made significant contributions. Small wonder that the Austrian economy, led by banks and insurance companies, has acted as a trail blazer too.

Among EU partners, Austria enjoys a reputation for expertise and analytical skills with regard to the Balkans. Our voice is being heard. In foreign politics, the time of spectacular solo flights is over for countries like Austria—if ever it existed. Today, it is more important to make our distinct voice heard in international decision making bodies. Under the leadership of Foreign Minister and Vice Chancellor Michael Spindelegger, the Balkans' European future has become the trademark of Austria's commitment to the UNO and the EU. The recognition of the Danube area strategy as an EU macro region is one of his lasting achievements.

The Thorny Issue of Security Policy

Over the last few decades, questions of security policy have been increasingly neglected if not openly disregarded **as serious socio-political** challenges and **matters of the state.** The end of the Cold War did nothing to change this. In fact, Austrian neutrality was transformed from a constitutional principle into a dogma if not the *sine qua non* of our international identity. Politicians who dared to re-interpret the traditional concept of neutrality were publicly snarled at. Any form of airspace monitoring—be that by Draken or Eurofighters—encountered entrenched criticism. The Federal Armed Forces suffered a severe loss of respect. The great coalition government (SPÖ-ÖVP) even conducted a referendum in 2013 about the future of compulsory military service after the issue had been a pawn in the short-lived daily politics of the Vienna municipal election campaign. The results, however, were clear: 59.7% of respondents supported compulsory military service or alternative civilian service. Today, Austria supports the training of Mali security forces against Jihadists with 10 medical doctors as part of an EU training mission. To this day, no political party has managed to escape the alarming dynamics of invisibility camouflage. Correspondingly, Austria continues to be profoundly ambiguous with regard to the EU's Common Security and Defense Policy.

The EU's limited capacity to act in matters of foreign and security policy became painfully manifest during the Yugoslav wars of the nineties. The economic giant EU was unable to solve the Balkan problems in its own backyard without the support of US troops. Against this backdrop, the 1997 Treaty of Amsterdam introduced a legal basis for the "Common European Security and Defense Policy" (CSFP). In the summer of 1998, just before the first Austrian EU presidency, the French-British summit in St. Malo brokered an important change of course in as much as the British abandoned their reservations against a European defense component outside of NATO. In the course of the next few years, Javier Solana, the first "High Representative for Joint Foreign and Security Policies" and former general secretary of NATO, steered the step-by-step build-up of European security and defense policies.

Inside Austria, the question of how a neutral Austria would fit into the emerging common security and defense policy remained essentially an open issue. Our previous "logical" partners Finland, Sweden, and Ireland had already adapted their concepts of neutrality to the new circumstances. They no longer served as a frame of reference for comparisons. In 1991, the German-French-Brigade had become the "Joint Euro-Corps." The 1992 Treaty of Maastricht distinctly assigned security policies to the EU, albeit in the context of the inter-governmental "second pillar." The EU and the Western European Union (WEU) worked closely together, with the former taking over the latter's Petersberg Tasks. However, unlike the WEU and NATO, the EU did not become a military alliance with obligatory mutual assistance. The EU was thus able to accommodate the special needs of neutral member states like Austria.

During the turbulent nineties nobody could foresee how the security-political framework and necessities in our part of the world would evolve. The Warsaw Pact had dissolved in July 1991. NATO was re-defining its role. Against the background of the Balkan wars, the debate about the possible option of **Austrian NATO membership**—so much reviled in our day—appears in a slightly different light. Hungary, the Czech Republic, and Poland were scheduled to join NATO on the occasion of its 50-year anniversary in 1999. Under these circumstances, it would have been negligent not to search actively for the most appropriate solution for Austria. The first EU presidency was at our doorstep. Agreeing to clarify Austria's position in security matters, the Austrian People's Party and the Austrian Socialist Party, in their 1996 coalition agreement, promised to present Parliament with a full report about our security policy options by April 1, 1998.[32]

In spring 1998, Ambassadors Thomas Mayr-Harting and René Pollitzer from the Foreign Ministry and the Federal Chancellors office worked hard to draft the so-called "options report," the basis for the report to Parliament. In essence, the only open question was whether eventual Austrian NATO membership was to be included in this report as one of the options to be examined. The government leaders at the time had to finalize the report in strictest secrecy. I am still uncomfortable when I remember Chancellor Viktor Klima's nonchalance on this issue. Then-Vice Chancellor and Foreign Minister, Wolfgang Schüssel, and the two delegations sat and waited for hours in Vienna's Palais Pallavicini, the secret meeting place, for the Chancellor. He had sent word that he would make an appearance at the opening of the *Kronenzeitung*'s first private radio station and then come to

---

32. The passage in the coalition agreement regarding the "options report" reads as follows: "Given the course of the EC Conference and the developments in European security politics, the Austrian government will thoroughly review all options, including the question of full Austrian membership in the WEU, and will report the findings to parliament before the beginning of Austria's EU presidency but no later than the first quarter of the year 1998, as requested by the Chancellor, the Minister for Foreign Affairs, and the Minister for Defense. Based on the conclusions of this report, the government will make a recommendation to parliament on the best course of action. Austria will continue to develop its relationship with other security organization that are part of the network within which the EU member states negotiate their security and defense policies." [trans. Inge Fink] Quoted in Heinrich Schneider, "Der sicherheitspolitische 'Optionenbericht' der österreichischen Bundesregierung: Ein Dokument, das es nicht gibt - und ein Lehrstück politischen Scheiterns," in *Die sicherheitspolitische Entwicklung in Österreich und der Schweiz*, ed. Hans Fuhrer, Heinrich Schneider, and Ernest Enzelsberger (Vienna: Landes-Verteidigungsakademie, 1999), 4.

the Palais Pallavicini immediately afterwards. He never did. Apparently, he had gotten "cold feet," but never bothered to let his coalition partner know.

For years, Austria saw many poisoned debates not only about the NATO question but also about possible participation in the European Security and Defense Policy. In essence, the debate revolved around the question whether, as a last resort measure, Austria would assist in EU military actions, as specified in the "Petersberg Tasks," without an explicit mandate by the UN Security Council. Despite legal clarity, this remains a toxic question in both Austrian foreign and party politics. It has not really been resolved on the political front to this day.

In the meantime, EU "battle groups"—hotly debated around the turn of the millennium—started to form in 2005. In 2012, Austria even took over the leadership for the logistics and transportation unit of the battle group formed with Germany, the Czech Republic, Croatia, Ireland and Macedonia/FYROM. Together with their comrades, 350 soldiers must be ready for action within five days. So far, for lack of political agreement, the EU battle groups have not seen any action. The closest they came to active deployment was during the Libya crisis of 2011 when they were supposed to help in the evacuation of EU citizens in accordance with a UN mandate. To be sent into action, battle groups require a unanimous deployment decision from all EU governments plus a UN mandate. In Austria, deployment of soldiers requires in addition a unanimous decision by the Council of Ministers and the Standing Committee of the National Council of the Austrian Parliament.

Through the years, the Federal Armed Forces of Austria have earned a solid reputation as reliable UN peacekeepers. The Middle East is a geographical focus (UNDOF in the Golan and UNIFIL in South Lebanon, UNFICYP in Cyprus). On the Balkans, Austrian soldiers participate in NATO's "Partnership for Peace," in EU Missions (EUFOR [European Union Force] Althea in Bosnia and Herzegovina), or even in special NATO units such as in Northern Kosovo. Austria's first larger scale participation in an EU mission in Africa in 2007 was a remarkable event: Under the command of Irish General Patrick Nash, some 160 Austrian soldiers provided protection for civilians as part of "EUFOR Chad." Participation in an African mission was an important—if testing—experience for the Federal Armed Forces as well as Austrian EU politics. Austria's participation in the EU training mission for security forces in Mali (EUTM [European Union Training Mission] Mali) continues this dimension of Austrian security politics.

A New International Identity?

The end of the Cold War, EU accession, and globalization not only fundamentally changed the parameters of Austrian foreign politics, they also changed **Austria's very international identity**. From a seemingly protected marginal existence at the intersection of two irreconcilable political rivals, courted by both for its neutrality, Austria, as a middleweight, net contributor to the EU budget, was thrown into a world of relentless competition. A gap opened between Austria's self-perception and its perception by others.

While the Austrian private sector quickly learned how to benefit from the new situation, Austrian political and social self-perception largely lagged behind. Instead of enthusiasm about new opportunities, we witnessed entrenched positions in security policy, sterile debates about neutrality, anti-Temelin hysteria, dissatisfaction about the EU, a public opinion largely uninterested in questions of foreign politics, and sensation-hungry tabloids. If during the first decades of the Second Republic the Cold War had limited Austria's options in foreign politics, Austria "in freedom" showed a dangerous tendency to self-imposed provinciality.

In early 2009, pollster Rudolf Bretschneider revealed that Austrian opinions about their neighbors in the East had changed for the better over the past 20 years. However, he criticized that "many intellectuals—exceptions prove the rule—have remained remarkably indifferent. Only small groups—for example, in the Institute for the Danube Region and Central Europe, in the Forum Alpbach, in the Institute for Human Sciences—or lone wolves like Paul Lendvai or Karl-Markus Gauß would consistently and systematically promote a better understanding of this region."[33]

Not many innovative ideas emerged from the ranks of the Socialist Party; a vague nostalgia for the 70s began to spread, characterized by the stereotypical demand for Austrian foreign politics to embrace the role of mediator. Hardly anybody pointed out that due to a total change of circumstances, this demand for "politics à la Kreisky" was a chimera in the new European context. In Austria, inferiority complexes alternated with delusions of grandeur.

The Social Democrats' waning interest in questions of foreign and European policy is difficult to understand. It resulted in some surprising

---

33. Rudolf Bretschneider, "Die neuen, alten Nachbarn," *Wiener Zeitung*, 21 Feb. 2009, 1 and 4.

changes of positions by the party. The disastrous joint letter to the *Kronenzeitung* by Chancellor Alfred Gusenbauer and his Minister of Infrastructure Werner Faymann in June 2008 on future ratification of EU treaties by referenda is a telling example for such a fundamental change of position. Chancellor Werner Faymann, underwent a conspicuous transformation from EU skeptic in 2008 to ardent EU supporter in 2012. Populist anti-EU sentiment even left its traces in the staunchly pro-European Austrian People's Party.

In the mid-90s, the Austrian Freedom Party under Jörg Haider did an about-face for purely populist reasons, turning from EU supporters into harsh EU opponents. His closest associate at the time reckoned Haider's turnabout to have been a purely tactical move: after the 1989 pro European "Rütli oath" of the People's Party and the Social Democrats, the position of EU-opposition had become vacant. Haider expected to mobilize a relevant electoral segment with some careful cultivation—an opportunity not to be missed. Anti-EU sentiment ran high, a constant temptation for any opposition party. I first met former Vice Chancellor Susanne Riess-Passer by chance when she entered a TV studio to participate in a television debate as the spokeswoman against the Euro. As a vice chancellor, she later took constructive EU positions, often against significant resistance within her own party.

The Austrian Green Party took the opposite route: Since the EU-accession, it has increasingly made a name for itself as pro-European force. Gone were the days of 1989, when seven Green Party members voted against Austria's application for EC membership. Andreas Voggenhuber turned from EU-Saul to EU-Paul; Alexander van der Bellen, Ulrike Lunacek, and Eva Glawischnig have emerged as committed—albeit not uncritical—EU supporters.

Wolfgang Schüssel deserves credit for putting the Freedom Party, at least for a few years, on a clear pro EU trajectory. Everybody in this party knew that there was a red line they must not cross. Still, the Freedom Party continued to stir the pot of critical opposition. Referenda became their favorite tool in this process. They ceaselessly registered demands for referenda for all and sundry, even for the revocation of EU sanctions in 2000. Working with Freedom Party representatives backstage used up a lot of political energy, but it brought about the desired effect for the People's Party, for Austria, and for Europe. The strategy proved especially useful during the delicate phase of enlargement. Austria supported every single EU decision during the years the Freedom Party was a partner in the coalition government. The ratification of the accession of our twelve new

EU members looked like a smooth process from the outside, but one can easily imagine that it involved a lot of arm-twisting by the Austrian People's Party and quite some teeth-clenching on the part of the Freedom Party and its voters. While in the first vote on July 9, 2003, the Austrian National Council unanimously approved EU enlargement, by December 2003, two parliamentarians of the Freedom Party voted against the ratification of the accession treaties of the ten new EU members because of the Czech Republic's position on the Temelin nuclear power station and the Beneš decrees.[34]

How to Become Confident Europeans

Austrian EU membership brought about an unprecedented push toward modernization and adaptation to the European mainstream. At the same time, letting go some of our beloved peculiarities caused unexpected tension at some quarters. On the domestic scene, the positive boost of EU accession faded rather quickly; uncertainty and dissatisfaction resurfaced yet again. The "EU-naysayers," one third of the population, became a welcome marketing niche for the opposition, especially the Freedom Party. Naturally, the Freedom Party profited from the Great Coalition's decline into immobility. The twin pressure to adapt to the West—the EU partners, and the East—the new "old" neighbors, had become a test of political endurance. The upheavals inside the other Austrian political parties were fueled by similar concerns.

Judging by reliable polls, one cannot fail to notice that Austrian public opinion about the EU has hardly changed throughout the years. About one third of the population are EU enthusiasts, one third lukewarm supporters, and one third opponents, with a few nuances here and there. Only a small minority advocates for Austria's leaving the EU. Opposition to the EU today often masquerades as some sort of conditional support: "Yes, but…"; in other words, these people would support the EU if it were different, better, slimmer, greener, more socially oriented, or less bureaucratic. This attitude constitutes a permanent challenge for all EU communication. "Europe emerges new every day"—every generation and every country has to reinvent Europe for itself, has to explain the European dream to

---

34. By the way, the only member of the National Council to vote against the ratification of a European constitution on May 11, 2005 was a delegate of the Liberal Party. The Liberal Party demanded a referendum after the Treaty of Lisbon had already been ratified. In both cases, the Austrian newspaper *Kronenzeitung* supported the Liberal Party with virtually hysterical fervor.

themselves and to others, time and time again.[35]

The influence of Austrian anti-EU tabloids on domestic and European politics should not be underestimated. The *Kronenzeitung*'s capacity for launching political campaigns is legendary. In a 2008 interview, its editor-in-chief Hans Dichand opined that he controlled a minimum of 3% of Austrian votes. Taking into account that in most elections the two main parties are usually less than 3% apart, one can imagine the repercussions of this kind of control of the electorate. Given that the *Kronenzeitung* reaches almost half of the Austrian population on a daily basis (which is the largest per-capita distribution of any newspaper worldwide), its vilification of the EU does not remain without consequences. Unfortunately, its influence extends also to those who bear political responsibility. Nowadays, tabloids represent a main vehicle of communication for positions and projects in both domestic and European politics.

The year 2000 with the EU partner's "sanctions" against the coalition government of the Austrian People's Party and the Freedom Party delivered a massive shock to the EU attitude of Austrians. This rather unappealing chapter in Austrian and European politics remains yet to be investigated more thoroughly. One day, the exact circumstances of the sanctions including possible involvement of politicians in office at the time will be analyzed. Doing so in this article would far exceed its purpose. It took a significant amount of political energy to shake off this aberration of the European spirit in September 2000. Yet the repercussions of the sanctions extended far beyond their actual existence. A little-regarded positive result of this experience can still be found in EU treaties. Together with Peter Moors, the chief of staff of Belgian Premier Minister Guy Verhofstadt, I drafted Article 7 of the European Constitution on the margins of the European Council in Nice in December 2000. Article 7 defines the conditions and procedures that apply to such cases today. Interestingly, they have not been formally invoked since. Could this be a positive example of a pan-European learning process?

Benita Ferrero-Waldner had to start her new job "under the most difficult conditions an Austrian foreign minister has ever faced."[36] She experienced first-hand the sanctions imposed by the EU partners and often downplayed as "measures." A particularly embarrassing "highlight" in the sanctions circus occurred at the formal opening of the "European

---

35. See also Ursula Plassnik, "Europa entsteht jeden Tag neu," in *Zukunft denken: Festschrift für Wolfgang Schüssel*, ed. Andreas Kohl, Reinhold Lopatka, and Wilhelm Molterer (Vienna: Verlag für Geschichte und Politik, 2005).
36. Gehler, *Österreichs Außenpolitik in der Zweiten Republik*, 872.

Monitoring Centre on Racism and Xenophobia" (EUMC) on July 4, 2000 in the Hofburg Palace in Vienna. In the turbulent spring of 2000, this EU organization was openly re-directed as an instrument for the mortification of the People's Party/Freedom Party coalition. The roster of speakers for the official opening ceremonies included Commission President Romano Prodi, EP President Nicole Fontaine, Austrian Federal President Thomas Klestil, and the Chair of the EUMC Management Council, Jean Kahn. Beate Winkler, the director of the EUMC, deliberately did not invite Austrian foreign minister Benita Ferrero-Waldner to this major international event in Vienna. This was an unprecedented affront. I will never forget the determination with which the uninvited foreign minister, flanked by her loyal General secretary for foreign affairs Hans Kyrle, and her chief of staff Michael Zimmermann, walked into the Hofburg Conference Centre and took a seat in the front row, smiling through gritted teeth. Ferrero-Waldner was not only a courageous and indefatigable fighter against the sanctions; in 2000, she successfully chaired the Organization for Security and Cooperation in Europe; she developed a new format of neighborly cooperation with the "Regional Partnership" and later became the respected and much-appreciated EU diplomat-in-chief.

Austria takes time to develop a **new type of international self-confidence**. Inside the EU, Austria's continuing positive economic development make it easier to score points and even serve as a role model for youth employment, export capacity, labor-market reforms, and social cohesion. In the long run, a sense of unity transcending party-political fixations will emerge as we focus on contemporary foreign-policy challenges like protection of civil society, rule of law, environmental protection, women, dialogue between religions, and the stabilization of fragile states. The traditional Austrian DNA of "mediator" and "bridge builder" finds new ways of expression in our self-definition as a strong EU partner and good neighbor with a keen preference for global multilateral approaches to problem solving and the willingness to show solidarity to the best of our abilities.

Global Foreign Policy

The end of the Cold War was not only the final impetus for the reunification of Europe; it also boosted hopes for efficient multilateral diplomacy. Many naively assumed that the UN would now be able to kick-start into action in the interest of world peace. However, the 1990s turned out to be years of open military conflict: on the Balkans, in the Middle

East (the invasion of Kuwait, the first Iraq war), and in Africa (genocide in Rwanda). 1989 also saw the Chinese student revolt in Tiananmen Square in Beijing.

The intense and time-consuming work in the EU never weakened Austria's commitment to the United Nations. Our membership in the UN Security Council, the 1993 Vienna World Conference for Human Rights, our active engagement in Geneva, New York, and Vienna, as well as our constant efforts to expand the UN headquarters in Vienna are illustrations of this profound and undiminished engagement.

In 1973/74, Austria served as a non-permanent member of the UN Security Council and, among other things, dealt with the Yom Kippur War (October 1973) and the Cyprus Crisis (1974). When Austria applied for a second term in the UN-SC in 1990, its profile was still defined as that of "active mediator tasked with building bridges, encouraging dialogue, and negotiating compromises." In 1991, Austria joined the Security Council for another two years. During this phase, it faced the Gulf War and a series of regional conflicts in its immediate neighborhood, including the crisis in Yugoslavia. Despite such serious challenges, Austria voted in favor of all 116 resolutions adopted by the UN-SC at the time.

In October 2008, after the successful EU enlargement, Austria prevailed against its competitors Iceland and Turkey, with 133 votes in the first ballot, in its application for a seat on the UN Security Council. In 2009/10, the UN-SC focused on improved protection of civilians during military conflicts, the integration of women in the political process, and the rule of law. In intervals of two decades, Austria thus successfully served the International Community as a member of the UN SC. The tight coordination of Austrian diplomacy between Vienna, New York, and Brussels has long been a fixture on our day-to-day foreign-policy agenda. There is no such thing as Austrian "UN abstinence."

In the course of its work for sustainable peace, Austria has consistently advocated disarmament and arms control and has repeatedly added innovative ideas to the discussion. The world-wide condemnation of anti-person mines and cluster munitions serves as an example for Austria's successful contributions. We have also contributed significant political and professional expertise to the Comprehensive Nuclear-Test-Ban Treaty Organization (CTBTO) and the Treaty on the Non-Proliferation of Nuclear Weapons (NPT). In addition, the suggestion to multilateralize the nuclear fuel cycle is still on the table. This suggestion would offer a constructive approach to negotiating the nuclear question with Iran.

Citizens' Services and New Partners: The New Foreign Ministry

During the EU-membership negotiations, the Austrian foreign ministry proved its mettle as a competent motor and honest broker for inner-Austrian coordination. Clearly, the ministry was useful as a direct line to the permanent representative in Brussels and as a resource for professional synthesis. The EU-briefs regularly produced by the ministry's staff for members of government and parliament, as well as the daily directives to Brussels, found broad approval throughout the republic. In this way, the Austrian foreign ministry became the "ministry of Europe."

In order to express the new nature of our work on a symbolical level, I initiated a legislative amendment in March 2007 changing the official name of the Ministry for Foreign Affairs to "**Ministry for European and International Affairs**." As EU members, Europe and all things European have long ceased to be "foreign affairs."

Globalization brought new professional challenges for the European and foreign ministry. The demand for citizens' services increased as people became ever more mobile (mostly thanks to air travel). In case of plane crashes, terror attacks, the taking of hostages, natural disasters, and armed conflicts, people had to be evacuated at short notice and often under dramatic conditions. We had to assist our citizens during the East Asian tsunami disaster on December 26, 2004, the 2006 Danish Cartoon Crisis, and the 2006 Lebanon war. In 2003 and 2008, Austrian citizens held hostage in the Sahel zone by Al Kaida of the Islamic Maghreb could be liberated and brought out of the country only after extensive negotiations. Of course, in many cases, these disasters affected citizens from other EU countries as well, which meant that several EU foreign ministries were active in crisis management, albeit without much opportunity for coordination.

Unfortunately, an Austrian-led initiative of the Regional Partners for improved consular protection during a crisis never got off the ground. To this day, a study about rapid humanitarian relief units named "Europe-aid," written by the former EU Regional Commissioner and Foreign Minister Michael Barnier and commissioned by Austria, is still gathering dust in the drawers of the EU. The basic idea was to create a kind of humanitarian task force of "EU blue helmets" which would help EU citizens in a non-military crisis. Conceptually, this was similar to the "EU battle groups" that were being set up to help manage military crises outside the EU. Such relief units could give a boost to European identity as EU citizens would have a chance to experience EU providers of humanitarian help. Who knows, maybe there are still courageous EU politicians left, who, undaunted by problems of bureaucratic competence, will manage to get this project up and running. The next giant leap forward must lie in common EU consular representation in the world. This would make the EU more visible and tangible for its citizens.

During the 90s, the new information and communication technologies dramatically changed foreign policy, long the exclusive domain of diplomats and a few professionals in parliament and universities. When I joined the foreign ministry in 1981, I still learned the art of manual encryption so I would be able to communicate confidentially with headquarters in case of crisis. I saw my first ever computer at the end of the 1980s in the Austrian representation to the Council of Europe in Strasbourg, which boasted state-of-the-art equipment. I marveled at a computer monster named "Wang," which took up an entire room and was operated by a specially-trained secretary, who sat at a giant control board like a train operator. I will never forget the first laptop, which the Finnish delegation proudly showed off to less-fortunate fellow delegates at the CSCE conference on human contacts in Bern in spring 1986. All of this happened long before the invention of cell phones and round-the-clock accessibility. Today, all Austrian diplomatic representations are well equipped with modern communication technology; after the passing of the Electronic Administration Act (ELAK), the foreign ministry even became the first "paperless" Austrian ministry.

Public space as such also underwent a profound change. In the wake of the 60s, this found expression in new forms of self-organization. The age of Non-Governmental Organizations (NGOs) had arrived. Amnesty International was founded in 1961, its Austrian chapter in 1970.[37] Through the US Congress, American NGOs had already established themselves as new players during the CSCE process. They drew attention to specific issues and problems and became partners of governments and diplomatic services.[38]

---

37. Peace activists in Vancouver, Canada founded Greenpeace in 1971; Transparency International was founded in 1993 in Berlin.
38. Karel Schwarzenberg is a textbook example of the new alliance between the work of NGOs and top politics. Very early on, he supported the resistance against the Communist government in Czechoslovakia, intervened on behalf of the opposition, and became active in the international human-rights movement. He had caught my attention when he was the president of the International Helsinki Foundation for Human Rights (1984 and 1991). Personally, I mistook the mustachioed, mumbling old-Austrian for a hopelessly passé figure from an operetta. Then, in the early fall of 1989, I first experienced "Schwarzenberg live" at the awards ceremony for the Human Rights Prize, awarded by the European Council in the Strasbourg Hemicycle. Back then, I was primarily interested in the luminous figure of Lech Walesa. However, Walesa was anything but a born orator; his performance in front of the large Strasbourg audience was lackluster at best. Schwarzenberg, on the other hand, gave a brilliant three-minute speech, which completely captivated me. I have rarely changed my

Austrian diplomats learned to deal with their new partners and their specific ideas mainly by working with domestic help organizations and through multilateral diplomacy at the UN, CSCE, the Council of Europe, and the Organization for Economic Cooperation and Development (OECD). Today, no politician can imagine Austrian development aid Policy without taking into consideration its close cooperation with active NGOs. On the contrary, the Austrian government repeatedly had to keep committed NGOs from dipping into the taxpayers' pockets. The Austrian Development Agency (ADA) often walks a thin line between general taxpayers' interests and NGO requests. There is no doubt that Austria has to substantially increase its financial share in development cooperation. It is a collective failure of several Austrian governments to never have implemented the 0.7% benchmark. However, Austrian development cooperation is right in focusing on key countries and key topics, as stipulated in the Austrian Development Cooperation Act.

New Topics in the Global Village

Mixing the voluntary and the involuntary, all of us have moved closer to each other in the global village. The end of the Cold War has made this evolution more visible for Europeans and their immediate neighbors. The ideological straightjacket having disappeared, underlying cultural, religious, and social differences have reappeared. New frictions arose; new lines of separation emerged.

The new proximity needs smart management. Here, too, lies a big challenge for modern foreign policy. The dialogue between cultures and religions can significantly contribute to constructive conflict management and sustainable peace. Austria has hundreds of years of experience with cultural and religious diversity. This positive legacy of the Habsburg monarchy could benefit all of Europe. We are only slowly starting to judge this legacy objectively and without false glorification or random condemnation. During the days of the Cold War, the Catholic Church, particularly Cardinal Franz König, has the merit of having cultivated the dialogue with orthodox churches. Based on his personal experience, Alois Mock, a practicing Catholic, engaged in the dialogue with Islam, which was recognized as a religious community in Austria since 1912. The Austrian-Iranian dialogue between theologian Father Andreas Bsteh and Mohamed Khatami further advanced the cause in the 1990s. Following in their wake,

---

mind about a person in such a short amount of time. Much later, as foreign ministers, we harmoniously worked together on difficult topics like Temelin.

the challenge was to bring this highly intellectual and specialized dialogue down to the everyday level of ordinary citizens. This was even more important because, in domestic politics, integration and mutual understanding had become crucial issues that called for constructive management.

The dialogue between religions became a new interface of foreign, domestic, and European politics. For Austria, it offered the opportunity to make a valid contribution in a completely new context. Personally, I thought it important to include women and young people in this dialogue and to put to practical use existing Austrian expertise in research (universities, the Academy of Sciences), media, and civil society (two conferences of European Imams, 2003 in Graz and 2006 in Vienna). As the dialogue between civilizations also took place at the UNO level under the leadership of SG Kofi Annan, I pursued two long-term goals: setting up an appropriate UN unit and establishing a "Center of Excellence for Inter-Religious Dialogue" – both in Vienna. This would have opened up possibilities to exchange best practices on specific questions of living together, such as the construction of mosques and the improved integration of young immigrants into the school system and job market. When I proposed this to the Austrian Parliament, however, the mere suggestion provoked jeers and heckling.[39]

Four uncommonly competent people Gudrun Harrer, Sabine Kroissenbrunner, Ambassador Ralf Scheide, and Consul General Ernst-Peter Brezovsky helped me organize a series of international events to further the dialogue between religions: the big conference "Islam in a Pluralistic World" in November of 2005 (attended by the presidents of Iraq and Afghanistan, Iranian Ex-President Mohamed Khatami, and Nobel-Peace laureate Shirin Ebadi); the conferences "Islam in Europe" in March 2007 and "Muslim Women and Youths in the West" in Salzburg in May 2007; the workshop "Inter-Cultural and Inter-Religious Dialogue Seen from a Gender Perspective" in June 2008; the Salzburg Trilogue on the question "Do We Speak the Same Language?"; the EU-Arabian League ministerial conference in Vienna in December 2008 on the topic "Women, Youth, and Civil Society."

In my function as the chairwoman of the EU Council of Foreign Ministers, I met with Danish Foreign Minister Per Stig Møller and religious leaders from Bosnia and Herzegovina, Syria, Denmark, and Austria during the tense period of the Danish Cartoons Crisis. The 2008 Culture Conference of the Austrian Foreign Ministry was deliberately dedicated to the "Dialogue between the Cultures as Most Important Challenge of

---

39. See the minutes of the 85th meeting of the National Council, XXIV. legislative period, for November 18, 2010.

Our Time." Initiated by Vice-Chancellor and Foreign Minister Michael Spindelegger, the important dialogue conference of the "Alliance of Civilizations" in February 2013 in Vienna successfully continued this well established tradition of Austrian foreign policy.

"Every other person is a woman" - this catchy slogan was suggested by a French TV station in February 2013 to raise awareness for the situation of women in the global village. Considering that they make up 50% of the world's population, women have not received nearly enough attention as a subject matter of international politics. If we strive for successful development cooperation and sustainable peace, we have to make women's voices heard and support their participation in public space. This is not a "women's issue" but an issue for our entire society, which requires equal commitment from men. Even Communism might have had at least this advantage: it established women's participation in the working world as normal, which is still not the case in many regions of the world. Austria is well-placed for international leadership in this issue as well.

The continued engagement for implementing UN Security Council Resolution 1325 on "Women, Peace and Security" constitutes another important feature of contemporary Austrian foreign politics. In May 2007, US Secretary of State, Condoleezza Rice, traveled to Vienna specifically to participate in the international conference on "Women Leaders in the Middle East," along with Israeli Vice Prime Minister and Foreign Minister Tzipi Livni, Palestinian leader Hanan Ashrawi, and a good dozen female ministers from the region and from Europe. This was a new and fruitful experience for all participants. A lot of challenging work remains to be done, especially in the light of the Arab Spring, which has again brought women's precarious situation to the public's attention: a rewarding task for future European and Austrian foreign politics.

Concluding Remark

In many ways, Austria made the best of the double chance offered by the magical year 1989. As on previous occasions (the 1955 State Treaty), Austrian politicians had a "good nose" for the strategic potential of the moment. The Austrian economy did not lag behind either. With astonishing speed, Austrian businesses established themselves in Eastern and Southeastern Europe. They became leading investors in the entire region, out-stripping all other European competitors. Cultural affinity? Geographical proximity? Ancient ties? Whatever may have made the difference, the Austrian economy profited greatly from Eastern enlargement; at least 5% additional growth was achieved due to this development during these years. Hundreds of thousands of jobs were created or saved. The export ratio climbed rapidly from 36.4% in 1989 to 57.3% in 2011 and now still lies above the EU average of 46.6%.[40] Austrian investments abroad have multiplied: Since 1995, Austria has strongly increased its direct investments and closed the much-cited investment gap by the end of 2004.[41] In addition, as long as our neighbors' standard of living is not equal to ours, there will be further opportunities for economic growth.

Throughout the last decades, Austrian foreign policy has received neither the public attention nor the acclaim is deserved. The reasons may lie more in the eye of the beholder than in the actual accomplishments. Day to day the media—television in particular—submerge us with images and news of horrendous events from all over the world. Clearly, explanations regarding the context and background of such events get short shrift. Despite the increasing complexity of our world, the media employ fewer and fewer foreign correspondents, political analysts, and well-informed academics—often for budgetary reasons. Even foreign policy professionals show little interest in the views of those politically responsible for Austrian foreign policy. Throughout my term in office and afterwards, I have never been consulted by a single Austrian political scientist or historian on the background of specific foreign-policy issues (like the Turkish EU-negotiations in 2005).

Could it be that the socialization of those professionally interested in foreign policy has a part in this state of affairs? Most of them grew up during the Kreisky era; their view of the world has often not completely made the transition to the new conditions and complexities of the 21st century. Most of them are amazingly unfamiliar with the practical dimension of Austrian EU membership. For some, it is still a "thorn in their side" that most of the key figures in Austrian foreign politics over the last few years were mostly members of the People's Party. Why approve of anything a politician does if he or she does not share the views of one's political family? It is so much easier to succumb to nostalgia for a time irretrievably past. The reception and analysis of contemporary Austrian foreign policy continues to suffer from the "1970s filters."

Whoever built or destroyed a sandcastle as a child knows the fundamental principle of architecture: building is much harder than destroying. And it generally takes a lot longer. The same is true for international politics.

---

40. Statistik Austria.
41. Austrian direct investments abroad by the turn of 2004/2005 amounted to € 51.2 billion, as compared to €8.7 billion in 1995. In 2010, Austrian direct investments abroad amounted to €132.5 billion, see Österreichische Nationalbank, *Statistisches Sonderheft Statistiken Direktinvestitionen 2010* (As of the end of 2010).

Whenever a political system dies—for whatever reason—it takes a long time for a new system to take its place, especially if the transition involves questions of identity and democratic processes. Democracy is a living thing; it requires transparency and the involvement of the greatest possible number of people in complex decisions. Every society develops the rules by which it wants to live, including the right to further question, change, and develop these rules.

During the last twenty-five years, Austrian politicians and diplomats, together with their European partners, had the truly unique privilege to write the script by which we want to live. Step by step, this process has made Austria freer, more committed to solidarity and more self-confident. Those active in Austrian foreign politics deserve credit for making major contributions to the new international positioning of our country. But let us not forget the contributions made by immigrants. State Secretary Reinhold Lopatka recently remarked that the 1.6 million people with immigrant background form a bridge between Austria and their countries of origin: "We can read the connection between foreign and integration politics in numbers: today, about 450,000 people from former Yugoslav countries live in Austria."[42]

In the course of this process, Austria has come closer to implementing the original mission statement of the Second Republic, which was spelt out as a leitmotif in the Government's Statement of April 27, 1945: "Austria wants to live its identity in unalloyed friendship with the peoples of the Danube region and work together with all its neighbors in peace and friendship, to the benefit of all." If Austria's 1995 EU accession opened the door to the Slavic-Byzantine dimension of the new "old" Europe, the EU accession of Croatia on July 1, 2013 will link Central Europe with the Mediterranean. We must and will succeed in fully integrating the 18.5 million inhabitants of the remaining six Balkan states—Bosnia and Herzegovina, Serbia, Montenegro, Macedonia/FYROM, Albania, and Kosovo—into the European Union.

Young diplomats and future foreign politicians might heed the encouraging words by Austrian star painter Maria Lassnig: "Change your vocabulary, your pre-conceived notions about your fellow man and about politics daily; change your way of living every week; change your job; get ahead of the changes time has in store for us!"[43]

---

42. BMeiA press release of September 18, 2012.
43. Quoted from Maria Lassnig, *Die Feder ist die Schwester des Pinsels, Tagebücher 1943-1997* (Cologne: Dumont, 2000), 30.

Austrian Cultural and Public Diplomacy After the End of the Cold War

Emil Brix

Since the beginning of the Second Austrian Republic, cultural and public diplomacy played a central part in positioning Austria in an international context and in rebuilding reputation after the Second World War. The conscious decision to communicate internationally Austrian culture and heritage (including natural landscape) became a part of national identity building and complemented Austria's status of neutrality after 1955.[1] This priority agenda was upheld throughout the time of the Cold War, but in the 1970s the idea of a modern globally orientated Austria was added and in the 1980s the emphasis shifted from presenting Austria in the West[2] towards a cautious re-evaluation of cultural and mental contacts with Central and Eastern Europe. But only the end of the Cold War brought a fundamental change to the scope, direction and dimension of Austria's possibilities to project the self-understanding and the image of the country internationally.

The New Position in Central Europe

The end of the Cold War and the ideological division of Europe in 1989 also marked the end of Austria's special position as a Western but neutral country with long borders with Warsaw Pact countries which had created artificial cultural fault lines. World politics made Austria a "normal" European country in the heart of Europe. This offered new chances for making even more use of traditional Austrian "soft power" assets in the field of culture and cultural heritage. The chances and challenges were twofold. For the first time since the end of the Habsburg Monarchy there was a clear rationale to concentrate cultural and public diplomacy efforts

---

1. Ernst Bruckmüller, *Nation Österreich. Kulturelles Bewusstsein und gesellschaftlich-politische Prozesse*, 2nd ed. (Wien-Köln-Graz: Böhlau, 1996); Gerald Stourzh, *Vom Reich zur Republik. Studien zum Österreichbewußtsein im 20. Jahrhundert* (Wien: Geschichte und Politik, 1990).
2. For Austrian cultural diplomacy in the United States see: Walter Seidl, *Zwischen Kultur und Culture. Das Austrian Institute in New York und Österreichs kulturelle Repräsentanz in den USA* (Wien-Köln-Weimar: Böhlau, 2001).

on the newly established democracies in transition in Central Europe, and later in the Balkans, and to build on long-term multinational traditions (cultural plurality[3]) which had had little chance to come into play during the time of ideological confrontations in Europe. Overall, Austrian foreign policy concentrated on the country's effort to join the European integration resulting in the EU-membership in 1995. But at the same time cultural diplomacy became a major tool to redefine Austria's position as a Central European country.

The Institutional Expansion of Austrian Cultural Promotion Abroad

Under the leadership of the Austrian Foreign Ministry (which has been on the level of the federal government since 1974 responsible for promoting Austrian culture abroad) the end of the Cold War was the beginning of an era for the "institutional expansion" of Austria's cultural presence abroad. The then Austrian Foreign Minister Alois Mock (ÖVP) seized the chance of newly opened borders to the east and started to substantially increase the budget and the role of cultural diplomacy ("one of the pillars of Austrian foreign policy"). To consolidate these increased international activities some years later for the first time an official strategy paper was published (*Auslandskulturkonzept Neu*, updated in 2011[4]) which outlines the objectives, strategies, and instruments of Austria's international cultural policies. Its main emphasis lies on the classical objective of public diplomacy: "winning friends and influencing people."

Since the early 1990s the network of "Cultural Institutes" (since 2002 "Cultural Fora") has been gradually enlarged from eight "Institutes" to now thirty "Fora." The majority of them are situated in Central and South Eastern Europe. The first of these new representations opened in 1990 in Cracow and soon became a model for strongly intensified cultural diplomacy in former Warsaw Pact countries with more than a hundred projects annually which ranged from street festivals to expert seminars on modern city administration. Worldwide Austrian cultural representations organize or support more than 4000 projects every year with budget money and strategic input from the department for international cultural policies in the Foreign Ministry (*Kulturpolitische Sektion*).

---

3. Emil Brix, "Pluralität. Die Erneuerung der Moderne," in: *Pluralität. Eine interdisziplinäre Annäherung*, ed. Gotthart Wunberg and Dieter A. Binder (Wien-Köln-Weimar: Böhlau, 1996), 273-296.
4. <http://www.bmeia.gv.at/fileadmin/user_upload/bmeia/media/3-Kulturpolitische_Sektion_-_pdf/Broschueren/Broschuere_Auslandskulturkonzept_2011.pdf> (February 21, 2013).

From 1988 onwards Austria also began opening "Austrian libraries" in cooperation with local partners in most Central and South Eastern European countries (today there are sixty-one libraries in twenty-eight countries).[5] A special agency (*Österreich Institut Gmbh*) was established to open language schools in neighboring countries (today nine language schools in Bratislava, Brno, Budapest, Cracow, Ljubljana, Rome, Warsaw, Wroclaw, Belgrade). The Foreign Ministry established cultural cooperation offices as well in Sarajevo and in Lviv, and in cooperation with other government departments an "Office of Science and Technology" in Washington DC.

In 2001 the Foreign Ministry initiated the "Platform Culture Central Europe" as a permanent forum of cultural cooperation between the foreign ministries of Central European countries. The Platform for Central European International Cultural Policy was founded on the occasion of the first foreign minister's conference of the "Regional Partnership" countries (Austria, Poland, Czech Republic, Hungary, Slovakia, Slovenia) on June 6, 2001, as a forum for cultural dialogue with the purpose of providing support for bilateral and multilateral cultural projects that focused on common Central European cultural interests. The goals of the platform are:

– to distribute information and raise awareness of the cultural life in the participating Central European countries, the European Union and beyond

– to exemplify the creative power and strength of expression of our artists

– to highlight the common cultural identity of Central Europe within the context of European integration.

Since its foundation, the platform has supported about fifty projects worldwide; in two major annual meetings—held in the capitals of the respective EU Council Presidency—the platform member countries convene for key issue conferences and the presentation of common artistic projects.

From the early 1990s onwards, the Ministry of Education started to support "Austrian Schools" in the Czech Republic, Slovakia, and Hungary, and established a cooperation organization for educational and cultural contacts with the new democracies to the east and southeast of Austria (*KulturKontakt Austria*). Various "artist in residence" scholarship programs give young Austrians the chance to live and work for a few months in artists' studios abroad and provide young foreign artists with studio spaces in Vienna.

---

5. See: <http://www.oesterreich-bibliotheken.at> (February, 21 2013).

The Ministry of Science and Research started to send Austrian lecturers to universities in Central and South Eastern Europe to support German language departments and to create a network of university cooperation in the region (including grants for regional student mobility). The Ministry also increased efforts to support Centers for Austrian Studies and "Austrian Chairs" especially in countries with close historical ties or where closer academic cooperation promised to have a positive impact for the "Austrian image" and for Austria's positioning as a Central European country (from the US to Israel).

From the early 1990s onwards the government has also provided funds for young Austrians who work in Holocaust-related institutions abroad as an alternative to the obligatory military service in Austria (*Gedenkdiener*).

Most of these new institutional arrangements have been an immediate response to new possibilities of cooperation with neighboring countries in transition after the end of the Cold War. All of the regional initiatives had clear objectives to help neighboring countries in their transition to democracy and to strengthen Austrian influence in the region. From the point of view of public diplomacy the success of this strong new input in cultural diplomacy depended also on a strong involvement of regional governments, city administrations, Austrian business interests in the region, and private initiatives. The opening of the "Iron Curtain" also led to increased initiatives of the Austrian Public Broadcasting Corporation (ORF) to provide more information about the Central European neighbors.[6] Even the big traditional institutions in Austrian culture such as the "Salzburg Festival" and the "Vienna Philharmonics" began to support public diplomacy efforts by working more closely with partners in Central Europe. Re-establishing close contacts with Central and South East European countries became in the 1990s the driving force for putting public diplomacy at the heart of Austria's foreign policy, more so than Austria's public diplomacy efforts to support the joining of the European Union.

This period of catching up and responding to a new open neighborhood with Central and South Eastern Europe was never formally ended, but by the end of the 1990s cultural diplomacy opened to a more European and global agenda while trying to maintain the new contacts in the neighborhood (although with less public money).

Yet culture remained the focal point. Major global changes which

---

6. After the first years of transition in Central and South Eastern Europe ORF soon reduced the number of foreign correspondents (for instance closing of offices in Prague and Warsaw) and this was accompanied by a general reduction of programs in foreign languages of Austrian public radio.

resulted from the end of superpower confrontation, such as the increased impact and recognition of globalization processes, and related renewed discourses about cultural identities contributed worldwide to a new interest in "soft power," thus, turning public diplomacy into a major factor in modern foreign policy,[7] which could support the national interest by communicating directly with diverse foreign audiences. Austria as a country with limited means of "hard power" but a long and treasured tradition of classical diplomacy faced the dilemma that Austrian diplomats were not always well prepared for the necessary changes towards "public diplomacy." Working as a press or cultural officer meant to accept junior positions in the Foreign Ministry and was somewhat, until nowadays, not seen as an advantage regarding one's diplomatic career. But surprisingly policies changed quickly in spite of lagging human resources.

New Policy Priorities and Strategic Shifts

As a consequence of the end of the Cold War, the political and intellectual position of Austria in Europe changed significantly from a neutral "outpost of the west" to a member state of the European Union, a promoter of "Central European" cooperation, and of Balkan integration into European structures. After the end of the East-West divide, Austria was one of many European countries which experienced that the increasing speed of change triggered off a roll back towards political re-evaluation of cultural heritage (history, geography, faith, ethnic loyalties) and cultural narratives of plurality and differentiation.

European Issues

As the main official agent for cultural and public diplomacy, the Austrian Foreign Ministry was remarkably swift in a deliberate shift of policies towards
– rediscovering and establishing cultural networks and cooperation projects within the Central European region
– interpreting "Central Europe" and the "Danube region" as a viable identity option which supported Austrian business efforts in the region and political objectives (good neighborhood policy; regional partnership)
– less interest in special cultural relations with Germany (less

---
7. Joseph S. Nye Jr., *Soft Power. The Means to Success in World Politics* (New York: Public Affairs, 2004).

need for a clear ideological separation from the idea of a common German culture)
– a renewed cultural discourse about politics of memory and politics of identity
– reducing the traditionally strong dominance of the public sector (etatistic tradition) in foreign cultural politics and cultural cooperation
– interpreting Europe as a "cultural project."

These strategic shifts have to be seen in the context of the specifics of European integration since 1989:
– The European integration process after 1945 deliberately avoided cultural issues. Since 1989 the idea of necessary "emotional bonds" (Ralf Dahrendorf: *Europe is a cold project*) to get popular support for the European project has significantly gained ground (still more among analysts and intellectuals than among policy makers).
– Present day discussions about Europe seem to center around spaces of identity and interest rather than on ideas of progress. The dynamics of "time" have given way to the dynamics of "space" and of "interest." Urban sociologists such as Edward Soja and historians such as Karl Schlögel formulated a "spatial turn" in cultural studies. In Europe, space has become more interesting than time: "seek and learn to recognize who and what, in the midst of the inferno, are not inferno, then make them endure, give them space" (Italo Calvino).[8]
– As a result, there is renewed interest in "politics of memory" (in the increasing accumulation of knowledge of the past /Aleida Assmann) and in issues related to identities and borders. At the same time some political parties in Europe gather momentum by mobilizing "fears of proximity."
– Critical concepts about European traditions and European perspectives all deal with the question of borders. If there is something specific that can be learned from the manifold traditions of European cooperation, it is the question of how Europe deals with borders, be they internal, external, real, or imagined. Have Europeans developed a specific ethics of borders? The key question is to understand borders not only as identity markers or as lines of separation between different identities, but to see them as spaces of transition between identities that have something in common. On

---

8. Italo Calvino, *Invisible Cities* (London: Harcourt Trade Publishers, 1974), 10.

a continent proud of cultural diversity, it is worth working towards a situation where borders stand for integration and not for rupture. Europe has much to do in order to find some balance between centers and peripheries. Who decides on where the centers or peripheries are in Europe? What is the core of a national or a European identity, and does the center or the periphery decide on this question?

– There is a need for European discussions about neighborhood as a potential for cross-border solidarity and for cross-border conflict. The myriad of visible and invisible borders turns everybody into a neighbor, and may force Europeans to interpret borders as places of transition. Europe revisited may provide exactly this message: borders are unstable identity markers even if they take the very physical shape of a Berlin Wall or of the "peace walls" which separate the religious communities in Belfast.

– Europe is moving east. The present crisis of the idea of Europe is often interpreted as a belated consequence of the fundamental changes of 1989. After the fall of communism, Europe has not developed common visions for its future but has been trying to simply enlarge the Western model of European integration.

– Can all major normative social trends in Europe (notion of sustainability, mobility of labor force and capital, service orientation of society and economy, change towards knowledge based societies, location competition/creative milieus, civil society/social capital, leisure society, and secularization) be interpreted as creative rediscoveries of past conditions which Europe and the West may successfully implement universally?

– The cultural specifics in the history of Central European cities (ethnic and religious plurality, strong cross-border relations with neighboring cities, strong symbolic presence of history in the form of myths and rituals, late modernization, similarities in architecture and urban planning, potential for middle class dissent throughout the 20th Century, appreciation for "being different," tradition to understand cities as narratives, functioning city centers) have become attractive for today's policy makers in Europe, at least for those who interpret our post industrial condition as a chance to overcome the political dynamics and economic rhetoric of a uniform global village.

– Responding to the continued dominance of "national loyalties" communication efforts in many European countries devote

themselves to the pursuit of a European idea which would be capable of drumming enthusiasm for the "European Project" into 500 million people. The Austrian writer Elias Canetti probably would have described the narratives that are currently under discussion as an indigestible mixture of illusion and dangerous, new formulas for crowds and power. Popular are stories about "allegedly specific European values" (democracy, market economy, and rule of law), "Fortress Europe" (with the keywords "global player" and "most competitive economy") and about an idea, which has lost its enemy (Communism) and now seeks a new "European soul," but in the process only encounters new foreign enemies (asylum seekers, Islamists, terrorists). If European stories are reinvented in this way, it is not surprising that the wish of states such as Turkey and Ukraine to become part of the European Union is regarded as a threat by majorities in EU member states. Europe promotes "fear of contact" since it fails to bring about a common idea bearing more than an economic rationale. After 1945, the "rousing" idea of peace and reconciliation between European nation-states marked the beginning of European integration. The fact that Europe overcame its ideological division back in 1989 led to enough enthusiasm to realize fifteen years later a substantial enlargement of the European Union to the east but in many countries (such as the United Kingdom) this did not create a common drive for "more Europe."
– From an Austrian perspective today's major European cultural challenges are fully integrating all Balkan countries in the European project, avoiding the use of so-called "cultural fault lines" in the context of decisions about future EU enlargement and dealing with migration issues and Muslim populations in Europe not only as potential or real security risks.

In 2007 in order to underline the significance and special character of European affairs the Austrian Foreign Ministry even changed the official name of the ministry to "Federal Ministry for European and International Affairs" and started to regularly communicate European matters directly with diverse home audiences (schools, local politicians, meetings with employees, NGOs). The change of ministers from Ursula Plassnik to Michael Spindelegger at the end of 2008 (both ÖVP) resulted in slight changes regarding the government communication of EU matters in Austria which is still strictly pro-European but more strongly concentrating on factual information and on an interactive dialogue with the Austrian public. Such a pragmatic approach is accompanied by an increased use of the traditional name "The Austrian Foreign Ministry."[9]

A Difficult Return of the Past

Informing and influencing foreign audiences about Austrian identity and foreign policy priorities after the Cold War could not only concentrate on positive Central European and European traditions of the country. The role of Austrians in the Second World War and in the Holocaust and especially the ambiguous perception of having been the first victim of Nazi Germany blurred a positive Austrian image in most Western countries.[10] It was only after the "Waldheim Affair" that the then Austrian Prime Minister Franz Vranitzky (SPÖ) in the early 1990s publicly acknowledged that Austrians participated in the Holocaust and that there are moral consequences for Austria that followed from this.[11] Following increased compensation and restitution efforts, public diplomacy could start to communicate that Austria shared a collective responsibility for the good and the bad in the past. Since the early 1990s it has become a constant in Austrian public diplomacy to communicate internationally that modern Austria has learned from history and that official Austria as well as Austrian society have learned this lesson. Austrian representations abroad regularly collaborate with Jewish organizations and academic institutions in organizing common projects on Holocaust-related issues and also on the strong Jewish contribution to Austrian culture. No concerted action was taken to start specific image campaigns but the contact with Jewish Austrian emigrants and second and third generations of emigrants has become a constant part of the work of embassies and cultural representations abroad.

The question of a specific public diplomacy campaign was only really raised when in the year 2000 all other EU-member countries decided on the "so-called sanctions" against Austria because of the fact that Jörg Haider's rightwing FPÖ became part of a coalition government. The negative reaction of European and other Western governments, and of the public opinion in many European countries, proved that Austria was still under scrutiny regarding rightwing politics. A normalization of relations could not be achieved by immediate public diplomacy responses[12] but by a

---

9. See the homepage of the Ministry website: <http://www.bmeia.gv.at/en/foreign-ministry/startpage.html> (February, 21 2013)
10. Anton Pelinka, *Austria: Out of the Shadow of the Past* (Boulder: Westview Press, 1998).
11. Steven Beller, *A Concise History of Austria* (New York: Cambridge University Press, 2006), 296.
12. As examples for public diplomacy reactions see the following publication which was

formalized procedure of advisory opinion ("group of wise men") and by the fact that the center-right coalition government of the time followed a strict course of confidence building measures regarding Austria's commitment to democracy and further increased measures for Jewish compensation and restitution.[13]

Opening Public Diplomacy to Global Issues

Following the events of 9/11 Austrian public diplomacy significantly widened its scope to communicating more strongly Austria's traditions and initiatives in the dialogue between cultures and religions including efforts to promote Vienna as a leading venue for international dialogue.[14] As a host country for many international organizations (UN-institutions, OSCE, IAEA, OPEC) and with her multinational and multi-religious traditions from the time of the "Danube Monarchy" (for instance being the first European country which officially recognized Islam in 1912) Austria strongly supports a dialogue of activities between religions and on wider humanitarian issues.

These activities are in line with the longstanding tradition to lay particular stress on cultural relations in public diplomacy. Cultural cooperation and cultural relations with foreign publics are seen as crucial for the image and perception of Austria abroad. Cultural exchange—as a means which is promoted but not controlled in its contents by governments —promises access to diverse target groups, high credibility and the creation of trust which is an ever more valuable commodity in international relations. Culture respects and furthers the two-way-relationship which is pertinent for modern communications.

Cultural Diplomacy is More than an Image Transmitter

In his introduction to the "Austrian Foreign and European Policy Report 2011," Foreign Minister Michael Spindelegger underlines the

---

financially supported by the Foreign Ministry: Hubert Feichtlbauer, *The Austrian Dilemma. An Inquiry into National Socialism and Racism in Austria* (Vienna: Holzhausen, 2001) and the topical title of Austria's annual cultural diplomacy conference in the autumn of 2000: "Heiss umfehdet, wild umstritten. Zur aktuellen Debatte um Österreich: Ziele und Perspektiven der Kulturdiplomatie."

13. For a summary of events and further literature see the introductory essay of Bischof in this volume.

14. See Eric Frey, "Konferenzplatz Wien: Vienna as an International Conference Site," in *Global Austria. Austria's Place in Europe and the World*, ed. Günter Bischof et al. (New Orleans: UNO Press, 2011), 147-160.

public diplomacy relevance of cultural projects:

"Culture is an essential factor in the international perception of Austria and thus an indispensable element of foreign policy. With the new International Cultural Policy Concept 2011, we have defined the goals of our international cultural activities for the coming years: In addition to showcasing the innovative-creative potential of Austrian cultural players, we above all want to support projects that contribute to fostering European integration according to the idea of Europe as "Unity in Diversity." Furthermore, we want our cultural activities abroad to make a sustainable contribution to the global formation of trust and the keeping of peace by means of initiatives targeted at fostering the dialogue between cultures and religions."[15]

This official statement of the Austrian Foreign Minister indicates that cultural and public diplomacy has gone a long way from simply trying to create and transmit a "positive image" of the country (as requested in the ministry's cultural guidelines until the 1980s) towards making good use of images and stereotypes for the formation of trust and the fostering of dialogue. Making good use of images and stereotypes is relevant because Austria does not only see itself as a *Kulturnation* but it is also internationally identified by its rich traditions in the arts and culture. When, in today's fast-paced media society, these take the form of simplified positive images, then they become all the more an asset for Austria's foreign cultural policy. The strong international recognition and appreciation of its heritage allows Austria to place present-day cultural and scientific achievements and ideas from a strong civil society at the very center of its foreign cultural policy. For this task all new methods of communication and technology should be exploited, so that information about Austria can be conveyed quickly and to targeted audiences. An international comparison shows that states often have very different goals in their cultural diplomacy. These range from ideological competition to attempts to make their own state-identity better known, from making one's own country more international and more open to the world to economic considerations like investment policy, promoting tourism, and boosting exports or even supporting ideas of an "ethical foreign policy."[16] Foreign cultural policy is often used by smaller states to

---
15. <http://www.bmeia.gv.at/en/foreign-ministry/foreign-policy/foreign-and-european-policy-report.html> (February 21, 2013)
16. Emil Brix, "Cultural Work Abroad: Between Management and Diplomacy," in *Public Diplomacy* (Favorita Papers 01/2004), ed. Gerhard Reiweger (Vienna: Diplomatic Academy,

distinguish themselves from their politically and economically powerful neighbors. The goal is always to be able to "tell our own stories" and this is also relevant to Austria. It is not possible for a smaller state to define its image abroad mainly on its own terms. But in the question of "trust" and "confidence building," smaller countries with less "hard power" often have a competitive advantage which can be utilized in mediation processes and in conflict resolutions.

A "high touch" understanding of public diplomacy favors projects which engage the individual directly and is ideally based on personal and group interests of engaged private actors (including non-governmental organizations and also religious communities and multinational corporations) at home and abroad.

In the field of dialogue activities it is necessary to at least partly change objectives for public diplomacy from presenting national images or directly trying to influence international opinion towards supporting intercultural dialogue within Europe and worldwide. Major new objectives are actively promoting a respectful "dialogue between cultures" and supporting projects which concretely show the value of cultural diversity in Europe as a specific strength of European integration.

The implementation of these new objectives can be exemplified by a Foreign Ministry initiated series of conferences of Islamic communities and organizations in Europe (first meeting in 2003) to strengthen the discourse on European Islam and its commitment to European values (including projects to establish standards for Islamic religious education in Europe). Regarding cultural cooperation within Europe, Austria strongly supports the new collaboration in the framework of EUNIC (European Union National Institutes of Culture, established in 2006) which develops common projects (with Austria as a lead country) to strengthen the knowledge about cultural traditions and the cultural potential of the Western Balkans.

New technologies and new expectations of instant communication via the internet create opportunities for better service from Foreign Ministries for their own citizens abroad (tourists and expatriates). Austria is among the growing number of countries which uses public diplomacy not only to communicate with foreign publics to establish a dialogue designed to inform and influence, but also to offer direct contact and support for Austrians abroad especially in crisis situations from natural catastrophes to political unrest. Austria also offers networking possibilities for Austrian researchers and scientists who live and work in the United States or for academics related to "Austrian libraries" who want to cooperate in the fields of Austrian literature and history.

2004): 41-45.

For specific target audiences the branding and marketing activities of the "Austrian Development Agency" (ADA) and its cooperation offices abroad as well as the international network of the "Austrian Economic Chambers" and of the "Austrian National Tourist Office" play a significant role in supporting the main objectives of Austrian public diplomacy. Already for some years attempts have been under way to better coordinate national branding between all interested public partners in Austria.

Perspectives

For a prosperous but small country in the heart of Europe it is an obvious choice for Austria to concentrate its public diplomacy efforts on national assets which are either well known internationally or sought after in international relations. Thus the self understanding and perception of Austria as a *Kulturgroßmacht* (cultural superpower) will continue to serve as the core asset for public diplomacy. With the end of the Cold War, Austria seized the chance to communicate its renewed Central European position by means of a strengthened cultural cooperation in the region. European and global consequences of a more fragmented world order with a growing number of non-state actors will not fundamentally change Austrian foreign policy priorities but public diplomacy will have to further strengthen its use of "new social media" and more generally its impact on foreign audiences by communicating Austrian perspectives on the future of Europe and on trust-building through a dialogue between cultures.

The challenges for the diplomatic service are obvious because today diplomats have to be foremost "mediators" and "communicators." At the same time direct relations with the public at home (*Bürgerservice*) become essential which includes an even more pro-active attitude towards helping Austrians abroad. The Austrian Foreign Ministry communicates on its website a very clear though ambitious message: "worldwide at your service."

Austrian Security Policy after the End of the Cold War

Erwin A. Schmidl

Introduction

Austrian security policy evolved gradually and in several phases after the Second World War.[1] For a long time it was shaped by Austria's specific geographical position during the Cold War, directly on the "front line" between the two blocs, and by the neutrality policy adopted in 1955.[2]

Whereas the military always saw its main task (as formulated in the Constitution and the Army Law[3]) in preparing for military defense in the

---

1. Walter Feichtinger, "Österreich im sicherheitspolitischen Wandel – von der Landesverteidigung zur solidarischen Friedenssicherung," in *Military Power Revue der Schweizer Armee* 3 (2007), supplement to *the Allgemeine Schweizerische Militärzeitschrift* 12 (2007) and *Schweizer Soldat* 12 (2007): 18-27. For the background and the period up to 1989, see Andrew Earl Harrod, "Felix Austria? Cold War Security Policy between NATO, Neutrality, and the Warsaw Pact, 1945-1989," Dissertation, Fletcher School of Law and Diplomacy, 2007; Manfried Rauchensteiner, ed., *Zwischen den Blöcken: NATO, Warschauer Pakt und Österreich* (Vienna: Böhlau, 2010); Erwin A. Schmidl, "Österreichs Sicherheitspolitik und das Bundesheer 1918 bis 2008: ein Überblick," in *Österreich: 90 Jahre Republik: Beitragsband der Ausstellung im Parlament*, ed. Stefan Karner and Lorenz Mikoletzky (Innsbruck: Studien Verlag, 2008), 481-95; and Erwin A. Schmidl, "The Warsaw Pact and Austria: Threats and Threat Perceptions," in *"Peaceful Coexistence" or "Iron Curtain"?: Austria, Neutrality, and Eastern Europe in the Cold War and Détente, 1955-1989*, ed. Arnold Suppan and Wolfgang Mueller (Vienna: LIT Verlag, 2009), 203-17. As the author is a civil servant in the Austrian Ministry of Defense, the usual disclaimer has to be made that this article reflects only his personal views and in no way seeks to transport any official standpoint on the part of the Austrian government.
2. An interesting comparative workshop about the neutral countries Austria, Finland, Sweden, and Switzerland in the Cold War was organized by Thomas C. Fischer and Jussi Hanhimäki in Geneva in October 2010; the resulting book will be out soon. For Austrian foreign policy in general, the reader is referred to the standard *opus magnum* by Michael Gehler, *Österreichs Außenpolitik der Zweiten Republik: Von der alliierten Besatzung bis zum Europa des 21. Jahrhunderts* (Innsbruck: Studien Verlag, 2005).
3. The Austrian Constitution goes back to the text adopted in 1920 and amended in 1929; it was re-adopted in 1945 following the separation from the Third Reich, to which Austria had belonged since the *Anschluss* (annexation) of March 1938. Likewise, the main elements of the Army Law adopted in 1955 were based on the earlier Army Law of 1920. See Felix Schneider, "Der Weg zum österreichischen Wehrgesetz von 1955," in *B-Gendarmerie, Waffenlager und Nachrichtendienste: Der militärische Weg zum Staatsvertrag*, ed. Walter Blasi, Erwin A. Schmidl and Felix Schneider (Vienna: Böhlau, 2005), 171-90.

case of war in Europe, the political leadership never truly expected the Austrian Armed Forces to fight. Under the impression of barely having survived two major defeats, in 1918 and 1945, the political leadership by and large always hoped to stay clear of future wars. This becomes evident from a discussion held in the Parliamentary Defense Committee in February 1958: Chancellor Julius Raab described the military's main assignment as serving as "an educational tool for youth" (Austria had re-instituted obligatory national service in 1955[4]). In the event of a war or crisis in the neighborhood (such as had been the case during the Hungarian uprising of 1956), soldiers would assist border police in caring for refugees and disarming armed groups. In the case of a major war, any defense was to be only "symbolic" in nature. Raab's view was shared by most members of the government (with the laudable exception of Defense Minister Ferdinand Graf). This explains, in part, why the military never received adequate defense funding.[5]

In addition to military defense, the Austrian Armed Forces always had the secondary task of assisting the civil power, usually during natural disasters and occasionally to support the police in controlling the border, such as during the crisis in Hungary in 1956, or to prevent cross-border supply for the South Tyrolean "activists" ("terrorists" or "freedom fighters," depending on one's point of view) in 1967. A third task for the military, initially taken on very reluctantly, was the deployment of personnel to United Nations peacekeeping operations. In 1960, a medical contingent was dispatched to the UN operations in the Congo for the first time, later followed by other medical units, police and military observers. With the deployment of two battalions to UN operations in Cyprus and the Middle East, Austrian participation in international missions increased dramatically in 1972-73, from about 115 to 900 men.[6]

Varying Concepts of Military Defense

In 1961, the concept of "comprehensive defense" (*Umfassende Landesverteidigung* or ULV) was officially adopted by the Austrian

---

4. A referendum held on 20 January 2013 confirmed the system of obligatory conscription (as well as the parallel alternative community service in a civilian organization) by a 60:40 majority.
5. The protocol of the meeting of the Defense Committee on February 25, 1958 was published by Manfried Rauchensteiner, ed., *Das Bundesheer der Zweiten Republik: Eine Dokumentation* (Vienna: Bundesverlag, 1980), Document no. 26, 41-42.
6. Erwin A. Schmidl, *Blaue Helme, Rotes Kreuz: Das österreichische UN-Sanitätskontingent im Kongo, 1960 bis 1963* (Innsbruck: Studien Verlag, 2010); Christian Ségur-Cabanac and Wolfgang Etschmann, eds., *50 Jahre Auslandseinsätze des Österreichischen Bundesheeres* (Vienna: BMLVS, 2010).

government, following the example of other neutral countries such as Finland, Sweden, and Switzerland.[7] "Comprehensive defense" consisted of four components: apart from the military, there were also psychological, civilian, and economic aspects. In the 1970s and early 1980s, this concept was developed further, and was embodied in the official National Defense Plan (*Landesverteidigungsplan*) of 1975, published in 1985, which was and, in theory, still is a binding document.[8]

In May 1965, three different "contingency cases" were defined: (1) international tensions with mainly economic consequences (the "crisis case"), (2) a war in the vicinity, which might lead to refugees crossing the border and to political, economic, and possibly, military consequences ("the neutrality case"), and (3) direct military aggression ("the defense case").

A new defense concept was adopted in the 1970s, officially entitled "territorial defense" (*Raumverteidigung*), but better known as the "Spannocchi Doctrine," after its initiator, Army Commander Emil (Count) Spannocchi.[9] In the event of war in Europe, the aggressor was to be "dissuaded" from entering Austria, where he might expect massive resistance throughout the country, including guerrilla-style attacks from the rear by small, mobile groups. In 1972-78, the army was reorganized along these lines, comprising two different elements:

- the "Readiness Force" (*Bereitschaftstruppe*) of three mechanized brigades plus three specialized infantry battalions (one airmobile and two mountain battalions) and air support, numbering altogether some 15,000 soldiers; and
- the "Reserve Force" (labeled "Militia" after the Swiss model), consisting of mobile and territorial elements and eventually supposed to number more than 300,000 trained reservists.

However, for various reasons the army was never able to attract a sufficient number of reservists to fulfill this structure.[10] In 1987, well before the end of

---

7. See the study by Johanna Rainio-Niemi, "Small State Cultures of Consensus: State Traditions and Consensus-Seeking in the Neo-Corporatist and Neutrality Policies in Post-45 Austria and Finland," Dissertation, University of Helsinki, 2008.
8. *Landesverteidigungsplan* (Vienna: Bundeskanzlcramt, 1985).
9. Emil Spannocchi, *Verteidigung ohne Selbstzerstörung* (Vienna: Hanser, 1976). See also Wolfgang Wildberger, *Emil Spannocchi: Engagiert und Eloquent* (Graz: Vehling, 2006).
10. In 1971, obligatory national service was shortened from nine to six months, with an additional service of two months for refresher call-ups and exercises. However, many young men chose to serve in the Readiness Force for a total of eight months, thus avoiding later call-ups. At the same time, conscientious objectors were allowed not to serve in the military (in non-combatant functions, as had been the case before), but to choose an "alternative service" (in a hospital, with the Red Cross, etc.). This further depleted the number of recruits available to build up sizeable reserves. Also, lacking budgetary means delayed the acquisition of necessary equipment.

the Cold War, a new military structure was adopted, with an establishment of only 187,000 troops in the event of mobilization (240,000, including reserves and logistic elements).[11] This figure was more realistic, but insufficient to fulfill the dual task of blocking an aggressor's advance through the Danube valley into Bavaria and defending the central "redoubt" at the same time. Adequate supplies, including ammunition and medical back-up, were lacking.[12]

The years 1989-90 not only brought about major changes in Europe, but also important ones in the ministry. Robert Lichal was succeeded as Minister of Defense by Werner Fasslabend—which was as much a generational change as the retirement of the former Chief of Staff, General Othmar Tauschitz (who had served in the German Luftwaffe in World War Two), whose successor, Karl Majcen, already came from the postwar generation. On July 2, 1991, surprisingly in the midst of the Slovenian crisis,[13] the army command was abolished (the move had originally been scheduled for the autumn, but was taken earlier), with the forces being directed straight from the ministry through the corps commands.[14]

Subsequently, the brief war in Slovenia in the summer of 1991 was seen as a conceivable "model" for future crises: ethnic conflicts in the neighborhood, with possibly large numbers of refugees crossing into Austria, rather than direct aggression. As the dangers of an all-out war in Europe receded, the army structure was reduced again. Instead of the 1975 organization (one army command in Vienna and two subordinate corps commands in Graz and Salzburg), three corps commands were established (in Graz, Salzburg, and Baden, responsible for the south-eastern, western, and north-eastern borders respectively). This formed the basis for the "New Army Structure" (*Heeresgliederung Neu* or HG Neu), which was officially decreed on July 14, 1992. The army's main task switched from outright defense to border surveillance in times of crisis, and the intended mobilization strength

---

11. This and the following notes about army structure reforms follow the excellent study by Friedrich Hessel, *Strukturentwicklung des Bundesheeres von der „Wende" 1989/90 bis zum Jahr 2003* (Vienna: BMLV/LVAk, 2004). For a critical view, see also Walter Mayer, "Zur Entwicklung der Gliederung des Bundesheeres," <http://www.bmlv.gv.at/facts/geschichte/pdfs/entwicklung_mayer.pdf> (15 Nov. 2010).
12. A good account of these developments is the article by ret. General Hannes Philipp (Army Commander in 1986-91), "Der Operationsfall 'A': Gesamtbedrohung im Zeichen der Raumverteidigung, 1973-1991," in *Zwischen den Blöcken*, ed. Rauchensteiner, 325-86.
13. The events in Yugoslavia are not dealt with in any detail here because they form the topic of another article in this book.
14. I am grateful to several high-ranking officers, some of them already deceased, for granting me interviews over the years that have helped me to better understand what happened "behind the scenes." Some of them have asked not to be named, however.

was reduced to 120,000 (plus 30,000 reserves). Active strength was set at 10,000 troops, with an additional 5,000 reservists being available at short notice. There were still three active mechanized and twelve reserve infantry brigades, but the massive territorial organization of the 1980s (which had largely relied on reserve formations for guard and protection duties) was abolished. (Later on, with the new threat of terrorist attacks on crucial infrastructure, some observers questioned whether this move might not have been premature.)

EU Accession, "Neutrality Debate" and Looking Towards NATO

Parallel to these organizational measures, it became obvious that the future would bring increased participation in international peace missions. From the early 1970s on, Austria had always contributed two battalions plus some observers to UN operations in Cyprus and the Middle East, usually ranking on places two to five on the monthly UN lists of troop-contributing nations. To better organize future deployments, the "Prepared Unit" (PREPUN or VOREIN for *Vorbereitete Einheiten*) concept was authorized in 1993: module-like sub-units could be formed into contingents at short notice. Here it must be added that from the very outset Austria had always maintained that only volunteers were to be sent on such missions; therefore, Austrian peacekeeping battalions were always (and are still to a large extent) not standing units, but ad-hoc formations. Also in 1993, participation in international exercises started and has since become the norm for the Austrian Armed Forces. Beforehand, international cooperation in training had been limited to preparation for traditional peacekeeping operations. Courses held at the peacekeeping training center established in Vienna-Stammersdorf in 1987 had always attracted participants from abroad, and Austrian trainers had increasingly been invited to other countries.

In 1995, Austria joined the European Union (EU) and the NATO-Partnership for Peace (PfP). These moves coincided with intense discussions about the possibility of joining NATO as well.[15] Opinions differed across the political spectrum, but for a certain time even high-ranking Social Democrats could envisage Austrian membership of NATO—ideally without abandoning permanent neutrality which had developed far beyond its legal meaning and become an important part of Austrian identity over the four decades since 1955.[16] However, during the last phase of the "Grand

---

15. Erich Reiter, *Neutralität oder NATO: Die sicherheitspolitischen Konsequenzen aus der europäischen Aufgabe Österreichs* (Graz: Styria, 1996).
16. Gunther Hauser, *Österreich – dauernd neutral?* (Vienna: Braumüller, 2002).

Coalition" government of the 1990s, with the increasingly frosty climate between the dominant SPÖ and its minority partner ÖVP,[17] in April 1998 both parties failed to agree whether the intended joint report on future security policy options (the *Optionenbericht*) should even mention joining NATO as one of the alternatives or not, even though the meaning and relevance of Austrian neutrality had already been severely restricted in practice by Austria's accession to the EU and by the latter's evolution from an economic into a political and defense community. An important step in this regard was the Treaty of Amsterdam, signed on October 2, 1997, which took effect on May 1, 1999. That Austria officially clutched to neutrality despite insisting on European solidarity was not always easy to explain abroad—such as during the Kosovo crisis of 1999, when Austria welcomed NATO's air campaign of March 1999 in the context of the EU, but closed its air space to NATO aircraft for reasons of neutrality.

In 1996, the mechanized components of the Austrian Armed Forces were re-equipped with modern "Leopard II" main battle tanks (instead of the obsolete M-60s), "Ulan" armored fighting vehicles and "Jaguar" tank destroyers. Many observers questioned the rationale behind this decision at a time when it was already clear that the military's main task in the future would lie in increased participation in peace operations. Another major change was the opening of the army to women. Currently, 369 women are serving in the armed forces in various functions, including combat duties and officers.[18] Women are still far from being accepted as equals in the military, and recent studies have shown that women suffer from mobbing and discrimination to a higher degree than men.[19]

The 1992 army structure was changed once more when the government reduced mobilization strength to 92,000 (or 110,000 including reserves)

---

17. Traditionally, the Social Democrats (*Sozialistische*, later *Sozialdemokratische Partei Österreichs*, or SPÖ) and the Christian Socials (the Austrian People's Party or Österreichische Volkspartei, ÖVP) were the two strongest parties. Over the years, the right-wing and increasingly populist Freedom Party (*Freiheitliche Partei Österreichs*, FPÖ) attracted up to one quarter of the electorate, but it later split into two parties, the Freedom Party and the slightly more liberal Union for the Future of Austria (*Bündnis Zukunft Austria*, BZÖ). Since the 1980s, the Green Party has also been represented in Parliament.
18. This is the current figure according to the official homepage of the Austrian Armed Forces: <http://www.bmlv.gv.at/karriere/frauen/images/pdf/verwendung_weibl_soldaten.pdf> (14 Nov. 2010). The total is misleading; however, as it includes 73 professional athletes, who are soldiers for formal reasons only.
19. According to a study published by the Technical University in Vienna in mid-2010, one fifth of female soldiers have suffered from workplace bullying, otherwise known as mobbing. Out of 838 women who joined the army after 1998, more than half have already quit the job. See <http://www.tt.com/csp/cms/sites/tt/%C3%9Cberblick/Politik/PolitikContainer/949986-8/soldatinnen-leiden-unter-mobbing-im-bundesheer.csp> (14 Nov. 2010).

on April 1, 1998.[20] The three corps commands were reduced to two, and the three mechanized brigades to two. The infantry battalions were reorganized in three infantry brigades, with twenty additional territorial reserve battalions. This reform was known as "structural readjustment" (*Strukturanpassung* or StrAn).

On October 3, 1999, the federal elections yielded significant losses for the two (former) major parties. As a consequence of general frustration with the "Grand Coalition's" weak performance, the populist Freedom Party reached second place. When negotiations between the former coalition partners failed, a new "reform government" was formed by the ÖVP and the FPÖ under Wolfgang Schüssel in February 2000. In order to respond to developments in the fields of European cooperation and security, but also in view of the terrorist attacks of September 11, 2001, the new government (with a competent Defense Minister, Herbert Scheibner, from the Freedom Party) managed to adopt a new Security and Defense Doctrine in December 2001.[21] This Doctrine was intended to replace the old Defense Plan of 1975, but was adopted by parliament with only a simple majority (whereas the old Defense Plan has the rank of a constitutional law, which would have required a two-thirds majority to be changed), so—at least in theory—the old Plan is still in effect.

Continuing the Reforms

In 2002, the Defense Ministry and the General Staff were reorganized again ("Reorganization 2002"). The remaining two corps commands were abolished and six new higher commands instituted instead (land forces, air forces, special operations forces, international operations, logistic support and IT support). A year later, an Army Reform Commission was established under a former mayor of Vienna, Helmut Zilk, which led to the creation of a reform project team within the ministry, entitled "Management 2010" at a time when 2010 still lay far in the future.

Acting on the Commission's and the project team's recommendations, a

---

20. These figures themselves point to a compromise, as SPÖ negotiators had aimed at a final figure fewer than 100,000, whilst the ÖVP wanted more than 100,000. Hessel, *Strukturentwicklung*, 24.
21. See the official description of the Security and Defense Doctrine on the homepage of the Austrian Ministry of European and International Affairs <http://www.bmeia.gv.at/aussenministerium/oesterreich/staat-und-politik/sicherheitsdoktrin.html> (15. Nov. 2010), and the article by Brigadier General E. Gustav Gustenau (who was actively involved in the preparation of the doctrine), "Ein Paradigmenwechsel in der österreichischen Außen- und Sicherheitspolitik? Zur Ausarbeitung einer neuen Sicherheits- und Verteidigungsdoktrin", <http://www.bmlv.gv.at/pdf_pool/publikationen/03_jb01_48_gus.pdf>.

further reduction of forces was announced in May 2005, with mobilization strength of 55,000. In 2006, the six higher commands created in 2002 were amalgamated into two (joint forces and logistic support), and the number of brigades further reduced from five to four (two mechanized and two infantry brigades). Instead of fifty-seven battalion-sized units, there were now thirty-nine.

The issue of obligatory national service had been excluded from the Reform Commission's agenda, but the minister reduced national service from eight to six months in 2006. This actually led to protests from the Red Cross and other non-government organizations, as the length of the civilian alternative service was reduced accordingly, and many organizations count on the availability of sufficient numbers of young men opting to take this alternative instead of serving in the army. At the same time, higher professionalization of the forces was sought by creating active duty units composed of volunteers declaring their willingness to serve abroad, if ordered to do so (and receiving financial bonuses in return).[22] Participation in international operations became a clear priority, with the aim of permanently deploying two to three battalions (two for more robust operations, consisting mainly of professional soldiers, and one for more traditional peacekeeping duties, formed mainly from reservists) and in a position to deploy a "framework brigade" (i.e., the brigade command and important support elements) every two to three years.[23]

Participation in International Operations

For Austria, taking part in international operations was anything but new. Indeed it goes back to the 1960s, being one element of the "active neutrality policy" propagated by Bruno Kreisky. Within the armed forces, however, this view was not readily accepted—many saw these missions as "well-paid holidays" for those wanting to escape their real duties back home, and able personnel were often prevented from going. These opinions changed dramatically in the 1990s: after the end of the Cold War, participation in international missions has clearly become one of the main assignments (and, some would say, even the *raison d'être*) for the armed forces. For career

---

22. These units are known as *Kaderpräsenzeinheiten* (KPE), whereas the traditional ad-hoc formations are now labeled *Formierte Einheiten* (FORMEIN). KPE and FORMEIN are the two elements of KIOP (*Kräfte für Internationale Operationen* or "forces for international operations").
23. These aims were formulated in the 2004 White Paper: *Weißbuch 2004: Analyse – Bilanz – Perspektiven* (Vienna: BMLV, 2005), which is accessible via the internet: <http://www.bmlv.gv.at/cms/artikel.php?ID=2425>.

soldiers, participating in international operations has become a fact of life, and is now actually a prerequisite for making a career—exactly the opposite of what it used to be twenty years ago.

The Reform Commission of 2003 called for the ability to participate in the whole spectrum of international operations, from robust combat missions to traditional peacekeeping and humanitarian assistance.[24] In November 2000, Austria declared its willingness to contribute up to 1,500 soldiers and 110 police officers to the projected EU intervention forces of some 60,000 troops and 5-6,000 police officers. These "Helsinki headline goals" were modeled on the force deployed by NATO in Kosovo in 1999. Some years later, in 2004, in view of the need for smaller task forces quickly available for interventions in Africa and elsewhere, the EU created the concept of "battle groups" of some 1,500 troops, to which Austria agreed to contribute in November 2004. In 2011 and 2012, Austria indeed had contingents ready for deployment, but so far these battle groups have not yet seen action.

The number of personnel deployed abroad has remained fairly stable over the years. For obvious reasons, the emphasis is now on South-Eastern Europe, where Austria deploys some 800 soldiers and twenty-five police officers in Kosovo and Bosnia-Herzegovina at the time of writing (late 2012), and where Austrians also hold top international positions (for the second time, an Austrian diplomat, Valentin Inzko, is the High Representative,[25] and an Austrian general, at present, Major General Dieter Heidecker, the third Austrian in a row, is Commander EUFOR in Bosnia-Herzegovina). In addition, Austria contributes a battalion to the UN Disengagement Observer Force (UNDOF) on the Golan Heights in Syria, which has served there since 1974, and numerous smaller contingents and observers. In 2008, the deployment of 170 Austrian soldiers to the EU Force in Chad for the first time led to heated discussions in Austria about the motives for this decision. Up to then, participation in international missions had by and large been supported by all political parties as well as the public.[26]

Since 1974, fifty Austrian soldiers have been killed "in the service of peace," and more have been wounded or injured. In addition, there is a

---

24. In this context, the whole scope of the so-called "Petersberg missions" is sometimes mentioned. This is actually a misnomer, as the Petersberg Declaration (made by the foreign ministers of the Western European Union at the Petersberg guest house of the German government near Bonn) of 1992 is not really a clear definition, but rather a vague listing of military tasks. However, the wording of this declaration as well as the term "Petersberg tasks" has become a standard formula in European Union security parlance.
25. Before him, Ambassador Wolfgang Petritsch was OHR in 1999-2002.
26. Ségur-Cabanac and Etschmann, *50 Jahre Auslandseinsätze*.

"social price" to be paid, in terms of failed marriages or relationships. This is offset by the experience and international reputation gained by the service of altogether ca. 80,000 Austrians—all volunteers—in international operations since 1960. This has certainly boosted Austria's status in the international arena: that Austria was three times elected a non-permanent member of the Security Council (in 1973-74, 1991-92, and 2009-10) is just one indicator of this respect. Although the proportion has varied over the years, only about one third of these volunteers have come from the active duty forces, and the remainder from the reserves. Reservists are actually better suited for peacekeeping operations than many active duty soldiers, as they are slightly older and can provide more life experience. For the future, it remains to be seen how the reduction of the reserve forces over the past years will affect the ability to recruit qualified reservists for these missions.

Austria contributed an infantry battalion to the UN Peacekeeping Force in Cyprus (UNFICYP) from 1972 to 2001, and another battalion to the UN operation in Syria (UNDOF) since 1974. Larger contingents have also been sent to Bosnia-Herzegovina (since 1996) and Kosovo (since 1999) as well as to Albania (1997), twice to Afghanistan (in 2002 and 2005), to Chad (2008-09) and to Lebanon (since 2011). Austrians commanded the brigade-sized Multinational Task Force North in Tuzla (Bosnia) in 2005-06 and the Multinational Task Force South in Kosovo in 2008-09. Since 1974, Austrians have served as force commanders in UN operations on numerous occasions; and since December 2009, an Austrian has been in charge of the EU Force Althea in Bosnia-Herzegovina. The increasing importance of international operations has had repercussions on training and infrastructure in Austria as well. Participation in international exercises has become a standard element of most officers' training courses.

For Austria, participation in international missions has also led to better cooperation with neighboring countries. From 1996 on, contingents from Hungary and Slovenia have served with the Austrian battalion in Cyprus, and a Slovak company formed part of the Austrian battalion on the Golan Heights. In 2008, the Slovak company there was replaced by a company from Croatia. Likewise, German, Swiss, and Slovene contingents have formed part of the Austrian battalion in Kosovo. Following the Danish-led model of establishing a multinational brigade structure for future UN missions (the "Stand-by High-Readiness Brigade," or SHIRBRIG) in 1996, Austria initiated a similar cooperation in 1998, called "Central European Nations Cooperation in Peace Support" or CENCOOP.[27] Over

---

27. For SHIRBRIG, see <http://www.shirbrig.dk/html/plaque_0.htm> (14. Nov. 2010); for CENCOOP, see <http://www.cencoop.at/history/index_history.htm> (14 Nov. 2010).

the years, however, enthusiasm for these structures has waned. SHIRBRIG was formally ended in 2009, while CENCOOP still continues, at least on paper.

Ongoing Debates

A listing of Austrian commitments abroad would not be complete without some mention of the many humanitarian missions in the wake of earthquakes and other disasters. Experts such as Brigadier-General Norbert Fürstenhofer have been actively involved in institutionalizing international cooperation in this field.

In Austria itself, the army has often been committed to disaster relief and humanitarian efforts. This is in fact the role most readily supported by the population. In addition, a border surveillance mission launched in autumn 1990 to curb illegal migration on the Austro-Hungarian border was extended to the Austro-Slovak border in 1997. When Austria implemented the Schengen Agreements in 1997/98, Austria's eastern borders became "Schengen frontiers" for ten years, and the military deployment was dubbed the "Schengen frontier mission." Although the Schengen area was extended further east to include all neighboring countries in 2007, the border assistance mission continued for three more years in the form of an increased military presence in the border districts in order to curb petty crime.

To a certain extent, the discussions about this border mission mirror the discourse on the armed forces as a whole following the end of the East-West confrontation. The armed forces' mission and their very *raison d'être* in times of seemingly eternal peace have been repeatedly challenged, and downsizing has exacerbated conflicts within the army that have existed for a long time, but were previously less visible.

The debate about abolishing the system of obligatory national service continues. Some political leaders already advocated a switch to a professional army in the 1990s, following the example of most European nations. Many observers warned, however, that the current army budget would be insufficient to support a professional army. Until the summer of 2010, most political leaders, especially from the Social Democratic Party, adhered to the principle of obligatory national service.[28] During the last phase of the

---

28. In the autumn 2010 issue of *Der Offizier: Die Zeitschrift der Österreichischen Offiziersgesellschaft*, the president of the Austrian Officers' Organization (the leading organization of reserve officers) could still praise the defense minister for his "*einhellige Abfuhr*" to any ideas of abolishing national service (4), and in his article "Wehrpflicht bestätigt! War's das schon?," Udo Ladinig could cite, "*dass verstärkt ab Mitte Juni heurigen*

Vienna election campaign in September 2010, however, the Vienna Mayor (a Social Democrat) surprised everybody by performing a complete turn-around and announcing that obligatory national service would soon come to an end. By saying this, he forced his party and the defense minister to follow suit, although the latter had proclaimed obligatory national service to be "set in stone" just a few weeks earlier.[29] All this led to virulent discussions between apologists and critics of the present system. In fact, there has been frequent questioning regarding the value of a system that gives recruits a few weeks of basic military training, after which the majority is usually employed for often frustrating maintenance and office duties. Currently, according to figures given by General Edmund Entacher, the Chief of Staff, some 60 percent of the 25,000 recruits undergoing basic training every year are employed for basic duties such as clerks, drivers or cooks.[30] Obligatory military service now serves mainly as a tool for enlisting volunteers to serve for longer periods or to opt for a non-commissioned officer career.[31]

The social acceptance of the military in Austria is not very high; consequently, the Minister of Defense is not exactly seen as the most important cabinet post. Quite often in the past, it has been delegated to the minor partner in a coalition government, such as during the SPÖ's coalition governments with the Freedom Party in 1983-86 and with the ÖVP in 1987-99, or during the latter's coalition with the Freedom Party in 2000-02. In 2002, Günter Platter (ÖVP) became minister of defense; he was followed in 2007 by Norbert Darabos (SPÖ). The ministry, together with the top levels of military command, has been restructured several times over the past years. In 2008, responsibility for sports affairs was also transferred to the ministry of defense. This move surprised many, but is less weird than may first appear because many high-level sports and training activities have always been supported by the military.[32]

As in the 1990s, when Austria bought aged Saab J-35 "Draken" interceptor aircraft, their overdue replacement twenty years later led to

---

Jahres von maßgeblichen Politikern und von der Führungsspitze unseres Heeres klare Bekenntnisse zur Wehrpflicht abgegeben wurden" (6-7).

29. On July 3, 2010, he told the *Tiroler Tageszeitung*: "*Für mich ist die Wehrpflicht in Stein gemeißelt. Mit mir als Verteidigungsminister wird es kein Ende der Wehrpflicht geben.*" See <http://www.tt.com/csp/cms/sites/tt/%C3%9Cberblick/Politik/938884-6/f%C3%BCr-mich-ist-die-wehrpflicht-in-stein-gemei%C3%9Felt.csp> (14 Nov. 2010).

30. *Wiener Zeitung*, 31 July 2010 <http://www.wienerzeitung.at/DesktopDefault.aspx?TabID=4097 &Alias=wzo&cob=509944> (14 Nov. 2010).

31. Unlike future commissioned officers, who usually join the army with the clear intention of making their career there, the majority of future non-commissioned officers is recruited during their national service period.

32. For similar reasons, the Swiss defense minister is also responsible for sports affairs.

heated discussions. Eventually, modern Eurofighter "Typhoon" planes were acquired in the midst of heavily politicized debates, but the number purchased was reduced from twenty-four to fifteen aircrafts. These became operational in 2008. The old "Draken" had to be retired for technical reasons already in 2006, and Swiss Northrop F-5E "Tiger" fighters were leased for the bridging period. As the maintenance costs of the "Typhoon" fighters were very high, their acquisition placed an additional burden on the already over-depleted defense budget.

A View to the Future

In closing, one positive aspect has to be mentioned. During the Cold War, the political and the military leadership differed widely in their expectations. Whilst the latter prepared for defense in times of war, the former thought it highly unlikely that the Austrian army would ever fight a war, and therefore withheld the necessary budgets. After 1990, the overlap between political and military intentions appears to have increased. Both the political and the military leaderships are in agreement about the importance of increased participation in international peace and crisis management operations, notwithstanding still existing differences in detail. This does not mean, however, that these views are automatically shared by the public at large, as became evident during the discussions about participation in the Chad mission in 2007-08.

"Comprehensive security" and now "comprehensive approach" were catchwords often heard after the end of the East-West conflict. The terrorist attacks in New York and Washington on September 11, 2001 and the subsequent attacks in Madrid (March 11, 2004) and London (July 7, 2005) have shown how vulnerable highly developed societies are. With no immediate conventional threat visible, non-conventional threats have flourished, from terrorist attacks to cyber warfare. In times of ever-deepening European integration, better cooperation in the fields of defense and security will become increasingly paramount in the foreseeable future. Defense of the democratic and enlightened values of society take different forms today than they did in the past, but they are no less urgent.

What Does It Mean To Be Neutral? Postwar Austria from a Comparative Perspective

James J. Sheehan

In the closing paragraph of an essay on the study of international relations, first published in 1977, Stanley Hoffmann listed a number of subjects that the discipline has neglected. "Another zone of relative darkness," he wrote, "is the functioning of the international hierarchy [...] the nature of relations between the weak and the strong." The strong, Hoffmann argued, are less successful in dominating the weak than simple calculations of power suggest—or it might be better to say that calculations of power are rarely simple.[1] The strong, to modify Thucydides's famous, and often misunderstood formulation, do not always do what they can nor do the weak always suffer what they must: as the history of international relations clearly shows, there are sometimes significant limitations on strength and effective strategies for overcoming weakness. A study of these limitations and strategies can tell us things about the functioning of the international system that a concentration on the role of the great power sometimes overlooks.

In this paper, I want to examine a particular policy employed by what I will call "small states," that is, a policy of permanent—as opposed to occasional—neutrality, in other words, neutrality in every potential conflict rather than in any particular one.[2] And here it is worth remembering that

---

1. Stanley Hoffmann, "An American Social Science: International Relations," *Daedalus* 106, no. 3 (1977): 41-60, here 58. Compare John Mearsheimer: "The particular international order that obtains at any time is mainly a by-product of the self-interested behavior of the system's great powers," *The Tragedy of Great Power Politics* (New York: Norton, 2001), 49. For a recent discussion of how small states function in the international order, see the essays in Kristen Williams et al. ed., *Beyond Great Powers and Hegemons: Why Secondary States Support, Follow, or Challenge* (Stanford: Stanford University Press, 2012).
2. I am aware that the category "small state" is an elastic one, embracing a wide variety of political units in between "microstates" such as San Marino and "middle-sized states" such as France. For an introduction to the policies of small states, see Robert Rothstein, *Alliances and Small Powers* (New York: Columbia University Press, 1968), David Vital, *The Survival of Small States: Studies in Small Power/Great Power Conflict* (London: Oxford University Press, 1971) and the essays in A. Schou and O. Brundt, ed., *Small States in International Relations* (Stockholm: Nobel Symposium, 1971). In this collection, Gerald Stourzh's brief essay on "permanent neutrality" is a good introduction to the problem.

for most of history, permanent neutrality was a policy only available to small states, whose primary interest was to preserve their autonomy rather than to project their power. A major state, as the United States discovered in 1917 and 1941, usually cannot remain on the sidelines during a struggle among the great powers.

The Latin roots of the term, *ne uter*, neither one nor the other, invite us to think of neutrality as a negative condition, characterized by the absence of alliances and the ability to stay outside of international conflicts. But that condition is the result, not the source of neutrality. Effective neutrality is not a condition, but a policy, a way of behaving in international affairs that, far from being passive, often requires a great deal of political skill and strategic investment. Eternal politics, Thomas Jefferson once said, is the price of liberty. Eternal politics is also the price of effective neutrality: it does not just happen; it must, like every successful security policy, be carefully crafted and energetically sustained.[3]

Three factors are involved in a policy of effective neutrality. The first, and the most important, is geography, especially what Jean Gottmann identified as the most significant characteristic of any territory, its position.[4] There is, of course, a certain tautology in emphasizing geography since without geographical advantages most of the small states that managed to survive into the nineteenth century would have joined that long list of polities that were absorbed by their larger neighbors during the early modern period. In the case of neutrals, geographical position is especially significant. One is reminded of the old joke about the three most important things in evaluating real estate: location, location, and location. Obviously the best location for a potential neutral is to be as far away from strong powers as possible. The worst is to be directly between two competing powers. It is unlikely, for instance, that neutrality was ever a viable option for the Poles, no matter how skillful their policies. Most neutrals, in fact, are what we might call

---

3. On neutrality and the policies of neutral states, see the following: Arnold Wolfers, "Allies, Neutrals, and Neutralists," *Discord and Collaboration: Essays on International Politics* (Baltimore: Johns Hopkins University Press, 1962), 217-32; Daniel Frei, *Dimensionen neutraler Politik Ein Beitrag zur Theorie der internationalen Beziehungen* (Geneva: Droz, 1969); Hanspeter Neuhold and Hans Thalberg, ed., *The European Neutrals in International Affairs* (Vienna: Wilhelm Braumüller, 1984); Efraim Karsh, *Neutrality and Small States* (London: Routledge, 1988); Alan Leonhard, ed., *Neutrality: Changing Concepts and Practices* (Lanham: University Press of America, 1988); Sigmar Stadlmeier, *Dynamische Interpretation der dauernden Neutralität* (Berlin: Duncker and Humblot, 1991); Michael Gehler and Rolf Steininger, ed., *Die Neutralen und die europäische Integration, 1945-1995* (Vienna: Böhlau, 2000).
4. Jean Gottmann, *La politique des états et leur géographie* (Paris: Éditions du CTHS, 2007), 119.

rim states, that is, states that border one great power, upon which their neutrality often must depend. Position, therefore, together with the nature of the terrain, shapes a neutral's security needs and its military strategy.

Second, a policy of neutrality usually involves some kind of legal agreements, international, multilateral, or with a single great power. Few neutrals are able to depend on their own resources; most require the support or at least the toleration of outsiders. Acquiring and maintaining this support or toleration are the key tasks of a neutral's foreign policy. In this enterprise, neutrals must reassure their potential opponents that they have the ability and will to remain neutral, while at the same time resisting their friends' efforts to enlist their support. This is a very difficult balance to maintain, particularly in times of international conflict.

Finally, effective neutrality always has a domestic foundation. Without some degree of political consensus, neutrality is impossible since in deeply-divided states the opposing sides are tempted to seek allies among external powers, thus contaminating domestic conflict with external alignments. Avoiding the perils of this situation was what George Washington had in mind when, in his famous "Farewell Address," he warned against both entangling alliances and factions, which he regarded as two sides of the same dangerous coin. The Wars of Religion, the French revolution, and the Cold War provide vivid examples of this fusion of internal and external conflicts. Not surprisingly, these were all difficult times to be neutral.

During the long nineteenth century from 1815 to 1914, when the European society of states attempted to establish rules and create institutions to regulate international behavior, the character and conditions of wartime neutrality were codified. These efforts culminated in the two Hague Conferences of 1899 and 1907, where the great powers tried to define the differences between combatants and non-combatants on the high seas, the battlefield, and the international arena. In October 1907, the conference agreed to a "Convention Respecting the Rights and Duties of Neutral Powers and Persons in the Case of War on Land," which declared the territory of neutral powers to be "inviolable" and at the same time set rather generous limits on what was permissible to any would-be neutral.[5]

Less than a decade later, Europeans learned just how fragile these agreements would turn out to be. The First World War began with Germany's violation of Belgium's neutrality, which demonstrated the ease with which

---

5. "Laws of War: Rights and Duties of Neutral Powers and Persons in Case of War on Land" (Hague V), 18 Oct. 1907. Available on the *Avalon Project Website*: <http://avalon.law.yale.edu/20th_century/hague05.asp>. For a survey of the status of neutrality in international law, see Stephen Neff, *The Rights and Duties of Neutrals: A General History* (Manchester: Manchester University Press, 2000).

international guarantees (what the German Chancellor Bethmann Hollweg infelicitously referred to as a "scrap of paper") could be swept aside by the strategic imperatives of a great power. In the course of the war, a number of small states abandoned their neutrality and joined one side or the other in pursuit of territorial expansion. The results were uniformly catastrophic, both for those, like Italy, who were among the winners, and those, like the Ottoman Empire, who were on the losing side.[6]

In light of this experience, it is understandable that a large number of small states attempted to remain neutral when the international situation deteriorated in the late 1930s, hoping, as Winston Churchill put it, "that the storm will pass before their turn comes to be devoured."[7] Most of these attempts failed, once again, with unfortunate results for those states caught in the path of the major belligerents. Of the twenty states that proclaimed their neutrality in 1939, only a handful survived: the five powers that enjoyed an advantageous position on the periphery of the conflict—Sweden, Ireland, Spain, Portugal, and Turkey—and that persistent exception to every political generalization, Switzerland.[8]

After 1945, when the Cold War began to divide Europe once again, the dismal historical experience of neutrals during the second war encouraged a number of small states—Norway, Denmark, Belgium, the Netherlands, Luxembourg, Portugal, and Turkey—to join the Western powers. This meant that throughout the postwar era, there were only five important European neutrals: the Republic of Ireland, Sweden, Finland, Switzerland, and, after 1955, Austria. In what follows, I will illuminate the origins and character of Austrian neutrality by comparing it to the geopolitical, legal, and domestic dimensions of its four neutral counterparts.

Neutrality and the Cold War

Ireland is a typical rim state, and like most rim states, its security depended on one great power. At least for the first half-century of its existence, Ireland's politics, both foreign and domestic, were dominated by its relationship with Great Britain.[9] In 1920, while the Irish insurrection was

---
6. On neutrals during the war, see David Stevenson, *The First World War and International Politics* (New York: Oxford University Press, 1988).
7. Rothstein, *Alliances*, 233. Churchill's remark reflects the contemptuous attitude towards neutrals characteristically taken by the Great Powers, particularly in times of war.
8. See Annette Fox's classic analysis, *The Power of Small States: Diplomacy in World War II* (Chicago: University of Chicago Press, 1959).
9. On Irish foreign policy, see the essays in M. Kennedy and J. Skelly, ed., *Irish Foreign Policy, 1916-1966. From Independence to Internationalism* (Dublin: Four Courts, 2000), Patrick

still going on, Eamon de Valera, a fierce and uncompromising nationalist, defined the essential tension in this relationship when he pointed out that a dependent Ireland must hope that Britain's international position would become weaker, but an independent Ireland would necessarily depend on Britain's strength as a defense against outside intervention. "Mutual self-interest," he argued, "would make the people of these two islands, if both were independent, the closest possible allies in a moment of real danger to either."[10] De Valera's nationalist comrades sharply attacked him for apparently accepting British superiority, yet his assessment, while perhaps tactlessly expressed, was largely correct. Because Ireland was a small and weak state, it would always need British power as a shield against potential aggressors. At the same time, lingering resentments from the past and persisting sources of contention in the present continued to divide the two nations, precluding an alliance between them. Irish neutrality was the product of this complex blend of dependence and antagonism.

Ireland established its independence from Britain gradually and incompletely. The original peace treaty signed in 1921 granted the Irish Free State "Dominion" status, allowed Britain to retain three "treaty ports," and, most important, left the six Protestant counties in Ulster under British sovereignty. The treaty ports were abolished by a new agreement in 1938; even before its formal declaration as a republic ten years later, the Irish Free State became a fully sovereign, autonomous entity. This autonomy was severely tested during the Second World War, when Ireland struggled to preserve its neutral independence without provoking either of the belligerents. With some reluctance and a great deal of bitterness, London finally decided that the cost of violating Irish neutrality was substantially higher than the military advantage of using Irish ports during the Battle of the Atlantic.

Immediately after the war, the Irish came close to joining the Western alliance. Firmly anti-Communist, sympathetic to European Christian Democracy, and clearly in need of economic and political support, Ireland seemed to be a natural partner for the North Atlantic Treaty Organization when it was established in 1949. After considerable debate, however, the Irish remained neutral. On the one hand, whether a formal member of the alliance or not, the Irish knew they could count on a security umbrella

---

Keatinge, *The Formation of Irish Foreign Policy* (Dublin: Institute of Public Administration, 1973), Brian Girvin, "National Interest, Irish Neutrality, and the Limits of Ideology" in *Die Neutralen*, ed. Gehler and Steininger, 87-112, and the excellent brief summary by Conor Cruise O'Brien, "Ireland in International Affairs," in *Conor Cruise O'Brien Introduces Ireland*, ed. Owen Dudley Edwards (London: Deutsch, 1969), 104-34.
10. Quoted by Ronan Fanning, in Kennedy and Skelly, *Irish Foreign Policy*, 310.

provided by the Western powers; they were, in fact, not directly threatened by Soviet expansion or Communist subversion. On the other hand, a formal alliance with the West was politically unacceptable. As the Minister for External Affairs put the matter in February 1949: "As long as partition lasts, any military alliance or commitment involving joint military action with the state responsible for partition must be quite out of the question as far as Ireland was concerned."[11]

The geopolitical basis of Irish neutrality is clearly revealed in the republic's security policy. The Irish military is the weakest among the neutrals. Its defense expenditures, which are among the lowest in Europe, are largely devoted to covering personnel costs, leaving it totally without the capacity to project power. Unlike Switzerland or Sweden, Ireland does not pretend to be able to deter a potential aggressor. Instead, its small professional army performs two tasks: first, the army patrols the border with the north and battles subversion by nationalist extremists; second, it provides peacekeepers for the United Nations, thus helping Ireland to assert a limited but not insignificant influence over world affairs. Protected from external threats by the accidents of geography, Ireland can afford to concentrate its energies on local conflicts and global aspirations.[12]

In comparison to Ireland's turbulent history, Switzerland's past may seem placid, even a little dull—an assessment memorably expressed by Orson Welles's character in *The Third Man*, who remarked that after five hundred years of peace and democracy all the Swiss could produce was the cuckoo clock. In fact, for most of their history, the Swiss were a divided and contentious people; their territory was the site and source of considerable bloodshed. In 1815, Swiss neutrality was founded on a blend of international and domestic arrangements similar to what we will find in Austria a century and a half later: in March, the twenty-two Swiss cantons formed a Confederation under a weak, rotating directorate; seven months later, the Five Great Powers committed themselves to a policy of non-intervention, thus increasing the Confederation's chances of survival by guaranteeing its autonomy. In the Swiss case, therefore, neutrality was a contribution to, rather than a reflection of, domestic stability.[13] It was by no means obvious that this enterprise would succeed: well into the

---

11. Quoted in O'Brien, "Ireland," 126.
12. For a good introduction to Irish security policy, see Paul Sharp, *Irish Foreign Policy and the European Community: A Study of the Impact of Interdependence on the Foreign Policy of a Small State* (Aldershot: Dartmouth Publishing Group, 1990) and Roisin Doherty, *Ireland, Neutrality, and European Security Integration* (Aldershot: Ashgate, 2002).
13. See Paul Schroeder, *The Transformation of European Politics, 1763-1848* (Oxford: Oxford University Press, 1994), 570-72.

nineteenth century, the Swiss Confederation was beset by civil conflict at home and aggressive neighbors abroad. Metternich, for example, declared in 1845 that the Confederation "represents for itself and for its neighbors an inexhaustible spring of unrest and disturbance."[14] Only in the century's second half were Swiss stability and neutrality firmly established and, even then, had to be vigorously defended.

Swiss security policy is democratic, decentralized, and defensive. According to the Constitution of 1848, the Confederation cannot have a standing army; except for a small number of professionals, the Swiss depend on a militia, based on universal military obligations with a twenty-year reserve commitment. While decisions about war and peace are made by the central authority, the administration of the army remains in the hands of the Cantons. In 1914, Switzerland mobilized its force to defend its borders against foreign intervention, but the major threat to its neutrality came from the divided loyalties among some of its citizens, especially the pro-German sentiments prevalent in the officer corps. In 1940, as German armies swept across Western Europe, the external threat was much more acute. Annoyed by reports of secret agreements between Switzerland and France, and by Swiss actions against the German warplanes that entered their airspace, the Germans considered military action. The Swiss army responded by formulating a deterrent strategy based on mass mobilization, a vigorous defense of mountain redoubts, and the threat of a scorched earth policy. Because Germany eventually decided that the military—and more importantly, the political—costs of conquest outweighed the benefits, Switzerland remained a peaceful and prosperous island in the middle of the war-torn continent.[15]

The successful defense of Swiss independence during the Second World War greatly strengthened the domestic consensus on which neutrality rested. As the Federal Council declared in April 1983, "Swiss neutrality is not only the application of the law of nations and of international conventions. It is first and foremost the expression of the profound conviction and determined will of the Swiss people."[16] The army, which touches the lives of virtually every Swiss household, is the most important expression of this national will. The slow but apparently steady decline of the army's popular

---

14. Quoted in Jonathan Steinberg, *Why Switzerland* (Cambridge, UK: Cambridge University Press, 1976), 4.
15. In addition to Steinberg, see the relevant sections in *Handbuch der Schweizer Geschichte* 2 (Zürich: Verlag Berichthaus, 1977).
16. Quoted in Jean Freymond, "Swiss Neutrality and the Future of Europe in a Changing Europe," in *Neutral States and the European Community*, ed. Sheila Harden (London: Brassey's, 1994), 4.

support (and military effectiveness) has, therefore, profound implications for the nation's political identity, as well as for its strategic posture and international position. Among these implications, as we will see, are changes in Switzerland's relationship to the international community and especially to the European Union.

Like Switzerland's, Sweden's neutrality was built on a long history of war and conquest. For a brief moment in the seventeenth century Sweden had been a major player on the European stage, and, at least until the emergence of Russia in the eighteenth century, it remained a formidable regional power. By 1815, however, after Sweden had sold most of Pomerania to Prussia and ceded Finland to Russia, it had been pushed to the periphery of the European state system, both geographically and politically. Swedish neutrality gradually emerged as a response to this condition. Unlike the other neutrals, it has never had a legal basis, either in international agreements or constitutional provisions. Instead, it was, and continues to be, a consciously chosen and persistently reaffirmed policy, which certainly takes advantage of Sweden's geographical location, but essentially rests on political consensus and military strength.[17]

The two world wars tested Sweden's neutrality just as they did Switzerland's. In 1914, Sweden was almost drawn into the war when its navy came close to being attacked by the Russians, but in the end managed to remain on the sidelines. During the Finnish-Soviet war of 1940, deeply ingrained habits of neutrality and a careful calculation of national self-interest kept the government from yielding to popular pressures to come to Finland's aid. After Germany attacked the Soviet Union, the Swedes felt obliged to allow the movement of German troops across their territory and were more than willing to supply critical materials to the German war effort. When the fortunes of war turned against Germany in 1943, Swedish sympathies to the allied cause grew; their neutrality, once tilted towards Berlin, now shifted in the other direction.

During the Cold War, Sweden, despite its political sympathies and economic ties with the West, retained its neutrality. Originally it had hoped to join with Norway and Denmark in a Nordic bloc of non-aligned states, but these two states joined NATO while, as we will see, Finland signed a limited security agreement with the Soviet Union. As a result, Sweden became the keystone in a remarkably stable arch of countries across northern Europe, stretching from Norway (allied with the West but without nuclear

---

17. On Swedish neutrality, see Neil Kent, *A Concise History of Sweden* (Cambridge, UK: Cambridge University Press, 2008) and the essays in Bengt Sundelius, ed., *The Committed Neutral: Sweden's Foreign Policy* (Boulder: Westview, 1989).

arms) to Finland, formally neutral but diplomatically dependent on the Soviets. Like Switzerland, Sweden devoted a relatively large share of its resources to defense, with a conscript army and a well-equipped and well-trained air force. And, again like the Swiss, Swedish neutrality was closely bound up with the nation's sense of itself. Non-alignment, combined with an affinity towards, but frequent criticism of, the West was the foreign political equivalent of Sweden's "third way" between American style capitalism and Soviet Communism. Both were regarded by Swedes as the expression of their nation's political independence and moral superiority.

Finland, which had become a semi-autonomous part of the Russian Empire in 1809, took advantage of imperial Russia's collapse in 1917 to assert its independence, a status that was eventually recognized by the Bolshevik regime. Like the other newly independent Eastern European states, Finland's security in the 1920s was enhanced by the relative weakness of both Germany and the Soviet Union, and like the rest of Eastern Europe, it was threatened by the revival of German power under the Nazis. In the face of the deteriorating European situation, Finland declared its neutrality in 1938, but swiftly found itself drawn into a long struggle against the Soviet Union, first in defense of its territorial integrity during the so-called Winter War of 1939-40, and then, as part of an uneasy alliance with Germany, between 1941 and 1944. After Nazi Germany had collapsed and the Western powers showed little or no interest in their fate, the Finns were left alone with the Soviets. At this point, the central question about Finnish security became painfully simple and extraordinarily difficult: how could a small, politically isolated, and relatively poor state live in the shadow of its overwhelmingly more powerful former enemy?[18]

In its search for a solution to this question, the Finnish government operated on the assumption that the major issue in their relationship with the Soviet Union was strategic. They hoped that if Moscow's legitimate strategic concerns were allayed, the Soviets would be willing to let the Finns maintain their own social, economic, and political system. They were, in other words, prepared to exchange some degree of foreign political dependence for a large measure of domestic autonomy. In April 1948, after long and difficult negotiations, this exchange was ratified in a Treaty of Friendship, Cooperation, and Mutual Assistance between Finland and the Soviet Union.[19]

---

18. See David Kirby, *A Concise History of Finland* (Cambridge, UK: Cambridge University Press, 2006).
19. Max Jakobson, *Finnish Neutrality: A Study of Finnish Foreign Policy since the Second World War* (New York: Praeger, 1968).

In comparison to the other bilateral agreements that the Soviet Union made with its Eastern European neighbors in 1948-49, the treaty with Finland was more limited and permissive. In the first place, the treaty did not establish an alliance, that is, Finland was not compelled to provide support for the Soviet Union in the event of a war. Instead, in Article 1, paragraph 1, Finland pledged to fight if its territory became the object of military aggression on the part of Germany or its allies. Unless and until it was itself attacked, therefore, Finland did not have to fight. Moreover, Article 2 stated that, in the case of attack, Finland must consult with the Soviet Union, but retained the right to approve any assistance the Soviets might offer. While the term "neutrality" did not appear in the treaty, the substance of the agreement seemed to affirm what the preamble calls "Finland's aspiration to stand aside from the contradictions of interests of the Great Powers."[20]

Even more than most successful security policies, permanent neutrality depends on credibility rather than formal agreements. For forty years, the Finns had to convince the Soviets that they were both willing and able to prevent their territory from being used by any potential enemy. This required the maintenance of armed forces that would be sufficient to deter aggression. It also involved Finland's voluntary acceptance of limits on its freedom of action in the international arena and of occasional Soviet interference in its domestic affairs. We should not underestimate the difficulties and deceptions that punctuated Soviet-Finnish relations, but there seems little question that Finland's security policy provided the foundation for decades of peace, prosperity, and stability. Geography dealt the Finns a difficult hand, which they played with great skill and courage.

Like Finland's, Austria's neutrality was the product of those two closely connected developments that dominated Europe's international history in the postwar era: the rivalry between the United States and the Soviet Union and the disappearance of Germany as a potential European hegemon.[21] In 1945, Austria's prospects for joining the small group of European neutrals seemed bleak. Unlike Switzerland or Sweden, Austria could not draw on experiences that had, in the course of time, embedded neutrality in the nation's identity; unlike Finland, Austria could not base its neutrality on a bilateral arrangement with a single powerful neighbor; and, unlike Ireland,

---

20. See Wladyslaw W. Kulski, "The Soviet System of Collective Security Compared with the Western System," *American Journal of International Law* 40, no. 3 (July 1950): 453-76, quoted here 458.
21. For the centrality of the German question, see Rolf Steininger, *Austria, Germany, and the Cold War: From the Anschluss to the State Treaty, 1938-1955* (New York: Berghahn Books, 2008).

Austria was in the middle of Europe, along the seam of the increasingly intense conflict between east and west.²² Militarily defeated, morally implicated in the horrendous crimes of National Socialism, and occupied by the victorious powers, Austrians faced an uncertain future. Who could have predicted that an economically prosperous, politically stable, and internationally secure state would emerge from these ruins?

In retrospect, two factors seem especially important for the development of Austrian neutrality. The first was the commitment, formally agreed upon by the allies in Moscow in 1943 and persistently restated thereafter, that Austria would return to its pre-1938 status as an independent state. The second was the fact that an independent Austria was never at the center of either superpower's essential interests. Some degree of marginality—political, military, and often geographical—is an important element in the survival of every neutral. In the case of Austria, marginality meant that while neither the United States nor the Soviet Union was fully satisfied with the final resolution of the Austrian question, both were willing to compromise for the simple reason that the cost of a better outcome was higher than they were willing to pay.

Needless to say, each side would have liked to see Austria firmly embedded within its own sphere. How to do this was the problem. The Soviets recognized early on that they could not take over legally: in the first postwar elections of November 1945, the Austrian Communist Party polled just over five percent. But neither a coup like those that had brought Communists to power in much of Eastern Europe, nor a partition on the German model seemed possible. The Americans were unwilling to risk a violent conflict in order to force the Soviets out. For their part, while most Austrians wanted a Western style political and economic system, they were prepared to give up formal ties with the West in order to end the occupation and regain their national independence. In the end, after a decade of fruitless negotiating, neutrality turned out to be everyone's second choice.

The final breakthrough came in 1955 when Nikita Khrushchev, after having consolidated his position as Stalin's successor, began a series of new foreign political initiatives, which included an opening to Yugoslavia and a renegotiation of the Finnish treaty. The Soviets realized that Austrian neutrality was strategically advantageous because it would, in combination with a neutral Switzerland, separate the northern and southern components of NATO. Equally important, they recognized that neutrality would

---

22. For some interesting comparisons, see the essays in Friedrich Koja and Gerald Stourzh, ed., *Schweiz-Österreich. Ähnlichkeiten und Kontraste* (Vienna: Böhlau, 1986) and in Günter Bischof et al., ed., *Neutrality in Austria* (New Brunswick, N.J.: Transaction Publishers, 2001).

confirm Austria's separation from Germany and thus became the final step in the dismemberment of Hitler's Greater Germany that included the annexation of Königsberg, the transfer of territory and population between Germany and Poland, and, most importantly, the transformation of the Soviets' occupation zone into the German Democratic Republic. While the Soviets had by no means abandoned the hope that they might dislodge West Germany from the Atlantic alliance, they could at least be sure that the Third Reich was now permanently and irretrievably lost.[23]

The *Staatsvertrag*, which was signed in May 1955 in Vienna by Austria and the four occupying powers, defined the new state's past, present, and future. The Soviet leaders had agreed on signing the Treaty only after an Austrian delegation had given in to their demand that Austria declare neutrality. In the Preamble, the State Treaty established the historical fact on which Austrian autonomy was based: "Hitler's Germany forcibly annexed Austria on 13 March 1938." Article One recognized Austria as "a sovereign, independent, and democratic state," but then restricted its sovereignty by prohibiting any future political and economic connections to Germany. Neutrality was not mentioned in the *Staatsvertrag*; it was adopted by the Austrians themselves in a constitutional law passed by the Austrian parliament on 26 October 1955, immediately after the last of the occupying forces withdrew. Neutrality was not, therefore, formally imposed by outsiders but, in theory at least, voluntarily embraced by the new state. At the same time, the October law was circulated to, and accepted by, every state with which Austria had diplomatic relations, thus giving it a kind of international legal status.[24]

As these two documents suggest, Austria's international position and national identity, like those of every postwar neutral except Sweden, were based on a complex blend of foreign and domestic political arrangements. In the Austrian case, this blend had a particular significance because it involved that quintessential fusion of national and international issues, the German question. After 1945, the Austrians, for the first time in their

---

23. For the evolution of Austrian question, see Wolfgang Mueller, "Stalin and Austria: New Evidence on Soviet Policy in a Secondary Theatre of the Cold War, 1938-53/55," *Cold War History* 6, no. 1 (February 2006): 63-84; Gerald Stourzh, "The Austrian State Treaty and the International Decision Making Process in 1955," *Austrian History Yearbook* 38 (2007): 208-28; and the essays collected in Arnold Suppan, Gerald Stourzh, and Wolfgang Mueller, ed., *The Austrian State Treaty 1955: International Strategy, Legal Relevance, National Identity* (Vienna: Verlag der Österreichischen Akademie der Wissenschaften, 2005), especially the essay by Georges-Henri Soutou.
24. The classic work on the treaty is Gerald Stourzh, *Um Einheit und Freiheit: Staatsvertrag, Neutralität und das Ende der Ost-West-Besetzung Österreichs, 1945-1955* (4th ed. Vienna: Böhlau, 1998), which also provides the most important documents.

history, formally severed the bonds of interest and affection that had, on several occasions and under several different auspices, joined them to the rest of German Europe. Austrian neutrality, therefore, was part of a historic reformulation of the German question that was caused by the total defeat and disintegration of German power and expressed in the emergence of three postwar German states. 1955 opened new chapters in Austrian and German history, which gave a new shape to both the past and the future. For the Second Austrian Republic, the key date in this new past was 1938, when its predecessor supposedly became Nazi Germany's first victim and not, as might plausibly be argued, its first and most enthusiastic ally. In the future, independence would mean, above all else, independence from the possibility of an *Anschluss*.[25]

The State Treaty expressly prohibited Austria from acquiring a long list of weapons (including submarines, which might be thought to have limited utility for a landlocked state). Nevertheless, the Western powers insisted that Austria take responsibility for its own defense, which the Austrians acknowledged in their constitutional declaration of neutrality. In fact, the military component of Austrian neutrality was always weak and became weaker over time. Among the neutrals, only Ireland spends less on defense and has a more modest and less effective military force. From the start, Austria's autonomy depended not, like Sweden's or Switzerland's, on its own efforts, or, like Ireland's, on the accident of geographical location, or, like Finland's, on the tolerance of its more powerful neighbor. Instead, Austria's existence as an independent state rested on the same explicit and implicit agreements among the superpowers that had produced the *Staatsvertrag* in the first place. Neutrality, which was frequently invoked by Austrian statesmen and remained firmly embedded in the Second Republic's remarkably consensual political culture, was both the precondition and the product of these international agreements.[26] Among the postwar neutrals, Austria had the most difficult geopolitical location and was, therefore, most dependent on international guarantees and domestic consensus.

---

25. On postwar Austria's historical self-image, see Fritz Fellner, "Das Problem der österreichischen Nation nach 1945," in O. Büsch and J. Sheehan, eds., *Die Rolle der Nation in der deutschen Geschichte und Gegenwart* (Berlin: Colloquium, 1985).
26. Hanspeter Neuhold, "The Neutral States of Europe: Similarities and Differences," in Leonhard, ed., *Neutrality* (1988), 111-14, on the origins of Austrian security policy; for its development, see the material collected in Erich Reiter, *Österreichische Sicherheits- und Verteidigungspolitik* (Frankfurt: Peter Lang, 1993). On the evolution of Austria's international position after 1955, see the essays in Arnold Suppan and Wolfgang Mueller, ed., *Peaceful Coexistence or Iron Curtain? Austria, Neutrality, and Eastern Europe in the Cold War and Détente, 1955-1989* (Vienna: LIT Verlag, 2009).

Neutrals and the Problem of International Organizations

Neutral states are by necessity in favor of peace and stability. As the two world wars clearly demonstrated, disruptions in the international order undermine neutrals' domestic consensus and encourage both their friends and their enemies to exert unwelcome pressure for support. Because neutral states need peace and stability to survive, they must be non-revisionist powers, committed to retaining the status quo. Among the postwar neutrals, Ireland might seem to be an exception to this commitment since the Republic does not accept the legitimacy of Britain's sovereignty over the northern counties. But while they may be revisionist in theory, the Irish have learned to live with—if not to love—partition, which has become a fact of political life. During the Second World War, for example, only a small minority was prepared to jeopardize Irish neutrality by joining with the Germans in an effort to force the British off their island.

A major goal of every neutral's foreign policy must be to strengthen the international order without becoming directly engaged in international disputes. Neutral states, therefore, characteristically seek uncompromising ways to affirm their international solidarity. In the nineteenth century, for example, Switzerland provided the site for a number of international organizations including the Red Cross, and the International Postal and Telegraph Unions. In the wake of the First World War, many neutrals hoped that the League of Nations would offer new opportunities for solidarity. After a close vote in favor of their own membership, the Swiss allowed the League to establish its headquarters in Geneva, where it coordinated a web of international social, economic, and cultural organizations. When it came time to apply sanctions after the Italian invasion of Ethiopia, however, the Swiss did not go along; they remained in the League, but reaffirmed a strict definition of neutrality that precluded participating in the defense of collective security.

Despite the League's dismal record in the protection of small states, most neutrals participated in the United Nations. Sweden joined in 1946 and quickly became one of the UN's most generous and energetic supporters, providing funds, civil servants, and peacekeepers to a number of international projects. Ireland was significantly less enthusiastic about the UN; when it somewhat reluctantly applied for membership in 1946, its application was vetoed by the Soviet Union, supposedly because of Ireland's sympathy for the Axis during the war. Ireland, together with Austria and Finland, finally joined in 1955 as the result of a complex deal between the superpowers. Like the Swedes, the Irish and the Austrians express their international solidarity by regularly supplying troops for peacekeeping missions and officials for the UN's civil service. Among the European neutrals, only Switzerland held back; as late as 1986, three-fourths of Swiss voters opposed joining the UN. But while it did not become a member until 2002, Switzerland (like the Vatican) held non-member observer status in the General Assembly and participated fully in ancillary institutions such as UNESCO and the Food and Agriculture Organization.[27]

Neutrals sent money, diplomats, and sometimes soldiers out to encourage international peace and stability, but they knew that their security, indeed even their existence, ultimately depended on peace and stability in their immediate European neighborhood. Small states can think globally but they are forced by the inexorable logic of power to act locally. After the traumatic violence of the Second World War, therefore, the neutrals supported efforts to encourage reconciliation and cooperation on the continent, especially between the superpowers and their European allies. Throughout the Cold War, the continental neutrals did their best to encourage diplomatic solutions to global conflicts by offering their capitals as sites for summit meetings, arms control negotiations, and conferences. Austria and Finland also played important roles in preparing the Conference on Security and Cooperation in Europe, which finally met (in Helsinki and Geneva) between 1973 and the summer of 1975 and ended in the agreements signed in the Finnish capital. All the neutrals participated in the conference and at its follow-up meetings, four of them (Ireland was the exception here), joined with non-aligned states to form a neutral bloc among the CSCE members.[28]

Belonging to the CSCE did not compromise a state's permanent neutrality, in part because the superpowers and their respective allies all belonged, and because membership did not commit anyone to anything. Neutrals also felt able to join the Council of Europe, which had been established in 1949 to promote international understanding, democratic values, and European integration. Ireland and Sweden were both founding members of the Council, Austria joined in 1956, Switzerland in 1963, and Finland joined May of 1989. The neutrals also supported the European Commission on Human Rights and the European Court on Human Rights

---

27. Stadlmeier, *Dynamische Interpretation*, has a good account of neutrals in the United Nations.
28. See Harto Hakovirta, *East West Conflict and European Neutrality* (Oxford: Oxford University, 1988) and the relevant essays in Richard Davy, ed., *European Détente: A Reappraisal* (London: Sage, 1992). The Helsinki Accords are available online: <http://www.osce.org/documents/mcs/1975/08/4044_en.pdf>. The essays in Suppan and Mueller, ed., *Peaceful Coexistence*, give an excellent analysis of the Austrian role in détente.

and signed the Council's various conventions and protocols (over 200 as of June 2009) on a wide range of social, economic, and cultural issues. Like the Helsinki Accords, these were declarations of principles, promises of consultation, and exhortations to common action, not commitments that might interfere with a state's sovereign independence or international autonomy.[29]

Much more problematic than these agreements were the efforts at economic integration that began with the Coal and Steel Community in 1951 and led to the European Economic Community established by the Treaty of Rome six years later. In the first place, the EEC was part of the Western alliance system; all of its original members were also members of the North Atlantic Treaty Organization. Moreover, the EEC was both an international organization of independent sovereign states and, potentially at least, a supranational organization with aspirations to assume sovereign powers of its own. Nevertheless, in 1961, Sweden, Switzerland, and Austria applied for associate status with the EEC. All of them eventually withdrew their applications, in the Austria case as the result of intense pressure from the Soviets. It was now assumed that belonging to the EEC was not compatible with their neutrality. Instead, the neutrals became members of the European Free Trade Area (until 1986, Finland was an affiliate), a much looser and more exclusively economic organization.[30]

Given Ireland's geopolitical position, it is not surprising that during the Cold War it was the only state that was both avowedly neutral and a member of the European Community. Indeed, given Ireland's close economic ties with Britain, the imperative to join the EEC seemed so overwhelming that neutrality was not an issue when its application process began in 1970; after over eighty percent of the electorate voted in favor of joining the Community, Ireland, together with Great Britain and Denmark, became a member in 1973 as part of the EEC's first expansion.[31]

During the 1980s, the neutrals' relationship with the European Community was complicated by two countervailing trends. First, especially when the Community further expanded to include Greece, Spain, and Portugal, its economic power, and therefore its pressure on non-members, increased. Second, as the Community expanded, its leaders made renewed efforts to create a federal state that would fulfill the founders' ambitions

---

29. Further information can be found on the *Council of Europe website*, <http://www.coe.int/>.
30. On the evolution of neutral policies towards European institutions, see the essays in Gehler and Steininger, *Die Neutralen*.
31. Paul Sharp, *Irish Foreign Policy*.

for a politically united Europe. In other words, the economic cost of staying outside the EEC increased at the same time as the political price of membership. Even Ireland was concerned about the potential political costs: after the Irish parliament had approved the Single European Act of 1986, widely seen as a major step towards closer integration, the Supreme Court declared it unconstitutional; an impasse was avoided when the Act was approved in a national referendum. Nevertheless, the economic logic of integration was difficult to withstand. Sweden, for example, made preliminary moves towards the EEC, thereby potentially undermining the bargaining power of the European Free Trade group and putting pressure on both Austria and Finland.[32]

The Soviets viewed these developments with considerable alarm. In July 1988, Moscow's ambassador to the Federal Republic of Germany warned that "more and more European states may begin to be sucked into the EEC and via the EEC into NATO, that is, there could be the construction of an all-European branch of NATO [...]."[33] Nevertheless, a year later, Austria applied for EEC membership with the understanding that it would not jeopardize the neutrality provisions of the constitutional law of October 1955. Soviet pressure did undermine Finnish efforts to move closer to the EEC. In September 1989, the Finnish Foreign Minister, while maintaining that "neutrality is not a term known to trade policy," was compelled to acknowledge that trade policy should not be allowed to compromise neutrality, adding that Finland was not, at the moment, considering membership in the EEC.[34]

Although the rapid and remarkable collapse of Soviet power that began in 1989 transformed the whole European security environment for every neutral state, it had particular significance for Finland and Austria, whose international position was most closely tied to the Cold War. In September 1990, the Finns renounced important elements in the peace treaty of 1947 and the Friendship Treaty with the Soviets of 1948; they negotiated a new treaty, this time with the Russian Federation, in 1992. Austrians continued to celebrate the State Treaty of 1955 as the basis of their statehood, but

---

32. Bo Huldt, "Sweden and European Community Building, 1945-1992," in *Neutral States*, ed. Harden, 104-42.
33. Quoted in Vladislav Zubok, "The Soviet Attitude towards the European Neutrals during the Cold War," in *Die Neutralen*, ed. Gehler and Steininger, 42.
34. On Austria, see Peter Jankowitsch, "The Process of European Integration and Neutral Austria," in *Neutral States*, ed. Harden, 3-37; on Finland, Paavo Lipponen, "Finish Neutrality and EC Membership," in ibid, 69. Nicole Alecu de Flers compares the Irish and Austrian relationship to Europe in *EU Foreign Policy and the Europeanization of Neutral States: Comparing Irish and Austrian Foreign Policy* (London: Routledge, 2012).

were clearly no longer bound by the implicit or explicit restraints imposed by the Soviet Union. In 1994-95, Finland, Austria, and Sweden joined the European Union. Now only Switzerland remained an associated rather than a formal member, although in 2009 the Swiss did become part of the Schengen Agreement that abolished border controls (including in airports) with its neighbors in the EU. Given the deep historical significance of the Swiss border, this marked an extraordinary reassessment of the Confederation's national and international position.[35]

Unlike the Soviet Union's former allies in Eastern Europe, the neutrals did not join in the extraordinary expansion of NATO that provided new European security architecture in the 1990s. Beginning with Finland and Sweden in 1994, the neutrals (Austria in 1995, Switzerland in 1996, and Ireland in 1999) did agree to participate in NATO's Partnership for Peace program, which consists of a set of bilateral agreements through which European states agree to cooperate with each other and with the alliance on political and, to varying degrees, military matters. The basis of the partnership are regular consultations between the partners' diplomatic representatives at NATO headquarters and the Euro-Atlantic Partnership Council, established in 1997, which includes the twenty-eight member countries of NATO and the twenty-two partner countries. Some of the partners, including all the neutrals except Switzerland, contribute troops to NATO's peacekeeping missions. Perhaps more than any other institutional change, participation in Partnership for Peace underscores how neutrality has been redefined in the years after the end of the Cold War.[36]

Does Neutrality Have a Future?

It is appropriate to conclude by asking if neutrality continues to have any meaning in the post Cold War era: is it possible to be "neither one nor the other," when otherness seems to have disappeared?[37] To think about this question, let us return to those three elements in the formulation of neutral politics with which we began: geography, international agreements, and domestic politics.

---

35. See the essays in Hanspeter Neuhold, ed., *The European Neutrals in the 1990s* (Boulder: Westview, 1992).
36. Doherty, *Ireland*, has a good account of the Partnership from the Irish perspective. More information is available on the *NATO website*, <http://www.nato.int/cps/en/natolive/topics_ 50349.htm>.
37. For some interesting reflections on this question, see Laurent Goetschel, "Neutrality, a Really Dead Concept?," *Cooperation and Conflict* 34 (1999): 115-39; and Michael Gehler, "Quo Vadis Neutralität? Zusammenfassende Überlegungen zu ihrer Geschichte und Rolle in europäischen Staatensystem sowie im Spannungsfeld der Integration," in *Die Neutralen*, ed. Gehler and Steininger, 711-54.

From the neutrals' perspective, the end of the Cold War transformed Europe's geopolitical landscape in two important ways. First, by removing the ideological, economic, and strategic boundary between east and west, it resolved the major security problem faced by every neutral state throughout the postwar period. Second, and at least as significant, the end of the Cold War changed the strategic meaning of geography, which now lost the military significance it had had throughout modern European history. After the collapse of Communism, the neutrals, like other European states, no longer saw threats to their security in the form of invading armies, but rather as terrorist attacks, organized crime, and environmental disaster, threats against which even the most formidable geographical barriers offered little protection.

The end of the Cold War also reshaped the network of agreements and institutions that had regulated the neutrals' role in the society of states after 1945. All of the bilateral agreements signed between the Soviet Union and Eastern European states in 1948-49 disappeared, including, as we have seen, the Treaty of Friendship with Finland. Some Cold War institutions, such as the Organization for Security and Cooperation in Europe, survived, but with much diminished significance. Western European institutions expanded to fill the political vacuum created by the collapse of the Soviet imperium, so that within a decade most European states belonged to, or sought membership in, the North Atlantic Treaty Organization and the European Union. For the neutrals, with the highly qualified exception of Switzerland, European values and institutions became the essential framework within which their foreign political issues and interests were defined and defended.

It is, I think, largely in the realm of domestic politics that neutrality continues to have meaning. In the first place, neutrality remains politically popular because it is identified with the remarkable stability and prosperity enjoyed by all five states in the postwar period and, in the case of Ireland, Sweden, and Switzerland, with the achievement of avoiding the punishing violence of the Second World War. Second, neutrality is closely connected to each neutral state's sense of its particular historical identity: in Ireland, to the Republic's hard won independence from Great Britain; in Switzerland, to a carefully constructed balance between nationalities; in Sweden, to a long history of profitable non-alignment as well as the creation of a third way between Communism and capitalism; in Finland, to the struggle for independence from Russia, first through a heroic if ultimately doomed military campaign, then through skillful diplomacy; and in Austria, to the end of its postwar occupation, the reordering of its long and complex relationship with Germany, and its status as the Nazis' "first victim." Finally, even after losing its significance as a policy of non-alignment, neutrality remains important as part of a broader set of attitudes about the nature and practice of international relations. Even more than their European neighbors, the neutrals are civilian states, deeply suspicious of the utility of force in the resolution of conflicts.[38] All the neutrals, even those with relatively vigorous security forces, emphasize defense and deterrent strategies in which force projection does not play a role. That is why, as we have seen, none of the neutrals has joined NATO, although all of them do cooperate with the alliance to some extent. Moreover, in different ways, the formerly neutral states have expressed reservations about the EU's persistent commitment to developing a common foreign and security policy. These reservations are one reason why even the most robust formulations of a common European foreign policy become highly tentative when they describe how and when force might be used. Permanent neutrality is not just a residue from the past, it remains part of Irish, Swiss, Swedish, Finnish, and Austrian political culture and as such will continue to play a role in the development of the European society of states.[39]

---

38. On the concept of the "civilian state," see James Sheehan, *Where Have All the Soldiers Gone?* (Boston: Houghton Mifflin, 2008).
39. See for example, Sean Boyle, "Ireland Edges Towards EU Security Identity," *Jane's International Defence Review* 28, no. 4 (April 1995): 56-60. On the Austrian case, see the essays in Günter Bischof and Anton Pelinka, ed., *Austrian Historical Memory and National Identity* (New Brunswick, N.J.: Transaction Publishers, 1997).

Eastern Europe
and the Balkans

Austria and Eastern Europe in the Post-Cold War Context

Between the Opening of the Iron Curtain and a New Nation-Building Process in Eastern Europe

Arnold Suppan

The opening of the Iron Curtain did not happen in a day. The first experience for the Viennese population came already in mid-December 1988 when tens of thousands of Hungarians with new passports flooded the main streets in the Austrian capital to buy Christmas gifts. Even though one could cross the city faster by foot than by car, the mood shared by Austrians and Hungarians was excellent. Later, the Austrians enthusiastically greeted the symbolic opening of the Iron Curtain by the Foreign Ministers Alois Mock and Gyula Horn in June 1989. On 19 August 1989, when the Pan European Union of Otto von Habsburg organized a cross-border picnic in the west of Sopron and hundreds of German Democratic Republic (GDR) citizens on holiday in Hungary used the opportunity to flee to the West, many residents of the Burgenland applauded. After midnight on September 11, 1989, Austrians welcomed tens of thousands of GDR citizens in their *Trabi* cars crossing into Austria with permission from the Hungarian government, on the way to West Germany. At the time no one knew that an accord had been made between the West German chancellor Helmut Kohl and the Hungarian prime minister Miklós Nemeth. Both had phoned to Moscow and received assurance of support from Secretary General Mikhail Gorbachev and Prime Minister Nikolai Ryzhkov.[1] Even the governments of Austria and the GDR were informed of this agreement only days before the border was to be opened.

In December 1989, the episode was repeated when Mock and his new Czechoslovak colleague Jiří Dienstbier opened the border near Znojmo and tens of thousands of Czechs and Slovaks came for a first visit. The following weekends tens of thousands of Viennese, Lower and Upper Austrians visited Bratislava, Brno, Znojmo, Český Krumlov, České Budějovice and

---

1. István Horváth, *Die Sonne ging in Ungarn auf: Erinnerungen an eine besondere Freundschaft* (Munich: Universitas, 2000), 317-34; Helmut Kohl, Kai Diekmann, and Ralf Georg Reuth, *Ich wollte Deutschlands Einheit* (Berlin: Propyläen, 1996), 74.

Prague. Larger Austrian enterprises, such as the gas producer OMV, the supermarket chains Billa, Spar and BauMax, as well as the upscale firms Meinl and Palmers established shops in the Czech Republic, Poland, Slovakia, Hungary, Slovenia, Croatia, the Serbian Vojvodina, Romania, the Ukraine, and Bulgaria. Bank Austria, Raiffeisen, and Erste Bank also decided to "go east."

In the second quarter of 2008 the share of Austrian banks in Western investments in East-Central, Southeast and Eastern Europe was 19.5% (over 200 billion Euro), ahead of Germany with 15.8%, Italy 15.6%, France 11.5%, Belgium 9.5%, the Netherlands 8.1%, Sweden 7.2%, Greece 4.2%, and Great Britain 3.0%. The Austrian share was 66% in Croatia, 52% in Bosnia-Herzegovina, 47% in Slovakia, 38% in Romania, 36% in the Czech Republic, 32% in Albania, 29% in Serbia, 25% in Bulgaria, 22% in Hungary, 18% in Slovenia, 13% in the Ukraine, 8% in Belarus and Kazakhstan, 4% in Russia, 3% in Lithuania, and 2% in Poland. The terrible history of the twentieth century seemed to be forgotten. The imminent world financial crisis, however, brought new dangers.[2]

Austrian politics did not react only by opening the Iron Curtain. Starting in May 1989, the new Minister for Science and Research, Erhard Busek, met his new Hungarian colleague, Ferenc Glatz, to agree on sending about three-dozen German lecturers to Hungarian universities and *gymnasia*. In June 1989, Minister Glatz—educated partly in Mainz and Vienna—cancelled the special status of the Russian language, making it equal to English, German, French, Italian and Spanish as a foreign language option in Hungarian schools. Thousands of Hungarian teachers of the Russian language were forced to learn another European language. Minister Busek also supported the establishment of bureaus of the Austrian Institute for East and Southeast European Studies at Bratislava (1990), Budapest (1990), Ljubljana (1991), Brno (1991), L'viv (1992), and Sofia (1994).[3] The quickest negotiations happened in Bratislava, where there are few, if any, negative stereotypes about "the Austrians." When the Austrian delegation visited the university in Ljubljana, some older Slovenian professors asked behind the scenes whether the Austrians wanted to reestablish the Habsburg Monarchy. Nevertheless, the Austrian Ministry of Science and Research

---

2. Sandra Dvorsky, Thomas Scheiber, Helmut Stix, "The OeNB Euro Survey in Central, Eastern, and Southeastern Europe—The 2008 Spring Wave Update," *Focus on European Economic Integration* 2 (2008): 83-93. Available online at: <http://www.oenb.at/en/img/feei_2008_ 2_dvorsky_tcm16-95551.pdf> (10 Dec. 2010).

3. In the first draft a scientific bureau was planned in Belgrade, too. But when Milošević blocked foreign accounts in December 1990, it became impossible to pay the rent for this bureau.

organized scholarships, announced scientific projects and supported many bilateral publications. The Austrian Foreign Ministry established so-called "Austrian libraries" between České Budějovice and Liberec, Znojmo and Olomouc, Bratislava and Prešov, Cracow and Wrocław, L'viv and Černivci, Cluj and Timişoara, Pécs and Szeged, Maribor and Osijek, Sarajevo and Ruse. A new generation of Hungarians, Slovaks, Czechs, Poles, Ukrainians, Romanians, Slovenes, Croats, Serbs, and Bulgarians started to learn German. After twenty years of experience we can state that the great majority of the educated youth in East-Central Europe decided to learn English. The German language plays only a secondary role compared with the popularity of English as a second language, not to mention French, Russian, Spanish, and Italian. English became the first colloquial language in East-Central Europe, not only in Prague and Warsaw, but also in Bratislava, Budapest, Ljubljana, Zagreb, and Belgrade. Even in Bucharest English is the dominant foreign language. Scholars and students from Slavic origin are also using English as their colloquial language.

The first major item on the post-Communist East-Central European agenda was the fast proliferation of new nation states: the Yugoslav disintegration process, the dissolution of the Soviet Union, and the split of Czechoslovakia. In the beginning, there was hope that the new process of national self-determination would go hand in hand with the democratization of the societies concerned. To the most shocking extent, primarily Yugoslavia but also—albeit to a lesser degree—many of the post-Communist countries showed signs of xenophobia and authoritarian leaders emerged with popular support (Milošević, Tuđman, Mečiar, Iliescu, etc.). It was clear that in order to prevent greater disasters direct or indirect external interventions could not be avoided. Consolidation, peace, and security could be implemented only if the EU and NATO made substantial financial, political, and military efforts in the region. This became an axiom for the political leaders and most of the leading intellectuals of the countries of the former Soviet bloc.[4]

Soon after the establishment of the new coalition between the Social Democratic Party (SPÖ) and the Austrian People's Party (ÖVP) in January 1987, Vice-Chancellor and Foreign Minister Alois Mock (ÖVP) pushed forward Austria's preparation to join the European Union. Although the government feared some dissatisfaction from nationalists after the opening of the Iron Curtain in 1989, in spring 1994 sixty-five percent voted in favor

---

4. Attila Pók, "East and West as Historical-Political Concepts in Late and Post Communist Hungary (1968-2006)," in Iskra Schwarcz and Arnold Suppan, ed., *Quo vadis EU? Osteuropa und die EU-Erweiterung* (Vienna: LIT Verlag, 2008), 223-35.

of joining the European Union. In particular the older generation—the so-called "war generation" (now more the widows than the veterans) that was the target of so much criticism in 1986—voted on behalf of their grandchildren for a Western orientation. The coalition government of Franz Vranitzky and Erhard Busek feared especially the voter impact of EU austerity measures as well as the anti-immigrant propaganda of the new Freedom Party (FPÖ)-leader, Jörg Haider. Indeed, Haider garnered increasing support in the national elections in 1990 (16.6%) and 1994 (22.5%) with the help of the popular resentment against the coalition government and their policies. Nevertheless, the Second Austrian Republic had overcome the crisis of national identity that plagued the period between 1918 and 1945. Celebrations over the country's spurious millennium in 1996 were nonetheless decidedly muted. The exhibitions in St. Pölten and Neuhofen: Man-Myths-Milestones (*Menschen-Mythen-Meilensteine*) were presented not simply as an antiquarian exercise but as a dialogue between past and present, and the questions it posed could be asked of other European states as well.[5]

The dissolution of the Eastern bloc, of Yugoslavia and the Soviet Union suddenly raised the immigration question. Between 1990 and 1992 the number of immigrants to Austria reached almost 100,000 a year, more than one percent of the population. Between 1989 and 1994 the number of non-Austrian residents doubled from approximately 350,000 to 700,000. The Social democratic trade unions did not derive pleasure from this development; the ÖVP and FPÖ business and landowner clientele profited from immigrant workers; the left-wing Social Democrats and the Greens demanded more rights for immigrants. But Haider, who had spoken in 1988 about "the concept of the Austrian nation" as "an ideological miscarriage," cancelled the Germandom-article in the party program (Austria defined as a part of the *deutsche Kultur- und Volksgemeinschaft*), and in the fall of 1992 started an "Austria first" petition with a ten point program on the subject of immigration, collecting 417,000 signatures. In response, the new platform *SOS Mitmensch* protested against Haider's initiative and propaganda, organizing a huge demonstration on January 23, 1993 at Heldenplatz with a quarter of a million holding candles. Although the FPÖ historically had always been very pro-European, including support for a NATO security arrangement, when negotiations between Vienna and Brussels started in 1993, Haider rejected the centralism of Brussels and any attempt to enforce

---

5. Gordon Marsden, "Whose Austria?" *History Today* 45, no. 10 (October 1996): 22-28; cf. Ernst Bruckmüller and Peter Urbanitsch, ed., *Ostarrichi, Österreich 996-1996: Menschen, Mythen, Meilensteine: österreichische Länderausstellung* (Horn: Verlag Berger, 1996).

cultural homogeneity. In 1997, Haider initiated another voter initiative that asked for yet another referendum before joining the Euro currency, but this time only 254,000 signed.[6]

Perhaps the Western state chancelleries and media were more disturbed by Haider's infamous statements relating to Hitler and National Socialist rule. In a debate in the Carinthian Diet in June 1991, Haider praised the "orderly employment policy" of the Third Reich. In response, the SPÖ and ÖVP voted him out of office as governor of Carinthia. And again in February 1995, Haider referred to the "punishment camps of the National Socialism," perhaps implying that concentration camp inmates had been guilty of crimes. At the same time, however, he attacked the government for not doing more to ease the integration of Roma and Sinti. In September 1995, Haider spoke to World War II veterans, including former members of the *Waffen SS*, and praised them for having "remained true to their convictions until today." Even after the building of the ÖVP-FPÖ coalition government on February 4, 2000 and the subsequent "sanctions" of fourteen EU members against Austria, Haider reminded German television viewers of his belief "that if Jews receive reparations for their sufferings under Nazism, then Germans expelled from postwar Czechoslovakia and former Austrian prisoners of war in the Soviet Union should be similarly recompensed." Obviously, Haider didn't study enough the disastrous history of the National Socialist regime and the involvement of many Austrians. There is also much in Haider's language that mimics word for word some politicians of the war generation. But even this generation ultimately recognized Hitler's ruinous war economy, the mass murder in concentration camps, misleading and sending soldiers to the slaughter, and the differences in suffering.[7]

The Dissolution of Yugoslavia

Contrary to a notorious caricature in the Belgrade magazine *Nin – Čas anatomije* (The Time of Anatomy),[8] neither the Austrian government

---

6. Lothar Höbelt, *Defiant Populist. Jörg Haider and the Politics of Austria* (West Lafayette: Purdue University Press, 2003).
7. Cf. Ernst Hanisch, *Der lange Schatten des Staates. Österreichische Gesellschaftsgeschichte im 20. Jahrhundert* (Vienna: Ueberreuter, 1994), 337-94; Hans-Ulrich Wehler, *Deutsche Gesellschaftsgeschichte* 4: *Vom Beginn des Ersten Weltkriegs bis zur Gründung der beiden deutschen Staaten 1914-1949* (Munich: Beck, 2003).
8. The cover "Čas anatomije" (Time of Anatomy), *Nin*, Belgrade, September 18, 1992, contains two pictures: in the first, six men symbolizing the USA, Germany, France, Austria (sic!), Great Britain, and the United Nations are dividing Yugoslavia, with "the Austrian" playing a leading role as adviser. In the second picture, the six men are washing their bloody hands.

nor the Austrian population wished a violent breakup of Yugoslavia. Of course, many bankers, industrialists, merchants and intellectuals in Vienna, Graz, and Klagenfurt were in some ways informed about multiple threats to the stability and longevity of Yugoslavia. But, when the charismatic Marshal Josip Broz Tito died in May 1980, nobody foresaw the collapse of his Yugoslavia in the early 1990s. And looking at the Olympic winter games in Sarajevo in February 1984, nobody could imagine that this city will be besieged less than a decade later. However, familiar with tourism along the Adriatic coast, the export harbors in Rijeka and Koper, the fair in Zagreb and more than one hundred thousand Yugoslav "guest workers" in Austria, Austrians did not overestimate the so-called "artificial creation" of Yugoslavia and the existence of what came to be called "ancient hatreds." More attention has been given to the contrary state visions: the Serbs' vision of a centralized, unitary state, and the federal model of the Croats and the Slovenes.[9]

Because during World War II many former Austrians were engaged in the occupied and divided Yugoslavia—as *Höhere SS- und Polizei-Führer*, Wehrmacht generals, *Reichsstatthalter*, administrators, bankers, teachers, soldiers, and policemen—there existed not only specific knowledge of the distrust among ethnic and confessional groups within Yugoslavia, but also of the clashes between the Ustashe and the Chetniks, the Partisans and the Chetniks, the Ustashe and the Partisans, the Chetniks and the Muslims, the Slovene partisans and the Slovene homeguards, etc. Later as prisoners of war or expelled Lower Styrians and *Gottscheer*, many of these "Austrians" also experienced the mass slaughtering at the end of the war, still a debated topic in present-day Slovenia and Croatia. When the Serbs focused their discussion on World War II around the massacres of Serbs by the Ustashe, the Croats tended to minimize the extent of wartime persecutions of Serbs in Croatia and to speak only of the slaughter of Croats by the partisans at the end of the war (the tragedy of Bleiburg is one such instance). But the division of the Yugoslav kingdom between Germany, Italy, Hungary, and Bulgaria certainly worked to reinforce the idea that Yugoslav unity was necessary to fend off rapacious neighbors.[10]

---

9. See Ivo Banac, *The National Question in Yugoslavia. Origins, History, Politics* (Ithaca and London: Cornell University Press, 1984); cf. Arnold Suppan, "Yugoslavism versus Serbian, Croatian and Slovene Nationalism: Political, Ideological, and Cultural Causes of the Rise and Fall of Yugoslavia," in *Yugoslavia and Its Historians: Understanding the Balkan Wars of the 1990s*, ed. Holly Case and Norman M. Naimark (Stanford: Stanford University Press, 2003), 116-39.
10. See Jozo Tomasevich, *War and Revolution in Yugoslavia, 1941-1945: Occupation and Collaboration* (Stanford: Stanford University Press, 2001); Jože Dežman, ed., *Poročilo Komisije*

The totalitarian leader, Tito, began immediately in 1945 with the establishment of a centralized Communist state with six Socialist republics and the idea of "brotherhood and unity." Although the party, the army, and the bureaucracy tried to propagate a new, anti-religious Yugoslavism, the nationalist thinking from the interwar period did not disappear. The project of creating a Socialist Yugoslav national identity was undermined by Yugoslavia's constitutional decentralization since 1963, and with the constitution of 1974 the central power of the Belgrade government was replaced by the power of the republican governments. As long as Tito lived, the centrifugal force of the republics and the centripetal force of brotherhood were in equilibrium. In the 1980s, especially the second half, Austrian politicians, economists and intellectuals saw three harmful developments: the ineffectiveness of the central state in competition with new power centers such as Ljubljana; the inability of the Yugoslav state to generate wealth and prosperity for its citizens; and the growth of separate national narratives which directly competed with a Yugoslav narrative. On the other hand, the split between Stalin and Tito in 1948, as well as the Soviet invasions in Hungary 1956 and Czechoslovakia 1968, provoked fear of the USSR. Consequently this fear was an important unifying factor for Yugoslavia. But since the 1988 meeting between Reagan and Gorbachev in New York, a new geopolitical climate was created that led to the end of the Cold War. Therefore, a strong state was no longer necessary for external security and prosperity. In this environment, the various peoples of Yugoslavia began to recall a series of grievances that they interpreted in national terms.[11]

Perhaps even the Austrians underestimated the new (and old) Serbian national narrative around the "sacrifices" in the Ottoman period (the battle on the Kosovo Polje in 1389), in World War I (the Serbian "Golgotha" in the winter 1915-16), and in World War II (the slaughtering of the Serbs by the Ustashe). But when I invited the secretary general of the Serbian Academy of Sciences and Arts, Dejan Medaković, and two Belgrade professors to Vienna to explain the "Memorandum" of the Serbian Academy

---

Vlade Republike Slovenije za rešavanje vprašanj prikritih grobišč 2005-2008 (Ljubljana: Družina, 2008).

11. Andrew Wachtel and Christopher Bennett, "The Dissolution of Yugoslavia," in *Confronting the Yugoslav Controversies*, ed. Charles Ingrao (West Lafayette: Purdue University Press, 2009); cf. Aleksa Djilas, *The Contested Country: Yugoslav Unity and Communist Revolution, 1919-1953* (Cambridge, MA.: Harvard University Press, 1991); Andrew Wachtel, *Making a Nation, Breaking a Nation: Literature and Cultural Politics in Yugoslavia* (Stanford: Stanford University Press, 1998); Dejan Djokić, ed., *Yugoslavism: Histories of a Failed Idea, 1918-1992* (London: Hurst and Company, 2003).

of Sciences and Arts—the first draft was published in September 1986—they complained that Tito's Yugoslavia had discriminated against Serbs in a variety of ways, supposedly permitting Serbia's economic subjugation to Croatia and Slovenia, as well as the "genocide" perpetrated by the Albanians against the Serbs of Kosovo. Slobodan Milošević did not start his political career in 1986 with a developed plan to destroy Yugoslavia, but to recentralize the country under his own leadership. When he saw that this project was unrealistic, he turned to a policy of uniting all Serbs in a single state, meaning also the Serbs in Croatia and Bosnia-Herzegovina. Already in April 1987, Milošević posed as a "national savior" by protecting a group of Kosovo Serbs and he revamped Serbia's Communist Party with nationalism; in 1988-89 he orchestrated mass marches by paying unemployed young men to go around the country from meeting to meeting and gained full control over the Serbian autonomous provinces of Kosovo and the Vojvodina, as well as Montenegro. The peak of these marches was reached with the one-million-person rallies in Belgrade and on the Kosovo Polje (on June 28, 1989). Milošević's use of mass politics fascinated and attracted the Serbian intelligentsia, but this popular enthusiasm for Milošević's approach to the national question blocked any possibility of a democratic solution to Yugoslavia's crisis.[12]

Most Austrian and other Western spectators did not recognize that the suppression of the "Croatian Spring" in the fall of 1971 was taken by many Croat intellectuals as evidence that the Communist Yugoslav state was not willing to tolerate the particularity of Croatian literature and history, let alone Croatian autonomy. We should not forget that the Croatian Spring had shown the alignment between Croat national identity and the Catholic Church in Croatia and that the suppression of the Croatian Spring helped to delegitimatize the Partisan legacy upon which postwar Yugoslavia was based. On the other hand, the 1974 Yugoslav Constitution incorporated much of what had been demanded by Croats. Nevertheless, "Croatia descended into political apathy from which it did not emerge for almost two decades."[13]

---

12. Kosta Mihailović and Vasilije Krestić, *Memorandum of the Serbian Academy of Sciences and Arts: Answers to Criticisms* (Belgrade: SANU, 1995); Laura Silber and Allan Little, *Yugoslavia: Death of a Nation* (New York: Penguin Books, 1995), 58-81; Sabrina Petra Ramet, *Balkan Babel: The Disintegration of Yugoslavia from the Death of Tito to Ethnic War* (Boulder, CO: Westview Press,1996); Lenard J. Cohen, *Serpent in the Bosom: The Rise and Fall of Slobodan Milošević* (Boulder, CO: Westview Press, 2002); Florian Bieber, *Nationalismus in Serbien vom Tode Titos bis zum Ende der Ära Milošević* (Vienna: LIT Verlag, 2005).

13. Dušan Bilandžić, *Historija Socijalističke Federativne Republike Jugoslavije: Glavni procesi* (Zagreb: Školska knjiga, 1979); Ivo Goldstein, *Croatia, A History* (London: McGill-Queen's University Press, 1999), 183.

Slovene intellectuals also feared denationalization. Belgrade's call for repressive measures against opposition intellectuals and for centralization in the fields of education, science, and culture did more to mobilize public opinion than did economic problems. A Belgrade newspaper summarized the basic attitude: "We Slovenes will alone decide about our schools, and nobody should dictate to us." In this atmosphere, the Slovene educated strata formulated a national program—in some sense an answer to the Serbian Memorandum. Slovene intellectuals pushed for "realization of the Slovene right to self-determination" and for an independent, democratic state following the Western model. Admiral Branko Mamula, the Yugoslav defense minister, condemned this national program but unintentionally did more for Slovene independence than anyone else. When, in the spring of 1988, the Yugoslav National Army (JNA) and the military counter-intelligence ordered the arrest of one JNA sergeant and three journalists from the weekly magazine *Mladina*, the trial in Ljubljana—conducted in Serbo-Croatian instead of Slovene—became a catalyst for the creation of a Committee for the Defense of Human Rights, which collected a hundred thousand signatures. The result was a remarkable unification of Slovene society and national mobilization in support of the accused. Milošević's onslaught against the Albanian leadership and the striking miners in Kosovo in the spring of 1989 shocked even Milan Kučan, the head of the Slovenian Communists, and he took a firm stance against the attempts of Milošević to pressure Slovenia into submission.[14]

As Serb militants from Kosovo, in collusion with Serbian authorities, announced that they would organize a "rally of truth" in Ljubljana on December 1, 1989, and on the way there would stop in Zagreb, where they also wanted to stir up disorder, the Slovene authorities denied them entry and the Croatian authorities announced that they would use police force against the demonstrators. In response to Slovenian media and political criticism of the Serbian use of force in Kosovo, Serbia broke off economic relations with Slovenia in December 1989. Kučan hoped to expand regional autonomy within Yugoslavia by turning the League of Communists into a loose association of separate Communist parties. But in January 1990, as it became clear that there could be no negotiations, the Slovene and Croat Communists walked out of the fourteenth Congress of the League of Communists of Yugoslavia. A main pillar of Tito's Yugoslavia broke away. Now, new parties in Slovenia and Croatia demanded multi-party elections, and the Slovenian as well as the Croatian Communists agreed.

---

14. Peter Vodopivec, "Slovenes and Yugoslavia, 1918-1991," *East European Politics and Societies* 6, no. 3 (fall 1992): 220-40; *Politika Ekspres*, 21 Sept. 1983, 7.

In Slovenia, a coalition of six opposition parties called Demos defeated Kučan's reformed Communists; but in the presidential election Kučan was the victor. Milošević's pressure on Croatia helped Franjo Tuđman's Croatian Democratic Union (HDZ) win the first free parliamentary elections since 1927 in April-May 1990, the constitutional status of Croatia's Serbs was downgraded from that of a "nation" (with equal rights in comparison with the Croats) to that of a "national minority." At the same time, when the republics' new governments were established in Ljubljana and Zagreb, the JNA began to disarm the Slovene and Croatian Territorial Defense forces. This helped the Serbs in the Krajina to separate them from Zagreb.[15]

After the split of the League of Communists and the different results in the elections, the third—and for the bankers decisive—break came with Milošević's assault on the federal financial system in the fall of 1990. Serbia's main bank gave an illegal loan to the Serbian government, "effectively stealing 18 billion dinars, or 1.7 billion dollars at prevailing exchange rates, from the rest of the country."[16] This action also put an end to the reform program of Ante Marković, Yugoslavia's last prime minister. When Slovenia's Prime Minister Jože Peterle and Croatia's President Tuđman visited Vienna in January 1991, both remarked that they did not see the possibility of any compromise with Milošević. Yugoslavia had disintegrated even before Slovenia and Croatia formally declared their independence.

Already on December 23, 1990, 88.2 percent of the Slovenes decided for the independence of their republic, and the Slovene parliament declared its intent to secede from Yugoslavia in six months. But in the spring of 1991, the Serbs in the *Krajina*, as well as in Slavonia, revolted and clashed with Croatian policemen. Milošević, together with the federal president Borisav Jović, tried to impose a state of emergency. The Bosnian representative—a Serb (!)—, however, refused to support the representatives of Serbia, Montenegro, Vojvodina, and Kosovo to achieve the majority. Yugoslavia was left without a head of state and commander in chief of its armed forces when the Serbian bloc rejected the appointment of the Croat Stipe Mesić on May 16. In this situation, Croatia's leaders hastily organized an independence referendum on May 19, and seventy-eight percent of the Croatian electorate supported the proposal "that the Republic of Croatia, as a sovereign and independent state, which guarantees cultural autonomy

---

15. Silber and Little, *Death*, 82-91.
16. Wachtel and Bennett, "The Dissolution of Yugoslavia," 37. After an open lecture in Vienna at the end of January 1991, I frankly asked Tuđman in a private forum if he saw any parallels to the situation of the Croats in 1848 or in 1918. He did not see any parallels and fully expected Croat sovereignty in the very near future.

and all civic rights to Serbs and members of other nationalities in Croatia, can enter into a union of sovereign states with other republics."[17]

The breakup of Communist-ruled Yugoslavia was not the fault of the international community. At the end of the Cold War, Yugoslavia had lost its strategic importance as a buffer state between East and West. Neither the United States, nor the Soviet Union, NATO, the European Community, the Vatican, Germany, or Austria were engaged in the dissolution process; quite the reverse. Since February 1990 Foreign Minister Mock called many times for political dialogue and tried to engage the Conference on Security and Cooperation in Europe (CSCE); in the first half of 1991 Mock held consultations with Gianni de Michelis in Vienna and Rome and cooperated in the Berlin declaration of the CSCE foreign ministers on June 20, 1991. When Secretary of State James Baker made an unscheduled stopover in Belgrade on June 21, 1991, he made it clear that the USA "will neither encourage or reward secession."[18] The civil wars as well as the successor wars in Yugoslavia were planned and waged by Yugoslavs, mainly by the Serbian leadership around Slobodan Milošević and the Yugoslav National Army. For analytical purposes, Vesna Pešić tried to separate the breakup of Yugoslavia and the war, but she had to admit, "the two processes are indisputably linked." She attributed the cause of the war "to the creation of new national states in which the leadership of the individual republics brought them into conflict over the distribution of Yugoslav territory, borders, and ethnic boundaries. The national heterogeneity of all the republics, with the exception of Slovenia, led not only to the problem of integrating the existing states, but also to the conflicts between them."[19] Nevertheless, one should emphasize that in June 1991, only Milošević and the JNA had sufficient weapons at their disposal to start a war, and "the historical record shows that it was Milošević and no one else whose actions pushed the country over the brink."[20]

On June 27, 1991 the JNA started to occupy Slovenian border stations at the frontiers to Austria and Italy. Both foreign ministries officially protested. Minister Mock invited the CSCE countries to an urgent meeting in Vienna; the EC Troika negotiated in Belgrade, Zagreb, and on the island of Brioni and settled an accord for the next three months. At the beginning of August, Austria engaged the Security Council, which

---

17. Silber and Little, *Death*, 134-46.
18. *Washington Post*, June 27, 1991; cf. Cohen, *Serpent*, 189.
19. Vesna Pešić, "The War of Ethnic States," in *The Road to War in Serbia: Trauma and Catharsis*, ed. Nebojša Popov (Budapest: CEU Press, 2000), 9-49.
20. Wachtel and Bennett, "The Dissolution of Yugoslavia," 29.

concluded on September 25, 1991, with resolution 713. Although the EC started a peace conference in The Hague, the JNA attacked Dubrovnik and Vukovar; the Croatian parliament activated the proclamation of sovereignty, as did the Slovenian parliament some days before. On November 10, 1991, Radovan Karadžić, the head of the Serbian Democratic Party in Bosnia-Herzegovina, organized a referendum to stay in a common state with Serbia, Montenegro, Serbian Autonomous Oblast (SAO) of Krajina, SAO Slavonia, Baranja, and western Syrmia. At the beginning of December the Badinter Commission of the EC stated that the SFRJ is in the "process of dissolution." On December 17, the EC foreign ministers declared "a catalogue of criteria for the acknowledgment of new countries in Eastern Europe and the Soviet Union." After Germany had decided to recognize the sovereignty of Croatia and Slovenia on January 15, 1992,[21] the EC and many other countries including Austria acknowledged Croatia and Slovenia as independent countries; Russia followed on February 14/17, the USA not before April 7, 1992—only one day before the state of emergency in Bosnia-Herzegovina was declared.

Although there existed many political, economic, social and cultural links between Austria and Bosnia-Herzegovina, Austrian diplomats were not directly engaged in searching for a political and military solution to end the war in Bosnia-Herzegovina because Austria was not a member of the EU or NATO. But Austria accepted and helped more than 100,000 refugees from Bosnia-Herzegovina and condemned the violations against human rights, especially the ethnic cleansing, mass rape, and the genocide at Srebrenica. Many Austrian diplomats were engaged in the post-Yugoslav questions: Wolfgang Petritsch was one of the chief negotiators at Rambouillet in 1999; Albert Rohan was the deputy head of the Ahtisaari mission in Kosovo.[22]

Multiethnicity and Multiculturalism in Austria

Although a majority of Austrians is of Germanic stock and speaks German (95%)—the "Austrian German"[23]—in many regional dialects, and

---

21. Federal Chancellor Kohl stated that because Germany received the right of self-determination this should be given to the Croats and Slovenes also.
22. Mark Almond and Dunja Melčić, "Dayton und die Neugestaltung Bosnien-Herzegowinas," in *Der Jugoslawien-Krieg: Handbuch zu Vorgeschichte, Verlauf und Konsequenzen*, ed. Dunja Melčić (Wiesbaden: Verlag für Sozialwissenschaften, 2007), 439-52.
23. Peter Wiesinger, "Das österreichische Deutsch im Rahmen des Gesamtdeutschen," in *L'Autriche et l'idee d'Europe: actes du 29e Congrès de l'AGES, 10 au 12 mai 1996 à Dijon*, ed.

profess the Catholic faith (2001: 73% Catholic, 5% Islamic, 4% Lutheran), Austria has grown from multiethnic, multilingual, and multicultural roots. Since the Middle Ages Slovenes have lived in the southern parts of Carinthia and Styria; Jewish merchants and craftsmen immigrated to many Austrian towns; migrants from the Swiss canton Wallis settled in the Walsertal (Vorarlberg), followed by Italian settlers from the Val Sugana to the Walgau in the nineteenth century. Under pressure from the Ottomans in the sixteenth century, about two hundred thousand Croats fled to the north and settled in the western parts of the Kingdom of Hungary, what is today the Austrian Burgenland and Western Slovakia, and in the Lower Austrian Marchfeld. In the nineteenth century, almost half a million Czechs and Germans from Moravia, Silesia and Bohemia migrated to Vienna and Lower Austria, especially as industrial workers, craftsmen, and domestic servants. At the same time, as many as 200,000 Jews came from Galicia and the Russian Ukraine to Vienna, as did Poles, Slovaks, Magyars, Croats, Slovenes, Italians, Bosnians, Romanians, Serbs, Bulgarians, Greeks, Armenians, Arumanians (Vlachs), and Gypsies (Roma). The majority of them were assimilated before 1914.[24]

The Treaty of Saint-Germain in 1919 left to the new Republic of Austria only seven hereditary provinces. Only half of the 12 million Germans of the Habsburg Monarchy lived in the new Republic of Austria with 83,858 km^2, while 3.5 million Sudeten- and Carpathian Germans came to Czechoslovakia, 750,000 Saxons, Danube Swabians, and Bukovina Germans to Romania, 550,000 Germans—mostly Danube Swabians—to Hungary, 450,000 Danube Swabians as well as 100,000 Lower Styrians and Gottscheer to Yugoslavia, 220,000 South Tyrolians and about ten thousand Carinthians to Italy, and 150,000 Galician and Teschen Germans to Poland. On the other side, about 100,000 Czechs and Slovaks "re-emigrated" from the new Austria to Czechoslovakia, approximately ten thousand Galician and Bukovina Jews to Poland and Romania, some ten thousand South Slavs to the new Yugoslavia, as well as about five thousand Magyar state employees from Burgenland to Hungary. Some ten thousand German-Austrian civil servants and railway employees "returned" to the new republic. The new

---

Michel Reffet (Dijon: Editions universitaires de Dijon, 1991), 7-30; cf. Michael Clyne, *The German language in a changing Europe* (Cambridge, UK: Cambridge University Press, 1995); Ulrich Ammon, *Die deutsche Sprache in Deutschland, Österreich und der Schweiz: Das Problem der nationalen Varietäten* (Berlin: W. De Gruyter, 1995).

24. Josef Breu, *Die Kroatensiedlung im Burgenland und in den anschließenden Gebieten* (Vienna: Braumüller, 1970); Michael John and Albert Lichtblau, *Schmelztiegel Wien – einst und jetzt: Zur Geschichte und Gegenwart von Zuwanderung und Minderheiten* (Vienna: Böhlau, 1990), 11-17.

minorities of the Republic of Austria now included about 201,000 Jews in Vienna, 81,000 Czechs and Slovaks in Vienna, 42,000 Croats, 11,000 Magyars, and approximately 10,000 Roma (Gypsies) in Burgenland, as well as almost 50,000 Slovenes in Carinthia and Styria—all together six percent of 6,534,481 inhabitants in the popular census of 1923. Considering the minority policy in the other successor states of the Habsburg Monarchy, the Austrian Republic respected more or less the minority rights according to the Saint-Germain Treaty. Only the question of the Carinthian Slovenes remained as a bilateral problem with Yugoslavia. In 2002, Haider fiercely denounced the Constitutional Court and its president for ruling that where Carinthian Slovenes make up more than a tenth of the populace in a particular community they should be allowed to have place names written in Slovenian as well as German. Unfortunately, the State Treaty of 1955 did not bind this minority right to any percentage, so the decision of the Constitutional Court gave reasons for discussion.[25]

The Nazi period left a legacy of unbearable physical and emotional suffering: 247,000 Austrian soldiers killed or missing in World War II; 24,300 civilians perished in air raids; 128,000 Austrian Jews banished from their home and country; 65,450 remaining Jews murdered in the Holocaust; 32,000 Austrian dissenters and outcasts (including some thousand Roma) driven to death in Gestapo jails or concentration camps; 2,700 Austrian patriots executed for resistance. Overall, more than 372,000 Austrians, or 5.6% of the population, lost their lives under Nazi rule. Astonishingly, most Viennese Czechs were able to stay clear of the *Wehrmacht*, while most Burgenland Croats and the Carinthian Slovenes shared the destiny of the German Austrians; but in April 1942, 917 nationally engaged Slovenes (178 families) were deported to Germany. On the other hand, in September 1944 the evacuation, flight, expulsion, and resettlement began of some hundred thousand Danube Swabians, Transylvanian Saxons, and Carpathian Germans from Yugoslavia, Romania, Hungary, and Slovakia; and in May 1945 that of more than 200,000 Sudeten Germans to Austria. On June 30, 1952, the U.S. High Commissioner reported the existence of 344,849 expelled Germans from Eastern Europe in Austria: 141,524 Danube Swabians; 128,910 Sudeten Germans; 18,000 Transylvanian Saxons; 11,000 Carpathian Germans; 10,000 Lower Styrians and *Gottscheer*; 10,000 Bukovina Germans; 9,485 Germans from Poland; 3,000 Germans

---

25. Arnold Suppan, *Die österreichischen Volksgruppen: Tendenzen ihrer gesellschaftlichen Entwicklung im 20. Jahrhundert* (Vienna: Geschichte und Politik, 1983), 16-21; Paul Jandl, "Tatbestand: gemischte Bevölkerung," *Neue Zürcher Zeitung*, February 5, 2002, 33.

from Bosnia; 1,457 Germans from Russia; 650 Sathmar Germans; 100 Germans from Bessarabia; and 10,723 other *Volksdeutsche*.[26]

After May 1945, the Second Republic of Austria saw many refugee movements from the East to the West: almost 100,000 Jews, fleeing Poland after the pogrom of Kielce in July 1946; 30,000 Jews from Romania, fleeing a famine; 180,000 Magyars in November and December 1956, fleeing the oppression of the Hungarian uprising by the Red Army; 160,000 Czechs and Slovaks after the invasion of the Warsaw Pact in August 1968; 120,000 Poles in 1981 after the introduction of martial law; 260,000 emigrating Soviet Jews in the 1970s and 1980s on their way to Israel or the USA; about 115,000 Croats, Bosnian Muslims, and even Serbs in 1991/95, fleeing the civil wars in former Yugoslavia; and some thousand Albanians in the spring of 1999, mostly expelled from the Kosovo. Almost one quarter of all these refugees stayed permanently, integrated and subsequently received Austrian citizenship. The other three quarters emigrated to other Western countries. Because by 1970 all displaced persons and refugees of the postwar period— as well as Hungarian refugees of 1956-57—had been naturalized, the number of "foreigners" in Austria decreased between 1951 and 1971 from 323,000 to 212,000, those numbers consisting mostly of *Gastarbeiter*, the so-called "guest workers."[27]

In the 1960s, the Austrian economy and society needed to import a foreign labor force. On the basis of bilateral agreements between governments, recruitment took place especially in Yugoslavia and Turkey. In 1973, at the first peak of labor migration, Austria employed 227,000 of these foreign "guest workers." During the first oil crisis, recruitment stopped and labor migration turned into long-term settlement migration with family unification. But, in order to give native citizens a better chance on the labor market, a waiting period was established for newly arriving family members before they could receive a work permit. Even the fall of the Iron Curtain

---

26. Raul Hilberg, *The Destruction of the European Jews* (New York: Quadrangle Books, 1961); Evan Burr Bukey, *Hitler's Austria: Popular Sentiment in the Nazi Era, 1938-1945* (Chapel Hill: The University of North Carolina Press, 2000), 227; Tony Radspieler, *The Ethnic German Refugees in Austria 1945 to 1954* (The Hague: Martinus Nijhoff, 1955), 35-36; Kulturstiftung der deutschen Vertriebenen, ed., *Vertreibung und Vertreibungsverbrechen 1945-1948: Bericht des Bundesarchivs vom 28. Mai 1974* (Bonn: Kulturstiftung der Deutschen Vertriebenen, 1989).

27. Ernst Bruckmüller, *Sozialgeschichte Österreichs* (Vienna: Oldenbourg, 2001), 376-77 and map; Gabriela Stieber, "Volksdeutsche und Displaced Persons," in *Asylland wider Willen: Flüchtlinge in Österreich im europäischen Kontext seit 1914*, ed. Gernot Heiss, Oliver Rathkolb (Vienna: Jugend und Volk, 1995), 140-56; Thomas Albrich, "Zwischenstation des Exodus: Jüdische Displaced Persons und Flüchtlinge nach dem Zweiten Weltkrieg," in Asylland, Heiss and Rathkolb, 122-39; Heinz Fassmann and Rainer Münz, *Einwanderungsland Österreich? Gastarbeiter – Flüchtlinge – Immigranten* (Vienna: Jugend und Volk, 1992).

in 1989 and the coming of some hundred thousand Poles, Czechs, Slovaks, Magyars, Serbs, Croats, and Slovenes as new "guest workers" (in 1991 the number was approximately 450,000)—the majority only to work, not to stay—didn't disturb the Austrian labor market so much because many Austrian enterprises needed them. As in the decades before 1914, Austria's economy (banks, industries, commercial companies and enterprises, smaller firms, tourism, and larger landowners) used its favorable economic-strategic position in East Central Europe. Concerning the differentiation of the occupational positions of the "Austrians" and the "foreigners from non-EU countries" in 1996, 50% of the "guest workers" worked as unskilled and semi-skilled workers, 24% as skilled workers, 12% as professionals, 11% in service occupations, and 2% as clerks; the figures for the "Austrians" were: 32% professionals, 24% skilled workers, 15% clerks, 15% unskilled and semi-skilled workers, 13% in service occupations.[28]

Integrating the approximately 120,000-140,000 Turks in Austria was a special challenge. Some of them—nearly all Muslims—are not willing to integrate fully into Austrian society or learn the German language. At the same time, they demand dual citizenship. The biggest challenge to integration is the concentration of large Turkish and Bosnian Muslim groups in some quarters of Vienna and some Austrian industrial towns (such as Hallein in Salzburg). From the 8,065,166 inhabitants in the census of 2001, 761,400 (or 9.3%) are foreigners, and from the 1,566,459 Viennese, 287,700, or 17.7% are foreign-born. Fortunately, in the 1990s there were no racist riots in Austria as there were in Britain, France, Spain and Germany; but there was also relatively little assimilation or mixing between Christians and Muslims.[29]

Obviously, European migration patterns are determined to a considerable extent by cultural, political and historical connections between the individual countries of origin and destination. Part of the migration is the result of the proximity between these countries; therefore, migrations between neighboring countries take place more frequently. When Poland, the Czech Republic, Slovakia, Hungary, Slovenia, Romania, and Bulgaria have all joined the EU, freedom of movement within the EU will also apply to citizens from these countries following a period of transition lasting about seven years. Perhaps emigration to Austria and the EU area will not reach the record level of the late 1980s and early 1990s. Bringing peace to Serbia, Kosovo, Bosnia and Herzegovina, Montenegro, and Macedonia, as

---

28. Heinz Fassmann, Rainer Münz, ed., *European Migration in the Late Twentieth Century* (Aldershot: E. Elgar, 1996).
29. "Alone, Together: Riots and Multiculturalism," *The Economist*, July 14, 2001, 37.

well as the future development of Moldova, Ukraine, Russia and Turkey will also influence the future of immigration for Austria and the EU. Therefore, two things are crucial: the regulation of immigration and the integration of those migrants who will wish to remain in the country.[30]

Austria Under EU "Sanctions"

Did the more than fifty years of political stability really end, as many internal and external observers stated in February 2000? Why and how can a democratic changeover of a governmental power cause such a big stir? In the parliamentary elections on October 3, 1999, the SPÖ dropped from 38% to 33% of all votes, the FPÖ increased from 22% to 27%, the ÖVP received 27% as well, and the Greens won 7.6%. After long talks and negotiations—supported by Federal President Thomas Klestil—a renewal of the SPÖ-ÖVP coalition failed because of disagreements regarding the finance minister and the unwillingness of the trade unions to sign the coalition pact. The possibility of a SPÖ minority government with some FPÖ ministers also failed, and at the beginning of February 2000 an ÖVP-FPÖ coalition was established. ÖVP chairman Wolfgang Schüssel became Federal Chancellor; Jörg Haider remained governor in Carinthia and made Susanne Riess-Passer Vice Chancellor and FPÖ chairwoman; SPÖ chairman Viktor Klima resigned. The appointment of the new government was accompanied by expressions of concern by Klestil and foreign leaders as well as by demonstrations at the Ballhausplatz.

The main reason why support for Haider leapt from 5% before the elections in 1986, when he became party chairman, to 27% in 1999 was—as *The Economist* on February 12, 2000 pointed out—not his unacceptable comments suggesting sympathy for Hitler and the Nazis and his ugly generalizations about immigrants, but Austrians' growing dislike of a grubby system known as *Proporz*, under which the Social Democrats and the Christian Democrats shared power and patronage between them since World War II. Although the socio-economic situation in Austria in 1999 was the best it had ever been in the twentieth century, a general dissatisfaction increased among workers, peasants, and the youth. Austrian workers began to worry about low-paid workers from Poland, the Czech Republic, Slovakia, Hungary, Croatia, and Slovenia, coming to Austria to "steal their jobs," while employers more and more took advantage of the cheaper foreign labor. Farmers criticized the EU agrarian policy, which

---

30. Rainer Münz, "Migration in Europe – Challenges for Austria," *Europäische Rundschau* 26 (1998): 105-11.

lowered prices for most agricultural products. And the youth felt the impact of three "austerity packages" between 1996 and 1998, which limited their professional chances in the civil service and in many institutions close to the state, the provinces, and the communities. The majority of the well-educated academic youth, however, did not vote for Haider's party. Although the ÖVP demanded and got from the FPÖ clear commitments to the EU, to the Euro, and to the EU-enlargement on February 4, 2000, the other fourteen members of the European Union, after an ultimatum on January 31, isolated Austria because its "anti-immigrant Freedom Party" was a part of the coalition government. The Portuguese prime minister informed the Austrian authorities that the other members of the EU "will not promote or accept any bilateral official contacts at a political level" with any Austrian government that includes Haider's party; Austrian candidates for posts in international organizations would find no support, and Austrian ambassadors "will only be received at a technical level."[31]

Of course, the Austrians were shocked. The threat of EU sanctions was made without diplomatically consulting Austria or warning the Austrian foreign ministry, intervening in the domestic affairs of a member state without any violation of EU conventions. The *New York Times* noticed in its February 4 edition "a clash of opinions from Vienna to the Alps": interviews in the more conservative and patriotic Alpine regions and in the streets of the more liberal Vienna produced "a range of musing—not just about the diplomatic crisis, but also about Haider's unpredictable personality and Austria's complex self-image as the one-time seat of a vast empire later reduced to a Nazi state and now to an Alpine chalet on Western Europe's frontier." Prompted by memories of World War II, French President Chirac and the Socialist-led governments in France and Germany led the punishment because of the FPÖ's intolerable xenophobia. The British foreign minister added in a television interview: "We don't want to return to the time of WWII!" Israel recalled its ambassador, but Washington didn't impose any punitive measures against Austria. The social scientist Immanuel Wallerstein warned against "the Albatross of Racism": "Precisely because the other member states [of the EU] were not that different from Austria, they were afraid that they might soon be faced with a similar choice […] At the same time, it is the Austrians' inability to understand that they had crossed a line which all of Western Europe had set for itself, not in 1999 but in 1945."[32]

---

31. Arnold Suppan and Friedrich Steinhäusler, "The Current Political Crisis in Austria and the International Response" (paper, Stanford University, February 24, 2000).
32. Immanuel Wallerstein, "The Albatross of Racism," *London Review of Books*, May 18,

Fortunately, some of Austria's neighbors, such as the *Neue Zürcher Zeitung*, Bavaria's Christian Social premier Edmund Stoiber, the *Frankfurter Allgemeine Zeitung*, and Hungary's prime minister Viktor Orbán, saw the dangers of an EU overreaction. Orbán cherished Hungary's historic links with Austria, and saw that Austria, as the EU's bridgehead into East-Central Europe, is far too important to annoy, whoever is running its government. A Christian Democratic Union (CDU) foreign policy speaker criticized the anti-Austrian decision, stating: "It jeopardizes the process of European integration more than Mr. Haider could ever do."[33]

Although the new ÖVP-FPÖ government under Federal Chancellor Schüssel launched an ambitious reform program,—after signing the Declaration "Responsibility for Austria—a Future in the Heart of Europe" on request of the federal president—the other fourteen EU members blocked all official bilateral political relations. It was not until July 12, 2000, that the President of the European Court of Human Rights—in cooperation with the Portuguese prime minister and the Austrian government— gave a mandate to Martti Ahtisaari, former president of Finland, Jochen Frowein, director of the Max-Planck-Institute for Comparative Public Law and International Law at Heidelberg, and Marcelino Oreja, former Spanish minister for foreign affairs, to "deliver, on the basis of a thorough examination, a report covering the Austrian Government's commitment to the common European values, in particular concerning the rights of minorities, refugees and immigrants; the evolution of the political nature of the FPÖ." After discussions with the Austrian government and representatives of the political opposition, the Catholic and Protestant churches, the Jewish and Islamic communities, the High Courts, the Trade Unions, the Chamber of Commerce, and the Federation of Industries, as well as with members of many non-government organizations, on September 8, 2000, the "three wise men" presented their report to the EU-presidency in Paris, which had strongly demanded punishment of the Austrian government in February. While Chancellor Schüssel called for the fourteen EU members to immediately end bilateral sanctions, the French minister of European Affairs and Belgium's foreign minister still argued for a permanent "monitoring mechanism" to keep an eye on Austria.

Concerning the rights of minorities (*Volksgruppen*), the report stressed that the Austrian legal system has specific protections at the constitutional level for national minorities (Croats, Slovenes, Hungarians, Czechs,

---

2000, 11-14.
33. Friedbert Pflüger, "Isolating Austria Puts European Integration at Risk," *Herald Tribune*, February 19-20, 2000, 6.

Slovaks, and Roma) "to a greater extent than such protection exists in many other European Union countries." Besides German, Croat is being taught at elementary schools in Burgenland, Slovene in elementary and secondary schools in Carinthia. Similar to what happened earlier in Carinthian villages with Slovene minorities, in the summer of 2000 bilingual place names were put up in some dozen Burgenland villages with Croat and Hungarian minorities. In spring 2000, the Austrian parliament amended article 8 of the Austrian constitution with a new paragraph: "The Republic (Federation, States and Local Communities) recognizes its traditional linguistic and cultural plurality which is represented in its autochthonous national minorities. Language and culture, existence and preservation of these national minorities must be respected, secured and promoted."[34]

From 1988 until 1999 the yearly number of naturalizations has increased from 8,200 to 25,032. Therefore, the settlement ordinance for 2000 limited the maximum number of settlement permits, which are distributed among the Austrian provinces, to 7,860 applicants. More than 10,000 applications will not be granted. Nevertheless, the government has given "priority to the integration of foreigners residing legally in the country" and recognized "the principle that family reunification should be possible." Beyond that the government made clear commitments to the fight "against racism, anti-Semitism, discrimination and xenophobia," with the "Reconciliation Fund Law" to former slave and forced laborers of the Nazi Regime, with the restitution of works of art to their legitimate owners and with compensation for about 70,000 formerly Jewish-owned apartments in Vienna. After intensive negotiations between Chancellor Schüssel and Under Secretary of State Stuart Eizenstat, as well as representatives of the victims, in the fall 2000 and in January 2001 the new government found clear solutions on all three matters.

Although the EU report certified that the Austrian government's (including the FPÖ members) attitude toward the rights of minorities, refugees and immigrants, and the fight against racism, anti-Semitism, discrimination and xenophobia, conformed with the EU regulations, "the ambiguous language being repeatedly used by some high representatives of the FPÖ" is strongly criticized, especially of the former party leader Jörg Haider and Dieter Böhmdorfer, the minister of justice. The report emphasized "the positive obligation on the part of European governments to combat any form of direct or indirect propaganda for xenophobic and racial

---

34. Report by Martti Ahtisaari, Jochen Frowein and Marcelino Oreja, adopted in Paris on September 8, 2000, 9. Available online at: <http://www.mpg.de/pdf/commentsStatements/berichtOesterreich_en.pdf> (10 Dec. 2010).

discrimination, as well as to react against any kind of ambiguous language which introduces a certain trivialization or negative 'normalization' of the National Socialist past." According to the long-term Austrian prohibition law (*Verbotsgesetz*) and the jurisprudence of the Austrian Constitutional Court, all National Socialist organizations or organizations reactivating National Socialist ideas are prohibited. Although the FPÖ has been an applicant before the Court in many cases concerning electoral matters, the Court has not seen any reason to question the lawfulness of the FPÖ in relation to the *Verbotsgesetz*. In the party program of 1997 the FPÖ still described Austria as a non-immigration country and continued with this description in electoral campaigns—up to the national elections in October 1999. Posters with the expression "Stop Overforeignization" (*Überfremdung*) in Vienna had the immediate consequence that openly expressed remarks against foreigners became acceptable (*salonfähig*) and created feelings of anxiety among foreigners in Austria.[35]

In their concluding remarks, the "three wise men" stressed "that the measures taken by the fourteen Member States, if continued, would become counterproductive and should therefore be ended." The main reasons given were that "the Austrian Government is committed to the common European values" and that "in contradiction with past FPÖ behavior and statements made by other FPÖ officials, the ministers of the FPÖ have by and large worked according to the government's commitments in carrying out their governmental activities." The report furthermore states that: "The measures have already stirred up nationalist feelings in the country, as they have in some cases been wrongly understood as sanctions directed against Austrian citizens." Indeed, the great majority of the Austrian population could not understand (ideologically) one-sided measures within the European Union without a clear legal basis and without acts of violence against "foreigners" as had occurred in Germany, France, Spain, and the Czech Republic, all countries that had joined or supported the anti-Austrian punishment.

On September 12, 2000, the French president, Jacques Chirac, acting as current president of the EU, cancelled the sanctions. Great Britain, the Scandinavian member countries, and Luxembourg had all made clear that they supported a quick end to sanctions. It was no coincidence that the sanctions were being dropped just before Denmark's referendum on joining the Euro. On September 16, *The Economist* wrote that the main lesson deduced from the Austrian affair is that "They would do well to respect voters a little more. Voters do not put a Freedom Party into powers unless they are being badly served by their traditional parties. The EU's job in such

---

35. Report by Ahtisaari, Frowein, and Oreja, 27-31.

circumstances is to live with the result, not try to undo the election."[36] Caspar Weinberger, the secretary of defense during the Reagan administration, commented even more sharply: "The absurd attempt by the EU (led by France) to impose sanctions on Austria because some members did not like the center-right government voters elected last year did no damage. The total collapse of the sanctions effort weakened an already confused EU and was a principal factor in Denmark's rejection of the EU in its plebiscite vote earlier this year. An attempt to punish a democratic country simply because you do not like the way it votes demonstrates contempt for democracy that bodes ill for the future of the EU."[37]

On the Way to NATO and EU Enlargement

Ralf Dahrendorf's insightful forecast—one can build up democratic political institutions in six months, market economy in six years but to change deep-rooted attitudes calls for at least sixty years[38]—was not taken very seriously. From the perspective of changing mental borders of numerous East-Central European (and Austrian) intellectuals in the changing historical-political context of East and West, five events should be pointed out:

1) NATO intervention in Bosnia-Herzegovina in the summer of 1995, which led to the November 1995 Dayton agreement;

2) NATO air raids against Yugoslavia in the spring of 1999, which stopped the expulsion of hundreds of thousands of Albanians from Kosovo and opened the way to return of most of the refugees. While a part of the public praised this intervention as a humanitarian action, György Konrád and other intellectuals argued that although there was clear evidence for the crimes committed by the Milošević regime, external interference into the conflicts of radical nationalisms will only worsen the situation.

3) The attack against the World Trade Center in New York and the Pentagon on September 11, 2001. Although in the first moment all governments and newspapers condemned the terrorists, after some months structural differences appeared between the USA and Europe on the underlying causes for the attack.

4) The beginning of the Iraq war in the spring of 2003. Some East-Central European states supported the U.S. intervention.

5) The enlargement of NATO and EU with the accession of Poland,

---

36. *The Economist*, Sept. 16-22, 2000, 33.
37. *Forbes Global*, Dec. 25, 2000.
38. Ralf Dahrendorf, *Reflections on the Revolution* (New York: Crown, 1990).

the Czech Republic, Slovakia, Hungary, Slovenia, and the Baltic countries (as well as of Cyprus and Malta to the Union). The constraints on sovereignty resulting from EU membership turned out to be conspicuous, and furthermore the support came with a tremendous bureaucratic burden and great delays. The EU-15 was generally perceived as a tamed form of capitalism (a "capitalism with a human face"), where social solidarity is still a much more important issue than in the USA.[39]

Since the dissolution of the Soviet Union and Yugoslavia the Austrian security policy fluctuated between a vague neutrality policy (SPÖ and Greens) and approach towards NATO (ÖVP and FPÖ), sometimes joining common actions, sometimes hindering. The fundamentalist Austrian anti-nuclear politics provoked much irritation in neighboring countries—especially in the Czech Republic, Slovakia, and Slovenia. At the end of 2001 and the beginning of 2002, Austria staggered into a political conflict with the Czech Republic. Although Federal Chancellor Schüssel signed a treaty with Prime Minister Miloš Zeman to guarantee better safety measures at the nuclear plant Temelín in South Bohemia, Haider's Freedom Party—supported by the tabloid *Kronen Zeitung*—promoted a petition to close Temelín and to test the water for a referendum on whether the EU should take in new countries to the east. Thanks also to Zeman's angry words that Mr. Haider's "post-fascist" party should be tossed out of government, 915,220 (equal to 15.5%) of Austria's voters signed the petition. While the anti-nuclear Greens refused to sign, the split Social Democrats made no public recommendation. Schüssel openly warned the ÖVP-mayors and declared after the petition that enlarging the EU was one of his government's main aims.[40]

Since 1945, and especially since 1955, the Austrians have essentially found their way back from national fluctuations to their very particular identity by their own means. The new politics of the Second Republic were in some ways a new orientation to the West, in some ways a road back into Austrian history. In this respect, it was only logical that this new Austria has once again become a recognized interlocutor in the framework of the discussions concerning "Central Europe." But, as Charles Maier emphasized, Austria's *Mitteleuropa* is only one version. There existed also a German *Mitteleuropa*, led by Prussia and ending with the German Reich. And there existed in the time between the World Wars a third *Mitteleuropa*, "one emanating from East Central Europe, a shadowy realm radiating outward from Prague or Budapest, or even Warsaw, which embraces Vienna

---

39. Pók, "East and West," 230-33.
40. *The Economist*, January 26 - February 1, 2002, 28.

and Berlin but is not based upon them."⁴¹ In the 1980s, intellectuals from Poland, Hungary, Czechoslovakia, Slovenia, Croatia, and northern Italy, re-invented the phantom of Central Europe as a culturally powerful field between Cracow, Budapest, Vienna, Prague, Ljubljana, Zagreb, Trieste, and Trent. This *Mitteleuropa* of György Konrád, Václav Havel, Milan Kundera, Adam Michnik, Czesław Miłosz, and Claudio Magris, revolted against Yalta and the supposed division of Europe, and helped in the dissolving process of the Eastern bloc.⁴²

But what was to become of such a concept once the Communist empire ceased to exist? What configuration might the emerging Austrian version of Central Europe take? The Habsburg *Mitteleuropa* with its Baroque culture, its development of civilization, and its legal equality of nationalities and their single members, came to an end, although Musil's *Kakania* and Roth's *Radetzky Marsch* immortalized it in literature. With the destruction of the Central European Jews who, like the Germans, served as the integrative strength of this region, the old *Mitteleuropa* perished. And there remained the question of the new material basis, although Austria does enormous business with its neighbors. "What Austria needs is an injection of leadership to steer its democracy away from buffers, and forward into a less complacent, more dynamic, future," Hella Pick stated. But the new Austrian Republic with some 8 million prosperous Europeans cannot be the main finance and industrial center for 70 or even 120 million far poorer Europeans in East Central Europe. Austria can only widen the economic, social, cultural and scientific exchange, paving the way for the intellectual, political and economic elites of the former "successor states" to reenter the Western orbit of an enlarged European Union. As an EU-member since 1995, Austria has a new role to play as mediator between EU-Europe and East-Central Europe. Unfortunately, Austrian politics sometimes forgets the main goal of a real European policy: to overcome the division of Europe. Also, unfortunately, some other EU members sometimes forget this, too.⁴³

---

41. Charles S. Maier, "Whose Mitteleuropa? Central Europe between Memory and Obsolescence," in: *Austria in the New Europe*, ed., Günter Bischof and Anton Pelinka (CAS 1) (New Brunswick, NJ: Transaction, 1993), 8-18 (citation 9).
42. Timothy Garton Ash, *Ein Jahrhundert wird abgewählt: Aus den Zentren Mitteleuropas 1980-1990* (Munich: Hanser, 1990).
43. Hella Pick, *Guilty Victim: Austria from the Holocaust to Haider* (London: I. B. Tauris, 2000), 235.

The Return of History in the Balkans after the Cold War: International Efforts at Crisis Management and Conflict Resolution

Hanspeter Neuhold

The disintegration of the Socialist Federal Republic of Yugoslavia (SFRY) constituted the tragic exception to the otherwise rapid and peaceful end of the Cold War that had divided Europe since 1945. The collapse of the Communist regimes in Eastern Europe and the withdrawal of the Soviet Union from its zone of influence caught even experts by surprise. Equally unexpected was the implosion of three states created not after the Second but already after the First World War: the Union of Soviet Socialist Republics (USSR), Czechoslovakia, and Yugoslavia. But whereas the dissolution of the Soviet Union occurred with little and the "velvet divorce" between Czechs and Slovaks without any bloodshed, the dismemberment of the SFRY not only took almost two decades but was marked by large-scale violence and atrocities. Events in its southeastern neighborhood are of particular importance to Austria, for historical, geostrategic, political, and economic reasons.

What shocked enlightened, "post-modern" Europeans was the return of history in the western Balkans, the eruption of conflicts that had not been settled under the common Yugoslav roof but merely frozen during the Cold War. The hostile international environment of the East-West conflict had kept the people of the SFRY together. After Tito broke with Stalin, he opted for a "third way" between the two blocs. Yugoslavia was a founding member and one of the respected leaders of the Non-Aligned Movement to which the majority of Third World countries acceded. The economic policy of self-management resulted in higher prosperity than in countries practicing a Soviet-style command economy.

However, the disappearance of the common external threat, coupled with economic difficulties, brought issues to the fore that appeared obsolete in an integrating Europe: exclusive control over territory; violent nationalism and ethnicity; and religion. European integration within the framework of the European Community (EC)/European Union (EU) ought to have overcome these legacies of the continent's turbulent past.

With the four freedoms of the internal market[1] and the Schengen regime,[2] borders separating member states have become less and less relevant. A prosperous and peaceful "Greater Europe" ought to provide the alternative to "Greater" nation states, be they Serbia or Croatia. Multiple identities including a European dimension should downplay the importance of belonging to an ethnic group. Religion ought to be a person's private matter guided by tolerance for other denominations. A common vision of Europe should heal the wounds of the past, including those inflicted by violent strife between Serb Chetniks, Croatian Ustasha fascists, Communist partisans, and others during the Second World War.

A detailed account of the post-Cold War Yugoslav agony and its historic roots is beyond the scope of this essay.[3] Therefore, it will suffice to mention the main negative milestones.[4] The declaration of independence by Slovenia and Croatia in 1991 was followed by a brief armed conflict between the Yugoslav army and Slovenian forces in the former country where only a small Serbian minority lived. In contrast, Croatia, with a sizeable Serbian population of about 12%, experienced a protracted brutal war.

The fate of Bosnia and Herzegovina, once the showcase of a multiethnic and multi-religious constituent Republic of the SFRY, was even worse, marked by egregious atrocities of which the majority population, the Muslims, bore the brunt.[5] After military action by member states of the North Atlantic Treaty Organization (NATO) had turned the tables against the Serbs, the Dayton/Paris Peace Agreement was concluded in late 1995.[6]

This settlement failed to address another explosive issue, that of the status of the Serbian Province of Kosovo. In order to stop large-scale human rights abuses against the Albanian majority by Serb forces, in 1999 NATO members launched another air campaign which finally compelled President Slobodan Milošević to accept a great power peace plan. Subsequently, like

---

1. The free flow of goods, persons, services, and capital.
2. The Schengen Agreement abolishes border controls between the parties.
3. Robert Kaplan, *Balkan Ghosts: A Journey Through History* (New York: Vintage Books, 1994); Susan Woodward, *Balkan Tragedy: Chaos and Dissolution After the Cold War* (Washington D.C.: Brookings Institution, 1995); Misha Glenny, *The Fall of Yugoslavia* (London: Penguin Books, 1996); Laura Silber and Allan Little, *The Death of Yugoslavia* (London: Penguin Books, 1996); Mark Mazover, *The Balkans: From the End of Byzantium to the Present Day* (London: Phoenix, 2004); Robert Bideleux and Ian Jeffries, *The Balkans: A Post-Communist History* (London: Routledge, 2007).
4. On the legal aspects, see Marc Weller, *Twenty Years of Crisis: The Violent Dissolution of Yugoslavia in International Law* (Oxford: Oxford University Press, 2009).
5. They are called Bosniaks, a somewhat awkward name.
6. The Agreement was initialed in Dayton, Ohio, on November 21, 1995 and signed in Paris on December 14, 1995. Richard Holbrooke, *To End a War* (New York: Random House, 1998).

Bosnia and Herzegovina in 1995, Kosovo was placed under international administration by the Security Council (SC) of the United Nations (UN).

A major civil war was averted in Macedonia by a new constitution that the representatives of the Slav majority and the Albanian minority accepted, also under international pressure but without the use of armed force, in 2001. After a majority of the voters supported their country's independence in a referendum, Montenegro separated from the State Union with Serbia in 2006. Finally, in early 2008, Kosovo followed suit and declared its independence in accordance with the proposal submitted by the UN Special Envoy for Kosovo, Martti Ahtisaari.

The international community tried to stop the violence and help to solve these conflicts by peaceful means. Various traditional and new crisis management and pacific settlement methods were applied and tested in what might be called the "Balkan laboratory." Four international institutions were particularly active with a view to achieving these goals: the UN, NATO, the EU, and the Organization for Security and Co-operation in Europe (OSCE). It is on the efforts of these four "pillars" of the "European security architecture" that this essay will focus.[7] Moreover, the section on Austria's participation in the activities of these organizations in the former SFRY includes an overview of the development of the country's special international status, its permanent neutrality in the post-Cold War era. Although the political dimension of the topic will be emphasized, some legal aspects will also be discussed.

The United Nations: Collective Security after the Cold War

The first purpose of the UN mentioned in Article 1 of its Charter is to maintain international peace and security. To this end, effective measures are to be taken in the framework of a system of collective security established under Chapter VII of the constituent treaty of the World Organization. The SC is supposed to adopt non-military or military sanctions against member states responsible for a threat to the peace, breach of the peace or act of aggression.[8] However, the UN system of collective security remained paralyzed during the Cold War due to the "veto power" of the five permanent members of the Council: each of them may prevent the taking of a non-procedural decision by voting against it.[9]

---

7. On the early years, see Carsten Giersch, *Konfliktregulierung in Jugoslawien 1991-1995: Die Rolle von OSZE, EU, UNO und NATO* (Baden-Baden: Nomos, 1998).
8. Article 39 of the UN Charter.
9. Whereas a partial veto blocks an existing legal act, as, for instance, in the case of a veto

After the end of the East-West conflict, hopes that the SC would play its crucial role more effectively seemed to be justified because the main reason for its deadlock had disappeared. Yet the Council is still unable to take armed action itself, since it has failed to conclude the necessary agreements with member states on their contributions of troops and other military assistance.[10] Consequently, all it can do is to authorize UN members to resort to force. In contrast to a binding decision, such an authorization may, but does not have to be used. The most spectacular case where an ad-hoc coalition of able and willing states empowered by the SC mounted a military campaign was Operation Desert Storm, which drove Iraqi forces out of Kuwait in 1991.

The former Yugoslavia, which became a major testing site for SC measures in the 1990s,[11] also provided examples of such authorized military action, for example, Operation Deny Flight in 1993. This mission was successfully conducted by NATO states in order to enforce a ban on military flights in the airspace over Bosnia and Herzegovina after the prohibition imposed by the SC had been violated many times by Serbian aircraft.[12]

The SC agreed on non-military sanctions under Article 41 of the Charter much more frequently than during the East-West conflict. The Council adopted economic as well as non-economic, comprehensive as well as selective measures. Two of these enforcement actions taken in the "Balkan laboratory" may be mentioned in the present context. In its Resolution 713 of September 25, 1991, the SC imposed a general and complete embargo on all deliveries of weapons and military equipment to Yugoslavia. The wisdom of this ban affecting all former Republics of the SFRY was open to question. On the one hand, it could be argued that the fighting parties should receive as few arms as possible from abroad in order to limit human casualties and material damage. But on the other hand, the prohibition favored the obvious aggressor, since the Serbs had the arsenal of the JNA (*Jugoslavenska Narodna Armija*—Yugoslav People's Army) at their disposal, giving them a decisive military advantage.

After selective sanctions had failed to sway the government in Belgrade, the SC voted for a comprehensive boycott of the Federal Republic of Yugoslavia (FRY–Serbia and Montenegro) in Resolution 757 of May 30, 1992. These measures comprised a trade and financial embargo; a ban on

---

of the U.S. President against legislation adopted by Congress, the opposition of a permanent member prevents a SC decision from coming into legal existence.
10. In accordance with Article 43 of the UN Charter.
11. Hanspeter Neuhold, *The United Nations as a Security Organization: The "Balkan Laboratory"* (Gießen: Faculty of Law, 2007).
12. See SC Resolutions 781 of October 9, 1992 and 816 of March 31, 1993.

flights; the reduction of the level of staff at diplomatic missions and consular posts; the prevention of participation in sporting events; and the suspension of scientific and technical cooperation, as well as of cultural exchanges and visits.

However, such sweeping and indiscriminate sanctions may have unwelcome negative effects that were particularly evident in the case of measures taken by the SC against Iraq, but also noted in the case of those against the FRY. They tend to hurt the average citizens more than the regime and may result in lower life expectancy of the population largely due to malnutrition and starvation, as well as declining medical services.

These consequences raised the issue of the limits to the SC's competencies under Chapter VII of the UN Charter. Although a political organ in charge of collective security, the Council must also act in accordance with the Purposes and Principles of the UN.[13] These Purposes include promoting and encouraging respect for human rights.[14] That the right to life, which is enshrined in the principal human rights conventions, is affected by the fact that human beings die earlier is stating the obvious. That it is the most fundamental right, without which the other rights and freedoms cannot be exercised, is equally evident. Consequently, the SC has recently switched to so-called targeted sanctions. These measures are aimed at persons or entities responsible for or otherwise involved in major violations of international law, such as prohibited weapons programs or severe breaches of human rights and international humanitarian law. However, the effectiveness of these types of sanctions, such as travel restrictions, bans on luxury goods or the freezing of financial assets abroad, has been limited.[15]

Moreover, the SC further developed peacekeeping operations under its auspices. The "first generation" of these missions was the main innovation introduced by the UN in the area of security policy during the Cold War. Their tasks consisted of monitoring ceasefire agreements and inter-positioning, i.e., the deployment of "Blue Helmet" troops between conflicting parties that had agreed to a cessation of armed hostilities. Peacekeeping forces were required to observe impartiality and were only allowed to use force in self-defense. These operations were typical cooperative security activities that needed the consent of all parties involved: the SC, which had to provide their mandate; all parties to the conflict at hand; and the states participating in the mission.

---

13. Article 24 (2) of the Charter.
14. Article 1 (3) of the Charter.
15. As exemplified by the response—or rather lack of response—of the governments/regimes of Iran, North Korea and Sudan to UN sanctions in recent years.

The functions of "second-generation" peacekeeping operations mounted after the end of the East-West conflict were considerably enlarged. They included the recourse to armed force beyond self-defense of the peacekeepers; help with the maintenance of law and order and other contributions to state- and nation-building, especially the preparation, organization, and supervision of democratic elections, as well as with humanitarian assistance.

One of these operations was launched in the former Yugoslavia and provided a deplorable example of "mission creep," in other words, the continuous addition of new tasks by the SC without the necessary military resources. The United Nations Protection Force (UNPROFOR) commenced as a "first-generation" mission in Croatia. Subsequently, it was also deployed in Bosnia and Herzegovina; moreover, its mandate eventually was extended to the use of force to defend six cities that the SC had declared "safe areas" against bombardments or armed incursions.[16] UNPROFOR failed to provide adequate protection against militarily superior Serb forces, above all in Srebrenica. The city was conquered and its entire Muslim male population, approximately 8,000 men and boys, were massacred by Serb troops under the command of General Ratko Mladić in July 1995. UNPROFOR was further humiliated when some of its soldiers were taken hostage and used as human shields at strategic points against NATO airplanes after members of the alliance had decided to take military action.

The UN learned some lessons from its mistakes and authorized a new type of peacekeeping that could be called "enforcement by consent" and was also tested in the "Balkan laboratory." With the more or less voluntary agreement of the conflicting parties, peacekeepers were mainly tasked with enforcing ceasefires, the withdrawal of foreign troops and the disarmament of local fighters.[17] The crucial difference between these "third-generation" in comparison with "second-generation" operations was clear military superiority over the local forces. The Implementation Force (IFOR) in Bosnia-Herzegovina initially, in 1995, totaled approximately 60,000,[18] the Kosovo Force (KFOR) in Kosovo about 50,000 well-armed troops in 1999;

---

16. In accordance with paragraph 9 of SC Resolution 836 of June 4, 1993.
17. Consent was eventually given under the impact of NATO air campaigns, in the conflict over and in Bosnia and Herzegovina by the three parties in the Dayton/Paris Peace Agreement and by President Milošević in the Kosovo conflict against the backdrop of Operation Allied Force. Discussed further below.
18. One year later, this force was succeeded by the smaller NATO-led Stabilization Force (SFOR), which was in turn replaced by the EU Operation Althea in 2004.

both were led by NATO.[19] Local forces were therefore ill advised to renege on their commitments and to challenge the internationals.

Another variant of a peace force was also deployed in the former SFRY. UNPROFOR and later a separate force, the United Nations Preventive Deployment Force (UNPREDEP), were charged with helping to avert a spillover of armed hostilities from abroad to the Former Yugoslav Republic of Macedonia (FYROM).[20] Ironically, this mission was terminated when it seemed most urgently needed. In February 1999, China opposed the extension of UNPREDEP's mandate in the SC. The Chinese representative claimed that Macedonia had achieved sufficient stability domestically as well as in its relations with neighboring countries, although the crisis in adjacent Kosovo was reaching its peak at the time. The real reason for China's negative vote evidently was to punish the government in Skopje for opening official relations with Taiwan in exchange for much needed economic aid.

Such a preventive mission obviously is the most desirable form of peacekeeping, since it can assist in avoiding or at least minimizing human fatalities and material damage. Unfortunately, the Macedonian precedent is unlikely to set a new trend. It will probably not be followed by many other states, even if they find themselves on the brink or at the beginning of the resort to violence. For, as a rule, governments are reluctant to ask for international military assistance at an early stage of a domestic or international conflict. Such a request indicates the inability to maintain law and order within one's own borders or to deal with an external adversary. Therefore, conflicting parties usually agree on a peacekeeping operation after, and not before, the use of armed force with all its negative consequences, and only if military hostilities have not resulted in a clear victory for one side.[21]

The former Yugoslavia also served as the testing site for a new form of international administration. The concept as such is not new and was already applied to protectorates in the age of colonialism, as well as in the frameworks of the Mandate regime of the League of Nations and the

---

19. The mandates of these forces were contained in SC Resolutions 1031 of December 15, 1995 and 1244 of June 10, 1999, respectively.
20. The state calls itself Republic of Macedonia, but this name is opposed by neighboring Greece because of territorial problems, the flag of the new state and Greece's claim to be the only successor to ancient Macedonia ruled by Philipp II and Alexander the Great. FYROM is the name under which the state was admitted, *inter alia*, to the UN.
21. Operations in Burundi, Sierra Leone and the EU Operation Artemis in the Democratic Republic of the Congo (see below) are quoted as other examples of early consent-based deployment. "Implementing the responsibility to protect: Report of the Secretary-General," UN Doc. A/63/677, 12 January 2009, paragraphs 41 and 42.

Trusteeship system of the UN. However, several novel features characterize the formula adopted for Bosnia and Herzegovina as well as Kosovo. Their administration was neither entrusted to states nor to a single but to several international organizations under the umbrella of the SC, provided by the above-mentioned Resolutions 1031 (1995) and 1244 (1999).[22] In addition to the UN, NATO, the EU and the OSCE constituted the main "pillars" of the two administrative regimes. Each of these organizations[23] was entrusted with functions for which it was particularly qualified: NATO with military security, the EU with economic recovery and reforms, and the OSCE with democratization, human rights, capacity-building, confidence-building measures and arms control.

However, the center of power was placed in the hands of a single institution, for Bosnia and Herzegovina the High Representative, and for Kosovo the Special Representative of the UN Secretary-General. The competencies of the High Representative are based on the Dayton/Paris Peace Agreement that the SC welcomed and supported in Resolution 1031. They were substantially extended at a meeting of the Peace Implementation Council, which is composed of the principal stakeholders, in Bonn in 1997; they are therefore called the Bonn powers. For instance, the High Representative may enact legislation and dismiss public officials, and has done so in practice. Similarly sweeping powers were conferred on the Special Representative of the UN Secretary-General as head of the United Nations Interim Administration in Kosovo (UNMIK) by the SC in Resolution 1244 (1999).[24] The resulting paradox is the attempt to introduce democracy and the rule of law by extremely undemocratic means, made even more difficult by the population's lack of experience in these areas.

The record of these two experiments remains mixed. There have been positive results: some political, legal, and economic reforms have been implemented. But the drawbacks cannot be overlooked; there exists continuing political tension, economic backwardness and high unemployment, widespread corruption and organized crime. Moreover, only some refugees and internally displaced persons have returned to their homes, so the results of "ethnic cleansing" have not been corrected.

One of the main problems in Bosnia and Herzegovina is the constitution laid down in the Dayton/Paris Peace Agreement. It provides for one state

---

22. See footnote 19.
23. On the legal nature of the OSCE, see below.
24. The sources of the powers of the two Representatives and the roles of the UN vary in the two countries. While the competencies of the Special Representative in Kosovo are based on the authorization of the SC, those of the High Representative in Bosnia and Herzegovina stem from outside the UN.

composed of two "entities," the Republika Srpska and the Federation of Bosnia and Herzegovina. The latter, in turn, consists of ten "cantons," with an additional special regime for the Brčko District. Reaching agreement among or with fourteen parties is inevitably difficult and time-consuming. As a result of this complex structure, a large share of the budget of the poor country is spent on administration, which only worsens matters. Efforts to revise the constitution are deadlocked, above all, by the diametrically opposed demands of the Bosniaks and Serbs. While the former call for the transfer of additional powers to the weak central institutions at the federal level, the latter insist not only on keeping the competencies of their "entity," but they also want federal powers retransferred to it. Some Serb radicals, in particular Milorad Dodik, the President of the Republika Srpska, even threaten the secession of the Republic.

The principal issue in Kosovo was and is its legal status.[25] The only solution the Albanian majority would accept was independence; however, this was equally adamantly refused by Serbia and the Serb minority in Kosovo. SC Resolution 1244 (1999) provided for the substantial autonomy of Kosovo, but also reaffirmed the sovereignty and territorial integrity of the FRY, within which Kosovo was a Province of Serbia. It had enjoyed far-reaching rights as an Autonomous Province under the 1974 Constitution of the SFRY, which the Milošević regime abolished. The international community first proposed a "standards-before-status" approach. This meant that major reforms steering Kosovo towards a stable, functioning democracy and market economy had to be completed before the status question would be addressed. However, under the impact of riots and increasing unrest among the Albanians, it was decided to commence status negotiations without the achievement of those standards.

Since the gap between the Serb and the Kosovo Albanian positions could not be bridged, the UN Special Envoy Martii Ahtisaari eventually submitted his "Comprehensive Proposal for the Kosovo Status Settlement."[26] The Ahtisaari Plan essentially called for the independence of the former

---

25. David Harland, "Kosovo and the UN," *Survival* 52 (October-November 2010): 75-98; Hanspeter Neuhold, "Kosovo: A Testing Ground for International Crisis Management and Dispute Settlement," in *Völkerrecht und die Dynamik der Menschenrechte: Liber Amicorum Wolfram Karl*, eds. Gerhard Hafner, Franz Matscher and Kirsten Schmalenbach (Vienna: Facultas Verlags- und Buchhandels AG, 2012), 324-41; for the broader picture, see Ian King and Wit Mason, *Peace at Any Price: How the World Failed Kosovo* (Ithaca: Cornell University Press, 2006); Tonny Knudsen and Carsten Lautsen, *Kosovo Between War and Peace: Nationalism, Peacebuilding and International Trusteeship* (London: Routledge 2006). On the history of Kosovo, see Noel Malcolm, *Kosovo: A Short History* (New York: New York University Press, 1998).
26. UN Doc. S/2007/168/Add. 1.

Serbian Province under international supervision. This supervision was to be exercised by the International Steering Group comprising the major stakeholders and represented by the International Civilian Representative in Kosovo. The project also provided for far-reaching community rights, including establishing Serbian as the second official language of Kosovo, decentralization, and guarantees for the Serbian Orthodox Church. On the basis of the "Comprehensive Proposal," an assembly in Prishtina proclaimed the independence of Kosovo on February 17, 2008.

The independence of Kosovo was quickly recognized by the United States and most, but not all, member states of the EU.[27] It was vehemently opposed not only by Serbia but also rejected by Russia and China, two permanent members of the SC, and many other countries.[28] Serbia succeeded in obtaining the necessary majority support in the UN General Assembly for requesting from the International Court of Justice (ICJ), the principal judicial organ of the World Organization,[29] an advisory opinion on the following question: "Is the unilateral declaration of independence by the Provisional Institutions of Self-Government of Kosovo in accordance with international law?"[30]

To the surprise of some observers who expected a more nuanced response, the Court gave a clearly affirmative answer in 2010.[31] Put in a nutshell, the majority of the judges stated that general international law did not prohibit

---

27. Five members of the Union confronting problems with minorities have still not taken this step: Cyprus, Greece, Romania, Slovakia and Spain.
28. At this writing in late 2012, only about half of the 193 members of the World Organization have recognized Kosovo.
29. The ICJ was also involved in other disputes in the "Balkan laboratory." In 2004, the Court concluded that it had no jurisdiction to entertain claims by the FRY that ten NATO member states participating in Operation Allied Force had violated numerous obligations under international law. In 2007, the ICJ rejected the charge by Bosnia and Herzegovina that Serbia had committed genocide against the non–Serb population in the former country. It also ruled that Serbia had failed, however, to live up to its obligation to prevent the 1995 Srebrenica massacre which did constitute genocide. Serbia was found equally guilty of not arresting and transferring to the International Criminal Tribunal for the Former Yugoslavia the principal suspect responsible for the massacre, General Ratko Mladić. In 2010, the ICJ decided that Greece, by objecting to the admission of FYROM to NATO, had breached an obligation under a treaty, the 1995 Interim Accord, between the two states. Whether these judgments clarifying legal issues between the parties also contributed to mitigating the underlying political conflicts and emotional animosities is at best debatable. On this aspect with regard to the International Criminal Tribunal for the Former Yugoslavia, see below.
30. UN General Assembly Resolution 63/3 of October 8, 2008.
31. ICJ, *Accordance with International Law of the Unilateral Declaration of Independence in Respect of Kosovo*, Advisory Opinion of 22 July 2010, I.C.J. Reports 2010: 403-53; Richard Falk, "The Kosovo Advisory Opinion: Conflict Resolution and Precedent," *American Journal of International Law* 105 (2011): 50-60; Peter Hilpold, ed., *Kosovo and International Law: The ICJ Advisory Opinion of 22 July 2012* (Leiden: Brill, 2012).

the promulgation of a declaration of independence. They also held that the declaration of independence of Kosovo did not conflict with the special regime established by SC Resolution 1244, which was still in force. This is because the authors of the declaration, which the Kosovo President and the Prime Minister also signed, had not acted as the Assembly of Kosovo, one of the Provisional Institutions of Self-Government within the UNMIK Constitutional Framework, but as a different body, and therefore outside this special legal order.[32]

However, since Serbia has made EU membership a priority of its foreign policy, it gave in to international pressure and even submitted, together with EU member states, a draft resolution to the UN General Assembly in which the plenary organ of the organization acknowledged the content of the advisory opinion of the ICJ.[33] Furthermore, it welcomed the readiness of the EU to "facilitate a process of dialogue between the parties; the process in itself would be a factor for peace, security and stability in the region…to promote cooperation, achieve progress on the path to the European Union and improve the lives of the people."

Despite these edifying words from the World Organization, the present situation in Kosovo is anything but peaceful and stable. Apart from its continuing economic difficulties, the country remains divided, with the Serbs in the north refusing to recognize the authority of the institutions in Prishtina and maintaining parallel governance structures financed by Serbia. To make matters worse, violence, which KFOR could not prevent, flared up when the Prishtina government tried to extend its control over two border-crossing points with Serbia in 2011. Kosovo Serbs erected barricades on roads leading to the border; pipe bombs were thrown and shots fired, which caused injuries and even death on both sides.

On the positive side of the balance, a compromise was agreed on in February 2012 which enables Kosovo to take part in meetings between countries of the region.[34] Serb and Kosovar political leaders met, and some

---

32. To mention only one problem, under para. 19 of Resolution 1244, the international civil and security presences in Kosovo are to continue unless the SC decides otherwise. Another SC resolution would therefore have been necessary for a legally less controversial settlement of the status issue. However, such a Council pronouncement in favor of the independence of Kosovo was unacceptable, above all, to Russia, a permanent member with the right to block a decision to this effect.
33. UN General Assembly Resolution 64/298 of October 13, 2010.
34. It was mediated by the European External Action Service Counselor Robert Cooper. At these meetings, Kosovo's nameplate will simply read Kosovo (and not Republic of Kosovo). A footnote will be added that this name does not prejudice the status of Kosovo and is in accordance with SC Resolution 1244 (as demanded by Serbia) and the advisory opinion of the ICJ (as demanded by Kosovo).

agreements between the two conflicting parties were established. Thus in early December 2012, Serbian Prime Minister Ivica Dačić and his Kosovo counterpart Hashim Thaçi agreed on joint border controls and the opening of liaison offices in the two capitals.

Despite the still volatile situation and the need for more reforms, at a meeting in Prishtina on September 10, 2012, the International Steering Group terminated the international supervision of the independence of Kosovo. However, both KFOR and EULEX Kosovo, as well as the OSCE and the UN will remain in the country.

In a mid- and long-term perspective, eventual EU membership is the way out of the dilemmas of Bosnia and Herzegovina and Kosovo. However, the stumbling blocks on the road to Brussels are numerous and difficult to surmount.

The SC achieved a genuine breakthrough in the realm of international law, once more in the "Balkan laboratory," with the establishment of the International Criminal Tribunal for the Former Yugoslavia (ICTY) in Resolution 827 of May 25, 1993. One of the principal weaknesses of the traditional international legal order was the principle of collective responsibility. The sanctions inflicted for the breach of a state's international legal obligations affected the entire population and not only the responsible individuals.[35] The statute of the ICTY introduced individual criminal responsibility for serious violations of international humanitarian law.[36] Furthermore, the official position of any accused person, including that of head of state or government, does not relieve such person of criminal responsibility, nor does it mitigate punishment.[37] Unlike the Nuremberg and Tokyo War Crimes Tribunals after the Second World War, the creation of the ICTY was soon followed by the establishment of similar ad-hoc institutions for Rwanda, Sierra Leone, Timor-Leste, Cambodia, and Lebanon. This development culminated in 2002 with the entry into force of the 1998 Rome Statute of the permanent International Criminal Court (ICC).

The ICTY has not remained a "paper tiger" but has played an important role in dealing with the atrocities perpetrated in the former Yugoslavia. Both Presidents Slobodan Milošević and Radovan Karadžic, as well as General Ratko Mladić, were extradited to stand trial at The Hague. The Tribunal has sentenced several political and military leaders, for example Biljana Plavšić, the former President, and Momčilo Krajišnik, the former

---

35. Such as comprehensive non-military sanctions imposed by the SC.
36. Grave breaches of the 1949 Geneva Conventions, violations of the laws or customs of war, genocide and crimes against humanity.
37. Article 7 (2) of the Statute.

President of the Parliament of the Republika Srpska, to long prison terms. But on the other hand, in 2011 the Appeals Chamber of the ICTY acquitted Croatian Generals Ante Gotovina and Mladen Markač who had previously been sentenced to long prison terms for their involvement in Operation *Oluja* (Storm).[38] Similarly, in 2012, it confirmed, after a partial retrial, the acquittal of former Kosovo Liberation Army (KLA) leader and Prime Minister Ramush Haradinaj, also for lack of evidence of participation in a joint criminal enterprise.[39]

Theoretically, transferring disputes to the "legal front" may help to defuse a conflict by submitting it to the decision of an impartial third party on the basis of law; however, this is not a foregone conclusion. In the case of the former Yugoslavia, the involvement of the ICJ[40] and the ICTY only confirmed Serbs in their conviction of a widespread bias against them, so that they could not expect a fair treatment from international courts and tribunals. The judgments of the Hague Tribunal also added to the old truth that one side's heroes are the other side's criminals. Instead of paving the way to reconciliation, the UN court and the ICTY contributed to opening old wounds.[41]

NATO: An Alliance Surviving the "Loss" of its Enemy

For the Atlantic Alliance, the end of the Cold War meant the disappearance of the enemy against whom it had been established in 1949. The loss of its *raison d'être* as a collective defense organization against the threat posed by the Soviet bloc was expected to lead to the dissolution of NATO, following the example of its Eastern counterpart, the Warsaw Treaty Organization. In the words of the prominent political scientist Kenneth N. Waltz, not the days but the years of NATO were numbered.[42] It has to be borne in mind that alliance membership not only entails advantages for the allies, such as enhanced protection, a voice on important military decisions and access to state-of-the-art technology, but also costs, for example far-reaching restrictions on sovereignty, pressure by more powerful members and, in some cases, additional defense expenditures.

---

38. The operation restored Croatian authority over the Serb-controlled Krajina in 1995, leading to casualties and a mass refugee movement among Serb civilians.
39. One key witness was killed in a car incident, others refused to testify for fear of their safety.
40. See above (footnote 29).
41. In the words of Serb President Tomislav Nikolić, commenting on the acquittal of Generals Gotovina and Markač.
42. Kenneth N. Waltz, "The Emerging Structure of International Politics," *International Security* 18, no. 2 (Fall 1993): 44-79, see especially 76.

The alliance confronted the choice, as U.S. Senator Richard Lugar put it, between "going out of area or out of business." The political leaders of its members preferred the first option and decided "to stay in business," proving the prophets of the alliance's forthcoming demise wrong. This meant performing functions outside the territories of member states in addition to the defense of the latter against armed attacks. As a result, NATO has survived to this day, and its activities in the "Balkan laboratory" substantially contributed to its continued vitality.

Thus, the alliance helped with the enforcement of SC decisions in the framework of the UN system of collective security. Operation Deny Flight, mounted in 1993 in order to give military teeth to the flight ban in the airspace of Bosnia and Herzegovina, may be recalled as an example of such assistance.[43] Another was Operation Sharp Guard, which NATO conducted together with the Western European Union (WEU) from 1993 to 1996.[44] This naval and air mission was charged with monitoring the above-mentioned arms embargo and the economic sanctions imposed by the SC.[45] Operation Deliberate Force, an air campaign against Serb attacks on the safe areas and UNPROFOR in Bosnia-Herzegovina, at long last ended the siege of Sarajevo in August and September 1995 and tipped the scales in favor of the Bosniaks, paving the way for the Dayton peace talks.[46]

NATO also became active in the field of cooperative security. Its main project in this context is the Partnership for Peace (PfP) offered to non-NATO participating states of the Conference on Security and Cooperation (CSCE) in 1994.[47] They were invited, above all, to strengthen their ability to undertake peacekeeping, search and rescue, and humanitarian operations, for which joint planning, training, and exercises were suggested. Moreover, PfP participants are entitled to consultations with NATO if they perceive a direct threat to their territorial integrity, political independence, or security.[48]

---

43. See above.
44. The WEU was a European military alliance consisting of ten Western-oriented member states which was dissolved in 2011. It was founded in 1948 and always remained in the shadow of its "big brother" NATO. Arie Bloed and Ramses A. Wessel, *The Changing Functions of the Western European Union (WEU): Introduction and Basic Documents* (Dordrecht: Martinus Nijhoff, 1994).
45. In accordance with SC Resolution 787 of November 16, 1992.
46. SC Resolution 836 of June 4, 1993 served as the legal basis for this operation.
47. On the renaming of the CSCE, see below.
48. In 1997 NATO launched the Enhanced Partnership for Peace. It provided for a stronger role of the partners and added peace support operations (which range from conflict prevention, peacekeeping and peace enforcement to peacemaking and peace building) and a new institution, the Euro-Atlantic Partnership Council comprising all NATO members and partners.

For those partners who, unlike the neutral and alliance-free states,[49] aspired to NATO membership, PfP provided an opportunity to prepare for admission to the alliance. In the meantime, all states on the territory of the former SFRY joined the Partnership; two of them, Slovenia in 2004 and Croatia in 2009,[50] have already become members of the Atlantic Alliance.

NATO also undertook peacekeeping operations. Three "first-generation" missions were mounted in FYROM in order to stabilize the situation in the country, after the Slav majority and the sizeable Albanian minority had been on the brink of civil war. Under international pressure, also exerted by NATO Secretary-General Lord George Robertson, the two sides eventually agreed on the Ohrid Framework Agreement in 2001. The agreement provided for constitutional reforms granting the Albanians additional rights. NATO's Operation Essential Harvest was mandated to collect weapons Albanian fighters had consented to hand over. This mission was followed by Operation Amber Fox whose task was to protect approximately 200 OSCE monitors. It was succeeded by Operation Allied Harmony that was in turn replaced by the first peacekeeping operation of the EU, Operation Concordia.[51] The more demanding "enforcement-by-consent" operations led by NATO in Bosnia and Herzegovina and Kosovo, IFOR/SFOR and KFOR, also ought to be mentioned in the present context.[52]

Furthermore, members of the Atlantic Alliance embarked on a military operation in the "Balkan laboratory" without the consent of all parties involved and without the authorization of the SC. After the regime of Slobodan Milošević abolished the autonomy granted to Kosovo under the 1974 Yugoslav Constitution, the Albanians first practiced non-violent resistance under their leader Ibrahim Rugova, "the Gandhi of the Balkans," but to no avail. Finally, the newly formed KLA resorted to armed force, whereupon the Serbian side stepped up repression and proceeded to "ethnic cleansing" of the Albanian population.[53] After a peace agreement negotiated at Rambouillet and Paris had been accepted by the Albanian representatives but rejected by President Milošević, who also ignored a final ultimatum by NATO, Operation Allied Force was launched on March 24, 1999, and eventually forced the regime in Belgrade to agree to a settlement

---

49. The term chosen for their international status by Finland and Sweden instead of neutrality.
50. Together with Albania. Greece blocked the admission of FYROM, again because of the name issue.
51. Operation Concordia was followed by an EU police mission, Operation Proxima.
52. See above (footnote 29).
53. Tim Judah, *War and Revenge* (New Haven: Yale University Press, 2002).

drawn up by the G8.⁵⁴ Since the allies took for granted opposition by the permanent members Russia and China to a resolution authorizing the use of force, they simply bypassed the SC.

The advocates of the legality of NATO's massive air campaign tried to justify it as humanitarian intervention, i.e., the use of force in order to protect individuals on the territory of another state, first and foremost that state's citizens, against major human rights abuses by the authorities of that state. They pointed out that respect for human rights had become one of the cornerstones of modern international law and even a rule of *jus cogens*.⁵⁵ Although the latter contention is correct, the lawful use of armed force in order to protect human rights abroad is another matter. Such a claim could not be based on any treaty. Similarly, the necessary practice and *opinio juris*⁵⁶ were lacking as the required foundation of a right to provide a foundation under customary international law. In addition, critics of the operation argue that the prohibition of the threat or use of force is also recognized as one of the few peremptory norms of the international legal order. Unfortunately, there is no applicable criterion to determine which of the two contradictory principles has primacy over the other. However, it should be borne in mind that in the age of weapons of mass destruction the ban on armed force ought not to be tampered with lightly. Therefore this writer is of the opinion that Operation Allied Force was politically necessary, morally tenable, but unlawful.⁵⁷

---

54. The G8 comprises the main Western economic powers–Canada, France, Germany, Italy, Japan, the United Kingdom and the United States–and, since 1997, the Russian Federation.
55. *Jus cogens* norms enjoy a special "rank" in the system of international law. In particular, treaties conflicting with such peremptory rules are void under Articles 53 and 65 of the 1969 and 1986 Vienna Conventions on the Law of Treaties.
56. The conviction of the competent decision makers that following a given practice is required or a certain behavior permitted by international law.
57. Hanspeter Neuhold, "Collective Security After Operation Allied Force," *Max Planck Yearbook of United Nations Law* 4 (2000): 73-106, see especially pp. 95-103, and the literature quoted there. The debate on the legality of this military campaign led to the appointment of the International Commission on Intervention and State Sovereignty (ICISS). In its report of 2001, this commission put forth a legal concept that challenged the traditional definition of sovereignty: the responsibility to protect. According to this new notion, the focus of sovereignty, the main distinctive characteristic of states, has changed. It has been shifted from a state's supreme authority over its subjects and non-intervention in its internal affairs by other states to the obligation to provide for the safety and well-being of its citizens. The term has been widely accepted, in particular in the World Summit Outcome, the concluding document of the meeting of the UN General Assembly at the summit level in September 2005 (UN Doc. A/60/L.1). The General Assembly also agreed that if a state fails to live up to its protection obligations, a secondary responsibility may be exercised by the international community acting through the SC of the UN. See also "Implementing the responsibility to protect: Report of the Secretary-General" (UN Doc. A/63/677 of January 12, 2009).

The most effective contribution NATO can probably make to durable stability in the region is the admission of the Balkan states to the alliance, provided they meet the requirements for membership. Major steps on the road to joining NATO are participation in PfP and the Membership Action Plan. As mentioned above, this process is well underway, with two former Yugoslav Republics already admitted by now.[58]

Although KFOR remains deployed in Kosovo under the Ahtisaari Plan in order to guarantee security there, Europe is not the main theater of NATO's activities anymore. After turning sixty in 2009, the Atlantic(!) Alliance is facing its litmus test in Afghanistan and Pakistan against the Taliban and Al Qaeda.[59] Despite continuous reinforcements, NATO, which in 2003 assumed command over the International Security Assistance Force (ISAF) mandated by the SC in 2001,[60] the United States and local forces have been unable to defeat the insurgents. It remains to be seen whether, after the withdrawal of foreign combat troops to be completed by the end of 2014, the Afghan government will be able to maintain security in the country, or whether Afghanistan will share the fate of Vietnam after the pullout of American forces in the 1970s.

The EU: The First Steps in the Areas of Security and Defense Policy

After the fall of the Berlin Wall the political leaders of the EC realized that the end of the Cold War had not only positive effects, such as, above all, the implosion of the Communist regimes in Eastern Europe and the withdrawal of Soviet forces from the USSR's zone of influence.[61] It also meant that continued American interest in Europe as the main priority of U.S. security policy and consequently a massive military presence of the Western superpower on the Old Continent could not be taken for granted. Therefore Europeans had to shoulder a greater part of the burden if they wanted to keep order in their own house, with trouble in the former SRFY looming on the horizon. Moreover, EC leaders agreed that their Community not only ought to be a great economic power but should also become a major political and military actor in the international arena.

---

58. See above.
59. Mats Berdal and David Ucko, "NATO at 60," *Survival* 51, no. 2 (April-May 2009): 55-76.
60. Under SC Resolution 1386 of December 20, 2001.
61. Hanspeter Neuhold, "The European Union as an International Actor: Responses to Post-Cold War Challenges," in *Quo Vadis Europa? Twenty Years After the Fall of the Wall*, ed. Markus Kornprobst (Vienna: Diplomatic Academy of Vienna, 2010), 29-51.

The result was the inclusion of the "second pillar," the Common Foreign and Security Policy (CFSP), in the new EU created by the 1992 Maastricht Treaty on European Union (TEU).[62] The CFSP went beyond the modest beginnings of European Political Cooperation in the Single European Act of 1986. According to the vague provisions of Article J.4 of the Treaty, it shall include all questions related to the security of the Union, including the eventual framing of a common defense policy, which might in time lead to a common defense.

However, to this day the CFSP has remained intergovernmental and still has not become supranational like the other areas of activity of the Union. This means that the organs representing the governments of member states and their narrowly defined national interests, the European Council at the level of heads of state or government, and the Council at the ministerial level, dominate. Each member can still block the adoption of a basic decision by voting against it. The other principal organs of the EU are deprived of the key competences they hold within the supranational framework and relegated to secondary roles. The Commission in charge of the interests of the Union does not possess a monopoly on legislative initiative. The European Parliament is not endowed with co-decision powers. The Court of Justice of the EU does not have compulsory jurisdiction but is kept on the sidelines. The most recent version of the TEU, which was signed in Lisbon in 2007 and entered into force in 2009, has not changed this structural imbalance.

The new CFSP was soon to be tested in the EU's "near abroad," the Balkans.[63] Ironically, Jacques Poos, the foreign minister of Luxembourg that held the EU Presidency at the time, proudly announced in 1991 that the hour of Europe had dawned.[64] However, the actual record of the Union in the conflicts engulfing the former Yugoslavia was disappointing, to say the least. The EC Peace Conference on Yugoslavia chaired by former British Foreign Secretary and NATO Secretary-General Lord Peter Carrington, the EC/EU Monitoring Mission (EC/UMM) charged with supervising compliance with ceasefires and the release and return of prisoners of war, the so-called Badinter Commission tasked with deciding legal issues raised by the breakup of the SFRY,[65] and economic sanctions could neither prevent nor stop the fighting and the atrocities. The administration of the city of

---

62. Stephan Keukeleire and Jennifer MacNaughtan, *The Foreign Policy of the European Union* (New York: Palgrave Macmillan, 2008).
63. Steven Blockmans, *Tough Love: The European Union's Relations with the Western Balkans* (The Hague: T.M.C. Asser Press, 2007), especially 111-240.
64. Silber and Little, *The Death of Yugoslavia*, 159.
65. Named for its chairman, the French jurist Robert Badinter.

Mostar by the EU failed to achieve reconciliation between the Croatian and Muslim inhabitants of the city.

Later on the EU contributed to the above-mentioned peaceful settlement of the Macedonian crisis in 2001, with its special envoy, former French Defense Minister François Léotard, and the EU High Representative for the CFSP, Javier Solana,[66] contributing to the conclusion of the Ohrid Framework Agreement between the government and the representatives of the Albanian minority.[67]

Solana was also instrumental in the adoption of the 2002 constitution of the State Union of Serbia and Montenegro reconstituting the FRY. However, the attempt to keep the two countries together failed. In a referendum on May 21, 2006, 55.5% of the voters declared themselves in favor of independence, narrowly surpassing the 55% threshold rather arbitrarily imposed by the EU. Thereupon Montenegro declared its independence on June 3, 2006.

Against the backdrop of the Kosovo crisis in which the EU again cut a poor figure, the political leaders of the two principal military powers within the Union, France and the United Kingdom, took the initiative for what became the European Security and Defense Policy (ESDP).[68] At a meeting in Saint-Malo on December 3-4, 1998, President Jacques Chirac, Prime Minister Lionel Jospin, and Prime Minister Tony Blair called for the EU's capacity for autonomous action, backed up by credible military forces, the means to decide to use them, and a readiness to do so, in order to respond to international crises. This European crisis management capability was to be developed within the institutional framework of the EU, and not, as the United States would have preferred, that of NATO.

The new project was quickly endorsed by the other thirteen members of the EU, and steps to implement it were taken. In this context, the so-called Helsinki Headline Goal 2003 adopted by the European Council in the Finnish capital on December 10-11, 1999, was a milestone since it defined the relevant parameters of the EU's reaction force. The heads of state or government agreed that on the basis of voluntary cooperation, member states must be able, by 2003, to deploy within sixty days[69] and sustain for at least one year military forces up to 50,000-60,000 persons capable of

---

66. This post was created by the 1997 Amsterdam TEU.
67. U.S. Special Envoy James Pardew and, as mentioned above, NATO Secretary-General George Robertson were also involved in the settlement process.
68. Jolyon Howorth, *Security and Defence Policy of the European Union* (New York: Palgrave Macmillan, 2007).
69. Given this timeframe of two months for deployability, the EU force could hardly be called a "rapid" reaction force.

the full range of the Petersberg tasks.[70] One year later, at the Capabilities Commitment Conference in Brussels on November 20-21, 2000, member states pledged more than 100,000 troops, around 400 military aircraft and 100 naval vessels. Other commitment conferences were convened in the following years.

As a result, the EU was able to launch its first ESDP operations in the target year 2003.[71] That three of the operations were mounted in the former Yugoslavia could hardly come as a surprise at the time. The European Union Police Mission (EUPM) replaced the UN International Police Task Force (IPTF) in Bosnia-Herzegovina. It was charged with helping the local police to reach European standards and assisting it in the fight against various forms of organized crime. As already mentioned, Operation Concordia succeeded NATO's Operation Allied Harmony in Macedonia in order to maintain a safe environment for the implementation of the Ohrid peace agreement.[72] This peacekeeping operation was in turn replaced by the EU Police Mission Proxima, with a mandate similar to that of the EUPM.[73] The most difficult mission took place out of Europe. Operation Artemis was tasked with protecting civilians around Bunia, the capital of the eastern province of Ituri in the Democratic Republic of the Congo, from atrocities committed by ethnic militias. Finally, it may be recalled that the EU's Operation Althea followed SFOR in Bosnia and Herzegovina in 2004.[74]

In the meantime, the EU undertook, or is still conducting, twenty-seven ESDP missions, not only in Europe, but also several times in sub-Saharan Africa, as well as in the Caucasus, the Middle East, and even Indonesia. They include not only peacekeeping and police, but also border control, rule of law and security sector reform missions, as well as a counter-

---

70. These tasks—humanitarian and rescue tasks, peacekeeping tasks and tasks of combat forces in crisis management, including peacemaking—were first agreed on at a WEU ministerial meeting at the Petersberg near Bonn in 1992. They were included in Article 17 (2) of the 1997 Amsterdam TEU also as tasks of the EU. It should be noted that peacemaking normally means the peaceful settlement of disputes, but in the context of the Petersberg tasks is a euphemism for peace enforcement by combat forces. The term was chosen to make it easier for Germany to solve its constitutional law problems caused by participation in such missions.
71. For details see Gustav Lindstrom, "On the ground: ESDP operations," in *EU Security and Defence Policy: The First Five Years*, ed. Nicole Gnesotto (Paris: Institute for Security Studies, 2004), 111-29.
72. See above.
73. Another small police mission, the European Union Police Advisory Team in the Former Yugoslav Republic of Macedonia, followed in 2005.
74. See above.

piracy operation.[75] However, a typical EU mission is of limited duration, has a mandate that is not very challenging, and involves a low number of personnel, so that it cannot have a lasting substantial impact.

The most controversial ESDP operation was also launched in the "Balkan laboratory." The EU rule of law mission EULEX KOSOVO that is part of the Ahtisaari Plan, is a well-meant effort to help Kosovo reach some of the standards that it should have achieved prior to the settlement of the status issue. The project envisaged the dispatch of up to 2,200 police officers, judges, prosecutors, customs officials, and administrative experts whose manifold tasks are listed in the Special Envoy's Comprehensive Proposal. The operation was based on Council Joint Action 2008/124/CFSP of February 4, 2008. According to Article 5 of this Council decision, the operational phase of the operation shall start upon transfer of authority from UNMIK. EULEX KOSOVO was thus initiated on the assumption that the UN, more specifically its Secretary-General, would agree to the replacement of its administration in Kosovo by the EU.

Yet Ban Ki-moon hesitated to proceed to the expected transfer of powers, evidently mainly because of Russian opposition to a measure that was unacceptable to Serbia. Finally, a compromise was agreed on that provided for an enhanced operational role of the EU, but under the status-neutral authority of the UN. This meant that the powers of the reconfigured UNMIK, whose personnel were to be considerably reduced, would be substantially restricted to monitoring and facilitating. It would continue to operate within the framework of SC Resolution 1244 (1999) and be headed by the Secretary-General's Special Representative. This solution left the EU, which prides itself on respecting the law and calls on other countries to follow its example, in a rather awkward position.

To add to the embarrassment, in October 2012 the EU Court of Auditors issued a rather harsh assessment of EULEX KOSOVO. In addition to slow progress on the rule of law in general, the Court not only criticized the numerical size of the mission as too small but also found that staff members were not sufficiently qualified and that their presence in Kosovo was too short. The management of the mission by the EU Commission and the Union's recently established External Action Service at the disposal of the new High Representative for Foreign Affairs and Security Policy also left a good deal to be desired. Yet, the EU cannot allow the Kosovo experiment

---

75. Operation Atalanta against the Somali pirates off the Horn of Africa. Hanspeter Neuhold, "The Return of Piracy: Problems, Parallels, Paradoxes," in *Coexistence, Cooperation and Solidarity: Liber Amicorum Rüdiger Wolfrum*, eds. Holger P. Hestermeyer et al. (Leiden and Boston: Martinus Nijhoff Publishers, vol. 2, 2012), 1239-1258.

to fail, not only for political but also for financial reasons, having provided financial assistance totaling €3.6 billion since 1999 to Kosovo, making the latter its major aid recipient.

As in the case of NATO, inclusion of the countries of the region in the enlargement process is the most significant contribution the EU can make to lasting security, stability and prosperity in the "Balkan laboratory." The 2003 Thessaloniki European Council mentioned them among the applicants to which the doors of the EU would remain open, provided they fulfilled the criteria defined by this Council at its Copenhagen meeting ten years earlier. So far, only Slovenia has been admitted to the Union (in 2004); Croatia will become a member in 2013. The other states are also more or less advanced on the "road to Brussels," with Montenegro already engaged in membership negotiations and thus ahead of the rest.[76]

The OSCE: Variations on the Theme of "Softness"

The driving force behind the CSCE was the Soviet Union and its allies. They mainly aspired to multilateral recognition of the post-World War II territorial and political status quo in Europe by the West, and economic concessions from the capitalist countries, such as the abolition of trade obstacles and most-favored nation treatment. The West finally consented to the project; its main demands focused on the free movement of people, ideas, information, and reductions of conventional armed forces to lower common levels. The nine neutral and non-aligned (N+N) countries of Europe, including Austria,[77] also formed a group of their own in order to better defend and promote their common interests. They wanted, above all, to prevent the two blocs from deciding the continent's future over their heads. The N+Ns also tried to preserve and strengthen *détente*, so that they could maintain good relations with and avoid pressure from both East and West.

After preparatory talks at the ambassadorial level in Helsinki in 1972/73, the CSCE took place in three phases from 1973 to 1975, culminating in

---

76. However, a few days after the EU had received the Nobel Prize for Peace in Oslo for its peace project, on December 13, 2012, German Federal Chancellor Angela Merkel declared that the time was not ripe for enlargement negotiations after the admission of Croatia in 2013. EU member states suffer from "enlargement fatigue" at a time when they have their hands full with solving the most serious economic crisis the Union has faced so far.

77. The other members of this, in many respects, heterogeneous group were Cyprus, Finland, Liechtenstein, Malta, San Marino, the SFRY, Sweden, and Switzerland. Karl E. Birnbaum and Hanspeter Neuhold, eds., *Neutrality and Non-Alignment in Europe* (Vienna: Braumüller, 1981). For a recent study, see Thomas Fischer, *The N+N States and the Making of the Helsinki Accords* (Baden-Baden: Nomos, 2009).

the signing of the Helsinki Final Act at a summit meeting of the thirty-five participating states on July, 30-August 1, 1975. The conference was subsequently institutionalized through three follow-up meetings on the entire CSCE agenda in Belgrade (1977/78), Madrid (1980-83) and Vienna (1986-89), as well as several meetings of experts on specific issues; additional substantive agreements were reached at some of these conferences. The CSCE process became a diplomatic forum for comprehensive but limited cooperation[78] and peaceful political and ideological confrontation, notably over human rights. The "CSCE thermometer" measured the political Cold-War climate. In addition, the CSCE process was itself a factor which eventually contributed to the collapse of the Communist regimes in Eastern Europe, in particular by the agreements on human rights that the "Socialist" participants reluctantly accepted.

Another key document, the Charter of Paris for a New Europe, was signed at the end of the East-West conflict at a summit meeting in the French capital on November 19-21, 1990. The political leaders of all CSCE states now agreed on Western political and economic principles, from individual-oriented human rights and pluralist democracy to market economy, as the foundations for the future relations among participating states and their peoples. The Paris Charter also called for several new CSCE institutions. A multi-level structure, ranging from meetings of heads of state or government and a Ministerial Council headed by a Chairman-in-Office to a Permanent Council at the ambassadorial level in Vienna, and including a Secretariat also in the Austrian capital, was thereupon established. Moreover, some rather unique bodies were added: the Office for Democratic Institutions and Human Rights in Warsaw, the High Commissioner on National Minorities in The Hague, and the OSCE Representative on Freedom of the Media in Vienna.

The Budapest summit on December 5-6, 1994, decided to rename the CSCE the OSCE. However, despite its name, the OSCE is still not an intergovernmental organization, since it continues to lack a constituent treaty endowing it with international legal personality. Furthermore, its decisions are not legally binding but merely "soft law." From a diplomatic

---

78. Cooperation included 1) security; 2) economics, science and technology, and the environment; and 3) "humanitarian and other fields," the compromise term for human rights. At the same time, the scope of cooperation that could be agreed on in these three "baskets" was modest. For instance, security cooperation was restricted to a Declaration on Principles Guiding Relations between Participating States, a codification of ten key rules of international law that, however, failed to clarify numerous controversial issues. The first "basket" of the Final Act also contained military confidence-building measures, essentially the prior notification of major military maneuvers and the exchange of maneuver observers.

process in the framework of the East-West conflict, the OSCE has been transformed into the main pan-European cooperative security institution whose decisions are based on the consensus of, by now, fifty-six participating states.[79] It may therefore be called a "soft international organization" producing "soft law" mainly in the area of "soft (i.e., non-military) security."

The OSCE's main achievements are its field activities, first and foremost its Missions. At this writing, nineteen of these operations designed to promote stability and reforms in the target countries are going on. They fulfill these tasks, *inter alia*, by helping to strengthen effective respect for human and minority rights and by supporting democratization and the rule of law, notably through institution- and capacity-building, i.e., training police officers, judges, prosecutors, and other civil servants.[80]

As could almost be expected, the two largest of these Missions have been sent to the two most unstable testing sites in the Balkans, Bosnia and Herzegovina and Kosovo. In the former state, the OSCE was tasked, in accordance with the Dayton/Paris Peace Agreement, by the Budapest Ministerial Council in December 1995 to assist in the fields of elections, monitoring human rights, as well as security-building measures and sub-regional arms control. Subsequently, the mandate was extended to education, democratization, and the rule of law. The Mission also helped with the return of refugees and the restoration of property. Moreover, it took part in defense reform that led to the creation of a single, professional armed force.

In Kosovo, the Kosovo Verification Mission was deployed from October 1998 to March 1999 in order to verify compliance by the FRY with UN SC Resolutions 1160 of March 31, 1998 and 1199 of September 23, 1999 that had imposed an arms embargo and demanded a ceasefire. The current Mission was set up by the OSCE Permanent Council under SC Resolution 1244 (1999) as the "third pillar" of UNMIK. Its principal areas of activity are the development of human resources, *inter alia* by training police officers, judicial personnel and civil administrators; the promotion of democratization, especially elections; and respect for human rights. In particular, the Mission helped to establish and develop several major democratic institutions, such as the Central Election Commission, the Ombudsman and the Independent Media Commission, as well as the

---

79. Michael Bothe, Natalino Ronzitti and Allan Rasas, eds., *The OSCE in the Maintenance of Peace and Security: Conflict Prevention, Crisis Management, and Peaceful Settlement of Disputes* (The Hague: Kluwer Law International, 1998).
80. For more information, see OSCE Press and Public Information Section, *OSCE Handbook* (Vienna: OSCE, 2007).

Kosovo Police Service School and the Police Inspectorate. OSCE experts also provide training and advice to the local authorities. More recently, the focus of the Mission's activities has shifted from institution-building to monitoring. As pointed out above, the OSCE will remain present in Kosovo after the termination of international supervision in 2012.

The OSCE's contributions to the peace process in the former SFRY are undoubtedly useful. However, some of the projects, such as assisting education reform, are too ambitious, since the necessary personnel and financial resources are lacking, and therefore produce limited practical results.[81]

Austria: A Permanently Neutral Balkan Activist

Given Austria's long-standing manifold interests in the Balkans—from historic ties to concerns about political stability in a volatile neighboring region to economic opportunities—Austrian governments have consistently supported the efforts of the international community, in particular those of the above-mentioned international organizations, to end violent conflict and foster political reforms and prosperity in the former Yugoslavia.

As for its relations with these institutions, Austria was admitted to the UN in 1955, participated in the CSCE as a member of the N+N group from the beginning, became a member state of the EU in 1995, and joined PfP, also in 1995. In this context, the country's special international status, permanent neutrality, had to be taken into account as a potential obstacle to close ties to the four organizations, in particular membership.[82]

It must also be borne in mind that for a majority of Austrians neutrality constitutes a superior political value, even part of their national identity.[83]

---

81. Like other international organizations in the area of security policy, the OSCE has seen better days and is facing serious problems. It is criticized by Russia for its emphasis on human rights and for conducting its missions exclusively in former "Socialist" countries in the East. The U.S. position is characterized by "benign neglect" except for human rights issues. The EU has become a competitor, since it is increasingly active in the same areas as the OSCE and has the advantage of substantially more financial and other resources. Pál Dunay, *The OSCE in Crisis*, Chaillot Paper no. 88 (Paris: EU Institute for Security Studies, 2006).
82. On the period 1955-89, see Hanspeter Neuhold, "Austrian Foreign and Security Policy: Squaring the Circle between Permanent Neutrality and Other Pillars of Austria's International Status," in *"Peaceful Coexistence" or "Iron Curtain"? Austria, Neutrality, and Eastern Europe in the Cold War and Détente, 1955–1989*, eds. Arnold Suppan and Wolfgang Mueller (Vienna: LIT Verlag, 2009), 82-99.
83. Initially, however, permanent neutrality was the political price Austria had to pay to the Soviet Union for the conclusion of the 1955 State Treaty which restored the country's independence. This status, which was not welcomed by everybody in Austria, was defined as

Consequently, calling for the outright abolition of this cherished status would be a safe recipe for electoral suicide for any political party.[84] A closer look at the evolution of Austrian neutrality after the Cold War may therefore be appropriate in the present context.[85]

1) NATO membership would clearly be contrary to two cornerstones of the international law of neutrality, the principles of abstention from military support to belligerents[86] and equal treatment. Joining the Atlantic Alliance was nevertheless envisaged by the Austrian center-right coalition government formed in February 2000 in the context of the debate on a new Austrian security and defense doctrine. However, this option was abandoned and permanent neutrality "rediscovered"[87] in the wake of the controversies over Operation Iraqi Freedom in 2003. It should be recalled that this military campaign was mounted by a U.S.-led ad-hoc coalition, which included other NATO states, without an unambiguous authorization to use force by the SC.

2) In principle, neutrality is equally incompatible with the mutual assistance obligations in a system of collective security.[88] Yet, several solutions to this dilemma with regard to Austria's membership in the UN were put forth in the course of the past decades. Initially, Austrian international lawyers argued that the SC had to exempt Austria from taking part in sanctions contrary to its obligations as a permanently neutral state. They pointed out that Austria had been admitted without objection to the World Organization on December 14, 1955, after its neutral status, previously declared on October 26, 1955, had been widely recognized, also by four permanent members of the SC. Therefore the Council was under

---

means to an end, the maintenance of external independence and the inviolability of Austrian territory, in the Federal Constitutional Law of October 26, 1955 by which it was established. What was conceived as a security strategy later became an end in itself.

84. For the mayor of Vienna, Michael Häupl, neutrality is an old, perhaps also threadbare, but warm coat, *Der Standard*, 15 Feb. 2011. It may be objected that this coat was useful during the Cold War but that a milder climate prevails in Europe today.

85. For further details, see Hanspeter Neuhold, "Außenpolitik und Demokratie: Immerwährende Neutralität durch juristische Mutation?," in *Demokratie und sozialer Rechtsstaat in Europa: Festschrift für Theo Öhlinger*, eds. Stefan Hammer et al. (Vienna: Universitätsverlag, 2004), 68-91, and the literature quoted there.

86. Despite the watered-down wording of the collective defense guarantee in Article 5 of the 1949 North Atlantic Treaty: "[…] if such an armed attack (against one or more of the allies) occurs, each of them, […] will assist the Party or Parties so attacked by *taking forthwith*,[…] *such action as it deems necessary* (italics added), including the use of armed force […]"

87. The two governing parties had defined Austria's status as *bündnisfrei* ("alliance-free"), similar to that of Finland and Sweden after the Cold War.

88. Whereas collective defense is directed against an external aggressor, collective security requires joint action against a member of the system who attacks another member.

the obligation to use the discretion it enjoyed under Article 48 of the UN Charter with respect to participation in enforcement action.[89] Moreover, during the Cold War the problem remained largely theoretical anyway, since the SC never resorted to military and only twice to non-military sanctions, against the apartheid regimes in Southern Rhodesia and South Africa.[90]

When after the end of the East-West conflict the Council adopted the above-mentioned Resolution 678 (1990) authorizing member states to use force for the liberation of Kuwait, it also requested, in paragraph 3, all states to provide appropriate support for the actions undertaken in pursuance of this authorization. Withholding assistance would have placed Austria in an awkward isolated position within the international community. The circle was squared by arguing that the military campaign against Iraq was not a war as defined under international law; rather, it constituted a "police action," therefore Austria's neutrality did not materialize.

3) During the Cold War, Austrian membership in the supranational EC was generally considered highly problematic, if not contrary to permanent neutrality. One hypothetical example of conflicting obligations was an EC majority decision on certain unilateral trade restrictions against a belligerent in a war. Hence Austria settled for free-trade agreements with the European Economic Community and the European Coal and Steel Community in 1972. Paradoxically, despite enhanced integration within the EU created by the 1992 Maastricht Treaty, Austria eventually joined the Union in 1995 without any neutrality reservations. In a Joint Declaration on Common Foreign and Security Policy, Austria, together with Finland and Sweden, fully accepted the *acquis communautaire* in the field. It also refrained from invoking the so-called Irish clause. Neutral Ireland had insisted on the inclusion of paragraph 4 in Article J.4 of the Maastricht TEU, under which "the policy of the Union in accordance with this Article shall not prejudice the specific character of the security and defence policy of certain Member States," a general wording into which a reference to neutrality can be read.

Since its admission to the EU, Austria has sought to take part in the new CFSP/ESDP activities without abolishing its neutral status. The

---

89. Article 48 reads as follows: "The action required to carry out the decisions of the Security Council for the maintenance of international peace and security shall be taken by all the Members of the United Nations *or by some of them*, as the Security Council may determine" (italics added).

90. With regard to Southern Rhodesia, the Austrian government could claim that the unilateral declaration of independence by this British colony in 1965 led to an internal conflict within the United Kingdom and not an inter-state war, so that Austria did not have to comply with its obligations as a permanently neutral state under international law. The arms embargo imposed by the SC on South Africa in 1977 did not concern Austria, since it did not export any war material to this state.

solution to circumvent possible dilemmas was the continuous erosion of permanent neutrality, reducing it to its hard military core in line with the "avocado doctrine." Thus the Legal Adviser at the Austrian Federal Ministry for External Affairs, Ambassador Franz Cede, stated in 1995 that Austria's permanent neutrality was only based on constitutional, not international law.[91] The necessary intent to also establish a binding legal foundation at the international level was said to be lacking. Previously, it had been generally agreed, without objection by Austrian official representatives, that the notification of the 1955 Austrian Federal Constitutional Law on Neutrality to all states with which Austria had diplomatic relations at the time, and its recognition by the latter established an international legal obligation for Austria to comply with the rules of the law of neutrality.[92]

Thus the stage had been set for the unilateral interpretation, modification and even termination of permanent neutrality. In its efforts to make full participation with the evolving CFSP compatible with its neutral status, Austria enacted amendments to its constitution. Under a new Article 23 (f) added on the occasion of the country's admission to the EU, taking part in the CFSP includes measures with which economic relations with one or more third countries are suspended, restricted or completely terminated, in other words EU economic sanctions against non-member states. In 1998, participation in the Petersberg tasks, including the problematic "peacemaking" missions,[93] under the Amsterdam TEU was also inserted in this provision.

The Austrian government even tried to square the circle between the mutual assistance obligation in the event of armed aggression on the territory of an EU member under Article 42 (7) of the Lisbon TEU[94] and the maintenance of neutrality. According to the new magic formula,

---

91. Franz Cede, "Österreichs Neutralität und Sicherheitspolitik nach dem Beitritt zur Europäischen Union," *Zeitschrift für Rechtsvergleichung* 36 (1995): 142-48.
92. Moreover, the Moscow Memorandum of April 15, 1955, agreed on between high-level Austrian and Soviet delegations, should be mentioned in this context. According to this key "soft law" document, which paved the way for the readiness of the USSR to sign the Austrian State Treaty in exchange for the adoption of permanent neutrality by Austria, "the Austrian Government will make a declaration in a form which will oblige Austria *internationally* (italics added) to practice in perpetuity a neutrality of the type maintained by Switzerland." Translation in Alfred Verdross, *The Permanent Neutrality of Austria* (Vienna: Verlag für Geschichte und Politik, 1978), 26. Similarly, in its *avis* on Austria's admission to the EC, the EC Commission referred to the twofold basis of the country's neutrality under Austrian as well as public international law.
93. See above.
94. "If a Member State is the victim of armed aggression on its territory, the other Member States shall have towards it an obligation of aid and assistance by all the means in their power, in accordance with Article 51 of the United Nations Charter."

Austria will practice solidarity in Europe but remain neutral in the rest of the world—having its *Apfelstrudel* or *Sachertorte* and eating it, too.[95]

4) Participation in the OSCE, a cooperative security institution whose activities require the consent of all parties involved and do not include armed force beyond self-defense in the context of a peacekeeping operation,[96] does not pose any problems from the point of view of neutrality.

In any case, Austria has taken part in numerous missions undertaken by all four international organizations in the "Balkan laboratory." For instance, Austrian soldiers and non-military officials participated or are still participating in the EC/UMM, IPTF, EUPM, IFOR/SFOR, UN Mine Action Centre, OSCE Mission, Office of the High Representative and Operation Althea in Bosnia and Herzegovina; KFOR, OSCE Verification Mission, UNMIK, KFOR, OSCE Mission and EULEX KOSOVO in Kosovo, as well as Operation Concordia and Proxima in FYROM. However, in many cases the size of Austrian contributions was small and therefore more symbolic than substantial. Moreover, numerous civilian victims of the Balkan crises, above all from Bosnia and Herzegovina, found refuge in Austria. Austria also supports the admission of the states on the territory of the former SFRY to the EU.

On the one hand, Austria's neutral status did not raise any legal problems for participation in the above-mentioned missions, since all of them were cooperative security operations and therefore based on the agreement of all parties concerned, including the parties to the conflict that was to be managed or settled. Even an "enforcement-by-consent" operation such as IFOR/SFOR and KFOR, whose mandates include the use of non-defensive armed force, can hardly be qualified as war, even if international troops use their weapons against local forces. On the other hand, permanent neutrality, which in the past had been emphasized as a particular qualification for Austria's bridge-building services in international conflicts, was no particular asset for those activities because they were undertaken together with numerous other, non-neutral states in the framework of multilateral institutions.

With the end of the Cold War, Austrian neutrality lost its principal "conflict of reference" in which it had emerged and fulfilled useful functions for other states, in particular the two blocs opposing each other in Europe.

---

95. Instead of invoking the "Irish formula" reiterated in Article 42 (7). The Austrian writer Robert Menasse aptly called Austria the country of the "Either-and-Or" ("*Entweder-und-Oder*"). Robert Menasse, *Das Land ohne Eigenschaften: Essay zur österreichische Identität*, 3rd ed. (Vienna: Sonderzahl, 1993), 16.

96. The OSCE has not yet conducted a peacekeeping operation, although such a mission is envisioned in the context of the Nagorno-Karabakh conflict.

Austria served as a strategic buffer between NATO and the Warsaw Treaty Organization from which both alliances benefited. Furthermore, together with Switzerland, it formed a neutral wedge splitting NATO to the advantage of the Eastern bloc—one of the possible reasons why the Soviet Union agreed to withdraw its troops from Austria under the 1955 State Treaty. Today, Austria is almost completely surrounded by NATO members[97] and a nuisance factor, interrupting the direct transit routes between the neighboring members of the alliance. It still contributes to peaceful relations between states by offering its good offices, i.e., hosting international meetings and organizations. However, this and other bridge-building roles have increasingly been played by states that are members of military alliances. For instance, the ICTY and the ICC established their headquarters at The Hague.[98] Norway, another NATO member, mediated between Israel and the PLO and between the parties to the civil war in Sri Lanka. Furthermore, if European integration is taken seriously, and solidarity is the overarching principle, there will hardly be room left for the neutrality of individual member states. Either the EU as a whole takes sides in a conflict, or chooses to remain neutral.

Conclusions

The international community proved unable to prevent or stop at an early stage the tragic dismemberment of the SFRY, which subsequently exacted a heavy toll in human casualties, refugees, and material damage. It had no comprehensive strategy, and the steps taken by various international organizations, including those by the four institutions discussed in this essay, as well as by states individually, were tardy, half-hearted, and uncoordinated. However, some lessons were learned; new methods of crisis management and conflict resolution were successfully tested in the "Balkan laboratory," especially "enforcement-by-consent" peace operations and preventive peacekeeping missions. The establishment of individual criminal responsibility under international law first by the creation of the ICTY must also be included in the positive record. Moreover, the former Yugoslavia not only provided the UN but also NATO, the EU and the OSCE with opportunities to experiment with numerous new activities that ensured their continued relevance after the end of the Cold War, from NATO-

---

97. With the exception of permanently neutral Switzerland and Liechtenstein.
98. As well as the Organization monitoring compliance with the 1993 Chemical Weapons Convention (Convention on the Prohibition of the Development, Production, Stockpiling and Use of Chemical Weapons and on their Destruction).

led peace operations to various ESDP/CSDP activities as well as OSCE Missions. Austria was able to demonstrate in the conflicts in the former Yugoslavia that it could, in a spirit of solidarity, take part in numerous peace initiatives without abandoning its neutrality.

Two questions cannot be answered by this author in this essay. The issue of whether the international community could have prevented the post-Yugoslav tragedies if it had acted earlier and more vigorously must be addressed and answered by historians. Whether the new methods and instruments tested in the "Balkan laboratory" may also be successfully employed in other parts of the world merits further study and can only be ascertained by frequently using them in practice.[99]

---

99. This has already been the case with regard to some innovations. As pointed out above, several international criminal tribunals have been set up in other parts of the world in the wake of the ICTY. An "enforcement-by-consent" operation was also mounted in Timor-Leste in 1999.

Austrian Foreign Trade and Austrian Companies' Economic Engagement in Central and Eastern Europe (CEE) since 1989

Andreas Resch

The economic and political scenery in CEE has changed fundamentally since 1989. A massive influx of foreign direct investment (FDI) and a redirection of foreign trade were crucial for increases in productivity and shifts of the sectorial structure. Firms from Austria played an important part in this development which in turn boosted the internationalization of the domestic economy. Internationalization on the firm level can be carried out in different modes. Most important are exports and FDI. To understand these developments, geographic proximity and cultural factors must be kept in mind.[1]

In accordance with these considerations this paper is structured as follows. The first chapter gives an overview of the historical conditions that shaped the political, economic, and cultural environment of Austria-CEE relations since 1989. In the second chapter, FDIs in the region are analyzed with a focus on the Austrian investors, and thereafter the development of foreign trade is scrutinized. In the concluding section, characteristic general trends are summarized. The study concentrates on the most relevant Austrian trade partners among the new EU member states (EU-10) including Hungary, the Czech Republic, Slovakia, Poland, and to a lesser extent, Slovenia, Romania, and Bulgaria. Other states in Eastern and Southern Europe are only mentioned in passing.

Historical preconditions – Austria and CEE since the 19th century

The economic relations between Austria and CEE have a long tradition.[2] In the times of the Habsburg Empire, a specific regional pattern

---
1. See for example Schien Ninan, Jonas F. Puck, "The internationalization of Austrian firms in Central and Eastern Europe," *Journal for East European Management Studies* 15, no. 3 (2010): 237-259.
2. For an overview on the Austrian trade relations to Central and Eastern Europe see Andreas Resch, "Der Osthandel im Spannungsfeld der Blöcke," in *Zwischen den Blöcken. NATO, Warschauer Pakt und Österreich*, ed. Manfried Rauchensteiner (Vienna, Cologne,

of production and trade emerged. The Alpine and Bohemian countries provided a more than proportional fraction of the industrial production and financial services, while the other regions were generally more oriented towards agrarian production. In spite of successful industrialization schemes in Hungary from the 1880s on, this structural division of labor endured until the end of the Empire in 1918/19.

After the Great War the territory of the formerly unified market with more than fifty million inhabitants was shared among seven states, i.e. Austria, Czechoslovakia, Hungary, Italy, Poland, Rumania, and Yugoslavia.

During the 1920s the statistics of Austrian foreign trade continued to reveal an intensive economic interconnection with the other states in Central and Eastern Europe. In 1925 Czechoslovakia, Yugoslavia, Poland, Hungary, and Romania together provided for more than forty-seven percent of all Austrian imports and consumed around forty-four percent of Austrian exports.[3]

During the following decades, the Great Economic Crisis of the early 1930s, the politics of the National Socialists and World War II, and finally the division of Europe during the "Cold War" obstructed the traditional regional economic relations. In spite of these impediments, Austria maintained exceptionally strong economic relations to CEE, compared to other Western economies.

When Austria regained full political autonomy due to the State Treaty with the four Allied powers in 1955, a network of trade and payment treaties with member states of the Community for Mutual Economic Assistance (CMEA) was established in the short term. The portion of these socialist countries in Austrian foreign trade varied between nine and seventeen percent from the 1950s to the 1980s, which was one of the highest shares of all Western economies. During the early 1970s a further wave of trade liberalization between Austria and the Eastern countries followed, when international détente created a favorable political environment. Austria was the first European country, with the exception of Finland, which applied liberalized customs authorization procedures originally reserved for GATT imports to imports from CMEA members. Furthermore, bilateral clearing was replaced by payments in convertible currencies. At the same time a system of export financing and guarantees provided by the *Österreichische*

Weimar: Böhlau 2010), 497-556.
3. See *Der Außenhandel Österreichs in der Zeit zwischen den beiden Weltkriegen, Beiträge zur österreichischen Statistik*, ed. by Österreichisches Statistisches Zentralamt, Vol. 19 (Vienna: ÖStat, 1946): 20 and 31 ff; Felix Butschek, *Statistische Reihen zur österreichischen Wirtschaftsgeschichte* (Vienna: WIFO, 1997), table 15.3 and 15.4.

Kontrollbank was deployed. Firms located in Vienna, some of them owned by the small domestic Communist party, others owned by domestic banks, private owners or foreign investors became important players in all facets of the East-West-business. They organized imports, exports and all kinds of transit, barter and compensation deals.[4] During this period many Austrian managers, be it in the nationalized industries, leading banks or private firms, gathered business experience in CEE and knitted personal networks. Furthermore, during the 1970s the Vienna Institute for International Economic Studies (WIIW) emerged as a leading research institution with respect to CEE where Austrian scientists firmly worked together with emigrants from the entire region.[5]

To boost trade relations, Austria became one of the most important financiers of Eastern foreign debt in the West. Around 1980 Austrian institutions financed some ten percent of foreign-currency denominated debt of these countries. As a consequence, Austria was prominently involved in the restructuring schemes of Eastern debts from the early 1980s on.[6]

The economic collapse of state-socialism and the opening of the reform countries from 1989 onward launched a new era in Austrian economic relations with CEE. In this situation, the history of longstanding economic contacts and geographical nearness gave Austrian investors and businesspersons first-mover advantages from the early 1990s onward.

During the same decade, Austria's international position was dramatically changed by the country's accession to the EU in 1995.

Equally, reforms in CEE were stimulated by the perspective of international economic integration on a European and on a global level.[7] After a "transformal recession" during the early 1990s a successful catching up growth process began, which continued until the inception of the international financial crisis in late 2008. "The institutional participation in

---

4. Transit trade was recorded in the balance of payments and not in the trade balance. Marin and Schnitzer have shown that barter and countertrade may be efficient institutions to mitigate contractual hazards which arise in technology trade, marketing and imperfect capital markets. Dalia Marin, Monica Schnitzer, "Economic incentives and international trade," *European Economic Review* 42 (1998): 705-716.
5. <http://www.wiiw.ac.at/?action=content&id=organization> (March 4, 2013).
6. G. Fink, K. Mauler, *Hard Currency position of CMEA countries and Yugoslavia*. Sonderdruck der Ersten österreichischen Sparkasse, The Vienna Institute for International Economic Studies (Vienna: 1988); Jan Stankovky, "Der Osthandel," *WIFO Monatsberichte* 5 (1991), 245-255.
7. The following overview is based on Michael A. Landesmann, "Twenty Years of East-West Integration: Reflections on What We Have Learned," *Focus on European Economic Integration, Special Issue 2009: 1989-2009. Twenty Years of East-West Integration: Hopes and Achievements*, ed. Peter Mooslechner and Doris Ritzberger-Grünwald (Vienna: OeNB, 2009): 16-26.

an EU accession process was important for two reasons: (1) as a signal to the "internal actors," i.e. the economic and political actors within the countries, so that their expectations could be aligned, and (2) as a sign of reassurance to "external actors," in particular those which could provide capital, know-how ... , and support in the setting of new types of activities (e.g. in the banking system) or in the transformation of old types of activities."[8] The EU accession process lead to a first round of "Eastern Enlargement" in 2004, when the Baltic States, Poland, the Czech Republic, Slovakia, Hungary, and Slovenia became member states. In a second round in 2007 Bulgaria and Romania entered the EU. Above that Slovenia became member of the Euro zone in 2007; Slovakia followed in 2009.

Foreign Direct Investment

Foreign direct investment (FDI) has been functioning as one of the most important vehicles of change in the reform countries. During the first decade after 1989, the direct neighbors of Western Europe attracted the highest stock of FDI. Compared to domestic GDP in 2000 Estonia, Hungary, the Czech Republic, Latvia, and Slovakia had gained the highest levels of foreign investment. More recently, Bulgaria, which became an EU member in 2007, has experienced a massive inflow of FDI.

Table 1: Inward FDI stocks in selected countries by major home countries as of December 2010, share in percent

	Bulgaria	Czech Rep.	Hungary	Poland	Romania	Slovakia	Slovenia	EU-10
Austria	15.4	12.9	12.8	3.5	17.8	16.0	47.9	11.0
France	2.1	5.7	5.0	12.4	8.3	4.1	6.0	7.4
Germany	5.5	13.8	23.2	13.6	12.2	4.3	5.6	6.0
Luxembourg	2.5	6.1	8.1	8.7	1.9	4.3	1.9	6.0
Netherlands	20.3	29.6	17.1	17.8	20.7	26.0	5.1	20.3
United States	2.6	3.3	4.7	6.3	2.6	1.4	0.6	4.0
Other countries	51.6	28.6	29.1	37.7	36.5	43.9	32.9	45.3
Total, EUR mn	36,173	96,153	67,949	150,441	52,585	37,632	10,772	482,486

Source: *wiiw Database on Foreign Direct Investment in Central, East and Southeast Europe*, 2012. Table I/15, 53.

---

8. Landesmann, "Twenty Years," 18.

Table 1 shows the strong position of Austria among foreign investors in CEE. According to the data reported, Austria is number one in Slovenia, number two in Bulgaria, Romania, Slovakia, and number three in the Czech Republic and Hungary. In addition to the countries mentioned above, Austria also ranks first in Bosnia and Herzegovina, Croatia, and Serbia.

It must be noted that the official statistical data are distorted to a certain degree. Many multinational companies place their FDI via firms in the Netherlands. As a consequence, only a certain fraction of the FDI statistically assigned to this country does have an ultimate Dutch owner. This means that the weight of the Netherlands is exaggerated, while the other countries are underrated.[9]

In spite of the fact that the number of big multinational Austrian companies is quite limited, firms from this country were among the most important early movers as investors in CEE. During the first years after 1989 Greenfield investments dominated, from the mid 1990s on big privatizations gained momentum which allowed purchasing existing firms. Over time, the stock of Austrian FDI developed as follows.

Chart 1: Austrian FDI 1990-2011 (Stocks in mn Euro)

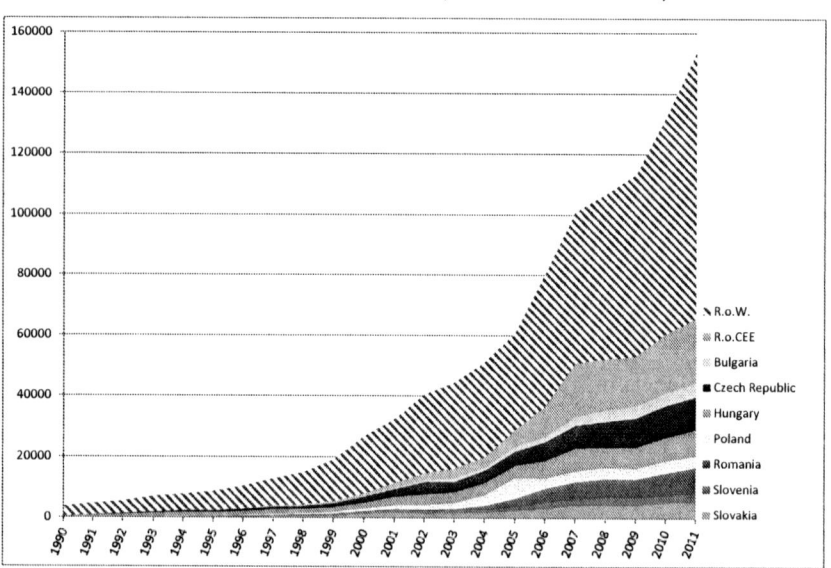

Source: Data by Österreichische Nationalbank CEE = Albania, Bosnia-Herzegovina, Bulgaria, Estonia, Latvia, Lithuania, Macedonia, Republic Moldavia, Montenegro, Poland, Romania, Russia, Serbia, Slovakia, Slovenia, Czech Republic, Ukraine, Hungary, and Belarus.

---

9. Gábor Hunya, "Short-lived Recovery," *wiiw Database on Foreign Direct Investment in Central, East and Southeast Europe* (Vienna: wiiw, 2012): 14-17.

Table 2: Austrian FDI in the Czech Republic, Hungary, Romania, Slovakia, Bulgaria, and Poland in mn Euros from 1990 – 2011

Year	1990	1991	1992	1993	1994	1995	1996	1997	1998	1999	2000
Czech Republic	10	32	206	363	604	693	850	997	1,112	1,291	2,108
Hungary	292	647	900	1,229	1,317	1,168	1,340	1,511	1,447	1,673	1,863
Romania	x	x	x	3	x	3	0	42	119	174	297
Slovakia	x	25	59	72	122	152	248	399	455	573	1,272
Bulgaria	x	x	6	1	x	4	8	20	18	113	137
Poland	12	25	41	65	77	120	192	342	378	558	914

Year	2001	2002	2003	2004	2005	2006	2007	2008	2009	2010	2011
Czech Republic	2,554	4,190	3,548	4,162	4,729	6,238	7,589	8,637	9,660	10,615	10,885
Hungary	2,724	3,429	3,453	3,962	3,934	5,714	7,429	6,477	6,922	7,621	8,593
Romania	431	568	555	1,589	2,843	4,772	5,682	6,238	6,311	7,487	8,449
Slovakia	1.769	1.382	1.515	1.828	2.456	3.258	4.325	4.464	4.354	5.175	5.507
Bulgaria	316	415	1,051	752	1,482	1,592	2,748	3,685	3,930	4,082	4,557
Poland	1,240	1,394	1,944	3,365	6,758	3,294	3,487	3,686	3,440	3,910	3,688

Source: Österreichische Nationalbank

Until the turn of the century Hungary was the most important CEE market for Austrian FDI. In Hungary Austrian firms had already started first small joint ventures during the communist era.

During the first years the growth rates of FDI showed strong fluctuations. While Austrian Investments in Czechoslovakia grew by 540 percent from 1991 to 1992, they diminished by 11.3% in Hungary from 1994 to 1995. Around 1995, when Austria entered the EU, Eastern investments tended to stagnate for a few years, but they re-gained momentum from the late 1990s on which led to a record level of FDI in 2007. Some of the changes are attributable to single big investments.

The international financial crisis of 2008 interrupted economic growth. In 2008 and/or 2009 a slight disinvestment occurred in many countries. Hungary lost 12.8% of all Austrian FDI in 2008 and in 2009 Slovakia, Poland and Slovenia witnessed a reduction in FDI of Austrian origin by rates between 2.5% and 6.7%. In 2010 investment has, more or less, recovered and since then, in all of the six countries mentioned in table 2 the stock of FDI surpassed the level of 2007.

The development of FDI flows shows the rapid growth until 2007 even more clearly. The 1990s brought full liberalization of international capital markets which allowed for a strong growth of FDI.

Table 3: Austrian FDI flows in mn Euro

	1995	1998	2001	2004	2007	2008	2009	2010	2011	Q1 12	Q2 12	Q3 12
FDI total	685	2,372	3,377	6,467	28,513	20,106	7,203	7,546	16,893	4,357	944	2,793
FDI to CEEC	395	762	3,061	4,096	16,736	10,654	2,060	3,748	7,206	1,917	714	723
Czech Republic	52	247	506	396	1,206	1376	379	828	375	331	-55	816
Hungary	196	185	708	634	1,731	950	-742	263	1629	-62	-141	-101
Slovenia	41	57	275	116	1,329	374	-26	128	516	251	-34	46
Slovakia	41	121	748	199	780	73	111	288	272	53	99	-148
Romania	1	62	97	1,779	1	980	607	511	1,272	287	276	128
Poland	56	127	246	287	447	286	389	-781	95	168	444	96
Bulgaria	-3	2	33	-174	1,573	1,604	382	131	475	84	52	-69

Source: Data by Österreichische Nationalbank; CEE as Chart 1

The total amount of Austrian FDI flows grew by the factor of five from 1995 to 2001 to some 3.4 billion Euros. Thereafter, it exploded to some 28.5 billion in 2007. Investments in CEEC grew more than proportionally from the turn of the century onward.

Chart 2: Share of CEE countries in total Austrian FDI stock in percent

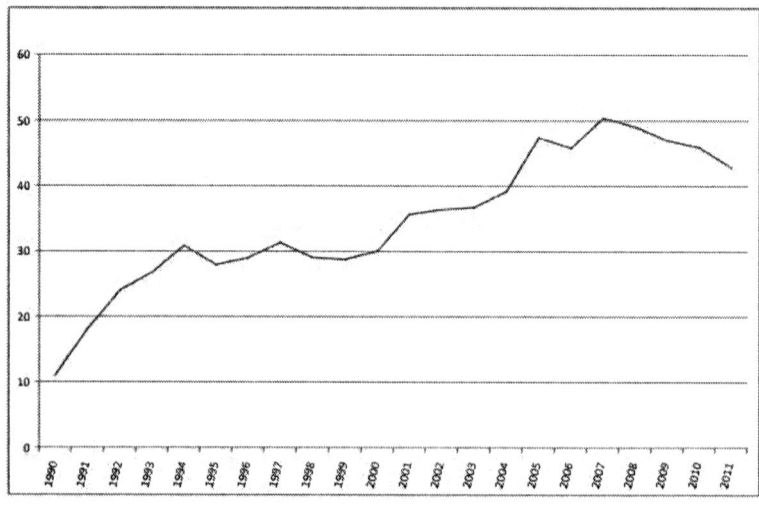

Data: Österreichische Nationalbank; CEE as Chart 1.

Chart 2 reveals an increasing share of Eastern investments in total Austrian FDI stocks as from the turn of the century. In 2007 around 10.6 billion Euros were directly invested in the Eastern economies, which made up for more than fifty percent of all investments.

The total of inward FDI stocks in CEE from all countries reached a record high of 112 billion Euros in 2008, but plummeted to some fifty-five billion Euros in 2009. Until 2011 FDI recovered to around seventy-nine billion.[10]

A study based on a sample of 109 Austrian firms with 1,271 market entries in the CEE region until 2008 shows that twenty-three percent of these entries occurred before 1990, testifying to the enormous importance of business contacts before the fall of the iron curtain. Forty-seven percent of the entries happened between 1990 und 1999, and thirty percent between 2000 and 2008.

28.4% of the firms have chosen direct investment as the first entry mode and have maintained this mode. 26.5% of the firms have begun with export deals and remained in this business, and 25.4% first entered the CEE markets with exports and moved on to higher modes like FDI (18.6%) or licensing and contract manufacturing (6.8%).[11] This makes clear that "a significant number of firms had sufficient market knowledge and commitment in order to enter CEE markets in higher modes from the beginning."[12]

During the first years, Austrian FDI in CEE were not very profitable. Building up new affiliates under the conditions of the transformal recession required patient commitment of the investors. From the second half of the 1990s onward, this strategy paid, and profitability far surpassed direct investments in the rest of the world. In 2005 all Austrian FDI produced an average return on equity of 8.3%. However, returns differed to a large extent by regions. They amounted to 5.1% in Western EU countries while they reached 9.7% in the four neighboring Eastern countries plus Poland (EU-5).[13] After the outbreak of financial crisis, in 2009 the average profitability of FDI has remained around ten percent in the Czech Republic while it plummeted to less than five percent in Bulgaria, Ukraine, Croatia, and Serbia and to less than one percent in Romania and Lithuania.[14]

---

10. *Der Standard*, June 8, 2011.
11. Ninan, Puck, "The internationalization of Austrian firms," 237- 259.
12. Ibid., 250.
13. Wilfried Altzinger, *The Profitability of Austrian Foreign Direct Investment – Reinvestment or Repatriation?*, FIW Research Report No 010 (June 2008): 8-12.
14. *Der Standard*, June 8, 2011.

Several studies have scrutinized the motives for direct investments. They have shown that just a small minority of Austrian FDI intended to profit from cheaper factor prices, above all from lower labor costs. The absolute majority of investments were motivated by the search for new markets.[15] Many industry and service sectors experienced saturated domestic markets in Austria, while CEE offered growing demand during the phase of the restructuring of the economies after the end of communism.

Mere outsourcing and buying input-goods from Eastern firms was not a feasible way to reap the fruits of cheaper labor, because lower productivity equalized lower wages, which led to equal labor unit costs in incumbent eastern sites as in Austria. In contrast, newly founded affiliates allowed for productivity increases. As a consequence, around the turn of the century, labor unit costs in new establishments in CEE amounted only to some forty percent of Austrian sites.[16] This makes clear that FDI provided for productive sites in CEE, which led to competitive networks of Austrian firms and Eastern affiliates.

In 2010, Austrian FDI employed 333,139 persons in CEE-12[17] and 478,116 persons in CEE 20.[18] Interestingly, the establishment of new sites was not merely oriented towards the employment of cheap unskilled labor. An important motive for FDI was the endowment of Eastern economies with skilled personnel, while this kind of human capital was scarce in Western Europe from the 1990s on. In Austria the share of high skilled labor force (tertiary education) amounted only to seven percent in 1998 and to eighteen percent in 2007, the respective percentages were fourteen and twenty-three in CEE. Due to the availability of highly qualified personnel, FDI did not lead to a kind of "Maquiladorization"[19] of CEE, but generated a substantial portion of jobs for skilled persons. While around 2000 Austrian firms

---

15. See for example Dalia Marin, *The Opening Up of Eastern Europe at 20 – Jobs, Skills and 'Reverse Maquiladoras' in Austria and Germany*, Munich Discussion Paper No. 2010-14 (September 2009); Ninan, Puck, "The internationalization of Austrian firms," 248; Österreichische Nationalbank, *Statistiken, Sonderheft, Direktinvestitionen 2010* (November 2012), 63.
16. Marin, *The Opening Up*, 6-8; Christian Bellak, Markus Leibrecht, Aleksander Riedl, "Labour costs and FDI flows into Central and Eastern European Countries: A survey of the literature and empirical evidence," *Structural Change and Economic Dynamics* 19 (2008): 17-37.
17. CEE-12 = Poland, Czech Republic, Slovakia, Hungary, Slovenia, the Baltic States, Cyprus, Malta, Romania, and Bulgaria.
18. CEE-20 = CEE-12 + Western Balkan and CIS-Europe. Österreichische Nationalbank, Statistiken, Table 13.1, 57.
19. A "Maquiladora" is a production site in a free trade zone in Mexico, where unskilled local laborers are employed. These factories usually pay low wages and offer poor working conditions and low job security.

with foreign affiliates employed an average share of 14.7% of persons with university and college graduation in their domestic sites, the share of highly qualified personnel was 16.3% in their CEE-branches. Obviously, a kind of "Reverse Maquiladorization" happened. As a complementary effect, Austria experienced a stable relation of wages for skilled and unskilled workers, while a pronounced exportation of unskilled jobs would have deteriorated this ratio.[20] In general, the development slightly stimulated labor demand in Austria[21] and led to more competitive structures of international division of labor, which strengthened sites in Austria and CEE.

The high percentage of qualified labor in the CEE affiliates came with a somewhat disappointing development of total demand for labor in the reform countries during the 1990s.

Table 4: Unemployment rates in selected countries 1995-2012

in % average	1995	2000	2005	2008	2009	2010	2011**	2012***
Bulgaria	16.5	16.9	10.1	5.6	6.8	10.2	11.2	12.0
Czech Republic	4.0	8.8	7.9	4.4	6.7	7.3	6.7	7.2
Hungary	10.3	6.4	7.2	7.8	10.0	11.2	10.9	10.9
Poland	13.3	16.1	17.8	7.1	8.2	9.6	9.7	10.2
Romania	n.a.	6.9	7.2	5.8	6.9	7.3	7.4	7.3
Slovakia	13.1	18.6	16.3	9.5	12.0	14.4	13.5	13.5
Slovenia	7.4	7.0	6.5	4.4	5.9	7.3	8.2	8.8

*Unemployed persons in % of labor force. Data refer to national labor force statistics definitions.
**Preliminary data
***Forecast
Source: *wiiw Handbook of Statistics 2006*, 19; *wiiw Handbook of Statistics 2012*, 5 and 23.

Only after the turn of the century a slight improvement of the job situation followed. In 2005, many countries still had two digit unemployment

---
20. Österreichische Nationalbank, Statistiken, Table 13.1, 19 and 22; CEE in this case is Hungary, Czech Republic, Poland, Slovakia, Slovenia, Lithuania and Estonia.
21. Fritz Breuss, *Ostöffnung, EU-Mitgliedschaft, Euro-Teilnahme und EU-Erweiterung – Wirtschaftliche Auswirkungen auf Österreich*, WIFO Working Papers 270 (Vienna: 2006); Martin Falk, Yvonne Wolfmayr, "Services and material outsourcing to low-wage countries and employment: Empirical evidence from EU countries," *Structural Change and Economic Dynamics* 19 (2008): 38-52; Wolfgang Koller, Robert Stehrer, *Trade Integration, Outsourcing and Employment in Austria: A Decomposition Approach*, wiiw Working Papers 56 (Vienna: wiiw, July 2009).

rates. Total employment in the ten new CEE EU member states did not regain the level of 1995 before 2008.[22] Furthermore, this sluggish demand for labor caused disappointing dynamics of wages for unskilled labor in CEE.[23]

Yet, foreign affiliates provided for strong impulses for the modernization and restructuring of the CEE economies. In 2009, some sixty percent of production and eighty percent of exports of countries like Czech Republic or Hungary were generated by foreign firms.[24]

An indicator for the strong commitment of Austrian investors to develop their affiliates was a high rate of re-investments of locally generated profits. While around 2000 approximately twenty percent of the profits generated by FDI in Western European countries were repatriated to Austria, the re-investments in CEE were significantly higher. Nearly ninety percent were re-invested in CEE5 and approximately sixty-nine percent in the other CEE countries.[25]

The structural change of Eastern economies after 1989 consisted of a modernization within all sectors of the economy and of a shift from secondary to tertiary businesses, which had been underdeveloped during the communist era. The structure of Austrian FDI shows that they have played an important role in this process.

Table 5: Structure of Austrian FDI (stocks) in December 2010 by economic activities

	EU-12	CEE-20	Total
	Market values in mn Euro		
Total FDI	45,411	6,0702	132,475
Food products etc.	1,919	2,034	2,561
Wood, paper	1,236	1,651	3,027
Chemical industry, oil	3,613	4,163	10,191

---

22. Landesmann, "Twenty Years of East-West Integration," 21.
23. Özlem Onaran, Engelbert Stockhammer, *The effect of FDI and foreign trade on wages in the Central and Eastern European Countries in the post-transition era: A sectorial analysis*, Department of Economics Working Paper Series 94, Vienna University of Economic and Business (2006).
24. *Der Standard*, June 8, 2011.
25. Other CEEC = Albania, Bosnia and Herzegovina, Bulgaria, Estonia, Croatia, Latvia, Lithuania, Moldavia, Romania, Russia, Serbia and Montenegro, Ukraine, and Belarus.

	EU-12	CEE-20	Total
	Market values in mn Euro		
Engineering*	1,513	1,860	7703
Construction	1,457	1,593	4055
Trade	4,196	5,135	19480
IT and communication	3,140	2,179	3817
Financial services	21,571	33,574	52285
Real estate business	2,474	2,473	4313
Others	4,292	6,040	25043
	Employed persons		
Total FDI	333,139	478,116	718,104
Food products etc.	10,019	10,882	14,557
Wood, paper	7,518	16,121	23,109
Chemical industry, oil	28,312	32,884	53,140
Engineering*	50,098	57,181	131,444
Construction	19,302	22,717	45,090
Trade	64,297	88,554	150,299
IT and communication	10,545	13,732	16,797
Financial services	88,045	161,902	175,972
Real estate business	638	611	919
Others	54,365	73,532	106,777

*Metal goods, electrical and optical equipment, mechanical engineering, vehicles.
Source: Österreichische Nationalbank, *Statistiken, Sonderheft Direktinvestitionen 2010* (November 2012), Table 13.1, 57.

Table 5 ascertains the strong weight of FDI in service sectors like trade and financial business. These two fields comprise more than fifty percent of all Austrian FDI in CEE and provide more than 250,000 jobs. Given the enormous amount of Austrian FDI, the following section can only go into a small sample of activities on the company level.

A big share of the jobs in chemical industries is located in affiliates of the Austrian oil and gas company, OMV. This company had already acted in the late 1960s as a pioneer of the European natural gas business when concluding the first gas import deal with the Soviet Union. Austria delivered steel tubes and know-how for pipelines, and the Soviets paid with natural gas. This was the beginning of huge export deals of Russian natural gas to Europe. As of the 1990s, OMV embarked on a strategy to become the leading oil and gas company in the Danube area. Between 2000 and 2007, OMV bought more than twenty percent of the Hungarian oil and gas company MOL, its main competitor in its core markets, and released a declaration of intent to merge with that firm. Yet, the Hungarian Parliament passed a law to prevent "strategic firms" from falling into foreign hands and OMV decided to sell its MOL stake in 2009, which at least brought a sixteen percent mark-up on the price which had been paid before. The most important acquisition of OMV in CEE came in December 2004. In this year the company acquired a controlling interest in Petrom, Romania's leading oil company. With this takeover OMV's workforce climbed from 6,137 in 2003 to 57,480, and daily oil and gas production increased from 120,000 to 340,000 boe (barrel of oil equivalents). Austrian FDI in Romania rose from 555 million Euros in 2002 to 4.8 billion in 2006 (Table 1). Over the years, the company also bought numerous gas stations in CEE and succeeded in gaining the leading position in its core market.[26]

Affiliates of Austrian technology firms employ some 57,000 persons in CEE. One of the biggest investors is Siemens Austria. This high tech company was an Austrian nationalized firm until the early 1970s, and was then bought by Siemens Germany. Siemens Austria holds operational responsibility for Siemens activities in nineteen CEE countries. In 2012 the company generated domestic sales of 2.9 billion Euros with 8,900 employees in Austria, while the CEE affiliates employed more than 36,000 persons and achieved sales of 8.2 billion Euros.[27]

Besides this big player, investments in CEE proved as a feasible growth strategy for numerous formerly small and medium sized enterprises in Austria. For firms in the automotive sector like Miba, for electronics companies like Kapsch Group or Fronius, and for many other Austrian high tech entrepreneurs, the foundation of new sites in CEE proved to be a worthwhile element of successful internationalization strategies.[28]

---

26. Alexander Smith, "OMV: A Case Study of an Austrian Global Player," in *Global Austria*, ed. Günter Bischof et al. (CAS 20) (New Orleans, Innsbruck: UNO Press/ IUP, 2011): 161-183.
27. Ferdinand Lacina et al., *Österreichische Industriegeschichte 1955-2005* (Vienna: Überreuter 2005): 60f and 224-230; Siemens Aktiengesellschaft Österreich, Facts and Figures 2012.
28. Lacina et al., Österreichische Industriegeschichte, 218; Andreas Resch, Reinhold Hofer, *Österreichische Innovationsgeschichte seit dem späten 19. Jahrhundert* (Innsbruck,

And yet, without a doubt, Viennese Banks can be seen as the most important Austrian investors in Eastern Europe.[29] In 2010 Austrian banks and insurance companies employed some 160,000 persons in CEE. During the 1990s structural change in the Austrian banking system was characterized by internationalization and mergers. Bank Austria, Raiffeisen Group (with Raiffeisen Bank International), and Erste Bank emerged as frontrunners in CEE. In 2000 Bank Austria was acquired by Bavarian Hypo Vereinsbank, which in turn was taken over by the Italian UniCredit Group. The Italian owner opted for a delisting of Bank Austria from the Vienna Stock Exchange. The business of Bank Austria now is recorded statistically as Italian, not as Austrian activity. Herbert Stepic, CEO of Raiffeisen Bank International (RBI) has accumulated experience in trading and banking in CEE since the 1970s.

During the 1990s, the big three banks acted successfully as "early movers," and they continued their expansive strategy until 2008. An important element of their strategies, to gain market shares was to buy additional local banks. Yet, competitive bids led to excessively increased purchase prices for some acquisitions after the turn of the century, which evolved into problematic investments during the recent crisis.

Especially in the directly neighboring Eastern countries, Austrian banks today hold the position of the market leaders. In 2002, approximately ten percent of the consolidated balance sheet of the Austrian banks was accounted for by transactions in CEE, and these ten percent generated twenty-two percent of the revenues and twenty-six percent of the earnings before taxes. Driver of high profitability were higher margins in the interest, provision, and trade business as well as the more favorable cost structure. While Austria was overbanked, and higher costs and stagnating business spoiled domestic earnings, the Eastern market allowed for expansion and profits. In turn, the banks invested in training of their new employees and built up the new structures with a mix of locals and expatriates.[30]

Vienna, Bolzano: StudienVerlag, 2010), 217f, 229-236, and 243-247.
29. The following section is taken for the most part from Andreas Resch, Dieter Stiefel, "Vienna: The Eventful History of a Financial Center," in *Global Austria*, ed. Günter Bischof et al. (CAS 20) (New Orleans, Innsbruck: UNO/ IUP Presse, 2011), 136-141; Marianne Kager, "A Banker's Take on Twenty Years of CEE Banking Sector Development", in *1989-2009. Twenty Years of East-West Integration: Hopes and Achievements, Focus on European Economic Integration, Special Issue 2009* (Vienna: Österreichische Nationalbank, 2009), 48-54; Stephan Barisitz, Sándor Gardó, "Banking Sector Transformation in CESEE," in ibid., 92-100; Gerald Krenn, Claus Puhr, "Austrian Banks' Activities in CESEE," in ibid., 101-108; Stephan Barisitz, *Banking in Central and Eastern Europe 1980-2006* (London et al.: Routledge, 2008).
30. Stephan Berchtold, Richard Pircher, and Christian Stadler, "Global integration versus

As a consequence of the financial crisis of 2008, Erste Bank and Raiffeisen participated in a supporting package by the Austrian government, and a program, named "Viennese Initiative" was launched which was borne by IMF, World Bank and EU-Institutions. Austrian banks committed themselves to continue their activities in CEE, and in turn they were supplied with cheap re-finance by the big international financial institutions.[31]

Austrian Banks plus Bank Austria have mounted a credit exposure of around 300 billion Euros in CEE, which approximately equals the Austrian GDP of one year or the cumulated balance of all Austrian banks.[32] In April 2009, the renowned American economist Paul Krugman was criticized for publicly doubting whether Austria could suffer a banking crisis and a consecutive fiscal crisis like Iceland and Ireland, due to this exposure. Above all, loans in foreign hard currencies appeared as a severe risk. When in January 2012 Standard & Poor's stripped Austria of its triple A rating, the reduced quality of eastern credits in foreign currency figured as important argument.[33] Fortunately, the real development did not match these worst case scenarios. Most of the loans were collateralized and Austrian banks endowed expensive reserves for the risks. In addition, it turned out that a high share of the foreign currency loans had been taken up by firms and households with income in foreign currency which acted as kind of automatic hedging of the exchange rate risk.[34] Yet, the rate of non-performing loans has risen substantially in a few CEE countries. During the second quarter of 2012 this rate remained at modest 5.3% in Slovakia and 6.1% in the Czech Republic while it moved up to 14.6% in Bulgaria, 15.4% in Hungary, and 21.6% in Romania.[35] This indicates that the Eastern exposure of Austrian banks must not be seen as one common lump risk but as a scenario, which is differentiated among the respective countries.

These different developments have left their traces in the balance sheets of the biggest Austrian banks during the recent years.

Andreas Treichl, CEO of Erste Bank, had to announce losses of 719 million Euros in 2011, the biggest losses in the entire company history. In 2012 the turn around succeeded. In this year the bank performed best in Austria, the Czech Republic, and Slovakia, while business remained in the

---

local adaptation: a case study of Austrian MNCs in Eastern Europe," *European Journal of International Management* 4, no. 5 (2010): 535-543.
31. *Der Standard*, Feb. 13, 2009; May 15, 2010.
32. *Die Presse*, May 30, 2012.
33. Ibid., Feb. 16, 2013; *Der Standard*, Jan. 14, 2012.
34. Raphael Auer et al., "Small man's carry trade in Central and Eastern Europe: Is he really taking the bet?," in *VoxEU.org*, <http.www.voxeu.org> (Jan. 29, 2009).
35. Österreichische Nationalbank, *Financial Stability Report* 24, December 2012, 17.

reds in Romania, Hungary, and Ukraine. In these three markets Erste Bank had already incurred most of the losses in 2011.[36]

Raiffeisen Bank International suffered the first negative quarter result in late 2012 since the outbreak of the international financial crisis. Quarter losses amounted to 117 million Euros but the company managed to produce a profit of 725 million Euros for the entire year 2012, after 968 million in 2011. The company had to write off 300 million Euro, most of it in Romania. Its Budapest branch had already produced losses in 2011 and during 2012 the fraction of nonperforming loans had risen. Furthermore, all foreign banks were negatively affected by the nationalist economic policy of the Hungarian Government, led by Victor Orban.[37]

Thanks to Bank Austria's profits of 247 million Euros in the second quarter of 2012, the UniCredit Group did not enter the reds. But the Austrian affiliate of the Italian Bank also had to digest some heavy losses in CEE. Above all, the acquisition of ATF-Bank in Kazakhstan in 2008 turned out as a source of heavy losses. Besides that, the company has reduced the number of jobs in Hungary and decided to concentrate on the core markets Russia, Turkey, Poland, and the Czech Republic.

Next to the big three, Österreichische Volksbanken AG (ÖVAG) has built up a group of affiliates in CEE. When the company had to be bolstered by the Austrian government due to heavy losses, the eastern activities were sold to the Russian Sberbank in February 2012.

Yet all in all, the Eastern affiliates of Austrian banks have proven worth their price, even during the most recent years. The value of their total assets in subsidiaries in EU-10 first shrank from 173 billion Euros on December 31, 2008 to 167 billion at the end of 2009. Since then they have recovered to 179 billion Euros as of June 2012. And in spite of several incidents which have caused heavy losses, the assets in total continued to contribute to the profitability of the Austrian banking sector. While the return on assets of the sector (on an unconsolidated basis) was zero in 2009, reached 0.4% in 2010, and a meager 0.1% in 2011 in Austria, the respective figures for assets in Central, Southern, and Eastern Europe were 0.7%, 0.8%, and 0.7%.[38] Profits in this region on average remained significantly higher than in Austria.

---

36. *Der Standard*, Jan. 16, 2013; Oct. 31, 2012; *Die Presse*, March 1, 2012; Feb. 28, 2013.
37. Sándor Richter, "Hungary: Sliding into recession," in *Fasting or Feasting? Europe – Old and New – at the Crossroads*, wiiw Current Analysis and Forecasts, 10 (July 2012), 67-70; *Die Presse*, Dec. 29, 2011; Jan. 4, 2012.
38. Österreichische Nationalbank, *Financial Stability Report* 24, 31 and tables A16, A24, and A25.

"The engagements of Austrian banks … in Central, Eastern, and Southeastern Europe were sustained despite some unfavorable legal amendments in those countries (e.g. in Hungary). Financial institutions have thus proved a factor of stability for those economies and maintain their engagements in order to support and leverage the still considerable growth potentials in those countries."[39]

Among Austrian insurance companies the Vienna Insurance Group (VIG) is the most successful player in CEE. This firm has begun investments in the early 1990s and now is market leader in Austria, the Czech Republic, Slovakia, Romania, Bulgaria, and Georgia, number two in Albania, and number four in Ukraine, Poland, Croatia, and Serbia, and has strong positions in Hungary and Macedonia.[40] In 2009 the profits were reduced as a consequence of the crisis,[41] but the company quickly recovered.[42] The total balance of the group has risen from 26.7 billion Euros in 2007 to 39.8 billion in 2011. In this year total earnings before taxes amounted to 559 million Euros of which 292 million were generated in Austria, 190 million in the Czech Republic, and fifty-seven million Euros in Slovakia.[43] In 2012 VIG achieved record profits of 585 million Euros before taxes.[44]

For all foreign investors active in CEE it was a difficult task to export products and processes, and simultaneously develop strong personal relationships and respect local cultures and traditions. Most useful strategies consisted in building in the younger generation in CEE, providing a wide range of training to enable the introduction of Western organizational practices and avoiding adaptations of imported Western products and process.[45]

For example, when the Austrian roof systems firm Bramac entered the Hungarian market as early as 1984, they hired former managers from VOEST Alpine, the Austrian nationalized steel company, who had already done a number of projects in CEE. Erste Bank set up local steering committees with locals and expatriates and Raiffeisen brought "senior staff for training to Austria, while lower levels receive training in their home

---

39. Resch, Stiefel, "Vienna," 141. See also Herbert Stepic, "Raiffeisen International: Bemerkungen eines Ostpioniers," in *Der "Ostfaktor": Österreichs Wirtschaft und die Ostöffnung 1989 bis 2009*, ed. Dieter Stiefel (Vienna: Böhlau, 2009), 47.
40. VIG, Konzernbericht 2011 / Vienna Insurance Group, Vienna 2011.
41. *Die Presse*, Jan. 26, 2010.
42. Ibid., Nov. 27, 2012.
43. VIG, Konzernbericht 2011, 14.
44. *Die Presse*, Jan. 24, 2013.
45. Berchtold, Pircher, Stadler, "Global integration," 524-549.

country." Personal relationships and cultural empathy foster the transfer of standardized organizational practices, while local adaptations of business processes threaten the value of the best practices. As a consequence, firms attempted a transfer of reporting systems, benchmarking, and business processes in an unadulterated fashion.[46]

Trade relations

As a consequence of the breakdown of the communist economies and of CMEA the CEE countries experienced a rapid reorientation of foreign trade from the early 1990s on. Sales in Eastern markets plummeted while the group of 15 EU countries became the most important trade partner.[47] Total exports of Austria's four Eastern neighbors plus Poland (EU-5) increased from forty-two billion Euros in 1993 to 361 billion in 2008. Germany absorbed some thirty percent, while Austria's share slightly diminished from 5.5% to 4.2%. Total EU-5 imports rose from fifty billion Euros in 1993 to 388 billion in 2008. Poland, Czech Republic, Slovakia, Hungary and Slovenia together purchased around thirty percent of their imports in Germany and Austria's contribution went down from 7.7% in 1993 to 4.9% in 2008. But still Austria's portion in foreign trade with these countries amounted to more than one sixth of that of Germany, while the size of the entire Austrian economy is just one tenth of Germany's. This reveals, that Austrian trade relations to CEE have maintained a more than proportional weight.

The EU-5 states, with exception of the Czech Republic, usually have recorded a negative trade balance. In 2008 their total deficit amounted to twenty-seven billion Euros, while the Czech Republic achieved a surplus of 3.2 billion. In this year, Austria recorded a surplus of 3.8 billion with regard to the group of 5 countries.

Trade development was strongly affected by the international financial crisis, which began in late 2008 and the consecutive economic downswing.

---

46. Ibid., 533-543.
47. The following figures were calculated on the basis of data given in *wiiw Handbook of Statistics*, CD edition, 2012.

Table 6: GDP, real change in percentage against preceding year

	1990	1995	2000	2007	2008	2009	2010	2011	2012*
Bulgaria	-9.1	2.9	5.4	6.2	6.2	-4.9	0.4	1.7	0.7
Czech Republic	-1.3	5.9	3.6	6.1	2.5	-4.2	2.5	1.9	-1.2
Hungary	-3.5	1.5	5.2	1.0	0.9	-6.7	1.3	1.6	-1.3
Poland	-11.6	7.0	4.2	6.8	5.1	1.7	3.9	4.3	2.3
Romania	-5.6	7.1	2.1	6.3	7.3	-7.1	-1.6	2.5	1
Slovakia	-2.5	5.8	2.0	10.4	6.2	-4.7	4.2	3.3	2.8
Slovenia	-4.7	4.1	4.1	6.8	3.7	-8.1	1.2	0.6	-2.0
EU-10	-6.3	5.4	4.0	6.4	4.3	-3.5	2.1	3.2	1.1
EU-25_27**	/	2.7	3.9	2.9	0.8	-4.2	2.1	1.6	-0.3

*Forecasts from summer 2012.
**Until 1995 without Bulgaria and Romania.
Source: *wiiw Handbook of Statistics*, various years.

After years of high growth rates, this crisis ushered in a severe recession. During all years reported in table 6, EU-10 countries in sum have outperformed the entire EU with respect to economic growth. Yet, some Eastern countries, like Romania, Hungary, Bulgaria, and Slovakia experienced a particularly hard backlash in 2009. In many countries, a second dip of the recession appeared in 2012.

The crisis forced the CEE states to balance their foreign trade and current account. To a certain degree, the reduction of current deficits was facilitated by the depreciation of local currencies in countries with flexible exchange rate regime. Furthermore, losses in real wages and increased unemployment improved the labor unit cost position.[48] After 2009, competitiveness trends and external demand for manufacturing exports have been acting as the most important factors for economic development of CEE.[49] A strategy of austerity in Western and Eastern Europe on the one hand has become necessary due to fiscal pressures, while on the other hand it has aggravated the slump.

As a consequence of the crisis, the total value of foreign trade of EU-5 plummeted from 2008 to 2009 by some twenty percent; exports and imports

---

48. Vasily Astrov, Mario Holzner, Sebastian Leitner, *Stabilisierung des verhaltenen Aufschwungs in den MOEL*, wiiw Forschungsarbeiten in deutscher Sprache (Vienna: wiiw, Juni 2011).
49. Leon Podkaminer et al., *Fasting or Feasting? Europe – Old and New – at the Crossroads*, wiiw Current Analyses and Forecasts 10 (Vienna: wiiw, July 2012).

contracted to 297 billion Euros. Thereafter, growth could be brought back again, and in 2011 total exports rose to 414 billion Euro, and total imports to 413 billion. Exports to Austria recovered from 12.4 billion Euros in 2009 to 18.6 billion in 2011 while EU-5-imports from the Alpine Republic at the same time developed from 14.3 to 18.2 billion Euro. As a consequence, Austria's trade balance has become slightly negative.

Austrian trade statistics show a complementary picture. Trade with Eastern neighbor states has gained weight after 1990. In 1993 (when Slovenia did not yet exist as a separate state and Czechoslovakia still was a common state), the portion of Poland, Hungary, and Czechoslovakia amounted to approximately five percent of Austria's foreign trade. Until 2008 the share of this region had risen to 12.1% of Austria's exports and ten percent of the imports. Until 2011 Poland, Hungary, the Czech Republic and Slovakia could slightly increase their quota as deliverers of Austrian imports to 10.8% while Austrian sales to the respective countries relatively declined to 11.8% of all exports. Austria's recorded trade surplus with the four countries diminished from 2.2 billion Euros in 2008 to 0.2 billion in 2011.

In 2010 Austria's most important foreign markets were Germany, Italy, Switzerland, USA and France. Ranks six, seven, nine, eleven, and thirteen were held by the Czech Republic, Hungary, Poland, Slovenia, and Slovakia.[50]

The total value of Austrian exports in 2011 amounted to 122 billion Euros and imports to 131 billion Euros.[51] The structures of imports and exports between Austria and CEE neighbors reveal a structural modernization of trade relations.

---

50. Österreichs Außenwirtschaft 2010, ed. by Kompetenzzentrum Forschungsschwerpunkt Internationale Wirtschaft (FIW) (Vienna: Dec. 2010), 308.
51. Statistik Austria, *Der Außenhandel Österreichs, Gesamtjahr, Serie 2, Spezialhandel nach SITC-revised 4* (Vienna: Statistik Austria, 2012), Table 5.

Chart 3: Structure of Austrian Foreign Trade with Czechoslovakia, Hungary and Poland in 1980, in mn Euro

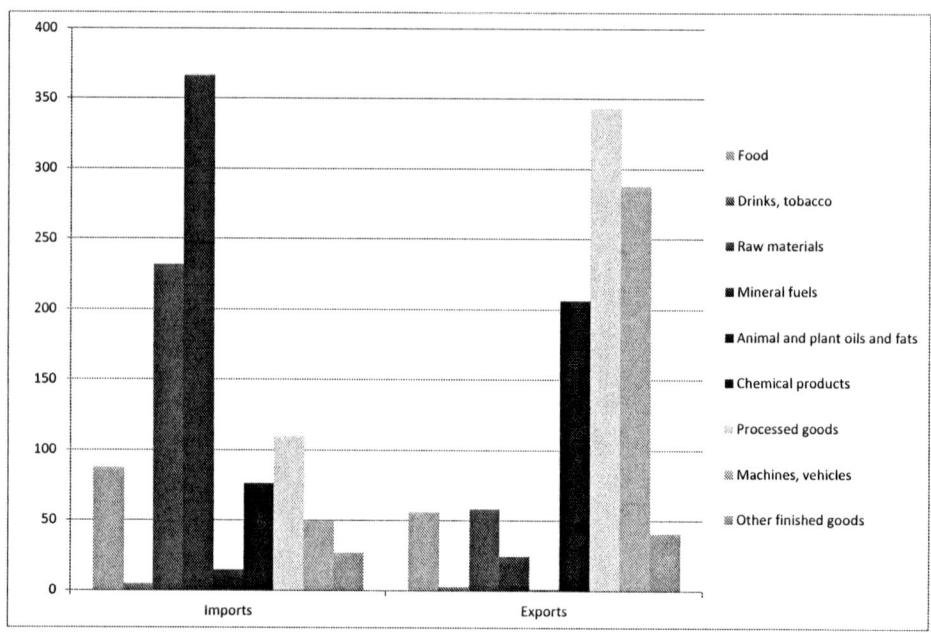

Source: Statistik Austria, *Der Außenhandel Österreichs, Gesamtjahr, Serie 2, Spezialhandel nach SITC-revised 3* (Vienna: Österreichisches Statistisches Zentralamt, 1981), Table 5.

Until the 1980s traditional complementary trade has dominated trade relations between Austria and CEE.[52] In 1980, still raw materials and mineral fuels made up for roughly sixty percent of exports from Czechoslovakia, Hungary, and Poland to Austria, while in the other direction among Austrian deliveries, chemical goods, processed goods, and machines and vehicles had a portion of more than seventy percent.

---

52. Resch, "Der Osthandel," 550-553.

Chart 3: Structure of Austrian Foreign Trade with the Czech Republic, Slovakia, Hungary and Poland in 2011, in mn Euro

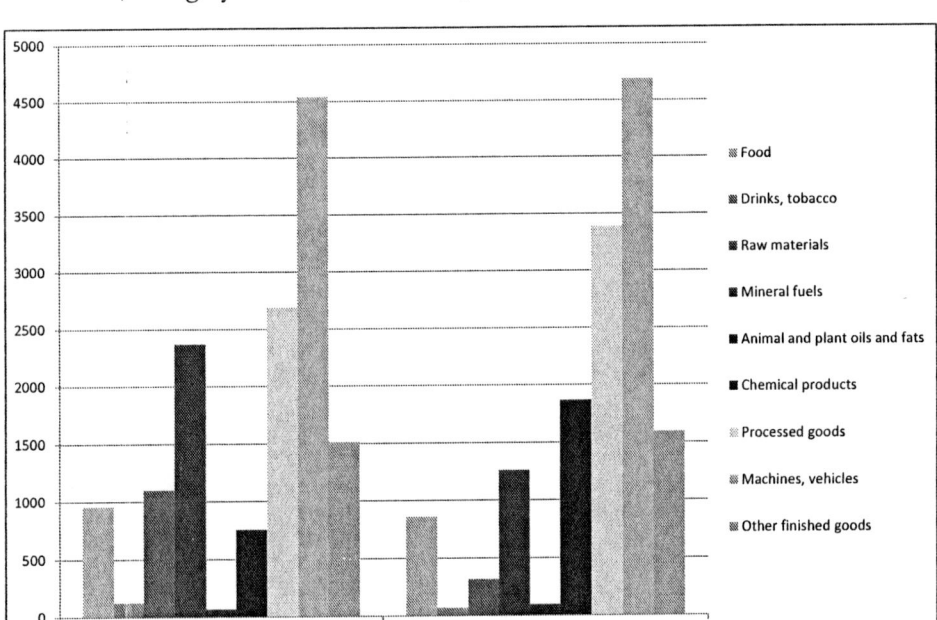

Source: Statistik Austria, *Der Außenhandel Österreichs, Gesamtjahr, Serie 2, Spezialhandel nach SITC-revised 4* (Vienna: Statistik Austria, 2012), Table 5.

Recent trade statistics convincingly show a radically changed pattern. From 1980 to 2011 the nominal value of foreign trade of Austria with the Czech Republic, Slovakia, Hungary, and Poland has increased more than tenfold. Until 2011, the import share of processed goods, machines and vehicles, and other finished goods has risen to sixty-one percent which nearly equals the weight of these goods among Austrian exports (sixty-six percent) to the four countries mentioned above. This structure of mutual trade shows a high level of inter-industry relations. With no doubt, the economic changes since the 1990s have ended the old scheme of exchanging Eastern primary goods for more sophisticated goods and provided for more complex relations of deliveries in cross border chains of creation of value.

On the company level during the recent decades foreign trade relations between Austria and CEE have been influenced by FDI and activities of numerous trading firms. The number of Austrian exporting firms has grown by a factor of five between 1995 and 2009 to 38,000.[53]

Foreign trade has emerged together with an increasing amount of FDI. Since around fifty percent of Austrian FDI have been focused in CEE, their development more than proportionally shapes the economic relations between Austria and Eastern Europe.

Roughly a quarter of Austrian exports and nearly a fifth of all imports are carried out by multinational firms with active FDI. Intra firm trade of industrial multinationals produces nearly eight percent of this trade. These developments have allowed for an increasing vertical integration of international groups of production sites.[54] As a consequence, more effective cross-border structures with competitive labor unit costs have emerged. This has provided for gains of market shares of Austria and the CEE region in world trade. Austria, for example, has increased her fraction in worldwide OECD exports from 1.5% in 1994 by forty percent to 2.1% in 2007.[55]

Apart from industrial firms, many commercial enterprises have seized the opportunity, to enter the growing Eastern markets. As mentioned above, affiliates of Austrian trading establishments in CEE have employed nearly 90,000 persons in 2010. For example, food store chains, furniture traders and DIY superstores have founded numerous branches in the region. The German REWE Group is active in Italy, Bulgaria, Croatia, Romania, Russia, Slovakia, Czech Republic, and Ukraine via Austria; the Austrian SPAR Group first began internationalization in 1990 with an affiliate in Switzerland. Shops in Italy, Slovenia, Hungary, the Czech Republic, and Croatia followed. In a similar manner, Austrian furniture groups like XXXLutz and Kika/Leiner have expanded towards CEE. The Austrian DYS superstore chain BauMax today is active in eight foreign countries, namely Slovakia, Hungary, Czech Republic, Slovenia, Croatia, Romania, Bulgaria, and Turkey.[56] Porsche Holding, Austria's largest car dealer, founded her first affiliate in Hungary in 1990. During the following years many other CEE countries followed, among others Bulgaria, Czech Republic, Croatia, Poland, Slovakia, and Slovenia. In 2010 the sales of the company amounted to 12.8 billion Euros of which eight billion were

---

53. Bundesministerium für Wirtschaft, Familie und Jugend, *Österreichs Außenwirtschaft 2012* (Vienna 2012), 6.
54. Wilfried Altzinger, *Österreichs Multinationale Unternehmen (MNUs) und deren konzernexterner und interner Handel*, Arbeitspapier für den "Forschungsschwerpunkt Internationale Wirtschaft (FIW), Arbeitspaket 2: Direktinvestitionen," FIW Studie Nr. 023 (June 2008).
55. Wilfried Altzinger, "Österreichs Wirtschaftsbeziehungen mit Mittel- und Osteuropa. Vom 'Goldenen Osten' zum Waterloo 2009?," *Kurswechsel* (4/2008): 33-34.
56. Günter Chaloupek et al., *Österreichische Handelsgeschichte* (Vienna: Styria, 2012), 275 f.

generated in foreign markets.⁵⁷

After years of successful expansion, the recession in 2009 has produced severe problems for many commercial enterprises. While the food store chains are still doing well, other sectors ran into trouble. The furniture chains suffered losses in 2011 and/or 2012 but intend to keep most of their shops in operation. The BauMax Company came close to a financial breakdown after having incurred losses of fifty-seven million Euros in 2011. The owner family had to invest more than fifty million Euro, and the banks agreed to grant extended loans to save the firm. Massive cost reductions seem necessary.⁵⁸ The Austrian shoe shop chain Leder & Schuh, which runs Humanic and Jello shops, was an early mover in CEE from 1991 onward. During the recent years, the group has achieved one quarter of total sales in the Eastern countries. After heavy losses disinvestments often follow. All Humanic shops in Poland, nine shops in Hungary and most shops in Croatia and Slovenia are to be closed.⁵⁹

Another field which has been hit hard by the recent recessions is the export of Austrian construction services. Since the 1990s, several Austrian firms have embarked on strategies of growth and internationalization. In this course, increased activities in CEE have played an important role. As is shown in table 5, Austrian FDI in 2010 employed 22,717 construction workers in the entire region. The formerly successful Maculan group broke down in the 1990s, due to massive losses in Eastern Germany. The leading Austrian companies, Strabag and Porr, have incurred some problems in CEE, as a result of diminishing demand and delayed payments. Most of all, the Alpine construction firm, which was acquired by the Spanish FCC group, suffered near bankruptcy around the turn from 2012 to 2013. The company had acquired high market shares by cheap offers, which resulted in numerous loss making projects. In March 2013, the owner group, together with forty-eight involved banks and insurances, agreed on a voluminous bailout package. At this moment the company, which had gotten close to insolvency, owed more than 500 million Euros to the banks.⁶⁰

Yet, while several stories of single firms reveal the depth of the crisis and while many companies are forced to massive disinvestments, in general, Austrian commercial enterprises try to persevere, in order to be ready for the

---

57. Chaloupek et al., *Österreichische Handelsgeschichte*, 188; <http://www.porsche-holding.com> (March 10, 2013).
58. *Die Presse*, Dec. 20, 2012; Bernhard Ecker, "Handel: Die große Flucht aus dem Osten," *format* (Dec. 28, 2012).
59. Ecker, "Die große Flucht."
60. *Der Standard*, March 4, 2013.

next phase of economic recovery and to prove their credible commitment as players in CEE. Experts agree that for players who outlast the present crisis, CEE, in the medium and long run, still holds an enormous potential for growth.

Résumé

The economic relations between Austria and CEE show that history matters. During the first years after 1989, activities of Austrian firms benefitted from traditional relations, cultural nearness, and personal experience of Austrian managers in Eastern Europe. As a consequence, FDI and foreign trade gained enormous significance during the first phase of the reform process and could maintain more than proportional shares since then.

FDI have provided for the emergence of productive networks in Austria and CEE, which contributed to economic growth, thanks to competitive labor unit costs and know-how intensive production. All in all, these developments have created jobs in Austria and CEE as well. The most important motive for FDI was to tap new growing markets. In contrast, investments were not primarily oriented towards the exploitation of cheap labor, but created a high share of jobs for highly skilled persons. Consequently, they did not result in a kind of "Maquiladorization." Yet, in the Eastern states demand for labor has grown at subdued rates, which lead to somewhat disappointing rises of wages.

FDI have supported the emergence of modern productive industries and the sectorial shift from secondary to service sectors in the reform countries. The highest share of jobs in Austrian FDI is recorded in the financial and trade sector.

In Austria, FDI provided for some job losses towards CEE, but at the same time new jobs were created or existing jobs secured, thanks to the emergence of competitive cross border networks and new growth opportunities. Altogether, FDI have slightly fostered domestic labor demand. The fact that not primarily low skill jobs have been exported has stabilized the wage relation between skilled and unskilled employees. Yet, the opportunity of the transfer of jobs has provided for wage restraints.

The development of FDI was complemented by increasing trade relations. Austria had maintained intensive trade with CEE during the communist era. After 1989, further growth followed. The pattern of trade flows has changed, from a mutual exchange of complementary goods to complex inter-industry trade. Thanks to productive networks, the entire region has gained shares in world trade.

The economic relations between Austria and CEE were strongly affected by the economic crisis, which followed the international financial crisis in 2008.

The necessity for austerity politics, tensions in the financial sector, increases in bankruptcy rates etc., led to a severe recession in 2009. Exports as well as internal demand plummeted in this year. Since then, a subdued recovery has begun, but in 2012 a second dip of recession was recorded. During this crisis Austria has more or less maintained her role in the CEE economies. Austrian banks had to digest heavy losses in some EU-10 countries. Yet, the Eastern exposure has not resulted as one single lump risk. Instead, the situation has to be perceived country to country. In spite of losses and risks, the leading banks have proved their commitment to stay on site and to be ready to participate in future developments. Commercial enterprises and construction firms have experienced differentiated consequences. While food store chains managed fairly well, DYS superstores and one chain of shoe shops were badly hit. Yet, most of the companies in these sectors are trying to continue their activities.

All in all, the cross border economic structures between Austria and CEE have suffered with the recent crisis, but they appear to be sufficiently intact to successfully participate in the next phases of growth in Central and Eastern Europe. Undoubtedly, this region still has potential for above average growth, thanks to a continuation of its catching up process with respect to Western Europe.

Foreign Policy and Memory

Historical Memory and the Debate about the *Vertreibung* Museum

Norman M. Naimark

The historical memory of the Second World War and its aftermath influences the politics and societies of Central Europe in ways that continue to baffle observers, both domestic and foreign.[1] The more that a new postpostwar period—to use Tony Judt's definitions from his important book, *Postwar*—dominates the continent, the more arcane and cranky seem the disputes about history from the now distant past, remembered literally by fewer and fewer citizens.[2] Battlefields have long since been covered over with suburban developments and shopping malls, and cities are fully rebuilt with hardly a sign of the catastrophes that befell them, except for the scattered memorials for school children, tourists, Jewish associations, and others that blend easily into the urban landscape.[3] The emergence of the European Union as a powerful motor for economic development and transnational interchange, of the easy movement of labor and capital between European neighbors, especially given EU expansion into East Central Europe in 2004, also makes historical disputes between Central European nations grounded in a distant war seem anachronistic and even silly.

In Germany, which was responsible for so much destruction of peoples and societies during the war, efforts to come to terms with the past, known by the misnomer, *Vergangenheitsbewältigung*, dominated intellectual and academic life for the last three decades of the twentieth century, producing a literary, historiographical, and memorial landscape of unparalleled intensity and subtlety. Despite the "divided memories" that characterized the

---

1. Istvan Rev appropriately notes that historical memory and history are two separate, if interrelated ways of thinking about the past. "Historical memory operates in the present; it maintains that the past is not past but an aspect of the present that can and should be redressed. Historical memory craves for justice: either legal or moral or both. Historical memory is an inherently moralizing attitude to the events of the past." Istvan Rev, "The Man in the White Raincoat," in *Past for the Eyes: East European Representations of Communism in Cinema and Museums after 1989*, ed. Oksana Sarkisova and Peter Apor (Budapest: CEU Press, 2008), 34.
2. Tony Judt, *Postwar: A History of Europe Since 1945* (New York: Penguin, 2005), 3, 10.
3. Heidemarie Uhl, "Schuldgedächtnis und Erinnerungsbegehren: Thesen zur europäischen Erinnerungskultur," in *Transit: Europäische Revue* 21 (2000): 6-22.

Federal Republic's and the German Democratic Republic's understanding of German culpability for Nazi genocide and aggression, both countries devoted considerable time and resources to ensuring that Germans not make excuses for their behavior.[4] Too many Austrians accepted the myth of being the "first victim" of Nazism until the late 1980s, when the Waldheim affair burst the bubble of Austrian innocence and highlighted the necessity of coming to terms with Austrian complicity in Nazi aggression and genocide.[5] At this point, a reasonably coherent and fair narrative of German and Austrian historical responsibility for the depredations of World War II infuse the intellectual life of German and Austrian society and have made their way into school textbooks and local politics.[6]

There is much to admire in the Germans' and now Austrians' attempts to come to terms with their common Nazi past. Yet the point also needs to be underlined that these efforts have been prompted by more than issues of conscience, historical memory, and generational change within these societies. The former victims of Nazi aggression and genocide have been over time increasingly vociferous in demanding recognition and compensation. The expansion of the European Union, while having brought nations closer together, prompted myriad points of contact and interchange, and fostered common European values and views of the past, has also provoked historical disputes and controversies. The European Union "sanctions" imposed against Austria at the beginning of 2000, as a result of the inclusion in the government of the right-wing populist Jörg Haider's Austrian Freedom Party (FPÖ), illustrate this interaction between domestic trends in dealing with the past and the pressure of international, in this case European, public opinion and law in the pursuit of historical justice.

The role of the victim nations of Central Europe in remembering World War II—in particular the Poles and the Czechs—is in many ways more complicated than that of the perpetrators. First of all, both societies got a much later start than the Germans and even Austrians in dealing with an honest and fair portrayal of the war. For decades after their "liberation" by the Soviet Union, the Poles' own immense suffering during the war was the

---

4. See Jeffrey Herf, *Divided Memory: The Nazi Past in the two Germanys* (Cambridge, MA.: Harvard University Press, 1997).
5. Gerhard Botz, Gerald Sprengnagel, ed., *Kontroversen um Österreichs Zeitgeschichte: Verdrängte Vergangenheit, Österreich-Identität, Waldheim, und die Historiker*, 2nd edition (Frankfurt: Campus, 2008).
6. Wolfgang Mueller notes that the Austrians do a much better job of dealing with the Nazi past than with the Stalinist one. See Wolfgang Mueller, "Memories of Stalinism: The Case of Austria," Institute für die Wissenschaften vom Menschen (2009): 1-3; and his "Stalinismus und europäisches Gedächtnis," *Transit: Europäische Revue* 38 (2009): 96-108.

only legitimate subject for discussion and commemoration, which suited the pro-Soviet and anti-German purposes of the Communist-dominated government. This was much the same in Communist Czechoslovakia, though the view of Czech victimization by the Nazis needs to be tempered by the wartime realities of a relatively healthy economy and a mostly complacent Czech population. In neither Poland nor Czechoslovakia was the fate of the Jews of much interest, either during or after the war. Polish martyrdom could only be shared publicly with the glorious exploits of the Red Army. Much was made of the small Czech resistance and the brotherhood of arms between the Czech underground and the Red Army. There was little talk of extensive Czech collaboration, while in Poland, complicity with the German occupation and the indifference among the majority to the murder of the Jews—the many instances when survival trumped morality—were wartime phantoms that were pushed into a deep psychological freezer. This was easier to do because the Poles had to contend with an unpopular Communist government, supported by the hated Russians. In both Poland and Czechoslovakia, the Communist governments, in search of legitimacy and support, were not interested in pointing out the culpability of Poles and Czechs for their own suffering, especially when it did not suit their political needs.[7]

Things began to change only in the 1980s, when the "Solidarity" movement inspired a fresh reading of the Polish past, one that challenged party-supported orthodoxies. Old mythologies about unalloyed Polish martyrdom were challenged and a series of important articles called into question the behavior of some Poles in connection with their Jewish neighbors.[8] On a smaller scale and in a narrower group of interlocutors, Czech dissidents, especially those associated with Charter 77, began to question the exclusive narrative of Czech victimhood, especially in connection with the expulsion of the German population of Czechoslovakia at the end of the war and beginning of the peace.[9] With the fall of Communism in both countries, the opportunities for researching and discussing wartime events broadened considerably. The floodgates opened for the kinds of public and

---

7. See my essay, "Die 'Killing Fields' des Ostens und Europas geteilte Erinnerung," *Transit: Europäische Revue* 30 (2005/2006): 57-70.
8. Most important was Jan Blonski's famous 1987 essay, "The Poor Poles Look at the Ghetto," which provoked a series of defensive protests, but also affirmations of Polish culpability and guilt in identifying and turning over Jews to the Nazi authorities. See Antony Polonsky, ed., *"My Brothers Keeper": Recent Polish Debates on the Holocaust* (London: Routledge, 1980).
9. See Bradley F. Abrams, "Morality, Wisdom and Revision: The Czech Opposition in the 1970s and the Expulsion of the Sudeten Germans," *East European Politics and Societies* 9, no. 2 (Spring 1995): 234-55.

academic debates that the Austrians and especially Germans had been involved in for decades.

The main blow in Poland came from the outside, when, in 2001, the Polish-American scholar, Jan Tomasz Gross, published his devastating study of the July 1941 massacre at Jedwabne, a small town in the Bialystok region. Not only were the Poles bystanders and even sometimes informers in connection with the Holocaust, they also sometimes brutally murdered Jews themselves. Gross's book provoked a wave of protests and criticism when it appeared in Poland. To the Poles' credit, many took his work seriously and began investigating the many similar episodes of mass killing involving Polish perpetrators. This was by no means an easy lesson for Poles to absorb. Polish-Jewish relations have been plagued with problems of Polish defensiveness and denial for a very long time indeed. Jewish anti-Polish prejudices have not helped. In this context, the strides made by the Poles in recognizing their complicity in the Holocaust over the past dozen years have been remarkable.[10] Significantly, this makes the Polish-German dialogue about wartime issues much more fruitful.

The Issue of *Vertreibung* (Forced Deportations)

Despite occasional setbacks and nasty polemics from the Right, the new openness in Poland to discussion of Polish-Jewish relations during the war serves the cause of bringing the country into synchronization with the Poles' new partners in the European Union. But just as in Germany, it has proven easier for the Poles to deal more straightforwardly with the destruction of the European Jews than it has with the expulsion of the Germans. Even after the fall of Communism, scholars and publicists came around to the issue of the German deportations more slowly and deliberately. Still, a number of excellent studies were published on the subject. Polish scholars enthusiastically embraced a German-Polish commission on the expulsion of the Germans. The report of the commission made great strides in constructing a common narrative of the *Vertreibung* (*wypędzenie* in Polish) that emphasized the crimes of the Nazis in Poland but also the harsh fate of the expellees at the hands of the Poles.[11] The joint publication of documents from the Polish archives has been one of the most important results of

---

10. Antony Polonsky and Joanna Michlic, ed., *The Neighbors Respond: The Controversy over the Jedwabne Massacre in Poland* (Princeton: Princeton University Press, 2004). For an understanding of continuing "denial," see Joanna Michlic, *Poland's Threatening Other: The Image of the Jew from 1880 to the Present* (Lincoln: University of Nebraska Press, 2006).
11. Wlodzimierz Borodziej, Artur Hajnicz, *Kompleks wypedzenia* (Krakow: Znak, 1998).

the new cooperation.¹² Polish textbooks were also rewritten to include the forced deportation of the Germans, and numerous bi-national conferences and symposia were held on the subject. In both Germany and Poland, there is an increasing scholarly sophistication and subtlety in writing about the deportations.[13]

At the same time that significant scholarly cooperation was creating a new basis for common discussions of the expulsions, "ethnic cleansing" in the Balkans played an important role in refocusing European public opinion on the evils of forced deportation. Media images of victims from Bosnia in 1992-95 and again from Kosovo in 1999 provided the German expellee association, the *Bund der Vertriebenen* (BdV), long known for its right-wing and revisionist views, with the opportunity to bring its particular interpretations of the history of German expellees to the attention of the press and government. Social Democratic Party (SPD) politician Markus Meckel, among others, believes that plans in the late 1990s for the building of the Holocaust Memorial near the Brandenburg gate also provided Erika Steinbach, Christian-democratic member of the Bundestag and president of the BdV, with the impetus to seek a memorial for German victims of forced deportation.[14]

The growing scholarly consensus in Poland and Germany about the causes, the costs, and the consequences of the *Vertreibung* masked deep unease in both Poland and Germany about the legitimacy of placing German suffering at the center of any historical understanding of World War II. The recently deceased Marek Edelman—veteran of the Warsaw Ghetto uprising—stated many Poles' views unambiguously: the Germans were the hangmen and the Poles were the victims, and there was nothing more to be said about German suffering.[15] Many Germans, fearful of the "relativization" of German responsibility for the war and Holocaust, think

---

12. Wlodzimierz Borodziej, Hans Lemberg, ed., *"Unsere Heimat ist uns ein fremdes Land geworden..." Die Deutschen östlich von Oder und Neiße 1945-1950: Dokumente aus polnischen Archiven*, 4 volumes (Marburg: Herder Institut, 2000).
13. There are too many excellent studies on various aspects of the forced deportations to be mentioned. Two stand out in my opinion: Witold Sienkiewicz, Grzegorz Hryciuk, ed., *Wysiedlenia wypedzenie i ucieczki 1939-1959: Atlas ziem Polski. Polacy, Zydzi, Niemcy, Ukraincy* (Warsaw: Demart S.A., 2008), and Gregor Thum, *Die fremde Stadt Breslau 1945* (Berlin: Siedler, 2003).
14. <http://www.dialogonline.org/Meckel-D.htm, 2>
15. See the translation of an extensive interview with Edelman in Tygodnik Powszechny, August 17, 2003 <http://www.freewebs.com/liberte-toujours/ZR%20-%20Interview%20Edelmann.pdf> (Dec. 10, 2010). Here Edelman states: "I don't like it when they [the Germans] portray themselves as victims, otherwise I would have to understand myself as a hang-man. The situation is reversed: they are my hangmen. For the same reason, the building of a Vertreibung center would contribute to an injustice."

the same. When, in 2000, Erika Steinbach proposed a fundraising campaign for building a museum in Berlin against forced deportations (Zentrum gegen Vertreibungen) to commemorate and document the *Vertreibung*, but also comparable events in twentieth-century Europe, the press in Poland and Germany raised a storm of protest. Before her visit to Poland in the fall of 2003, Steinbach was portrayed on the front of the popular Polish magazine, *Wprost* (August 17, 2003), as a Nazi leather-jacketed dominatrix riding on the back of her Trojan Horse, Chancellor Gerhard Schröder. There were counter-proposals from Germans (like Markus Meckel from the SPD) and "liberal" Poles (Adam Michnik, Adam Krzemiński, and Włodzimierz Borodziej) to build an all-European museum on forced deportation in Wroclaw (Breslau).[16] The "Copernicus Group," an association of Polish and German scholars and public figures suggested in a December 2003 report locating the center in Görlitz/Zgorzelec on the Polish-German border. Others suggested Strasbourg as the best site.

Meanwhile, a parallel initiative in 2003 came primarily from academic circles and cultural officials of the "Visegrad plus two" group, supported by resolutions of the Parliamentary Assembly of the Council of Europe.[17] This involved setting up a "European Network of Memory and Solidarity" that would integrate projects of research institutes and social organizations interested in developing an all-European approach to the history of ethnic cleansing, genocide, mass killing, and oppression in the region. Between the spring of 2004 and the early fall of 2005, the cultural ministers of Germany, Poland, Slovakia, and Hungary with the intermittent and wary participation of the Czechs and Austrians—worked on an alternative process to the Berlin Vertreibung museum idea, which both the Czech and Polish governments rejected out of hand. "The objective of the network," stated a resolution from the February 2005 founding meeting in Warsaw, "is the analysis, the documentation, and the dissemination of the history of the twentieth century, a century of wars, totalitarian dictatorships, and of the suffering of civilian populations […]." The idea was to develop a common history of mass killing and deportation and absorb it into a single European narrative of past, present, and future. The purpose of the network, as the then Cultural Secretary Christina Weiss put it in Warsaw, is "to broaden the narrow national view of the past into a European viewpoint."[18]

---

16. Piotr Madajczyk, "The Centre against Expulsions vs. Polish-German Relations," *The Polish Foreign Affairs Digest*, vol. 4, no. 2 (11) (2004): 43-78.
17. Stefan Troebst, ed., *Vertreibungsdiskurs und europäische Erinnerungskultur: Deutsch-polnische Initiativen zur Institutionalisierung. Eine Dokumentation* (Osnabrück: fibre Verlag, 2006), 22.
18. See Naimark, "Die 'Killing Fields' des Ostens," 67.

The Czechs proved unwilling to participate in any joint efforts that would, in their view, legitimate German claims that they were illegally expelled from Czechoslovakia after the war. They were incensed that the Association of Expellees and some German politicians, especially from the Christian Social Union (CSU) in Bavaria, had attempted to hold up Czech admission into the European Union until Prague abolished the so-called Beneš decrees, a series of ninety or so administrative regulations dating from the immediate postwar period that legitimated the expulsion and expropriation of roughly three million Sudeten Germans. The Czech government was annoyed by the claims of the Sudeten Germans. Prime Minister Vaclav Klaus quipped that the Beneš decrees should accompany the Czech accession to the EU.[19] In the spring of 1999 and 2000, some Austrian right-wing politicians also sought to use the imminent entrance of the Czech Republic into the European Union as a way to gain recognition of the expulsion of Austrians from Czechoslovakia at the same time. Roughly a million German-speaking refugees ended up in Austria, of whom only 320,000 could stay. One hundred forty thousand of these were the so-called Donauschwaben from former Yugoslavia and Hungary; 130,000 were so-called "Altösterreicher" from southern Bohemia, Moravia, and the Sudetenland.[20] Efforts to find some political traction in Austria on the *Vertriebene* issue came to naught, especially given the vehement Czech reaction. Meanwhile, the Austrian government showed little interest in inserting itself into the arguments between the Germans and the Czechs and Poles about how to deal with the *Vertreibung* controversy.

The change in government in Berlin in the fall of 2005 from the SPD-Green coalition to the Grand Coalition led by the CDU's Angela Merkel gave a shot in the arm to Erika Steinbach's BdV museum project. The politics of the museum debate were never so clear when, in the summer of 2006, the BdV's much-criticized traveling exhibit, "Erzwungene Wege: Flucht und Vertreibung im Europa des 20. Jahrhunderts" (Forced Paths: Flight and Forced Deportation in Europe in the Twentieth Century), was placed in Berlin in the Kronprinzessinenpalais right across the main Berlin avenue, Unter den Linden, from the German Historical Museum, which had sponsored a rival exhibit titled "Flucht, Vertreibung, Integration" (Flight, Forced Deportation, and Integration).[21] The exhibit of the highly respected and well-funded state museum, unlike the financially more modest BdV

---

19. Madajczyk, "The Centre against Expulsions," 54.
20. Manfried Rauchensteiner, *Das Neue Österreich: Die Ausstellung zum Staatsvertragsjubiläum 1955/2005* (Vienna: Österreichische Galerie, 2005), 121.
21. See *Erzwungene Wege: Flucht und Vertreibung im Europa des 20. Jahrhunderts* (Berlin: Zentrum gegen Vertreibungen, 2006), and *Flucht, Vertreibung, Integration: Material zur Ausstellung* (Berlin: Deutsches Historisches Museum, 2006).

exhibit, avoided comparative issues, and focused instead on the long-term history of Germans in Eastern Europe and the integration of the expellees into German society, rather than on their actual expulsion. The German Historical Museum exhibit, set up initially at Bonn's Haus der Geschichte at the end of 2005, had won considerable praise from historians and center and left politicians. It did not try to compare the German expulsions to similar nasty episodes in European history and said very little about Polish and Czech culpability for the expulsions. In short, the "Sonderweg" of German evil was underlined; the basic story was that Germans paid for German aggression.

The Poles, not unexpectedly, were very critical of the BdV exhibit and of the Germans in general for allowing the exhibit to be housed in a central location in Berlin. Complicating Polish reactions was the election in the fall of 2005 of a right-wing populist government of the Kaczyński brothers (Jarosław and Lech). Their nationalism and barely concealed contempt for German progressive culture made both formal and informal Polish-German relations much more difficult. In an interview with *Der Spiegel* (March 6, 2006), Polish President Lech Kaczyński stated that he was against any Center against Vertreibungen in Berlin because it would inevitably lead to "relativizing" German guilt for what happened between 1939 and 1945.[22] There was good reason to worry about a crisis in Polish-German relations, as members of the Polish government and public opinion circles attacked the museum idea, threatening to set up counter-exhibits in Warsaw, while collecting materials for demanding additional indemnities for the war and occupation from the German government. Even the much more modest and moderate scholarly Network was caught up in the bad atmosphere of relations between Warsaw and Berlin.

In the coalition agreement between the CDU, CSU, and SPD of November 11, 2005, the arguments about the museum and the Network were represented by compromise language: "The Coalition commits itself to the societal, as well as historical, coming to terms with [*Aufarbeitung*] forced migration, flight and forced deportation. In the spirit of reconciliation, we want to have in Berlin a visible sign [*ein sichtbares Zeichen*], in order—in connection with the European Network of Memory and Solidarity and in addition to the participating countries of Poland, Hungary and Slovakia [note the absence of the Czech Republic and Austria]—to remember the injustice of forced deportations and to proscribe forced deportations forever."[23] But the SPD and the CDU had different ideas in mind, while

---

22. Lech Kaczynski interview in *Der Spiegel*, reproduced in Troebst, ed., *Vertreibungsdiskurs und europäische Erinnerungskultur*, 243.
23. "Die Koalition bekennt sich zur gesellschaftlichen wie historischen Aufarbeitung von Zwangsmigration, Flucht und Vertreibung. Wir wollen im Geist der Versöhnung auch in

agreeing that the sensitive issues of the *Vertreibung* should be properly explored. Chancellor Merkel proposed going ahead with the building of a new exhibit in the "Deutsches Haus" outside the center of Berlin that would, in the best of circumstances, combine elements of the two exhibits. The SPD, on the other hand, believed that the original Bonn exhibit, with its exclusive attention to the German part of the story, and one that would be least offensive to the Poles and Czechs, should be the core of that effort.

Throughout 2006 and most of 2007, relations between Warsaw and Berlin remained prickly, in good measure because of the reverberations from the *Vertreibung* Museum issue. The Polish press reacted to every Steinbach speech and every meeting of the BdV as if the old revanchist Germans of the 1950s were in power.[24] The Germans interested in the museum project showed signs of being weary at being constantly lectured to by the Poles about the war. A December 2006 suit filed against Poland in the European Court of Human Rights by the "Prussian Trust" (Preußische Treuhand), which represents the property interests of expellees in former German lands in the east, did not help matters any. Although the claims for return of former German property were rejected out of hand by the German government and by the court in a October 4, 2008, decision, the Polish government quickly linked the property issue to the spectre of historical revisionism in Germany.[25] Jarosław Kaczyński warned: "If German elites don't react firmly, the nation could again move in a direction that has already ended once in a great European tragedy."[26]

Planning the Museum

The victory of the new Donald Tusk coalition government in Poland in the fall of 2007 gave impetus to a positive change in these relations. At the same time, Chancellor Merkel sought ways within the coalition to satisfy both the critics in the SPD and her supporters from the BdV.

Berlin ein sichtbares Zeichen setzen, um – in Verbindung mit dem Europäischen Netzwerk Erinnerung und Solidarität über die bisher beteiligten Länder Polen, Ungarn und Slowakei hinaus – an das Unrecht von Vertreibungen zu erinnern und Vertreibung für immer zu ächten." "Gemeinsam für Deutschland. Mit Mut un Menschlichkeit." Koalitionvertrag von CDU, CSU, und SPD, Berlin November 11, 2005, in Troebst, ed., *Vertreibungsdiskurs und europäische Erinnerungskultur*, 228.
24. Jan C. Behrends, "Geschichtspolitiken: Die Krise der deutsch-polnischen Verständigung in historischer Perspektive," *Berliner Debatte Initial* 6, no. 19 (2008): 53-67.
25. Pawel Lutomski, "Are the Ghosts of the Past Finally Banned by Law? The Case Prussian Trust v Poland at the European Court of Human Rights," (paper, German Studies Association, Washington D.C., Oct. 10, 2009).
26. Jan Puhl and Andreas Wassermann, "Suit Evokes Ghosts of War," *Spiegel Online*, 2 January 2007, http://www.spiegel.de/international/0,1518,456926,00.html (accessed December 10, 2010).

Her suggestion was to go ahead with building the exhibit as planned in Berlin's Deutschland Haus near the Anhalter Bahnhof, which would both be away from the very center of the city, and thus not "equate" it with the centrality of the Holocaust Memorial, and combine elements of both the BdV exhibit and the German Historical Museum exhibit. This would then be the "visible sign" promised by the coalition in 2005.

The exhibit itself would be assembled by a team of specialists under the aegis ("in der Trägerschaft") of the German Historical Museum; a board of the foundation of the project (Beirat der Stiftung "Flucht, Vertreibung, Versöhnung") would be formed from a variety of interested parties, including the BdV. A "scientific board" for the project, which would invite the participation of Poles and Czechs, would supervise the actual plans for the exhibit. Both the BdV and the SPD seemed to be mollified, though neither really gave up their quite distinct views of the story the exhibit should tell. In March 2008, Culture Minister Bernd Neumann seemed to think he had reached agreement with the Poles and the Tusk government that they would not raise protests against the new exhibit. The Polish elite remained mistrustful of German attempts to construct a narrative of victimhood, but was apparently ready to go along with the project. "The breakthrough," wrote *Die Zeit Online*, "is a result of a policy that could have come out of the handbook for achieving détente."[27]

But Polish sensitivities about German intentions, especially about the role of Frau Steinbach, did not evaporate so easily. The BdV, as one of the constituent members of the project's Stiftung, nominated Erika Steinbach to take one of their three assigned seats on the board. This raised a howl of protest in the Polish press, and more subtly, from the Polish government. There was a quick escalation of accusatory language from the Polish side. Władysław Bartoszewski, a highly respected former Polish Foreign Minister, an Auschwitz survivor, and special plenipotentiary for German affairs in the Tusk government, called Steinbach a "blond beast" and equated her appointment to the board with appointing the infamous Bishop Richard Williamson, a Holocaust denier, to be special representative to Israel.[28] Polish Foreign Minister, Radek Sikorski, reminded Germans that Steinbach's family came to Poland with Hitler and had to leave with

---

27. Alice Bota and Heinrich Wefing, "Entspannt euch!," in Zeit Online 13, 2008, 10. See also the press release: "Sichtbares Zeichen gegen Flucht und Vertreibung kommt!" Deutscher Kulturrat: aktuell. Kulturinformationszentrum des Deutschen Kulturrates und der ConBrio Verlagsgesellschaft, news release, March 19, 2008.
28. Lars Breuer and Astrid Homann, "Die Vertreibung der Frau Steinbach," in Jungle World 10, March 5, 2009 <http://jungle-world.com/artikel/2009/10/32784.html> (Dec. 10, 2010).

Hitler, a criticism leveled at her by the German left, as well. In an interview with *Der Spiegel*, Prime Minister Tusk let it be known that the Steinbach nomination would "jeopardize the very good relations that now exist between Germany and Poland." He explained: "We Poles are very sensitive when it comes to defending the truth about World War II. We are obsessive about it—and will always remain so."[29]

When Chancellor Angela Merkel met with Prime Minister Tusk in Hamburg on February 28, 2009, the issue of Frau Steinbach's place on the board dominated their conversations, instead of important international issues such as differences over the emplacement of a missile defense system in Poland and the Czech Republic, the impact of the world financial crisis on Poland, and the potential entry of Poland into the euro zone. The Germans and Poles showed good sense in seemingly finding a compromise, and Merkel prevailed upon Steinbach and the BdV in early March to withdraw their claim to Steinbach's seat on the board. Both sides were relieved, though they should have understood that the BdV's insistence that Steinbach's chair be left vacant boded trouble for the future. Steinbach noted that her chances of assuming a place on the board might change after the Bundestag elections in October.[30] Some Poles, at least, thought that the problem had been solved: Zbigniew Chlebowski, the head of Poland's ruling coalition stated: "I think we should now finally close the public debate on the subject."[31]

To some extent, the compromise solution held. The members of both the board of the foundation and the "scientific" advisory council were named by the German government. Every effort was made to include all of the important constituencies that felt they had a stake in the museum project, the Jewish organization, the Catholic Church, the Protestant Church, the BdV and representatives of the government. The scientific council significantly included, among others, a Polish, Czech, and Hungarian scholar. To renovate the Deutschland Haus for the exhibit was estimated to cost some 29 million euros; after that the costs of the museum would run about 2.5 million euros a year.[32] During the early fall of 2009, the museum project itself was launched within the walls of the German Historical

---

29. Interview with Donald Tusk, in Spiegel Online International, 2 Nov. 2009 <http://www.spiegel.de/international/europe/0,1518,610726,00.html> (Dec. 15, 2010).
30. "Steinbach beharrt auf Sitz im Stiftungsrat," in Spiegel Online, 30 June 2009 <http://www.spiegel.de/politik/deutschland/0,1518,633478,00.html> (Dec. 10, 2010).
31. *Tagesschau*, March 4, 2009 <http://www.tagesschau.de/ausland/steinbach>.
32. Daniel Brössler, "Zeichen im 'Geiste der Versöhnung'," in Sueddeutsche.de, Sept. 25, 2008 <http://www.sueddeutsche.de/politik/vertriebenen-stiftung-zeichen-im-geiste-der-versoehnung-1.694730> (Dec. 10, 2010).

Museum under the leadership of Manfred Kittel, a professor of History at Regensburg and a research fellow at the Institute for Zeitgeschichte in Munich. With both strong academic and centrist political credentials, Prof. Kittel was acceptable both to the government and to the BdV.

Yet with every new national election, a new twist in the story seems to emerge. The victory of the Christian Democratic Union (CDU)-Free Democratic Party (FDP) coalition in the October 2009 elections and the bitter defeat of the Social Democrats seemed to have empowered Frau Steinbach to try again to take "her" seat on the board. Moreover, the Bavarian CSU had become more aggressive in supporting Steinbach's nomination, criticizing FDP leader, Guido Westerwelle for his negative attitude toward the BdV president. CSU chief Horst Seehofer noted "We won't accept the fact that the FDP simply says no [to Steinbach's taking of a seat.]," threatening to make trouble in the new coalition if Chancellor Merkel did not take a firm stand on the issue.[33] But the cabinet of the new government decided who took a seat on the board, and it seems likely that the CSU's protests were easier to deal with than an aroused Polish government and society.

Conclusions

1) The story of the building of the *Vertreibung* Museum is far from over.[34] The controversies will continue, no doubt even after the exhibit is completed and open for public scrutiny. But differences of perspective and arguments about the past are always part and parcel of building museums of "historical memory." These are never fast and easy processes and maybe they shouldn't be. It took some fifteen years for all the parties to agree on the concept for and the contents of the Holocaust Museum in Washington D.C. before it finally opened in 2003. The result is a brilliant success: for the public, for the victims, for scholars, for legislators, and for the donors. One can hope the same for the Museum against *Vertreibung*.

2) Some Polish and Czech politicians and publicists are prone to polemical reactions to perceived German revisionist readings of the past. Old anti-German phobias and stereotypes can quickly capture the headlines and distort the real differences in perceptions about the past.[35] In the case

---

33. *Tagesschau*, Nov. 14, 2009 <http://www.tageschau.de/inland/vertriebene110>.
34. This essay does not cover the development of the Vertreibung Museum controversy after January 1, 2010.
35. See Pawel Lutomski, "The Debate about a Center against Expulsions: An Unexpected Crisis in German-Polish Relations?" *German Studies Review* 27, no. 3 (2004): 449-68.

of some Poles, there is the feeling that the Jews have unjustifiably seized the center stage of the victimhood drama. In this context, the attempts of the BdV to portray the fate of the Germans as that of victims is simply too much to take. A Catholic conservative newspaper, *Nasz Dziennik* (December 2003) wrote: "In several years we may be told that the Germans, just like the Jews, were victims of the Nazis. It will also be necessary to find co-perpetrators. This, however, should be no problem; after all the Poles are always handy."[36] Few victims are willing to accept the status of both victim and perpetrator; the more one admits to being a perpetrator, the less of a claim one has on being a victim. Thus both Poles and Czechs often reject the idea that during the war they could do serious harm to others, since they were clearly the victims of the Nazis. The distortion of the past during forty-five years of Communism in Poland and Czechoslovakia has not helped these societies form a more balanced picture of the past.

3) Internal German politics, left versus right, CDU versus SPD, CSU versus FDP, the Vertriebene Association versus its opponents, dominate the history of the development of the new museum. In the end, a fragile political settlement was reached based on a series of reasonable compromises. But inter-state relations in the new Europe frustrated the respective internal German players and complicated the outcome considerably. Moreover, many Germans are not without their insensitivities to the meaning of World War II for the peoples of East Central Europe, and for the Poles in particular.[37] The German public could also be much better informed about the past of their Polish neighbors and partners in the EU. As a result of frequent misunderstandings of the others' history and intentions, it has been remarkably difficult to reach consensus between nations that do pretty well with juridical, monetary, social, economic, and infrastructure agreements. Even the Parliamentary Assembly of the Council of Europe, which tried to set up a "European Center for Remembering Victims of Forced Deportations and Ethnic Cleansing," was unable to pass a resolution to that effect due to the opposition of the Russians, the French, and the Turks, each for their own reasons.

4) Symbolic politics play an enormous role, even in the new bureaucratized state system of Europe. Erika Steinbach, whatever her attributes or weaknesses as a political leader, has become larger than life, especially for those Poles have tended to view it as threatening their

---

36. Cited in Majdajczyk, "The Centre against Expulsions," 66.
37. See Jan P. Piskorski, *Vertreibung und Deutsch-Polnische Geschichte: Eine Streitschrift* (Osnabrück: fibre Verlag, 2005), 105 ff. Polish original: *Polacy i Niemcy: Czy przeszlosc musi byc przeszkoda* (Poznan: Wydawnictwo Porznanskie, 2004).

very existence. While most interested Germans look soberly—and at times cynically—at the new museum as a realistic outcome of a political compromise, the Poles view it as part of a tectonic shift in German views of the past. Coming closer together in Europe, even sharing the same European-wide laws, rules, and norms, does not guarantee that nations will get along any better than they did before. The common past continues to demand the attention of European citizens, leaders, and the historical profession.

Afterword

The original article covers the history of the museum controversy until the late fall of 2009. Since that time, remarkable progress has been made on the project. The Stiftung has its own headquarters on Mauerstraße in Berlin, and is supported by the office of the Federal Republic's State Secretary for Education and Media, Bernd Neumann. Although the original international Academic Advisory Council was disbanded as a consequence of accusations about the politicization of the discussions, a newly reconstituted one began meeting in January 2011 and included scholars from Poland and Hungary, though notably not from the Czech Republic.[38] Chaired by Stefan Troebst from Leipzig University, who had originally been associated with the Netzwerk initiative discussed above, the council represented a diverse group of scholars, primarily historians of 20th Century Europe familiar with the historiography of forced migration. In June 2012, after much internal debate and the eventual approval of the Stiftungsrat, the Director released a lengthy "Conceptual Framework" for the work of the Stiftung and the planned exhibit.[39] The document is not without its internal contradictions; "the devil is in the details," as several observers have noted. But these contradictions, like any legitimate arguments about the historical past, can, should, and no doubt will be carried over into the exhibition itself.

There are many indications that the museum will open as now scheduled, in 2016. The architectural plans for the redesign of the Deutschlandhaus were approved in November 2011. The annual budget of the project as 2.5

---

38. In the name of transparency, I should note that I became a member of this council in January 2011. With the exception of the "Afterword," the article was completed in its present published form before I was asked to join. It was originally drafted for a Stanford—Vienna University conference on "History and Memory," held at Stanford in March 2009.
39. The "Konzeption für die Arbeit der Stiftung Flucht, Vertreibung, Versöhnung und Leitlinien für die geplante Dauerausstellung" is available on the SFVV's website: <www.sfvv.de>

million Euros will reportedly be increased in 2013 to 3.75 million Euros.[40] Although the political hubbub around the project will certainly not disappear, there seems to be a willingness to compromise and include different points of view in both the academic advisory council and the Stiftungsrat. Meanwhile, Erika Steinbach's readiness to step into the background of the project and not insist on taking a seat in the Stiftungsrat helped ease the way to successful completion of the "Conceptual Framework." At the same time, there can be no question that the museum will owe its existence to her original proposals and activism.

The Polish reaction to the "Conceptual Framework" has been, on the whole, quite positive. Given the public statements by Prof. Kittel, Director of the Stiftung, and of State Secretary Neumann, there is every reason for Germany's neighbors to believe that there will be a clear presentation of the Nazi responsibility for the war and for initiating the cycle of violence and murder that ended in the expulsion of the Germans from Eastern Europe. The *Vertreibung* will also be cast in a comparative framework, which will give appropriate recognition to the suffering of Poles, Czechs, and other victims of both Nazi and Soviet depredations. Meanwhile, the history of forced migration in twentieth century Europe will serve as an important backdrop for understanding the calamities of the past and European hopes of the future. The new museum at Deutschland Haus will complement in important ways the landscape of historical museums and institutes in Berlin that seek to use history and memory to promote knowledge, understanding, and reconciliation.

---

40. <http://www.derwesten.de/politik/versoehnung-mit-den-vertriebenen-id7306170.html>

Nontopical Essay

The Rise and Decline and Rise of Austria's Radical Right

Ferdinand Karlhofer

Introduction

Up to some ten years ago, with good reason the Austrian Freedom Party (*Freiheitliche Partei Österreichs* – FPÖ) was considered a special case in Europe's landscape of political parties.[1] In fact, the pace with which Jörg Haider immediately after having unseated his predecessor in 1986 turned the party which had hitherto strived for a liberal profile into a populist one was astounding. Under his leadership the former five-percent party soon achieved double-digit results in national elections, peaking at twenty-seven percent of the vote in the 1999 election, and so becoming the second-strongest party. The FPÖ's rapid rise from a fringe party to, at least for a while, "Europe's most successful extreme-right party"[2] caught international attention when, in 2000, it entered into a government coalition with the ÖVP. Indeed, the FPÖ was not only the first successful right-wing populist party in Europe in terms of votes, but also the first one in government—a fact that made it a model for the far right in other EU-countries.[3]

Precisely the government takeover, though, marked a critical point in the party's populist success story. Already in the snap election 2002 it suffered a downfall from twenty-seven to ten percent. The FPÖ remained in office, but now in the role of a severely weakened junior partner for the ÖVP. The deep crisis that followed, culminating in a party split in 2005, gave rise to the assumption that the FPÖ's heyday was definitely over. Even

---

1. Anton Pelinka, "Die FPÖ in der vergleichenden Parteienforschung. Zur Typologischen Einordnung der Freiheitlichen Partei Österreichs," *Österreichische Zeitschrift für Politikwissenschaft* 31, no. 3 (2002): 281-90.
2. Thomas Schubert, "Extremismus in Dänemark," in *Extremismus in den EU-Staaten*, ed. Eckhard Jesse and Tom Thieme (Wiesbaden: Verlag für Sozialwissenschaften, 2011), 65-81.
3. Brigitte Bailer-Galanda and Wolfgang Neugebauer (1998): "The FPÖ of Jörg Haider – Populist or Extreme Right-Winger?," *Women in Austria*, ed. Günter Bischof, Anton Pelinka, and Erika Thurner (CAS 6) (New Brunswick: Transaction Publishers, 1997), 164-173. Switzerland, due to its unique Magic Formula applying to concordant government composition covering the four biggest parties (since the split of the populist SVP in 2007, five parties), is left out of consideration here.

profound experts expected the party to continue to exist in the medium run only at provincial level.[4] In the 2006 election, however, despite having split up just one year before, the populist right in total achieved fourteen percent of the vote: ten for the FPÖ and four for the Alliance for the Future of Austria (*Bündnis Zukunft Österreich* – BZÖ). Two years later, in the snap election 2008, they won more than seventeen (FPÖ) respectively eleven (BZÖ) percent, totaling even more than the FPÖ had gained in 1999.

Point of departure of the following analysis is the surprising rise and decline and subsequent rise of right-wing populism in Austria. The chapter focuses on two central questions: Firstly, there has been remarkable discontinuity with regard to the party's election results – what are the determinants explaining the ups and downs? Secondly, has the ideological profile changed over time, or has the traditional core of German Nationalism (in the sense of Nazi nostalgia) just merged with populist vote catching practices? In dealing with these questions, the chapter starts with a brief outline of the party's historical development until the takeover by Haider in the mid-1980s, eventually focusing on the populist turn. The article concludes with a look at the center parties' responses to the challenge, and a reflection on how far the FPÖ's populist agenda has changed the party system as such.

Party Formation with Nazi Veterans Taking the Lead

With good reason, the FPÖ was called into being only after Austria had been granted full sovereignty by the Allies in 1955. In 1945, roughly 524,000 ex-members of the NSDAP had been excluded from suffrage in the first democratic elections after the end of the NS regime. In the 1949 election about 480,000 "followers" were admitted,[5] many of them voting for the newly established League of Independents (*Verband der Unabhängigen* – VdU) which right away achieved eleven point seven percent (ten point nine in 1953). Rather soon the VdU, originally not just attracting former NS members but also returning war prisoners, became the focal point for the FPÖ's foundation process primarily pursued by proponents with NS background who established a Freedom Party (*Freiheitspartei*) in order

---

4. Kurt R. Luther, "Die Freiheitliche Partei Österreichs (FPÖ) und das Bündnis Zukunft Österreich (BZÖ)," in *Politik in Österreich: Das Handbuch*, ed. Herbert Dachs et al. (Wien: Manz, 2006), 364-388.
Cf. also Austrian Journal of Political Science (ÖZP) 3/2004, special topic "Rise and Fall of the FPÖ."
5. Dieter Stiefel, *Entnazifizierung in Österreich* (Wien: Europaverlag, 1981).

to underline a much stricter German national orientation than the VdU had. The FPÖ was formally founded as a merger of the two parties (in fact, though, the VdU was simply absorbed by the Freiheitspartei) at a convention in 1956 with Anton Reinthaler, a former high-ranking SS officer[6], and elected party leader. Reinthaler's successor after his death in 1958 was Friedrich Peter, a former SS-*Obersturmbannführer* whose unit allegedly had been involved in mass killings of civilians on the eastern front.

As for ideology and values, the FPÖ is to be classed as a German National party with roots back to the nineteenth century. In a sense, it forms —in addition to socialists and Catholics—one of the three political "camps" characteristic of Austria: "[...] Austrian society is divided historically into three ideologically diverse, equally hostile, watertight compartments called '*Lager*.' Each *Lager* found political expression in the form of parties, trade unions, and a network of voluntary associations following socialist, Catholic, and national traditions."[7] In democratic periods, the third *Lager* never managed to keep abreast with the socialist and the Catholic camps. What is more, is has also been divided into two streams: a (rather small) liberal one and a (dominant) German nationalist one.[8] What both streams have always had in common, though, is their pronounced criticism against consociational policy practices (i.e., negotiation rather than majority rule, corporatism, proportional power sharing, and preference for grand coalitions) as particularly characteristic for the Second Republic.[9] Between 1945 and 1955, however, right in the years when the foundations of the Second Republic were laid, the historically discredited third camp found itself an outsider, unable to influence the setting of the direction. The reconsolidation of the third camp simply arrived too late, and the experience of marginalization for the newly constituted democracy during this decisive period helps explain the FPÖ's proneness for populist attitudes, which

---

6. Reinthaler (1895-1958) had been SS-*Brigadeführer* resp. *Obergruppenführer* (1930-1945), Minister of Agriculture in the Seyß-Inquart "Anschluss" cabinet of 1938, and later a member of the NS-Reichstag (1938-1945). In two trials, 1950/1952, Reinthaler was charged with high treason and, in total, given five and half years imprisonment.
7. Piero Ignazi, *Extreme right parties in Western Europe* (Oxford: Oxford Univ. Press, 2003), with reference to Adam Wandruszka who coined the term in his famous book *Das Haus Habsburg* (Wien 1956).
8. Ibid.
9. Markus M.L. Crepaz and Hans-Georg Betz, "Postindustrial Cleavages and Electoral Changes in an Advanced Capitalist Democracy: The Austrian Case," in *The Marshall Plan in Austria*, ed. Günter Bischof, Anton Pelinka, and Dieter Stiefel (CAS 8) (New Brunswick: Transaction Publishers, 2000), 506-532 (here 514-517).

would unfold some three decades later.[10]

Between Pariah and Hinge Party

The step-by-step consolidation of the party in the late 1950s and the 1960s took place under ambivalent political conditions: The two dominant Lager parties ÖVP and SPÖ strived for winning ex-Nazis as voters, and furthermore, as party functionaries and office-holders in local, provincial and federal parliaments. In Austria, other than in Germany, de-Nazification has never been pursued systematically.[11] From the outset, the FPÖ was far from being ostracized by the grand coalition parties. Quite the contrary, already in 1953 the then Federal Chancellor Julius Raab (ÖVP) reportedly spoke for a three-party coalition under inclusion of the VdU, yet was vetoed by the SPÖ.[12] The other way round, the SPÖ is said to have actively supported the VdU foundation in 1949. Several more episodes of confidential agreements were recalled decades later by ex-FPÖ chairman Friedrich Peter.[13]

In the end, however, despite good informal contacts with both big parties, the FPÖ was in the role of a Pariah party left out of consideration in government formation processes. From 1956, the FPÖ's foundation year, through to 1966 (the year when the ÖVP achieved the absolute majority of seats in parliament), the outcome of invariably all elections would basically have allowed for a coalition between one of the big parties and the FPÖ as junior partner. Despite that, and although post-war consensus began to erode, ÖVP and SPÖ continued adhering to building grand coalitions.

Yet, as a matter of fact, over time it became increasingly clear that the lack of a German FDP-style hinge party, which was and has been open to centre-left and centre-right, significantly restrained the scope of options for coalition building in Austria's two-and-a-half-party system. A first attempt of cutting the Gordian knot was undertaken by Bruno Kreisky after the 1970 election that earned him a strong, yet not absolute majority of seats in parliament. By concluding a deal with the FPÖ, Kreisky managed his minority government to be supported by it in return for a franchise reform

---
10. Anton Pelinka, "Die FPÖ in der vergleichenden Parteienforschung: Zur Typologischen Einordnung der Freiheitlichen Partei Österreichs," *Österreichische Zeitschrift für Politikwissenschaft* 31, no. 3 (2002): 281-290 (here 283-284).
11. Stiefel, *Entnazifizierung in Österreich*.
12. Wolfgang C. Müller, "Parteiensystem," in *Politik in Österreich: Das Handbuch*, ed. Herbert Dachs et al. (Wien: Manz, 2006), 279-304 (here 299).
13. Peter in an Interview for the book by Pelinka (1993, 22-26).

favoring the small party.[14]

The ground for the breakthrough—albeit for one year only since the SPÖ in the snap election of 1971 gained the absolute majority—had been laid by the FPÖ itself. Party leader Friedrich Peter, with his distinct sense of pragmatism, made his party step by step a "normal," generally accepted force in parliament. For a while, the FPÖ had complained about being squeezed into a "parliamentary Ghetto [in a historical perspective a somehow inappropriate self-perception—FK] from which it had tried to escape, though with modest success."[15] Yet now, after the 1970 liaison with Kreisky, the breakthrough had come within reach. Peter consolidated the party insofar as he advocated for Nationals and Liberals peacefully coexisting, and acted as a go-between in case of party infighting. In 1979, one year after Peter's departure from chairmanship, the FPÖ was admitted a member of the Liberal International (LI).[16]

Populist Turn and Comeback of Right-wingers

Norbert Steger, elected chairman in 1980 (and in the same year, elected Vice-President of the LI), made further attempts to expedite the process of liberalization. An exponent of *Atterseekreis* (founded in 1973 and named after the location where the circle had its regular meetings), Steger entered into a small coalition with the SPÖ which had lost its absolute majority in the 1983 election. Based on an election result of just five percent, though, the lowest in the party's history, Steger's intra-party standing was weak from the outset. Although conscious of the unbroken presence of *Kellernazis*[17] as he called them later, Steger underestimated the network-based mobilization potential of the German National dueling fraternities spearheading the anti-liberalist countermotion. In order to appease intra-party rebellion, Steger incorporated pronounced right-wingers (e.g., Minister of Justice Harald Ofner) into his cabinet. In the end, however, he failed, and at the 1986 party convention, was ousted by challenger Jörg Haider who had gathered

---

14. Anton Pelinka, *Die Kleine Koalition: SPÖ–FPÖ 1983–1986* (Wien: Böhlau, 1993), 22-26. Sonja Puntscher Riekmann, "The Politics of Ausgrenzung, the Nazi Past and the European Dimension of the New Radical Right in Austria," in *The Vranitzky Era in Austria*, ed. Günter Bischof, Anton Pelinka, and Ferdinand Karlhofer (CAS 7) (New Brunswick: Transaction Publishers, 1999), 78-105 (here 85).
15. Friedrich Peter, "Wurzeln und Entwicklungslinien der Freiheitlichen Partei Österreichs," in *Der Spiegel der Erinnerung: Die Sicht von innen*, ed. Robert Kriechbaumer (Wien: Böhlau, 1998), 137-160 (here 150).
16. In 1993, the FPÖ under Haider cancelled membership in anticipation of a threatening exclusion by the LI.
17. Cf. "Das Problem mit den Kellernazis," *Profil*, May 10, 2010, 24-25.

a strong group of hardliners campaigning fiercely against the incumbent.

Steger's defeat marked a turning point in the party's strategic and ideological orientations. Contrary to Haider's expected coalition partner, SPÖ, under Chancellor Franz Vranitzky, promptly cancelled the coalition agreement. After a brief moment of shock, and after the SPÖ had made clear that a renewal of the red-blue coalition after the 1986 election was out of the question, the FPÖ immediately did an about-face and turned from a party heretofore trying hard to be accepted by others, to a populist party hitting out against SPÖ and ÖVP.[18] Though now as before with regard to structure and organization a fairly traditional party from every point of view, the more than three decades old FPÖ presented itself as an anti-party distancing itself from SPÖ and ÖVP, which henceforth were pejoratively denounced as power-hungry, clientelist *Altparteien* ("old parties"). With its harsh rhetoric the FPÖ met with a wide response and managed to double its share of votes. The party now being on course for further success, Haider on the election eve announced that from now on, as a party in opposition, "we are going to ride herd on the two old parties."[19]

The topics addressed with the populist turn of 1986 were anything but new in public discourse. Privileges, party patronage, political scandals, Lager parties as gate-keepers, erosion, and malpractice of SPÖ-ÖVP duopoly had been broadly thematized in media coverage since the 1970s. Haider and his entourage—despite the FPÖ being a clientelistic (but weak for long) party itself—had frequently referred to already before the 1986 party convention, yet had abstained from directly attacking the then coalition partner.

With the decomposition of traditional party affiliation and the big Lager parties' predominance eroding[20], the FPÖ started targeting the crisis of the party state and consociational politics.[21] The political rhetoric of the FPÖ, in particular of its leader, was twofold: On the one hand, it adopted elements of populist friend-or-foe simplification – populism defined "as an ideology that considers society to be ultimately separated into two homogeneous and antagonistic groups, 'the pure people' versus 'the corrupt elite', and which argues that politics should be an expression of the

---

18. Pelinka, *Die Kleine Koalition*, 91.
19. Which is to say "wir werden die alten Parteien vor uns hertreiben" (APA-Basisdienst, 23 November 1986).
20. Crepaz/Betz, "Postindustrial Cleavages and Electoral Changes in an Advanced Capitalist Democracy." Wolfgang C. Müller, "Wahlen und Dynamik des österreichischen Parteiensystems seit 1986," in: *Das österreichische Wahlverhalten*, ed. Fritz Plasser, Peter A. Ulram, Franz Sommer (Wien: Signum, 2000), 13-54.
21. Fritz Plasser, *Parteien unter Stress: Zur Dynamik der Parteiensysteme in Österreich, der Bundesrepublik Deutschland und den Vereinigten Staaten* (Wien: Böhlau, 1987).

volonté générale (general will) of the people".[22] On the other hand, with the return of the radical right which had been in the background during the liberal interlude, the party's German national continuity was emphasized. Countless political speeches with provocative statements purposefully breaking taboos by semantic gaffes,[23] from denying the existence of an Austrian nation through to downplaying the crimes of the NS regime, were quite deliberate allusions and signals to the old stock.[24]

McGann and Kitschelt identify two steps the FPÖ passed on the path to becoming a party of the new radical right: (1) Between 1986 and 1990, the new leader pushed the party in the direction of an anti-statist party. (2) Beginning with 1990, anti-statist populism gradually made way for a pattern far more typical of the new radical right. In this phase the FPÖ "added on to its anti-clientelist, populist appeal of the late 1980s distinctly right-wing socio-cultural appeals featuring the rejection of immigration and skepticism of European integration. These appeals resonated with the small business and lower middleclass constituency of the FPÖ, and added working-class support."[25] Like the Swiss SVP, the FPÖ now presented itself as a "*Heimatpartei*"[26] defending culture and identity against "foreignization."[27] As regards the liberal programmatic positions the party had emphasized under Steger, they were eliminated step by step. By 1996, "[w]ithin a decade, the FPÖ had shed its affinity for issues of the new left, and developed a mirror image position as new right party."[28] Eventually, the

---

22. Cas Mudde, "The Populist Zeitgeist," *Government and Opposition* 39, no. 3 (2004): 541-563 (here 543). See also Cas Mudde, "The Populist Radical Right: A Pathological Normalcy," *West European Politics* 33, no. 6 (2010): 1167-1186.
23. Florian Hartleb, "Extremismus in Österreich," in *Extremismus in den EU-Staaten*, ed. Eckhard Jesse and Tom Thieme (Wiesbaden: Verlag für Sozialwissenschaften, 2011), 265-281 (here 270).
24. Pelinka, "Die FPÖ in der vergleichenden Parteienforschung," 287-288.
25. Anthony J. McGann and Herbert Kitschelt, "The Radical Right in the Alps: Evolution of Support for the Swiss SVP and Austrian FPÖ," *Party Politics* 11, no. 2 (2005): 147-172 (here 151).
26. With regard to right-wing parties the emphasis on the term "*Heimat*" in the sense of "national sovereignty" clearly corresponds with efforts to mobilize anti-EU sentiments (De Vries/Edwards 2009).
27. Susanne Frölich-Steffen, "Die Identitätspolitik der FPÖ: Vom Deutschnationalismus zum Österreich-Patriotismus," *Österreichische Zeitschrift für Politikwissenschaft* 33, no. 3 (2003): 281-296 (here 297-289). Hans-Georg Betz, "Exclusionary populism in Western Europe in the 1990s and beyond. At threat to democracy and civil rights?," in *unrisd.org*, <http://www.unrisd.org/unrisd/website/document.nsf/%28httpPublications%29/17BFB81 6DA5CEF8B80256B6D005787D8?OpenDocument> (Oct. 12, 2012), 9. Susi Meret, "The Danish People's Party, the Italian Northern League and the Austrian Freedom Party in a Comparative Perspective: Party Ideology and Electoral Support," in *vbn.aau.dk*, <http://vbn.aau.dk/files/20049801/spirit_phd_series_25.pdf> (Oct. 12, 2012), 196-200.
28. Alexandra Cole, "Old right or new right? The ideological positioning of parties of the

harsh anti-immigration policy culminating in a petition for a referendum under the title "Österreich zuerst" ("Austria first") in 1993, prompted liberal delegates to split off and found a party of their own, the Liberal Forum (Liberales Forum – LIF).[29]

For the most part, except for the period when the FPÖ was in government as outlined below, the party still meets the criteria of phase 2 – aside from the fact that the party under its new leader Heinz-Christian Strache has moved from far right to the extreme right.

Issues, Voters, and Members

To say in advance, central in this chapter is the period of the party's continuous growth from 1986 through to 1999.

With regard to the central issues in the election campaigns of the FPÖ I follow, for the most part, the synopsis given by Müller:[30]

- *Political class*: since 1986 steadily denouncing the "old parties" for being aloof and ignoring the interests and needs of the "little man"; party as exposer of real as well as alleged scandals; party leader presenting himself as a kind of "Robin Hood" taking from the rich and giving to the poor.
- *Immigration*: as from 1989 with socialism in Eastern Europe collapsing potential threat through immigration (competition with jobs and housing, cultural clash and "*Umvolkung*") becomes issue number one; effects on voting behavior: generating a sense of community among FPÖ voters while dividing the electorates of SPÖ and ÖVP.
- *European integration*: in the run-up to the referendum on EU-accession (1994) the party turns from a former enthusiastic advocate of membership to a strict opponent, later on opposing further integration steps, particularly enlargement and monetary union; at present the FPÖ is the only anti-EU party in Austria's party system and, as an opposition party, has managed to mobilize disillusionment with EU politics better than populist parties in most other member states.[31]

---

far right," *European Journal of Political Research* 44, no. 2 (2005): 203-230 (here 217).
29. The LIF was present in parliament until the 1999 election where it failed to cross the 4 percent threshold of votes and eventually sank into insignificance.
30. Müller, "Wahlen und Dynamik des österreichischen Parteiensystems seit 1986," 32-35.
31. Elisabeth Ivarsflaten, "What Unites the Populist Right in Western Europe? Reexamining grievance mobilization models in seven successful cases," *Comparative Political Studies* 41, no. 1 (2008): 3-23 (here 13-14).

– *Cultural issues*: by contrasting "popular" culture with avant-garde art the party comes up to expectations of a voter potential emanating from the "silent counter-revolution" that followed the "silent revolution" of post-materialism as described by Ronald Inglehart.[32]
– *Catholicism*: for a short time the party addressed ultra-conservative Roman Catholics by calling for a defense of the Christian West against oriental infiltration; in the end, since provoking internal protests with regard to the party's anticlerical tradition the issue was removed from the agenda after a while.
– *Social policy*: for a while, the issue of the welfare state had primarily been communicated pejoratively with denouncing "welfare scroungers"; only in the 1999 election campaign welfare questions (pensions, child care, etc.) were focused in order to win SPÖ voters.
– *Economic policy*: parts of the party have cultivated excellent contacts with industrialists; a couple of neo-liberal topics on the party's agenda (e.g. privatization resp. outplacement of public services, flat tax) cemented ties with economic interest groups, particularly the Federation of Industrialists which sponsored the party financially.

All things considered, the FPÖ's discursive strategy under Haider, as Mouffe points out, "consisted in constructing a frontier between an 'us' of all the good Austrians, hard workers and defenders of national values, against a 'them' composed of the parties in power, the trade union bureaucrats, the foreigners, the left-wing artists and intellectuals who were, all in their own way, contributing to the stifling of political debate."[33]

The party's issue management and election strategy aimed at expanding the electorate while preserving the traditional old stock. In the first stage, the increase in votes was mainly at the expense of the ÖVP; in the second one the SPÖ recorded heavy losses.[34] Eventually, in the election of 1999, the FPÖ topped the SPÖ with its share of votes among skilled labor, prompting

---

32. See Ignazi, *Extreme right parties in Western Europe*; see also Simon Bornschier, *Cleavage Politics and the Populist Right: The New Cultural Conflict in Western Europe* (Philadelphia: Temple Univ. Press, 2010). Simon Bornschier, "The New Cultural Divide and the Two-Dimensional Political Space in Western Europe," *West European Politics* 33, no. 3 (2010): 419-444.
33. Chantal Mouffe, "Democracy in Europe: The Challenge of Right-wing Populism," in *cccb.org*, <www.cccb.org/rcs_gene/mouffe.pdf> (Oct. 12, 2012), 745.
34. McGann/Kitschelt, "The Radical Right in the Alps," 151.

observers speak of the FPÖ now being "the new labor party"[35] in Austria.[36]

The rapid surge of electoral support can be gathered from table 1. In 1983, the FPÖ under Steger had suffered an all-time low of just five percent (though, not too far below the results of previous elections).[37] With the 1986 election, now under Haider's leadership, the party managed almost to double the share, and in 1990 to increase threefold. Steadily growing (with a slight bump in 1995), in the 1999 election the FPÖ reached an all-time high of twenty-seven percent equaling more than five times the amount it had started with roughly a dozen years before.

Table 1: Voters and members 1983-2008

Election year	Voters			Members		
	abs. ('000)	% of total	1983=100	abs.	% of voters	1983=100
1983	241,789	5.0	100	37,233	15.4	100.0
1986	472,205	9.7	194	36,683	7.8	98.5
1990	782,648	16.6	332	40,629	5.2	109.1
1994	1,042,332	22.5	450	43,764	4.2	117.5
1995	1,060,175	21.9	438	144,541¹	4.2	119.6
1999	1,244,087	26.9	538	251,296	4.1	137.8
2002	491,328	10.0	200	344,959²	9.2	120.8
2006 FPÖ	519,598	11.0	220	n.a.	n.a.	n.a.
2006 BZÖ	193,539	4.1	82	n.a.	n.a.	n.a.
2006 FPÖ+BZÖ	713,137	15.1	302	n.a.	n.a.	n.a.
2008 FPÖ	857,029	17.5	350	40,000	4.7	107.4
2008 BZÖ	522,933	10.7	214	10,000	1.9	26.9
2008 FPÖ+BZÖ	1,379,962	28.2	564	50,000	3.6	134.3

¹ 1996; ² 2000; ³ 2004.
Sources: Pelinka *Die Kleine Koalition*, 88; Kurt R. Luther, "Die Freiheitliche Partei Österreichs (FPÖ) und das Bündnis Zukunft Österreich (BZÖ)," in: *Politik in Österreich: Das Handbuch*, ed. Herbert Dachs et al. (Wien: Manz, 2006), 364-388 (here 374); *Der Standard*, 31 Oct. 2008.

---

35. "Politologe Plasser: 'FPÖ ist die neue Arbeiterpartei,'" *Wiener Zeitung*, Oct. 5, 1999. The observation was revised after the 2002 election when the FPÖ suffered severe losses right among workers – see Fritz Plasser and Peter A. Ulram, "Analyse der Nationalratswahl 2002: Muster, Trends und Entscheidungsmotive," in *chello.at*, <http://members.chello.at/zap-forschung/download/NRW2002.pdf> (Oct. 12, 2012).
36. Müller, "Wahlen und Dynamik des österreichischen Parteiensystems seit 1986," 20.
37. 1956: 6.5%; 1959: 7.7%; 1962: 7.1%; 1966: 5.4%; 1970: 5.5%; 1971: 5.5%; 1975: 5.4%; 1979: 6.1%.

With regard to the development of party members the picture is quite different, clearly confirming that the FPÖ, other than ÖVP and SPÖ, has always been a voter rather than a member party (table 2).

Table 2: Austrian party membership as of 2008

Party	Membership
ÖVP	700,000
SPÖ	300,000
FPÖ	40,000
BZÖ	10,000
Grüne	4,600

Source: *Der Standard*, 31 Oct. 2008.

Even during the accelerated increase of voter support in the 1980s and 1990s membership figures rose only slightly. As a result, the share of voters who were also party members decreased from fifteen percent in 1983 to four percent in 1999. Clearly, the recruitment of members is a process that's demanding of a party's organizational capacities. Thus, recruitment can never keep pace with a quickly growing electorate. However, the fact that the number of voters could be increased more than fivefold in this period while party membership rose less than forty percent is puzzling and demands further explanation.

One explanation is in the fact that the FPÖ made use of widespread disenchantment with political parties, and in presenting itself as a movement deliberately fueling anti-party resentments. Exploiting electoral success for recruiting members would not have fit the anti-party image communicated in campaigns.

A second explanation is that the FPÖ, despite electoral success in its core, continued to be a German national milieu party. Given that this milieu now as before is the most important recruitment field for party functionaries,[38] the inner circle of the party had little interest in opening itself to the numerous protest voters flocking in, most of them ex-voters of SPÖ and ÖVP.

A third explanation is that the party leader claimed the electoral success as his personal merit and therefore had little interest to submit himself to formal party institutions and rules. Instead he preferred varying parallel advisory and decision structures not laid down in the party statutes.[39] In

---

38. Pelinka, "Die FPÖ in der vergleichenden Parteienforschung," 286-288.
39. Luther, "Die Freiheitliche Partei Österreichs (FPÖ) und das Bündnis Zukunft

other words, he was primarily interested in winning votes rather than members entitled to actively co-determine the party's political orientation.

The Center Parties' Response to the Populist Challenge

SPÖ and ÖVP, bound together in a grand coalition from 1986 thru 2000, reacted anything but consistent to the very sudden metamorphosis of a party that even in government (1983-1986) had played a marginal role in Austria's structure of party competition. In the first years after the populist turn, the center-left and center-right obviously had massive difficulties to coping with the successful course chosen by the new FPÖ leader, based on "an ideology mix made of pro-marketism, anti-statism and xenophobism embedded in a rhetoric oscillating between economic liberalism and political illiberalism, modernism and anti-modernism."[40] With its eclectic set of ideologemes primarily aiming at emotions and attitudes rather than on values the FPÖ eluded any attempt of rational political discourse. What is more, Haider's opponents again and again failed to stand up to his perfect media staging.[41] Clearly, it was his chameleon-like appearance: once in the role of a statesman when historically presenting a "Treaty with Austria"[42] ("*Vertrag mit Österreich*"), or claiming to be Bruno Kreisky's "real" heir (right when visiting dubious rulers such as Saddam Hussein and Gaddafi), another time making himself out to be a Robin Hood for the little man in the street, then again as an agitator stirring up dull resentments against immigrants and minorities, that earned Haider the permanent media attention he needed and wanted. There was also the fact that, quite in contrast with the picture of die-hard Nazis, "Haider's entourage was characterized by young, fashionable, mainly male, and, albeit politically inexperienced, faithful followers who would be game for anything or almost anything the new leader might dictate. [...] Haider's success would be unthinkable without the modernization of faces and forms."[43]

Österreich (BZÖ)," 366.
40. Puntscher Riekmann, "The Politics of Ausgrenzung, the Nazi Past and the European Dimension of the New Radical Right in Austria," 79.
41. An example par excellence of his sure feeling for surprise effects he delivered in the run-up to the 1994 election: During a TV debate with chancellor Franz Vranitzky (SPÖ) he lifted a plate displaying the exorbitantly high income of an SPÖ bureaucrat, and thereby not only confused his opponent in front of the live camera but in the end also contributed to the SPÖ losses in the election.
42. "Großer Haider-Auftritt gestern im Parlament: Vertrag mit Österreich," *Neue Kronen Zeitung*, Nov. 18, 1995.
43. Puntscher Riekmann, "The Politics of Ausgrenzung, the Nazi Past and the European Dimension of the New Radical Right in Austria," 86.

What made the FPÖ under Haider a case of whether to be ostracized or not by the other parties was the party's, and particularly its leader's, notorious propensity to deliberate break taboos.[44] With numerous sayings downplaying the Nazi past (e.g., the Austrian nation as an "ideological miscarriage," the "Third Reich" to have pursued a "proper employment policy," etc.) Haider made the FPÖ a clear candidate for being treated as a pariah party by the others.[45] Although "[t]he flashes of Nazi-rhetoric appear to be a well-calculated vote-maximizing technique,"[46] SPÖ and ÖVP (and, clearly, the Greens as well) could not simply ignore the provocations.

The response to the populist challenge was cautious, ambiguous, and different among and simultaneously within the parties in government. Given the FPÖ's success with making inroads even into the traditional electoral cores of both parties, the reaction of SPÖ and ÖVP was determined by concerns about possible further losses of wavering voters. Faced with the decision of whether or not to accept the FPÖ's swing to the far right, chancellor Vranitzky made a momentous decision when he cancelled the coalition agreement with the FPÖ immediately after Haider's takeover of the party. Despite suffering losses in the snap election of 1986 (and in following elections as well) Vranitzky did not change his stance; in denying any possibility of a coalition with Haider he provoked fierce attacks by the FPÖ which denounced the politics of *Ausgrenzung* as an offense to the voters of a "democratic" party.[47] Yet Vranitzky's position, despite becoming official party line, has never been complied with consistency. Again and again high-ranking party officials at the federal level rejected the party line by arguing in favor of cooperation and appeasement, while at the subnational level, a considerable share of the party organization continued to maintain good standing in borough councils and state parliaments. As a result, there is every indication that this striking inconsistency—ostracism on the one side, cooperation on the other—contributed to the FPÖ success since it gave rise to the expectation of many voters that the SPÖ sooner or

---

44. Florian Hartleb, "Nach Haider. Zur Bedeutung der charismatischen Person im Rechtspopulismus," *Vorgänge: Zeitschrift für Bürgerrechte und Gesellschaftspolitik* 47, no. 4 (2008): 127-137 (here 129-131).

45. With regard to "taboo-breaking" Haider sayings cf. Gudmund Tributsch, ed., *Schlagwort Haider: Ein politisches Lexikon seiner Aussprüche bis heute* (Vienna: Falter Verlag, 1992).

46. Puntscher Riekmann, "The Politics of Ausgrenzung, the Nazi Past and the European Dimension of the New Radical Right in Austria," 79.

47. Joost Van Spanje and Wouter van der Brug, "The Party as Pariah: The Exclusion of Anti-Immigration Parties and its Effect on their Ideological Positions," *West European Politics* 30, no. 5 (2007): 1022-1040. A strategy also pursued by Haider's follower Heinz-Christian Strache (see his personal website <www.hcstrache.at/home/?id=60&newsid=1677&p=105&s=0> [Oct. 12, 2012]).

later would abandon its isolation strategy.[48]

On the part of the ÖVP there has never been a strategy of holding the populist party at a distance. On the contrary, in 1989 the Carinthian ÖVP helped Haider to become governor of the state—a position that henceforth served him as an indispensable powerbase.[49] Occasional statements by leading representatives distancing themselves from the FPÖ by no means prevented them from taking a coalition with it into consideration. For instance ÖVP party whip Andreas Khol (rather sophistically) located the FPÖ "beyond the constitutional arch"[50] and at the same time, albeit "behind the scenes," contributed to paving the way for the formation of a common government.[51]

Beyond the question of whether or not the FPÖ was in line for becoming a coalition partner, the party successfully managed to influence the government policy from the oppositional benches. Comparative research on the new radical right provides evidence that there is some "contagion" impact on the other parties' political orientation, particularly of center-left and center-right parties.[52] With regard to immigration policy, the FPÖ already in the early nineties had accomplished becoming an agenda-setter demanding restrictive rules and practices.[53] Party leader Haider triumphed when he made a mockery of the interior minister's (SPÖ) restrictive asylum policy by claiming him to be "our best man in government."[54] Yet the populist attacks were also successful in other policy fields. Minkenberg lists numerous laws passed by parliament in the initiative of the FPÖ. "[E]ven when still in opposition, the FPÖ managed to shape part of Austrian

---

48. David Art, "Reacting to the Radical Right: Lessons from Germany and Austria," *Party Politics*, 13 no. 3 (2007): 331-49 (here 342). More general: David Art, *Inside the Radical Right: The Development of Anti-Immigrant Parties in Western Europe* (New York: Cambridge Univ. Press, 2011).
49. Cf. Reinhard Heinisch, "Success in Opposition - Failure in Government: Explaining the Performance of Right-Wing Populist Parties in Public Office," *West European Politics* 26, no. 3 (2003): 91-130 (here 120-123).
50. Andreas Khol, "Die FPÖ im Spannungsfeld von Ausgrenzung, Selbstausgrenzung, Verfassungsbogen und Regierungsfähigkeit," *Österreichisches Jahrbuch für Politik '95'* (1996): 193-222.
51. Cf. Kurt R. Luther, "Governing with Right-Wing Populists and Managing the Consequences: Schüssel and the FPÖ," in *The Schüssel Era in Austria*, ed. Günter Bischof and Fritz Plasser (CAS 18) (New Orleans/Innsbruck: Uno Press/IUP, 2010), 79-103 (here 81).
52. Joost Van Spanje, "Contagious Parties: Anti-Immigration Parties and Their Impact on Other Parties' Immigration Stances in Contemporary Western Europe," *Party Politics* 16, no. 5 (2010): 563-86.
53. Susanne Frölich-Steffen, "Rechtspopulistische Herausforderer in Konkordanzdemokratien," in *Populismus: Gefahr für die Demokratie oder nützliches Korrektiv?*, ed. Frank Decker (Wiesbaden: Verlag für Sozialwissenschaften, 2006), 144-164 (here 161).
54. Cf. APA-Basisdienst, Jan. 24, 1994.

policy-making in typical right-wing issues, an indication of the breakdown of the isolation policy by the other parties."[55] The SPÖ-led government's partial adoption of the populist agenda was a clear proof of the saying "if you can't beat them, join them."[56]

The FPÖ in Government and After—Failure without Collapse

In the 1999 election the FPÖ achieved twenty-seven percent of the votes, ranking second (with a small margin against the ÖVP) for the first time since its foundation. Despite ranking third, the ÖVP under Wolfgang Schüssel concluded a coalition agreement with Haider who in return accepted his claim to become chancellor. It was the first time in EU history that a party of the new radical right came to power in a member country. Although Haider, due to strategic considerations, abstained from seeking a government office for himself at this moment, and although the coalition partners accepted to formally pledge themselves to democratic values by placing a preamble in the coalition contract urged by the Federal President, the EU-14 responded with sanctions against Austria after the government had been sworn in in February 2000. What followed is well-documented, including the rapid erosion of unity within the EU which resulted in the breakdown of the *cordon sanitaire* after only seven months.[57] What is more, the ban provoked an unprecedented wave of chauvinism in Austria, even among voters who had been critical of the coalition before.[58] In the end, the widespread indignation against the sanctions helped the government, in particular the FPÖ, to divert from initial problems it obviously had.[59]

The FPÖ's decision to move from opposition to government meant a change of the primary goal from *vote* to *office*,[60] an about-turn that had an

---

55. Michael Minkenberg, "The Radical Right in Public Office: Agenda-Setting and Policy Effects," *West European Politics* 24, no. 4 (2001): 1-21 (here 13-14).
56. Tim Bale et al., "If You Can't Beat Them, Join Them? Explaining Social Democratic Responses to the Challenges from the Populist Radical Right in Western Europe," *Political Studies* 58, no. 3 (2010): 410-426 (here 419).
57. Ferdinand Karlhofer, Josef Melchior, and Hubert Sickinger, ed., *Anlassfall Österreich. Die Europäische Union auf dem Weg zu einer Wertegemeinschaft* (Nomos: Baden-Baden, 2001). Cécile Leconte, "The Fragility of the EU as a 'Community of Values: Lessons from the Haider Affair," *West European Politics* 28, no. 3 (2005): 620-649.
58. Günther Pallaver and Reinhold Gärtner, "Populistische Parteien an der Regierung – zum Scheitern verdammt? Italien und Österreich im Vergleich," in *Populismus: Gefahr für die Demokratie oder nützliches Korrektiv?*, ed. Frank Decker (Wiesbaden: VS-Verlag, 2006), 99-120 (here 105).
59. Cf., amongst others, Karlhofer et al., *Anlassfall Österreich*; Emmerich Tálos, ed., *Schwarz-Blau. Eine Bilanz des "Neu-Regierens"* (Vienna: Lit Verlag, 2006).
60. Kurt R. Luther, "Strategien und (Fehl-)Verhalten: Die Freiheitlichen und die

impact on the country's political culture as well as on the party itself. With regard to the policy style, the center-right coalition, referred to from the very beginning as confrontational rather than consensual, was emphasized by elements that had been characterized by the Second Republic. In particular during the cabinet Schüssel I (2000-2002), the political constellation between ÖVP and FPÖ on the one side, and SPÖ and Greens on the other, was polarized and tense. The Austrian party system, having turned from a multipolar to a bipolar system, was classed "a weak version of a two-bloc system."[61] It is worth noting that under the cabinet Schüssel II (2002-2007) relations eased slightly—not least because of the severe electoral setback of the FPÖ in 2002.

As a matter of fact, only a couple of months after the FPÖ had taken office in February 2000 it became apparent that it encountered hardships in managing the turn from an aggressive opposition party to a ruling party. There were several unfavorable conditions complicating the process of adaptation:

- Already in the process of negotiating the coalition agreement, the party had to lower its sights in various policy fields thereby laying the foundation for latent protest that eventually escalated to persistent party infighting.[62]
- Some of the members in government proved to be unable to cope with government business.[63] E.g., the minister of justice had to be replaced after two weeks already, the social affairs minister after eight and the transport minister after ten months.
- The members in government proving successful in office adopted a pragmatic, moderately rightist style that was perceived as being incompatible with ideological core values by the party's ultra-right wing. All things considered, alienation between the group officially representing the party and the fundamentalist faction acting behind the scenes increasingly eroded the party's unity.[64]
- Last but not least, it was the party leader himself who could not

---

Regierungen Schüssel I und II," in *Schwarz-Blau*, ed. Emmerich Tálos (Vienna: Lit Verlag, 2006), 19-37 (here 35).
61. Wolfgang C. Müller and Franz Fallend, "Changing patterns of party competition in Austria: From multipolar to bipolar system," *West European Politics* 27, no. 5 (2004): 801-835 (here 801).
62. Karlhofer et al. *Anlassfall Österreich*, 22.
63. Heinisch, "Success in Opposition - Failure in Government," 115.
64. Luther, "Strategien und (Fehl-)Verhalten," 30-31. Kurt R. Luther, "Of goals and own goals: a case study of right-wing populist party strategy for and during imcumbency," *Party Politics* 17, no. 4 (2011): 453-470 (here 461).

resist counteracting the policy of those very representatives he himself had nominated when negotiating the coalition agreement. Alone, the fact that at the request of Haider the party chairman was replaced five times between 2000 and 2005, indicates his unwillingness to abandon his claim of being the one and only real party leader regardless of the position he formally had at the time being.[65]

Already in 2002, as a consequence of the so-called *Knittelfeld* riot (named after the place in Styria where it took place), in line with Haider's "mercurial behavior"[66] against the government's policy, leading FPÖ ministers (including the FPÖ vice chancellor) tendered their resignation and hereby caused a snap election.

At first sight it appeared as if the FPÖ had failed because of a cunning approach by the ÖVP that started with integrating the populist challenger, followed by taming it and in the end causing its self-destruction. Yet it turned out that the ÖVP strategy of "co-optation and castration" that might even serve as an example for conservative parties in other countries in fighting right-wing populism[67] was successful for a limited time only. There's no question about the astounding success with which the ÖVP managed to boost its electoral support from twenty-seven to forty-two percent in the 2002 snap election while the FPÖ fell from twenty-seven to ten percent. And it is true, as well, that in the renewed coalition, with a shattered FPÖ as junior partner, the ÖVP had *de facto* the power of a single-party government. Around 2005, intra-party decision-making in the FPÖ followed anything but a hierarchical, not even a stratarchical pattern but rather resembled a "loosely coupled anarchy."[68] What is more, after the split-off of the Alliance for the Future of Austria (*Bündnis Zukunft Österreich* – BZÖ) founded by Haider in 2005 and, at the same time, the six FPÖ members in government joining the new party right-wing populism in Austria seemed to be close to collapsing definitely.

Against all odds, in the 2006 election it surprisingly "turned out that there was still life in the FPÖ after Haider and his followers had departed."[69] The FPÖ achieved eleven percent while the BZÖ—actually

---

65. Art, "Reacting to the Radical Right," 344-345.
66. Ibid.
67. Kurt R. Luther, "The Self-Destruction of a Right-Wing Populist Party? The Austrian Parliamentary Election of 2002," *West European Politics* 26, no. 2 (2003): 136-152 (here 150).
68. Luther, "Die Freiheitliche Partei Österreichs (FPÖ) und das Bündnis Zukunft Österreich (BZÖ)," 368.
69. Wolfgang C. Müller, "The surprising elections in Austria, October 2006," *Electoral Studies* 27, no. 1 (2008): 171-175 (here 175).

present in Haider's stronghold Carinthia only where it gained a quarter of the votes—by a narrow margin, managed to overstep the four percent threshold nationwide. In total, both parties held fifteen percent.

In the snap election of 2008 after the breakdown of the tension-filled coalition between ÖVP and SPÖ, the FPÖ gained nearly seventeen point five percent. Even the BZÖ, outside Carinthia virtually inexistent, ran for election, and due to Haider's sure feeling for favorable opportunity structures—and for last time, being at his best when presenting himself as the "original," while taunting Strache to be just a "copy"[70]—achieved ten point seven percent. In total, the radical right won more than twenty-eight percent.

No doubt, the radical right is back again, thus it's worth a closer look at the present state of the two parties. As regards the BZÖ, the party lost its charismatic leader in 2008 when Haider died in a car accident. In 2009, the Carinthian regional faction, by far the largest subunit, left the party and founded the Freedom Party of Carinthia (*Freiheitliche Partei Kärntens – FPK*), henceforth closely linked to the federal FPÖ while distancing itself from the BZÖ. At the time being, after having lost its regional stronghold, the BZÖ moderately successfully attempts to achieve a new programmatic profile with a mix of economic liberalism and political right-conservatism —yet upon closer inspection, hardly more than a copy of the FPÖ party program of 1999.[71] As of 2012, the BZÖ is present in none of the nine state parliaments and only in a small number of local councils.

As regards the FPÖ, the party, after the BZÖ and its followers had seceded, returned to be a party in a strict sense rather than a populist "movement." In April 2005, at a party convention, just a couple of weeks after the split, Heinz-Christian Strache took the lead and at the same time the party statutes were revised in the direction of strengthening the formal party hierarchy that had been ignored by Haider on every occasion. Strategically the FPÖ returned to the populist success orientation with focus on anti-immigration it had pursued in its pre-government phase. Its ideological reorientation can best be gathered from the parliamentary group's composition. While under Haider, die-hard Nazis had played a minor role and instead newcomers susceptible to the leader's populist political style had prevailed (albeit many of them withdrawing after a while), elite recruitment under Strache follows traditional ideology-based selection criteria. What is more, as a result of the 2008 election, fifteen out of the

---

70. Franz Fallend, "Austria," *European Journal of Political Research* 48 (2009): 884-902 (here 890).
71. Luther, "Governing with Right-Wing Populists and Managing the Consequences", 81.

thirty-four FP members in the National Council belong to extreme right dueling fraternities (including Strache himself),[72] some of them again and again embroiled in right extremist actions resp. suspected of re-engagement in National Socialist activities.

Conclusions and Outlook: No Escape from the Vicious Circle?

To observers the radical right's steep rise and fall and rise again over a period of two and a half decades must be puzzling. In 1986, when Haider took the lead, hardly anyone expected the hitherto five-percent party to boost its share of votes to twenty-seven percent as was the case in 1999. In 2002 then, when the FPÖ lost almost two thirds of its electorate, all indications seemed to be that the party's heyday definitely was over. Big was the surprise again in 2006, when the radical right, albeit split now, gained fifteen percent in total, and even twenty-eight percent in 2008. In recent opinion polls the FPÖ ranks second behind the SPÖ (occasionally even first) while the BZÖ moves around the four-percent threshold.[73]

The striking ups and downs of the radical right's electoral success obviously deserve more in-depth research on the hotbed of populism in Austria, and there is every indication that it is specifically the closed structure of party competition and the narrow variety of options for coalition-building in Austria that need to be investigated further. Attempting to do so in detail here would go beyond the scope of the article. However, the findings of this case study give cause to reconsider two questions central to comparative research on the new radical right:

The first question is about the effects of *ostracism vs. integration*. Based on their research about ten European anti-immigration parties (including the FPÖ), van Spanje and van der Brug arrive at the conclusion that the degree of radicalism with this type of party is substantially influenced by the strategies chosen by the other parties in the political system. Ostracism as one option tends to foster radical positions; integration, by contrast, favors moderation: "Anti-immigration parties that have been allowed to participate in normal politics have managed to escape from outright extremism, while their ostracized counterparts have not. Lacking any incentive to tone down their rhetoric, the latter parties can be dominated by their most radical factions."[74] Following this argument, government participation of a radical

---
72. Cf. "So rechts sind Straches Freiheitliche," *Die Presse*, Jan. 23, 2009.
73. <www.oe24.at/oesterreich/politik/OeSTERREICH-Umfrage-SPOe-und-FPOe-auf-Platz-1-OeVP-verliert-weiter/62104088>.
74. van Spanje/van der Brug, "The Party as Pariah," 1036-1037.

party eventually has a "taming effect" insofar as, given the coalition with a party pursuing less intransigent policy goals, it is, like it or not, forced to compromise.[75] No doubt, when in government, a populist party is structurally constrained in its communication with voters while in opposition there is no necessity to lower its sight. Hence, in government the FPÖ got into a dilemma since the center-right partner expected the party to mitigate its most radical xenophobe positions.[76] Yet this is not the whole story when taking into account that the dominant figure Haider continued to behave as if he was in opposition despite his own party being in government; he did not abandon, what is more, not even moderate his populist anti-government rhetoric.[77] In effect, the FPÖ, just as the Swiss SVP, was in government and opposition at the same time—with the one difference that the SVP, by making use of referenda, successfully managed to balance being "in" and "out" while the FPÖ failed in 2002. The lesson to be learned from the Austrian case is that a "static" approach neglecting the actual context cannot really grasp the varying dynamics determining specific situations.

The second question is about whether or not the mere presence of an aggressively attacking party has an influence on the other parties' political agenda, in other words: Do parties of the new radical right have a *contagion effect* on the mainstream parties' policy stances? Empirical research suggests that there is evidence supporting the hypothesis of close correlation: Based on comparative analyses of seventy-five parties' electoral support in eleven West European countries (including Austria), "it is found that the electoral success or failure of anti-immigration parties has a contagion effect on the immigration stances of other parties [...]. When in government, however, parties are not affected by this mechanism."[78] With regard to Austria the findings are ambiguous. Clearly, in the center-right coalition between 2000 and 2007 the ÖVP was the dominant force determining the general direction and, at the same time, averting radical attempts. Concurrently, though, the ÖVP gradually moved to the right.[79] In the same way the SPÖ in striving for winning back voters made concessions by adopting parts of

---

75. Michael Minkenberg, "Die radikale Rechte in Europa heute: Profile und Trends in West und Ost," in *Die Dynamik der europäischen Rechten: Geschichte, Kontinuitäten und Wandel*, ed. Claudia Globisch (Wiesbaden: Verlag für Sozialwissenschaften, 2011), 111-131.
Ivarsflaten, "What Unites the Populist Right in Western Europe?"
76. Elisabeth Ivarsflaten, "Populists in Power: attitudes towards immigrants after the Austrian Freedom Party entered government," in *New Parties in Government*, ed. Kris Deschouwer (London: Routledge, 2008), 175-189 (here 175-176).
77. Luther, "Strategien und (Fehl-)Verhalten," 32-33.
78. Spanje, "Contagious Parties," 578.
79. Pallaver/Gärtner, "Populistische Parteien an der Regierung," 117-118.

the right-wing populist agenda as outlined above. Once again, some general findings of comparative research deserve qualification: Just as the Danish case between 2001 and 2011 showed,[80] and the Netherlands in roughly the same time in return,[81] populist parties—be they in opposition or in government—have a contagion effect and, what is more, "remain part of the political spectrum as long as the conditions facilitating their growth persist."[82]

In conclusion, as concerns Austria, "Haiderism survives as a loose political ideology that has permanently changed the face of Austrian politics."[83] And going beyond this country's study, it's a fact that the populist radical right, other than expected in the 1980s and still in the 2000s, "should be seen as a radical interpretation of mainstream values, or more akin to a pathological normalcy."[84] The lesson to be learned is that the research focus concerning the new radical right is not so much the phenomenon as such but rather the hotbed that makes it grow. Any analysis of populism in general and the extreme right in particular, needs to direct the attention to the state of the party system as a whole.[85] In other words: Populism is a dependent variable of a country's political culture. There have been a lot of premature expectations, superficial diagnoses and misperceptions by observers about populism in Austria. Bearing in mind the *surprising* rise and *surprising* decline and *surprising* rise could be a good point of departure for further research on the preconditions of populist success.

---

80. Schubert, "Extremismus in Dänemark."
81. Paul Lucardie, Gerrit Voerman, and Friso Wielenga, "Extremismus in den Niederlanden," in *Extremismus in den EU-Staaten*, ed. Eckhard Jesse and Tom Thieme (Wiesbaden: Verlag für Sozialwissenschaften, 2011), 47-263.
82. Heinisch, "Success in Opposition," 125.
83. Art, "Reacting to the Radical Right," 345.
84. Mudde, "The Populist Radical Right," 1167.
85. Herbert Kitschelt, "Growth and persistence of the radical right in postindustrial democracies: advances and challenges in comparative perspective," *West European Politics* 30, no. 5 (2007): 1176-1206.

Postscript: The Carinthia debacle, March 2013

In the super election year 2013, with ballots in four of the nine states in spring and national elections scheduled for early fall, the radical right is facing a severe setback. Mainly responsible for the decline is the FPÖ's formally autonomous Carinthian faction FPK (*Freiheitliche Partei Kärntens*). During the party's ups and downs under Jörg Haider's leaderhip, Carinthia had always been a reliable stronghold, the only Austrian state ever ruled by an FPÖ governor (1989-1991, and then again 1999-2013). Haider himself had held office until his death in 2008. What followed in the aftermath of his accident (while driving drunk) came close to an apotheosis, if not a cult of a saint. His followers organized a pompous state funeral, hid the damaged car in a secret place and founded a Haider museum with devotional objects documenting his life. The politics of glorification paid: with a vote of 45 percent in the 2009 state election the party achieved its best election result ever. Soon, however, the state was shattered by trials over corruption scandals with leading FPK functionaries involved, and extensive fraud with roots tracing back to Haider's governorship. With several FPK leaders (including the party chairman) convicted, voter support rapidly eroded, eventually ending up in a loss of 28 percent in the election of March 3, 2013, and the governor office shifting to the social democrats.

At the same time as in Carinthia, the FPÖ suffered losses in the state election in Lower Austria, too—less dramatically (minus 2 percent), yet still painful since the party lost its single seat in government (which is composed proportionally). What is more, the FPÖ now ranks behind a political newcomer: the billionaire Frank Stronach who came close to 10 percent of the vote. Stronach, a populist having much in common with FPÖ-style anti-establishment attitudes (except for xenophobia) claimed the state elections of spring 2013 just to be a "test" for his plan to run for Parliament in the autumn election. For the national ballot the new player is well-prepared: In order to avoid tedious collecting of signatures to meet the requirements for candidacy, he decided to take a shortcut by simply recruiting five backbenchers coming from within the ranks of the BZÖ and now as MPs of a "Team Stronach" forming a parliamentary group of their own.

Altogether, with the collapse of the former stronghold Carinthia and an unexpected populist competitor entering the political stage nation-wide, Austria's rightist parties—both the radical FPÖ and the more moderate BZÖ—are not going to fly high in the near term.

Book Reviews

Dieter Stiefel. *Camillo Castiglioni oder Die Metaphysik der Haifische* (Vienna: Böhlau, 2012)

Harold James

Camillo Castiglioni was born in 1879 in the port city of Trieste, then part of the Austro-Hungarian Empire, as the son of a rabbi. He worked as a sales agent for the Viennese Continentale rubber factory, before becoming the director of its export department at the age of twenty-five. He was quickly fascinated by aviation and by ballooning. From 1912 he was an independent businessman, who built up an extensive range of industrial holdings, including the dominant Austrian steel company, Alpine Montan, the Munich aero engine manufacturer BMW, as well as briefly controlling one of the large Viennese banks, the Depositenbank, at the height of the Austrian hyperinflation. He led a larger than life existence, with a magnificent city palace in Vienna decorated with gigantic Tiepolos (now in the Metropolitan Museum in New York), and traveled regularly in the former railroad carriage of the Emperor. Not content with that, he ordered his own factories to make him a new, special carriage. He was supposed to be the richest man in Central Europe. He wrote on notepaper with a monogram C.C. Stiefel quotes the left-wing *Arbeiter-Zeitung* as valuing him at 80 m. Swiss francs, or more than enough to finance the whole of Austria's money-stock (p. 122). C.C. was a major patron of the arts, a sponsor of Max Reinhardt, and financed the early years of the Salzburg Festival. His third wife was a Burgtheater actress.

Inevitably his wealth and reputation attracted attention, and myths about C.C. sprouted like mushrooms. His substantial success was based on his ability as a salesman, but also on his skill in managing the complicated international politics of postwar Europe. In particular, he developed close links with Mussolini and with the Milan Banca Commerciale, and presented himself as a conduit for channeling Italian investment into southeast central Europe. Already before 1922, the Italian state had been interested in extending its economic influence; but the demand grew bigger with the establishment of the fascist state. The complicated business of dealing with unstable exchange rates in Central Europe, lent itself to a manipulation in which Swiss companies were established to channel foreign exchange receipts; the proceeds could be diverted away from the company and its investment plans to the owner or the manager. That is what seems to have happened in the case of both Alpine Montan and BMW. Rumors about Castiglioni's enormous influence focused on press corruption that plays a prominent role. He owned several Viennese newspapers, and paid a great deal of attention to the management of public opinion.

After the inflation, Castiglioni's affairs started to unravel. In 1922, he was forced out of the Depositenbank, which collapsed in 1924. He lost a large amount of money in speculation against the French franc in 1924, and was prosecuted for fraud (but never convicted) in relation to a complicated business involving trade in spirits. By the time of the Great Depression, he had lost a substantial amount of his fortune, and his possessions were sold off to pay tax arrears and other liabilities. He survived the Second World War first in Switzerland, which eventually expelled him, and then in Italy, where after the German occupation he hid in a Franciscan monastery. After the War, he restarted some of his old political intermediation—he helped Tito's Yugoslavia to a World Bank loan—but his natural environment had vanished and he died in Rome in relative obscurity in 1957. According to his daughter, he insisted to the end that he had never done anything wrong. Legally, that is a tenable position.

Dieter Stiefel's interesting and evocative book is in some ways a spinoff of a television film with the same title for which he had written the script in 1988. The film brought him into contact with Castiglioni's daughters, who provided some photographs of their family's interwar life. Unfortunately, there is almost no material produced by Castiglioni himself that survives and is accessible to historians, so it is difficult to write a real or deep biography. Stiefel's solution is perhaps necessarily somewhat choppy. The book is arranged by subject areas, rather than chronologically. It maintains a distinct literary character, in that many sections start with multiple contradictory accounts of a particular event. Did Castiglioni snatch his actress wife Iphigenie Buchmann off a steamer to America? Did he bribe the girl's father to get her hand? In fact, he seems to have met her at the port in Hamburg in 1915, when she was returning from a New York run of an Arthur Schnitzler play. Unfortunately, for many of the complex business cases, it is really impossible to establish the truth. As a consequence, the book relies extensively on very long quotations from newspaper articles, some from parts of the press influenced by Castiglioni, but much also from ideological and business critics and rivals. Castiglioni and the scribes he hired described the heroic entrepreneur as a victim, ultimately driven out by the old money aristocracy of Vienna; for socialists and anti-Semites on the other hand he was a predatory shark. For long stretches, Stiefel's account seems more of a scrapbook than an analysis, a multi-perspective view in which the central object is so mythological that it never becomes completely clear. The result gives a unique portrait of the atmosphere of the First Austrian Republic, of deep corruption portrayed in the rich and amusing prose in which baroque Austria is fused with modernism, of the upswelling of a poisonous anti-Semitism, and of economic, political, and moral collapse.

There are plenty of anecdotes, although we can never really know how reliable they are. One of Stiefel's most-used sources on C.C. apart from newspaper articles is the memoir of the German aeronautic engineer, Ernest Heinkel, which included vignettes on how C.C. sent messages of love to women written on high denomination banknotes. But there are also the memoirs of the banker Richard Kola, with a memorable vignette of Joseph Schumpeter as Austria's Finance Minister (p. 60) responding to Kola's suggestion on how to get foreign exchange without using the official exchange in the *Devisenzentrale*. "Isn't the purchase of foreign exchange forbidden?" Schumpeter asks. "Yes, indeed, but the prohibition is only there so that it can be circumvented," replies the banker, and Schumpeter gives him 50 million crowns to use as the state's banker.

The publishers present the book as containing "extraordinary parallels with the present." Perhaps. Fortunately, Stiefel lets this theme be implicit rather than explicit. Is it simply a question of the technical difficulty of prosecuting (and getting judges and juries to understand) in complex fraud cases—with many prosecutions in the U.S. or the U.K collapsing? Is it a case of a compromised and venal press? Is it a specific proclivity for Austria's political and business culture to produce constant *Affären*? Or is it rather that a great deal of regulation and bureaucracy will always create the opportunities for energetic and imaginative individuals to wreak havoc: the kind of lesson that the Austrian economist Friedrich Hayek drew from the sad story of the First Republic?

Brigitte Kepplinger and Irene Leitner (Eds.), worked on by Andrea Kammerhofer, *Dameron Report: Bericht des War Crimes Investigating Teams No. 6824 der U. S. Army vom 17. 7. 1945 über die Tötungsanstalt Hartheim* (Innsbruck: Studienverlag, 2012)

Gerhard L. Weinberg

In this, the first volume in a series of historical texts to be published by the memorial at the castle Hartheim near Linz in Austria, readers are offered a highly significant source on the German program of killing the handicapped. This 1945 report of an investigating team led by Major Charles H. Dameron was found in the U.S. National Archives, and with only one exception to be noted below, is published here in full with its annexes, photographs, and other related exhibits. This is of great importance for an understanding of both this particular portion of the so-called euthanasia program as well as that program as a whole because those in charge of the killing at the time quite deliberately and systematically destroyed the records created in vast quantities during the operation of the killing center. As the report and several of the exhibits make dramatically clear, this effort to cover up what had happened was not restricted to the destruction of records. The castle itself was quite carefully altered by removing or destroying all traces of its wartime function and making what had once been an institution for mental patients and had then been equipped with a gas chamber, crematorium, etc., into an orphanage with a contingent of orphans and an appropriate number of nuns to look after them.

The editors provide a very careful and thoughtful introduction to the history of the killing center as revealed by postwar investigation with special emphasis on how individuals were recruited and with one exception retained as individuals who participated in the killing of other human beings on a daily basis for high wages. They also explain how, after the halting of the centralized killing of the handicapped in August 1941 and the shifting of that process to hospitals and other institutions throughout Germany, the killing facilities that had been installed in the Hartheim castle were utilized to kill concentration camp inmates and others whom the regime wanted murdered. Most but not all of this second group of victims came from Mauthausen concentration camp, and, ironically, it was other prisoners from Mauthausen who were put to work restoring the castle to its former state in the winter of 1944-45.

The book contains the full text of the report by Major Dameron's investigation (in English) and also the statements and evidence of numerous individuals who had worked there or had in other ways been associated with it (in English and German). Only a statistical report on the program of killing the handicapped that was found by the investigating team is not included but is scheduled to be published separately. The materials presented in this book in full offer a real sense of how such an institution worked. In the process this document fully confirms the thesis of the late Professor Henry Friedlander in his book, *The Origins of Nazi Genocide: From Euthanasia to the Final Solution* (Chapel Hill: University of North Carolina Press, 1995), that it was in this killing program that the Germans developed the procedures subsequently applied in the systematic killing of Jews that we now refer to as the Holocaust. Thus one learns that already in Hartheim any gold teeth were knocked out of the corpses of the murdered victims to be sent to Berlin.

It was possible for Günter Bischof to interview Dameron before his death in 2002, and the book includes his short but helpful obituary on the head of the Investigating Team that produced the report. The volume also includes the text of a quite detailed and very interesting letter that Dameron wrote to his parents about his experiences in November 1945. Of the separate exhibits that follow the investigation report several deserve special mention. The written reports by Helene Hintersteiner (Nos. 9-10, 13, 28) and Hans-Heinrich Lenz (Nos. 41-42) provide important details because of their roles in the operation of Hartheim. No. 26 is a list of books sent from the Berlin headquarters of the euthanasia program to Hartheim and is in effect a bibliography on sterilization and so-called mercy killing, thus providing some insight into what those in charge of the whole killing program thought worthy of attention. Also to be noted because of their uniqueness are the pictures that are attached to the report with some explanations (Nos. 15-25, 27, 52, 53, 57).

One of the last documents (No. 54) records the suicide of the whole family of one of the central figures of the criminal activity at Hartheim, while few others suffered for their participation. That is why the original document was located among the "Cases not tried" in the files of the War Crimes Branch of Headquarters, U. S. Army Europe.

For each of the published documents, the editors have supplied a brief description of the document's contents as well as of the appearance of the original. It is all a very sad story about the killing of over 18,000 mental patients and many thousands of concentration camp inmates and other forced laborers, but in a way the victims have here at least a testimonial to their fate that sets a high standard for documentary editing.

Thomas König, *Die Frühgeschichte des Fulbright Program in Österreich: Transatlantische "Fühlungnahme auf dem Gebiet der Erziehung"* (TRANSATLANTICA 6) (Innsbruck: StudienVerlag, 2012)

Berndt Ostendorf

The book under review chronicles the early history of the Fulbright program in Austria, with a special focus on the formation of a transatlantic educational network and its impact on the Austrian system of higher education. A young Viennese political scientist, Thomas König, tells the story of the battle for the hearts and minds of the Austrian post-war academic elite. His inquiry has a dual thrust: It provides an important chapter on American cultural diplomacy in the early Cold War, and secondly, it offers a robust critique of the post-war history of Austrian higher education and its intrigue-ridden academic politics.

The book helps to understand the political choreography of the post-war period. During the Korean War the battle lines of the larger East-West conflict had hardened considerably; the Cold War became hotter, and as a consequence, the western occupying forces began the militarization of the occupation zones—a clear signal of the American determination to prevent Austria from becoming communist. Austria had to pay reparations to Russia, but in turn received help from the Marshall Plan. The force field changed drastically in 1955, a year which represents the *annus mirabilis* of post-war Austrian history. The occupational status ended; the retreat of the last Soviet troops and Austria's deliverance into neutrality had a dual effect. The exculpation created an instant democratic consensus and led to a repression of historical memory. Austria had become a victim rather than a supporter of fascism, hence there was no urgent need for any reeducation or what in Germany was labeled *Vergangenheitsbewältigung* (mastering of the past). All these developments were buttressed by the economic recovery of the late fifties and sixties. Under Bruno Kreisky as foreign minister, Austria began to carve out a new role as mediator and negotiator between the two power blocks which helped to stabilize the neutrality of Austrian foreign policy and encouraged the cognitive denial of guilt. These were the larger contexts in which the Fulbright program evolved.

Senator Fulbright, who gave his name to the program, was a former Rhodes scholar, who had spent time in England and Vienna during the twenties and thirties. The salutary effect of his educational experience gave rise to his concern that few Americans had studied abroad or knew foreign languages. Consequently he conceived of an imaginative use of the obscure Surplus Property Act of 1944. He proposed to use a portion of the monetary interest levied from war surplus overseas to start an educational exchange program. President Truman signed the P.L. 584 Amendment which set up a Board of Foreign Scholarship. The revolutionary new idea of the Fulbright Act was to bring young foreign students to study in the US and invite American scholars to go and study or teach abroad, and thus create a mutual network of cultural ambassadors. "We must seek through education to develop empathy that rare and wonderful ability to perceive the world as others see it." Such a visionary sentiment, coming from a conservative southern democrat, was unusual then, and seems rare today considering the new parochialism of his successors in office.

His logic was simple: get a mutual learning process going by reaching out to the educational multipliers and elites of various countries. The exchange program which began in 1952 gave annually forty Austrian young professionals the chance to get to know the US from the inside, study the newest scientific theories and methodologies and enjoy the free exchange of ideas. Likewise American students and scholars were invited to study Austrian or European history, the fine arts, politics, social sciences, and natural sciences or to teach in their respective fields of expertise. As is evidenced by the summary reports submitted by participants, the program was a resounding success from the start. Indeed, the visionary idea behind the Fulbright program has inspired subsequent exchange programs such as the current Erasmus and Socrates programs within the European Union. The Fulbright program became the master template for international student mobility programs.

König analyzes the reports of Austrian scholars who spent time at American institutions of higher learning from 1951 to 1964 and who later became respected scholars in Austria. The list at the end of the book reads like a who's who of academic leaders after the war. Equal attention is spent on visiting lecturers and research scholars from America who came to Austria to stimulate higher education in the country and impart innovative teaching and research approaches. Here the book is of particular relevance since it serves to unveil the provincial horizon and backward mind-set of the Austrian academic establishment. Two educational systems clashed. The old *Ordinarienuniversität* of Austria, which after the massive expulsion of Jewish scholars had atrophied intellectually under the Nazi years, was now confronted with competitive American institutions in a vigorous educational market. Most of the full professors at Austrian universities were *survival artists*; i.e. they had survived two authoritarian and dictatorial systems from 1934 to 1945. They were joined by an equally powerful network of hidebound civil servants from the Ministry of Education, among them first and foremost Heinrich Drimmel, the minister himself. These two cohorts actively resisted any change or innovation.

The Fulbright program was operated by a commission in Vienna with local and American members; this forced association introduced a breath of fresh air into the stuffy university bureaucracy. The program required a transparent merit-based selection process with public invitation and clear selection criteria. This procedure met with some resistance from the old boy network of professors. In Austria such appointments had been decided behind closed doors by officers of the ministry and the networked full professors. Here the classic principle of self-governance had resulted in institutional nepotism and intellectual stagnation, for those in power preferred to pick politically reliable candidates, both to go to the US and to come to Austria. The old guard was particularly hesitant to invite emigrees who had made successful careers in the US. Indeed such Fulbright lecturers were unwelcome competitors whose new methods and theories gave them a distinct feeling of inferiority. This was particularly true in the social sciences where the theoretical deficits and the stagnation in Austrian scholarship were glaringly evident. If these returnees were Jews this would add insult to injury. Those who were appointed in their jobs during the Nazi regime were under suspicion of having benefited from the wholesale expulsion of Jewish professors. As a result on top of the stagnation in personnel and academic knowhow there was a latent bad conscience caused by the mere presence of such Fulbrighters. The problem was not only the lack of civility, but also a tacit anti-Semitism combined with a residual Anti-Americanism which was part of the *esprit de corps* of the post-war professoriat.

No wonder then that in the early years of the program American visitors faced a strategy of benign neglect. They were simply ignored by the system. Their lectures were not listed in the course catalogs of universities; quite often their scholarship was considered not up to local standards; and, they were not included in the social life of the professoriat. The Princeton historian Eric Goldman who held a Fulbright at Vienna during 1953-4 gave up after a few weeks and reacted to the hostile reception by going back to America.

I remember well stories from Fulbrighters in Germany who never met the *Ordinarien* socially during their entire term. Thus the Americanization of the educational system as planned by American diplomacy did not proceed quite so smoothly as expected. But then a generational divide became effective, and things changed markedly during the rebellious sixties. For the younger generation marched to a different drummer and adopted American culture with an abandon that alarmed the old guard and increased their reserve. After all, Austria was let off the hook, it was a victim of Nazism. Hence their restorative impulse was supported by the quasi-wholesale denazification guaranteed by the Staatsvertrag. As victims of fascism, why should they accept reeducation. This initial resistance faded in the sixties when American guests were more welcomed and accomodated; even their courses were now listed in the catalogs and their lectures enjoyed overflow audiences. Students found the American pedagogy inspiring. Instead of reading from prepared manuscripts American professors invited discussion and accepted students as active participants in the scholarly debates. By then the program had become so successful that it was put on a secure financial footing by the Fulbright Hays Act and by ERP funds.

The study does an excellent job contextualizing the Fulbright program in Austrian education; but it also raises a host of additional questions that would merit further research. How did the program develop after 1964? How did Austrian Fulbrighters change the educational landscape after their return? Are the activists who were part of the Kreisky group during the 1970s reform a result of such influences? Of particular interest would be a comparison of the Austrian program with those in Germany and Italy. Many of the systemic obstructions that König describes for Austria are also relevant for Germany. During the fifties the response to the program was similarly reluctant. The lack of basic civility by the establishment had a positive long range effect: it fostered an active solidarity between German/Austrian students and their American teachers. At many universities an academic counter culture developed, an intellectual wetland that would spawn the new American Studies movement after the post-Fulbright students entered professional careers.

Currently American Studies is often dismissed as a child of the Cold War and hence accused of being complicit with American hegemonic designs. For us young graduate students, the reeducation offered by American Fulbrighters was a welcome alternative to the ruling canon. Noble principles such as the rule of law and democratic habits of the heart were planted in the souls of young Europeans. As an educational option after 1945 these seemed to hold more promise than the restoration politics of the old guard. The Fulbright program although embedded in the Cold War transcended its narrow, ideological killer opposition. In sum the creation of a transatlantic network of Austrian and American students and scholars who became knowledgeable about each other is one of the success stories of post-war Europe. American Studies, once a rarity in Europe, is now commonplace in university curricula. The European Association of American Studies is composed of twenty-two national associations from thirty-five countries and has spawned many research groups on all aspects of American culture and politics. Fulbright's vision initiated one of the most successful exports of the US: educational exchanges and American Studies, now coming into their global, transnational age.

The Expulsion of the Sudeten Germans from Postwar Czechoslovakia: A Review Essay.

Adrian von Arburg, Tomáš Staněk, ed., *Vysídlení Němců a proměny českého pohraničí 1945 - 1951 : dokumenty z českých archive; 1. Češi a Němci do roku 1945 : úvod k edici; 2.1. Duben - srpen/září 1945: "Divoký odsun" a počátky osídlování* (Středokluky 2010-2011)

David Schriffl

Not only did the expulsion of the Sudeten Germans set the stage for almost three million people to lose their homes and their homeland, but it also set the circumstances under which the relations between Austria and Czechoslovakia developed (or rather, didn't develop). The same can be said regarding the relations to the German states FRG and GDR. The situation of the German-speaking minority could have been important for Austria as the successor state of the Austro-Hungarian Empire, seeing as a vast number of people expelled who were—at least until 1938-1945—widely regarded as co-nationals, but it wasn't. Austria could have found itself in a position to defend a population and its political and cultural interest that in 1919 formed the provinces "Deutschböhmen" and "Sudetenland" (besides the German-speaking cities of Iglau/Jihlava, Olmütz/Olomouc und Brünn/Brno) which declared themselves part of the First (German-) Austrian Republic, but it did not. Not only had Austria's role changed on the international stage, it's self-consciousness had changed drastically, as well; this was partly due to the events of WWII, and partly due to a pragmatic emphasis on her mythical role as the "first victim" of Hitlerite aggression. Austria could not take a serious stand for the "German" population that was to be driven out from their century-long homeland. It only tried to take a stand for those who were eligible for Austrian citizenship. Even Austrian diplomats expressed their acceptance for the measures of the renewed Czechoslovak Republic, and followed the argument that the behavior of the German state and its former Czechoslovak citizens would make it impossible to live together in the same state.[1] Nevertheless, this expulsion

---

1. Memorandum, July 14, 1945, StKa-AA, Gr.Zl. 138-pol/45, Zl. 867-pol/45, Österreichisches Staatsarchiv, Archiv der Republik, Vienna; cf. David Schriffl, "*Tote*

and its repercussions have been the biggest burden for the relations between the two countries for decades after the war (besides and combined with the ideological confrontation in the Cold War). Mainly two facts or developments contributed: 1. Individuals with an Austrian citizenship or the entitlement to it were treated the same way as "Germans," and 2. By integrating some of the refugees from the Czechoslovak Republic as Austrian citizens, their physical and monetary losses became Austria's concern, too. The conflicts between the neighboring countries over these matters burdened the relationship that was already carrying a severe legacy from the times of the empire—a time Czech nationalist historiography always saw as a prison or *temno*, "the darkness." But for the Czechoslovak public, the expulsion was not very much put into question. The plan that has been developed to, as President Benes explained, "solve the problem," found wide acceptance amongst the Czech and Slovak people. Especially in the western part of the country, the trauma of the dictated surrender to German political and territorial wishes in Munich, 1938, together with the partly harsh measures against any political opposition and plans to Germanize Bohemia by way of the deportation of parts of the population, provided enough arguments for the post-war Czechoslovak society to feel the need to finally get rid of the unwanted neighbors.

The expulsion is divided into two easily distinguishable parts: The "wild" expulsion during the first months after the defeat of the German forces, and the more centrally organized expulsion, that happened with the consent and logistic support of the Allies, who, after the conference of Potsdam held in July/August 1945, agreed to large-scale deportations in Europe, mainly to make an end to German minorities in Eastern Europe as a possible threat to the post-war order in Europe.[2] The first phase was less organized and more violent, causing death, torture, and rape in a mixture of revenge for the wartime oppression, and an outburst of the lowest instincts of mankind which are often present under the thin surface of civilization. Very soon the Czechoslovak public and political sphere—widely united in acceptance of the expulsion itself—encountered several problems: 1. Violence against the expelled civilians corrupted the then accepted goal. Comparisons between the oppressive policy of the national-socialists and post-war Czechoslovakia were not welcome, even though the anti-German

---

Grenze oder lebendige Nachbarschaft? Österreichisch-Slowakische Beziehungen 1945-1968," in *Zentraleuropastudien* 16 (Wien: Austrian Academy of Science Press, 2012), 339.
2. For a bigger picture on the forced changes in populations in Europe after WWII including non-German minorities cf. Philipp Ther, *Die dunkle Seite der Nationalstaaten: "Ethnische Säuberungen" im modernen Europa* (Göttingen: Vandenhoeck & Ruprecht, 2011).

measures hit many people that explicitly should have been spared by the measures, such as Jews or proven Anti-Fascists.[3] Even more than the text of the presidential decrees, this made obvious that the only decisive factor was ethnicity. An attempt to confront that dilemma was Beneš speech in Mělník in October 1945, where he again rectified the transfer but condemned acts of violence, mainly to condole foreign observers. Even promises to foreign governments, such as the Austrian one to spare their citizens were widely ignored. In Slovakia the decision of the Prague government to exclude Austrians that had not acted against the Czechoslovak Republic from the anti-German measures was only formally accepted by the Slovak National Council and the local executive, but in 1945/1946 internal orders had been given that an Austrian citizenship was no reason for a different treatment of people formerly identified as Germans.[4] 2. The consent of the Allies gave a feeling of security that the measures would not have negative effects on the post-war Czechoslovak Republic. Nevertheless, there always has been the fear that some kind of revenge for the expulsion could occur in the future, via political organizations of the Sudeten Germans in the West or, decades later, by means of efforts to regain lost property in court. Consequently, the history of the expulsion in Czechoslovak society was always present, though simultaneously a great taboo, which is also a conviction of the editors. (cf. I., 220)

This is evidenced by the lack of research on the topic.[5] It also may not be coincidental that Václav Havel, the former dissident who became president after the fall of the communist regime, accounted for the greeting in the first pages of the books. He was one of the first important figures of the Czechoslovak civil society to openly address the guilt of Czechs and

---

3. Similar cases happened in the Slovak part of the country where f.e. Sisinio Pretis-Cagnodo, a land owner and candidate for the post of the Austrian representative in Slovakia in 1945, was dispossessed by the Soviets and had to leave the country like so many others, even though he actively fought on the side of the partisans in the "Slovak National Uprising" in 1944 and was decorated for this effort shortly after the war. Cf. Schriffl, *Tote Grenze*, 62-64.

4. Ibid., 47-48. For a more detailed view on the situation of the German-speaking minority in Slovakia and especially the question of the protection of Austrian citizens there confer to ibid., 333-352.

5. For research by Austrian scholars regarding that topic refer to: Gerald M. Sprengnagel, "Wenn die Toten die Lebenden packen: Zur Geschichte der Tschechoslowakei und Tschechiens nach 1945 aus österreichischer Sicht," in *Schlaglichter auf die Geschichte der Böhmischen Länder vom 16. bis 20. Jahrhundert: Ausgewählte Ergebnisse zu den tschechisch-österreichischen Historikertagen 2006 und 2008, Schriftenreihe der Waldviertel Akademie 6*, ed. David Schriffl and Niklas Perzi (Waidhofen a.d. Thaya/Wien/Münster: LIT, 2011), 268 FN 7; Niklas Perzi, David Schriffl, "Bunte Flecken auf weißem Feld? Österreichische Historiographie zur Geschichte der Böhmischen Länder 1914-1945" in Ibid., 145-159.

Slovaks in crimes committed in the expulsions, and dared to question the rightfulness of the population transfer or deportation in general—a posture that brought him harsh criticism from parts of Czech society. But with his posture he also gave impulse to critical scholarly research. (cf. I., 229)

It would be an improper simplification to blame only the communist regime for the long lack of scientific research; they had no interest to allow scholarly research on a topic that could corrupt the states master narrative of the collective suffering of a deeply democratic society and heroic resistance against the foreign enemy and his domestic supporters. It is also taboo to openly address the individual crimes of the expulsion and the general crime of "ethnic cleansing" as part of the post-war order that led to this delay. Under those circumstances, the outstanding role of Tomáš Staněk, who after 1989 soon became the leading scholar working on the topic including editing documents, has to be outlined explicitly.[6] And perhaps those conditions make it less surprising to find that the second driving force behind a number of remarkable works on the topic—including the one mainly addressed in this review—is a foreigner. The Swiss historian Adrian von Arburg already made the population exchange in the borderlands that followed the expulsion topic of his Master's thesis[7] and his dissertation.[8] The latter is—besides other works on the topic[9]—followed by the outstanding project, "The displacement of Germans and the metamorphoses of the Czech borderlands 1945-1951," which is partly discussed here. This project aims at collecting and editing the main sources related to the expulsion. Eight volumes will cover the years 1945-1951; three volumes have been published so far: II.3 about collective violence 1945 in 2010; I. about the common history of "Czechs and Germans until 1945" including a foreword for the edition in 2010, and II.1 covering the time from April to August/September 1945 of the "wild" expulsions and the origins of the population transfer in 2011. The edition is well structured and with its extensive introductory first volume it offers a broad study of the

---

6. I just mention his pioneering work here: Tomáš Staněk, *Odsun Nemců z Československa 1945-1947* (Prague: Academia, 1991).

7. Adrian von Arburg, "Osídlování: Die Besiedlung der Grenzgebiete der böhmischen Länder 1945-1950. Forschungsstand und ausgewählte Probleme," Master-Thesis, Vienna University, 2001.

8. Adrian von Arburg, "Zwischen Vertreibung und Integration. Tschechische Deutschenpolitik 1947-1953," PhD. diss., Prague University, 2004.

9. Adrian von Arburg, *Německy mluvící obyvatelstvo v Československu po roce 1945, Edice Země a kultura ve Střední Evropě 15* (Brno: Matice moravská pro Výzkumné středisko pro dějiny střední Evropy: prameny, země, kultura, 2010); Adrian von Arburg, Tomáš Staněk ed., "*Die Aussiedlung der Deutschen und der Wandel des tschechischen Grenzgebietes 1945–1951: Dokumente aus tschechischen Archiven*" (Brünn 2010ff).

societal circumstances of the Czech-German relations in the borderlands. The first volume explains the origins and backgrounds of the post-war events, and unintentionally reveals a part of the ancient master narrative of the Czechoslovak society regarding the expulsion: that it was well-founded in the events of the past, and that the Germans would have lost their right to live in the boundaries of the Slavic national state due to their behavior. Of course, I do not intend to imply that the editors follow the same pattern, and it is necessary to shed light to the history that has been abused to rectify "ethnic cleansing"; however, the sheer fact that the narrative in the volume follows the same deductive line speaks to the deep roots of this rectification in the public consciousness. Nowadays, almost every Czech citizen would deny the rightfulness of the principle of collective guilt. But asked for the reasons behind the expulsion of the Germans, still, many at least accept it as a logical consequence of the incidents between 1938 and 1945. Following the patterns of explanation, volume I goes back to the nineteenth century, plunging into the explanation of the rise of nations and nationalism in Europe. Many books have been written on that topic and perhaps it overstrains an editorial foreword—as voluminous as it is—to disentangle all those lines of development. An example being when in a footnote, Switzerland, amongst other (Western European) countries, has to prove the development of a political nation before the ethnic nation in Western Europe, while the development in Central and Eastern Europe followed the ethnic principle (cf. I., 72, FN 2.), a concept that is, to say it cautiously, disputed. When the Czech language and culture are displayed as threatened by extinction in the nineteenth century due to a combination of social mechanisms (the German language as a possibility to gain social status) and an initiating German nationalism, a rightful fight for the Czech nation gleams (cf. I., 72f.). Although the changing loyalties of the individual inhabitant of the Czech lands are addressed, the master narrative of the ethnic/cultural conflict between two groups defined by back-protection and amplified by processes of modernization stays in place. Looking back, Czechs stay Czechs, and Germans stay Germans. Already from those times a Czech fear of "losing" the borderlands to the Germans is, according to the authors, developing (cf. I., 75f.). The Germans are displayed as a threat and as an enemy. Out of this historical tradition it is not a surprise that the city of Brno still describes on its web-page its history with sentences like: "In the thirteenth century came foreign colonists: Germans, Flanders and Walloons […] The German dominance […] ended in 1919. […] Due to the nacistic occupation […] many Czech citizens died and were executed.

As a consequence the German population was expelled in 1945."[10] It seems that the old narrative has not changed much. More importantly are scholarly works that try to paint a more distinctive picture. The editors tried to do so, but, as I mentioned above, followed in the course of events that are presented as the pretext to the expulsion, the old narrative. Every chapter concludes with the list of secondary sources which makes the volume a useful guide through contemporary (prevalent Czech) historiography.

But the main undertaking, to present a carefully selected compilation of documents, is successfully achieved. The large number of documents explains the amount of time needed to publish all the planned volumes. One can already argue that these works are benchmarks in editing files related to the expulsion of the German-speaking minority after WWII. A strength of this edition is the broad base of physical sources. Sixty archives in the Czech Republic have been consulted, collecting 3,000 documents making material accessible that is out of reach for scholars with limited resources. Volume II.1 comes with more than 200 pages of historical framework and explanations of the events referred to in the documents. Comprehensive information on prior research on the topic can be found (besides the listing of secondary sources following the historical chapters) in volume I (p. 220-256). It is a goal of the edition to depict the social, cultural, and economic conditions in the borderlands between 1945 and 1951. One advantage is the explanation of all the major acting groups. In the respective parts of the texts the reader can find references to the documents regarding the specific group; in this way, the book can be used as an encyclopedia. For example, if we look to the fate of Austrian citizens, we find a distinction between them and the "Germans" that has been granted by the Czechoslovak government, and that was formally decided earlier in the Czech lands rather than in Slovakia, where contrary decisions had been made by the officials—facts that only recently have been taken into account by scholarly research (confer above).[11] Regarding the question of Austrian citizens, von Arburg already shows in his dissertation how difficult it has been to reach an agreement on this topic. With the decree of August 28, 1945 (determining that Austrians should not be deported), and the decree of October 2, 1945 (deciding that Austrians who didn't act against the Republic shouldn't be regarded as Germans anymore), the Prague

---

10. Cf. <http://www.brno.cz/turista-volny-cas/historie-mesta/historie-mesta-brna>.
11. For this topic cf. to Schriffl, *Tote Grenze*; also, see Jan Pešek, "Nemci na Slovensku po ukončení povojnového hromadného odsunu," in *Vynútený rozchod. Vyhnanie a vysídlenie z Československa 1938–1947 v porovnaní s Poľskom, Maďarskom a Juhosláviou*, ed. Detlef Brandes, Edita Ivaničková, Jiří Pešek (Bratislava: VEDA, 1999), 189-193.

foreign ministry did not to deport Austrian citizens, stating that Austrians should not be regarded as Germans anymore; he ends his investigation on this topic,[12] although the effects of these decrees varied largely due to geographical and structural differences. In volume II.1 of the edition in hand, the topic does not fill much space. The decision of July 24, 1945 by the foreign ministry is mentioned, which declared Austria a sovereign and free country; the decision from August 28th that guaranteed them free passage to Austria including parts of their belongings is also mentioned (cf. II.1, 166-168). In reality, their treatment did not change significantly; the majority had to leave the country the same way.

The editors concentrated their work on the Czech lands. This decision is understandable and arguable mostly due to the numbers of affected persons. The majority of the German-speaking minority in Slovakia (before the war approximately 140,000 people) had already been evacuated by the German authorities when the front approached. Nevertheless, it's worth mentioning that scholarly research needs to address the local specifics of Slovak policy-making, and the effects the different circumstances and the different historiographical approaches, had and still have today. Even though the measures in Slovakia have been similar—due to the fact that a smaller number of people were affected, the focus of public opinion and historical research on the Czech lands combined with different historical experiences lead to a different point of view, even by the expelled persons towards their former homeland. Conflict on the topic is less intense between Austria and Slovakia than between Austria or Germany and the Czech Republic. Conflicts that have been cultivated since the nineteenth century, and that have their roots in national battles over language and nation, and conflicts that have been ornamented with historical images like the Battle of White Mountain, or even older ambiguous events in the common history, played and still play a role in the perception of these events on both sides.[13] Because of this historiographical consideration, it is worthwhile to mention the Slovak situation.

The documents in volume II.1 are in chronological order and provide another specific feature of this edition: additional documents, often the full version of documents that have been shortened before being printed in the volume, are collected on a CD that comes with the book. The handling is easy, though it is necessary to install a small program on the computer to

---

12. Arburg, "Vertreibung," 131f.
13. Cf. Ota Konrád, "... alle unsere Rechnungen sind beglichen." Das Österreich-Bild in den ersten Jahren der Tschechoslowakischen Republik," in *Schlaglichter*, ed. Schriffl, Perzi, 207-216; Schriffl, *Tote Grenze*, 299-311.

view the documents. A complete coverage of the topic is achieved without overstraining the printed edition of documents. Of course, an important question becomes whether an edition should be printed, or solely be published online, and while it is not a question answered here, it's worth noting that the system used for this collection combines advantages of the analog and the digital world. Included are well-made Regesta, maps displaying the geographical allocation of the German-speaking minority and its changes in the period under observation, and a scientific apparatus that shows the amount of work that has been invested in the project making this edition, in content and form, an outstanding achievement. This project brings historical sources to the scholars and the students but also to an interested public that needs to develop a fresh, more critical and elaborated picture of the events of the expulsion of the Sudeten Germans in the years after WWII. Because this edition will have an impact not only in the Czech Republic, but also in Germany and Austria, the question becomes whether a bilingual publication of the documents[14] could have further increased the effect of the work towards a common elaborated and differentiated understanding of this dark series of events in the Czech Republic as in the German-speaking countries, particularly now that there's a willingness to develop such a common picture. But this is just a remark, not criticism due to the huge amount of work necessary for such an undertaking.

---

14. Such editions have been recently published on the topic of Slovak-German relations between 1938 and 1945—although with less emphasis on the accompanying historical description. Cf. Michal Schvarc, Martin Holák, David Schriffl ed., *Tretia ríša" a vznik Slovenského Štátu. Dokumenty I. – Das "Dritte Reich" und die Entstehung des Slowakischen Staates: Dokumente* I. (Bratislava: Ústav Pamäti Národa, 2008); Michal Schvarc, David Schriffl ed., *Tretia ríša" a vznik Slovenského Štátu. Dokumenty II. – Das "Dritte Reich" und die Entstehung des Slowakischen Staates: Dokumente* II. (Bratislava: Ústav Pamäti Národa, 2010); Eduard Nižnanský et al., ed., *Slovensko-nemecké vzťahy 1938 – 1941 v dokumentoch I: Od Mníchova k vojne proti ZSSR. Slowakisch-deutsche Beziehungen 1938 – 1941 in Dokumenten I: Von München bis zum Krieg gegen die UdSSR.* (Prešov: Universum 2009).

Benya und der Austrosozialismus: Erinnerungen und Gedanken, Edited by Heinzl Kienzl, Herbert Starke, (Vienna: Ögb Verlag, 2012)

Anton Pelinka

Anton Benya was one of the decisive figures of Austria's Social Democracy's golden years: When, from the 1950s to the 1980s, "social partnership" established itself as the all-important institution concerning economic, social, and financial policies; when, within this institution, organized labor (the Austrian Trade Union Association—ÖGB, and the Chambers of Labor) were under full control by social democratic labor leaders; and when, leading to the "Kreisky Period," the SPÖ was able to shift its overall image from a rather orthodox workers' party to a more flexible center-left catch-all-party: Benya was one of the key players in this time. It can be argued, that for this period of social democratic hegemony Benya was as important as Kreisky was.

Can this be called "Austro-Socialism," distinguishing it from "Austro-Marxism," the program of the Austrian Social Democrats in the years before 1934? Yes, as "Austro-Marxism" defined a strategy designed for a party in opposition—in opposition in parliament, between 1918 and 1933/34; for a party, which saw itself in antithetical, principal opposition to market economy as well as "bourgeois" democracy. "Austro-Socialism" stands for the process of reconciliation—between Austrian Social Democracy and a market economy, which became (due to the SPÖ's role in government and within "social partnership") a kind of "mixed economy"; but also for the reconciliation between the two major ideological camps, unable to stabilize a consensus prior to the civil war of 1934. The SPÖ had learned some lessons—as the ÖVP also had, making the successes of the Second Republic possible.

But is this pragmatic Austrian version of a democratic social- and welfare state "socialism"? It is up to the trends of semantic fashions, whether "socialism" is the right or even a possible term to characterize Austria in the second half of the 20th century. When soon after the collapse of soviet-style socialism the SPÖ became renamed—from "Socialist Party" to "Social Democratic Party," political semantics seem to count. But we must not forget that the party called itself "Social Democratic Workers' Party" until 1934, when it was in all possible respects more socialist than the "socialist" party of Kreisky and Benya. At the end, it is a name-game.

Bruno Kreisky represented the SPÖ's political victories as Anton Benya does the ÖGB's success story. But Benya was not only a man of organized labor, he also was one of the leading representatives of the party: In the 1970s and 1980s, he was (for the biggest party in parliament, the SPÖ) President (Speaker) of the National Council. The precondition of what the editors call "Austro-Socialism" was the synchronization between political party and labor unions; and between parliament and "social partnership."

The book includes six articles (among them analyses of Heinz Kienzl, Thomas Lachs, and Herbert Tumpel, representing the next leading generation of organized labor), reflecting Benya's personal political input; and ten interviews with some of Benya's most important colleagues and political friends (again: of course, from the next generation)—like Heinz Fischer, Hannes Androsch, and Ferdinand Lacina. At the end, the book offers a personal resume in the form of an interview Benya gave 1990, some years after the end of his political career, more than one decade before his death in 2001.

The book's focus is on Benya, the leader of organized labor; Benya, the ÖGB's president, who defined so many rules of the procedures called "social partnership"—an ongoing process of looking for compromises between business and labor. The major articles are following the argument that Benya's (and the SPÖ's) major interest was not creating a new economic and social order but improving the existing order by peaceful social engineering. "Austro-Socialism," Benya- (and Kreisky-) style, was not the agenda for revolution but for evolution.

It would have been of special interest to include some voices from "the other side"; from persons who have observed how business interests (especially organized in the Chambers of Commerce) perceive Benya's (and the ÖGB's) policies and politics. As "Austro-Socialism" was compromise-oriented, the view from the other side of the "green table" would have been most welcome. Concerning the stable, friendly, and professional relationship Benya was able to build, e.g. with Rudolf Sallinger, for a long time Benya's vis-à-vis as president of the Federal Chamber of Commerce, the interpretations coming from the ÖVP and its Wirtschaftsbund (Business Association) would have enriched the book.

Benya and "Austro-Socialism" stand for the re-definition of class warfare; for transferring class-based conflicts from the street to parliament and to the "green table," from open clashes to negotiations between employers and employees, between business and labor. What ever "Austro-Socialism" is: It is the success of social democracy and of organized labor; but it is not the defeat of "the others."

Margit Reiter and Helga Embacher, eds., *Europa und der 11, September 2011* (Vienna: Böhlau Verlag 2011)

Günter Bischof

The September 11, 2001, terrorist attacks on the World Trade Center in New York and the Pentagon in Washington were a fateful day on many counts—for those who perished and tried to save lives and for those who watched helplessly around the world. 9/11 unleashed a sea of change in American foreign policy. After the end of the Cold War in 1989/1991 the U.S. enjoyed a brief honeymoon—with intellectuals phantasizing about "the end of history" and asserting unique lonely superpower status. Intimations of "peace dividends" and a neo-isolationist retreat into fortress America were quickly rendered obsolete by the 9/11 attacks. After "the loss" of a long-time adversary during the American Cold War mission of the global containment of communism, 9/11 produced an instant new enemy with the "global war on terror." After the 9/11 attacks, the U.S. enjoyed a brief moment of a worldwide outpouring of sympathy and solidarity. Yet with President George W. Bush unleashing his punitive campaign against Afghanistan and his preemptive war in Iraq, the U.S. quickly faced a new upsurge of anti-Americanism. Many Americans, basking in the prosperity of the globalizing 1990s, asked after 9/11 "why do they hate us?"

The essays in this book assess the immediate reaction to the 9/11 attacks in a select group of countries in Western and East Central Europe as well as the often hostile consequences of "Bush's wars" in the bilateral relations of these countries with the United States. The two introductory essays by Hanna K. Ulatowska and Eugen Freund are anemic and self-absorbed and contribute little to the larger themes of the book. The former compares 9/11 with her experiences as a child in the ruins of Warsaw after the Nazi German attacks on Poland in September 1939 and dwells on "feelings of vulnerability in war and terrorism" (p. 26). The latter nostalgically recalls his visits with Austrian dignitaries to the World Trade Center towers as Austrian press attaché in New York as personal background to serving as an anchor in the coverage of the 9/11 attacks on Austrian state television.

Margit Reiter, one of the editors, provides much of the meat in this volume with her essays on both Germany's and Austria's reactions to 9/11.

Both countries' politicians quickly jumped on the bandwagon of declaring "absolute solidarity" ("*uneingeschränkte Solidarität*") with the United States. A German politician professed that "today we are all Americans" (p. 44). Much hyperbole was spilled in newspapers on the 9/11 events such as when Josef Joffe in *Die Zeit* compared 9/11 with the Holocaust when he spoke of a "civilizational breach" ("*Zivilisationsbruch*"). The Muslim community in Germany condemned the attacks and insisted the Muslims should not be equated with the Al Qaeda terrorists. However, the initial shock soon turned into "America bashing" and blaming the Americans themselves for the attacks. The "arrogance" of American capitalism as well as U.S. favoritism towards Israel in its Near Eastern policies became favorite tropes of German commentators for blaming the U.S. (pp. 54f). President Bush with his aggressive politics and missionary rhetoric—he had never been a favorite among most Europeans—was disparaged condescendingly as a "cowboy" and "Rambo" (p. 60). *Der Spiegel* dedicated a racy cover to "The Bush Warriors" and "America's Campaign against Evil" (p. 61).

With the frequent references to World War II, German commentators were different from all the other countries covered in this volume. While the Germans were never tired of thanking the Americans for their liberation from the Hitler regime, some also compared the destructive 9/11 attacks with American bombing of Dresden (p. 66)—off-setting contemporary American victimization with past German suffering. The pacifist Germans were gravely concerned to be pulled as "deputy sheriffs" into Bush's retaliatory "war on terror." The German government supported Bush's war against Afghanistan but not the war against Iraq. Both wars were highly unpopular with the German public. A German playwright phantasized about the Germans being "on their way back to the business of being war criminals" (p. 71). When Chancellor Gerhard Schröder (with the French) led the European front opposing Bush's preemptive war against Iraq, German-American relations slipped to their lowest point in the postwar period.

Austria's politicians and the public were as shocked as the Germans and professed their deep sympathy to the victims and the American public. Austrian state television ORF reported life from New York and Washington for forty-three hours straight—longer than German TV. The initial reaction among Austrians quickly morphed into a discourse about their neutrality. In a highly partisan debate many Austrians felt "lucky" to be neutral (p. 171), as their benign neutral status allowed the country to stay out of the looming conflict. While the government supported American retaliation against Afghanistan, the Austrian public at large did not. Austrians were even more critical about Bush's war against Iraq and public opinion slipped into dumb anti-Americanism and *Schadenfreude*. While anti-Americanism on the left fell back on its old patterns of blaming "U.S. imperialism," the right, which had never forgiven the Americans for defeating Hitler, blamed American "hubris, money and power" (p. 188) for having caused the 9/11 attacks. In a comparison with the German reaction, Reiter points out the Austrian lack of references to World War II as well as their lack of gratitude to the United States for liberation in 1945 and Marshall Plan aid.

Christian Muckenhumer's fine essay on French reactions shows many parallels in French and German reactions. French reactions were also characterized by a massive outpouring of empathy and solidarity with Americans after the attacks. *Le Monde's* famous September 13 pronouncement "*nous sommes tous Américains*" defined the French response. Yet among the 6 million Muslims in France—the largest Muslim community in Europe—responses were more controversial than among German Muslims. While Muslim organizations in France condemned the 9/11 attacks, they also harbored many conspiracy theories, blaming American and Israeli secret services for the attacks. There was plenty of *Schadenfreude* among marginalized French Muslims, "V" for "Victory" signs, and "*Allah Akbar*" ("God is Great") voices (p. 114). The French press soon began to dig deeper into the causes of the attack and often came up with the usual list of American transgressions of the past, blaming American capitalism, US-driven globalization, Washington's Near Eastern policies and its great power politics (American "*hyperpuissance*"). Given French intellectuals' uniquely elevated position in French society, Muckenhumer is particularly good in tracing their discourses. For the French media theorist Jean Baudrillard, America's "insufferable superiority" has spawned the "phantasies of the terrorists"—who saw the twin towers as "the multiplication of power" and therefore a target that invited its own destruction. Yet the even more famous "new philosophers" (Bernard-Henri Lévy and André Glucksmann) came to America's defense. Having supported America's policies towards Israel and American neoliberal capitalism and globalization—which earned them the sobriquet "new reactionaries"—they now grouped fundamentalist Islamism with Nazism and Communism and called it the "new evil" that needed to be fought (p. 114). France showed its solidarity with the NATO attack on Afghanistan to root out Al Qaeda's terrorist nests. The Chirac government, however, joined the Germans in condemning Bush's "preventive blow" against Iraq, carried out without a UN mandate (p. 129). This poisoned US-French relations for years to come and unleashed an enormous reservoir of resentment against the spineless "frogs" in the U.S.

The contributions by Helga Embacher on Great Britain and Filip Fetko on East-Central European reactions—in Donald Rumsfeld's terms the "new Europe" of Poland, Czech Republic, Slovakia and Hungary—suggest similarly pro-American governmental reactions in those countries. The British reaction was characterized by a considerable discrepancy between the obsequious reaction of Tony Blair's government and a much more complex popular response. Blair invoked "the special relationship" between the U.S. and Great Britain and acted as Bush's quasi-ambassador to Arab states and continental Europe. Blair had visions of greatness "standing shoulder to shoulder" with the Americans like Churchill had done during World War II (p. 81). Blair, argues Embacher, utilized the 9/11 crisis to reclaim British great power status and act as a "big player" (p. 81). The press on the left saw Blair as "Bush's lapdog". Commentators on the right wanted Blair "to lead the world to victory" in the war against terror (p. 83). Similar to continental European explanations, the more brainy British press made the American behavior and foreign policy responsible for the 9/11 catastrophe. Muslim organizations, too, argued that the Bin Laden supporters were terrorists "pure and simple" and had nothing to do with "the real Islam." The British worried, however, about more radical Muslim Imans who blamed "the CIA, freemasons, and Zionists" for the attacks and feared "a fifth column" illegal Arab-Muslim asylum seekers in their own midst. Blair's overeager support of both Bush's Afghanistan and Iraq interventions spawned massive antiwar protests on the British Isles and probably also were a cause for the Muslim terrorist attacks on the London subways on July 7, 2006 (the "7/7" attacks in British parlance) (pp. 102 ff).

Fetko ably summarizes the reactions of the "new Europe." Polish sympathy for the victims of 9/11 was enormous and their support of all of Bush's actions total. After their Cold War experiences these East-Central European countries were very pro-American, the Poles however most so. The United States was seen as an ally and protector against feared future Russian hegemonic drives in the region, and the Poles wanted to advance to become America's principal partner in the area. The Poles even hoped that the Americans would move their military bases from the "ungrateful Germany" to their country (p. 139). In the public debate anti-Americanism cropped up in Poland and East-Central Europe, too, but was usually muffled and in Poland coupled with anti-semitism. One Polish commentator even blamed "the Jewish lobby in the U.S." and their influence on American Near Eastern policies for the 9/11 catastrophe (p. 147). Blaming Hollywood and its love affair with violence and commercialism was a more popular form of anti-Americanism in the region. In the support of Bush's war policies, Poland became "the poster boy of solidarity with the U.S." (p. 154). The other nations in the region joined the "coalition of the willing" as well. When Chirac chided these nations for their support of the Iraq war,

Rumsfeld shot back the unfortunate metaphor of "the new Europe" that was on the side of the U.S., disparaging the Germans and French (and Austrians who did not open up their air space to American war planes crossing the Alps) as "old Europe." The East-Central European nations saw their support of Bush's war as part of the their Westernization strategy; they saw no contradiction in their pro-American policies with their next step of moving towards European economic integration and joining of the European Union (p. 158), which they proceeded to do on May 1, 2004.

Reinhard Heinisch's essay on Bush's foreign policy and its impact on American–European relations in the wake of 9/11 serves as a useful complement to the European perspectives. In a *tour de force* Heinisch marches the reader through the fateful months from the 9/11 attacks to the invasion of Iraq and the enormous "transatlantic discord" that the French and the German reactions to the Iraq invasion produced in Washington. Heinisch lived in the United States during the 9/11 catastrophe and its aftermath and is therefore sure-footed in characterizing the neo-conservative realist/geopolitical mindset that dominated Washington during the Bush presidency. Paul Wolfowitz's doctrine of preemptive blows against "rogue states" such as Saddam Hussein's Iraq was adopted by the Bush White House, as was Secretary of Defense Rumsfeld's notions of containing the "axis of appeasement" in the State Department (p. 198). Robert Kagan's essay of *Paradise and Power*, bemoaning European weakness and unwillingness to confront threats militarily, defined the condescending view of the neocons in Washington towards continental Europe. Given such arrogance vis-à-vis Europe, the Bush White House should not have been so miffed when their best allies – the Germans and French – did not follow them in their "preventive war" against Saddam, particularly without a UN mandate. When the occupation and "nation building" in Iraq went sour and turned very violent and dysfunctional, a chastened Bush recognized his mistakes in his second term and began to rebuild the damaged transatlantic bridges.

An essay by Wolfgang Aschauer about the terrorist threat and Islamophobia in Europe and Monika Bernold on 9/11 as an international media event conclude the volume. Aschauer provides a useful summary of the complexity of European discourses about Islam and a growing number of Muslim minority communities living in their midst (and estimated 12 to 20 million Muslims live in Europe [p. 234]). Some critics perceive of fundamentalist Islam spreading in Europe as potentially the biggest challenge the continent may face in the future. In Aschauer's summary of recent public opinion and value surveys about European responses to Muslims, Germany and Spain are in the lead of European nations with negative opinions about Islam, while Latvia and Austria are leading in xenophobia, rejecting multiculturalism and integration of minorities in their societies (p. 241). There seems to be a vast undercurrent of mistrust vis-à-vis Islam in Europe that does not bode well for integrating Muslims in European societies. Bernold follows the phases of "knowledge production" of the 9/11 events from the original dense coverage on television, as well as first analyses about the media coverage (2001-2003), to the cultural productions in films and popular culture of the war on terror and media representations of islamophobia and gender specific visual discourses (2003-2008), all the way to 9/11 as a "cultural chiffre" (2008-2010). Bernold covers the "cultural preconditions" of terror as well as "the effects of terror as provocations of cultural order" (p. 266). You get the idea—the discourses of cultural and media studies mystifying and diluting a sea change in history into realms of "knowledge production."

It is rare for Austrian scholars to leave their narcissistic, navel-gazing, small country perspective and produce an ambitious work with a comparative European scope. This collection of essays boldly does so and, on top of it, is unusually tightly organized and coherent. The responses to 9/11 in individual European countries show both communalities and differences. After an initial upsurge of solidarity, in most of these countries traditional patterns of anti-Americanism define their discourses, particularly after Bush unleashes his preemptive wars. The British response differs markedly from the German and French one. The German public is deeply stuck in its postwar antiwar stance and popular pacifism while the government refuses to act as a European power; the Blair government acts as the foremost warmonger in Europe and tries to resume its former great power status. The editors are to be commended for an unusually telling selection of cartoons and images that illustrate the particular country responses. More country studies (anti-war Russia, pro-war Spain, anti-war Belgium vs. the pro-war Netherlands, neutral vs. NATO Scandinavians), instead of idiosyncratic personal and fashionable cultural studies approaches, would have made the volume even richer. What the editors fail to deliver in their introduction is a thorough contextualization of the deteriorating transatlantic relationship after the end of the Cold War. They do not fathom American emotional reactions to 9/11 and Washington's strategic response to the global threat of terrorism. The old Cold War transatlantic consensus had collapsed long before 9/11. Europeans never quite contemplated how irrelevant they had become to American strategists after their failure to resolve the Yugoslav Wars on their own (eg. see Edwina S. Campbell, "From Kosovo to the War on Terror: The Collapsing Transatlantic Consensus, 1999-2002," *Strategic Studies Quarterly* (Fall 2007): 36-78).

Annual Review

Austria 2012-2013

Elections in Carinthia, Lower Austria, Tyrol and Salzburg

Referendum: Compulsory Military Service vs. Professional Army

Government Reshuffle

Again: FPÖ and Antisemitism

Ernst Strasser and Uwe Scheuch

Waltz and Haneke

Economic and Statistical Data

Reinhold Gärtner

Elections in Carinthia, Lower Austria, Tyrol, and Salzburg

After years without elections (the election for the EU-Parliament was in 2009, the country elections in Vienna and Burgenland were held in 2010), the year 2013 started with elections in Carinthia and Lower Austria on March 3rd.

In Carinthia, BZÖ (Bündnis Zukunft Österreich) had a considerable majority of 44.9%. In 2009, the party was led by Governor Gerhard Dörfler and his deputy Uwe Scheuch, and in December 2009 the prominent BZÖ-members changed to FPK (Freiheitliche Partei Kärntens), the regional branch of FPÖ (Freiheitliche Partei Österreichs). Early in 2010, though, Uwe Scheuch was suspected of having granted a Russian citizen the Austrian citizenship as a reward for a generous party donation ("Part of the Game Affair"). This led to Scheuch's retreat in August 2013 and his successor was his brother Kurt Scheuch.

In general, Carinthia had been shaken by various scandals during the last years—the biggest scandal was the mismanagement of Hypo Alpe

Adria; the bank had to be nationalized in 2009 – and this was the main reason that the FPK-result in 2013 was disastrous: From the 44.9% in 2009, only 16.8% were left, this was a loss of 28% (!!). SPÖ (Sozialdemokratische Partei Österreichs) got 37.1% (+ 8.4%) and Grüne got 12.1% (+ 6.9%). ÖVP (Österreichische Volkspartei)—traditionally weak in Carinthia— faced a moderate loss with 14.4% (- 2.4%) and the new Team Stronach —party of the 80 year old billionaire Frank Stronach—got 11.2%.

The new Governor of Carinthia is Peter Kaiser (SPÖ), SPÖ built a government with Grüne and ÖVP.

In Lower Austria ÖVP had to defend an absolute majority. In 2008, ÖVP got 54.4%, almost 30% ahead of runner up SPÖ (25.5%). The strategy of almost all other parties, thus, was to break ÖVP's absolute majority— but they failed. Though ÖVP lost some 3.6%, it kept the absolute majority of seats in the country parliament (30 of 56 seats). SPÖ lost again and got 21.6% (- 3.9%) and so did FPÖ with 8.2% (- 2.3%). Grüne got 8.1% (+1.2%) and Team Stronach 9.8%. The old and new Governor is Erwin Pröll; he's been Governor since 1992 already.

The elections in Tyrol were held on April 28th. For the first time, eleven parties were up for the election and thus it was doubtful if ÖVP could keep its 40%. ÖVP had suffered a serious loss in the 2008 elections (40.5%; -9.4% in comparison to 2003) but could barely this percentage with 39.6% in 2013. In 2008. Liste Fritz, an ÖVP separation, had gained 18.4% in 2008 but in 2013 it was minimized to 5.6% (- 12.7%). SPÖ lost, too, and got only 13.8% (- 1.6%; they had lost more than 10% in 2008 already) and another loser was FPÖ with 9.6% (- 2.8%). Vorwärts Tirol—a new center party with former ÖVP and SPÖ representatives—got 9.3%. Team Stronach faced an incredible internal chaos in the run up to the elections (with various competing lists and candidates) and got only 3.4%.

In Salzburg the election was dominated by a financial scandal. SPÖ and ÖVP were made responsible for the mismanagement and SPÖ faced a devastating loss: it got 23.8% only while ÖVP had to accept a smaller loss and got 29%. The outstanding winner in Salzburg was Grüne who almost tripled their result of 2008 with 20.2%. Governor Burgstaller (SPÖ) resigned and the new Governor will be Wilfried Haslauer (ÖVP).

	Salzburg		Carinthia		Lower Austria		Tyrol	
	%	seats	%	seats	%	seats	%	seats
ÖVP	29 (-7,5)	11 (-3)	14.4 (-2.4)	6	50.8 (-3.6)	30	39.4 (-1.1)	16
SPÖ	23.8 (-15,6)	9 (-6)	37.1 (+8.4)	16	21.6 (-3.9)	13	13.7 (-1.7)	5
FPÖ (FPK)	17 (+4)	6 (+1)	16.8 (-28)	7	8.2 (-2.2)	4	9.3 (-3.1)	4
Grüne	20.2 (+12,8)	7 (+5)	12.1 (+6.9)	5	8.1 (+1.2)	4	12.6 (+1.9)	5
Team Stronach	8.3	3	11.2	4	9.8	5	3.4	0
Liste Fritz							5.6 (-12.7)	2
Vorwärts Tirol							9.5	
BZÖ			6.4	2				

Referendum Compulsory Military Service vs. Professional Army

On January 20th, the first nationwide referendum (Volksbefragung) was held in Austria. In Austria we have three types of referenda, Volksbegehren is a bottom-up initiative to force the parliament to discuss certain topics (not compulsory); Volksabstimmung is a plebiscite (compulsory) on concrete laws and Volksbefragung is a nationwide referendum (not compulsory) on a special topic. Volksbefragungen are quite often made on regional or local levels but in January it was the first on a national level. The question was if a majority of Austrian voters would favor compulsory military service (since 1955) or a professional army. In most of the EU-member states there is a professional army, in Austria it is not. Young men have to serve in the army for six months or perform an alternative service (e.g. working for the Red Cross for 12 months).

SPÖ—in previous years in favor of compulsory military service—had changed its opinion in favor of a professional army in 2010 and ÖVP the other way round: in previous times it was for a professional army, now for compulsory military service. The referendum was held on January 20th and some 60% of the voters were for a continuing compulsory military service, 40% for a professional army. The turnout was 52.4%.

Government Reshuffle

On September 11th, 2012, Reinhold Lopatka replaced Wolfgang Waldner as Secretary of State in the Federal Ministry for European and International Affairs; on March 11th, 2013, Gerald Klug succeeded Norbert Darabos in the Federal Ministry of Defense and Sports.

Again: FPÖ and Antisemitism

In August 2012, Heinz Christian Strache, chairman of FPÖ, had this anti-Semitic cartoon on his facebook account. It shows the typical nose attributed especially by Nazis to Jews and the cufflinks are stars of David.

In the original version of this cartoon these discriminatory characteristics are not seen. Strache said that this wouldn't have anything to do with anti-Semitism and so did the prosecution office in Vienna. It argued, surprisingly, that it would be a legitimate critique on the Austrian government (!); it would not be an act of hatred against the Jewish community as a whole.

Ernst Strasser and Uwe Scheuch

Ernst Strasser was elected EU-MP (ÖVP) in 2009. In 2010 two Sunday Times journalists posed as lobbyists and tried to persuade sixty EU-MPs to support a bill in reward for €100,000. A few of them (among them Ernst Strasser) accepted the illegal offer. Together with two colleagues, Strasser, thus, had to resign as EU-MP in March 2011. Strasser was charged because of bribery by the Austrian prosecution office against corruption and on January 14th, 2013, Strasser was at first instance sentenced to four years in jail.[1]

Uwe Scheuch (FPK) was sentenced because of bribery to six months on probation and to a fine of €67,500 in December 2012 (at last resort and thus legally binding). As mentioned above, he had granted a Russian citizen the Austrian citizenship as a reward for a generous party donation.

Waltz and Haneke

And the Oscar went to Michael Haneke and—again—to Christoph Waltz in January 2013. Christoph Waltz got the award as best supporting actor in Quentin Tarantino's *Django Unchained*. It was Waltz's second academy award; the first one he was awarded in 2010 for the best supporting actor in Tarantino's *Inglorious Basterds*.

Michael Haneke, too, was awarded with an Oscar (and the Golden Globe) for the best foreign language film *Amour* (starring Jean Louis Trintignant and Emmanuelle Riva).

Economic and Statistical Data

Inflation was at 2.4% in 2012 (compared to 3.3% in 2011), HVPI was at 2.6% (compared to 3.6 % in 2011). The public deficit amounted 2.5% in 2012 (2.5% in 2011) and public debts amounted to 73.4% in 2012 (72.5% in 2011).

In 2012, GNP was at €36,640 per capita (compared to €35,750 in

---

1. Cf. Annual Review CAS XXI

2011); economic growth was 0.8% in 2012 (compared to 2.7 in 2011).

In 2012, imports amounted €132,000 million (€92,900 million from the EU-27) and exports amounted €123,500 million (€84,100 million to the E.U.). Imports from NAFTA were €4,743 million; exports to NAFTA €8,320 million.

In 2012 4,183,000 people in Austria were employed; the rate of unemployment was at 4.3% in 2012 (on average 4.2% in 2011).

At the beginning of 2011, 8,420,900 people were living in Austria, among them 946,587 foreigners (and among them 399,254 from EU/EWR/CH). In 2011 78,109 children were born alive in Austria and 76,479 people died. Life expectancy is at 78.3 years (men) and 83.9 (women).

List of Authors

Günter Bischof is the Marshall Plan Professor of History and the director of CenterAustria at the University of New Orleans.

Emil Brix is the Austrian ambassador in the United Kingdom and deputy chairman of the Institute for the Danube Region and Central Europe in Vienna.

Ferdinand Karlhofer is an associate professor and chair in the Department of Political Science at the University of Innsbruck.

Reinhold Gärtner is a professor at the Department of Political Science at the University of Innsbruck.

Harold James is the Professor of History and International Affairs, and Claude and Lore Kelly Professor of European Studies at Princeton University.

Norman M. Naimark is the Robert and Florence McDonnell Professor of East European Studies and the Fisher Family Director of the Division of International, Comparative and Area Studies at Stanford. He is also Senior Fellow of the Hoover Institution and the Freeman-Spogli Institute of International Studies.

Hanspeter Neuhold is a Professor Emeritus of International Law and International Relations at the University of Vienna.

Berndt Ostendorf is Professor Emeritus of North American Cultural History at Ludwig-Maximilians-Universität Munich.

Anton Pelinka is a Professor of Political Science and Nationalism Studies at the Central European University in Budapest.

Ursula Plassnik is currently the Austrian Ambassador to France, Monaco and UNESCO in Paris and was the Austrian Minister of Foreign Affairs from 2004 to 2008.

Andreas Resch teaches economic and social history at Vienna University of Economics and Business.

Erwin A. Schmidl is the director of the Austrian National Defense Academy's Contemporary History Unit and teaches at the Universities of Innsbruck and Vienna.

David Schriffl is a research assistant at the Institute for Modern and Contemporary History/Department of International History at the Austrian Academy of Sciences in Vienna.

James J. Sheehan is Dickason Professor in the Humanities and Professor of History Emeritus at Stanford University.

Arnold Suppan is the professor of East European History at the University of Vienna and Vice President of the Austrian Academy of Sciences.

Gerhard L. Weinberg is the William Rand Kenan, Jr., Professor of History Emeritus of the University of North Carolina at Chapel Hill.

Contemporary Austrian Studies
Günter Bischof and Fritz Plasser, Editors

Volume 1 (1992)
Austria in the New Europe

Volume 2 (1993)
The Kreisky Era in Austria
Oliver Rathkolb, Guest Editor

Volume 3 (1994)
Austria in the Nineteen Fifties
Rolf Steininger, Guest Editor

Volume 4 (1995)
Austro-Corporatism: Past—Present—Future

Volume 5 (1996)
Austrian Historical Memory & National Identity

Volume 6 (1997)
Women in Austria
Erika Thurner, Guest Editor

Volume 7 (1998)
The Vranitzky Era in Austria
Ferdinand Karlhofer, Guest Editor

Volume 8 (1999)
The Marshall Plan in Austria
Dieter Stiefel, Guest Editor

Volume 9 (2000)
Neutrality in Austria
Ruth Wodak, Guest Editor

Volume 10 (2001)
Austria and the EU
Michael Gehler, Guest Editor

Volume 11 (2002)
The Dollfuss/Schuschnigg Era in Austria: A Reassessment
Alexander Lassner, Guest Editor

Volume 12 (2003)
The Americanization/Westernization of Austria

Volume 13 (2004)
Religion in Austria
Hermann Denz, Guest Editor

Volume 14 (2005)
Austrian Foreign Policy in Historical Perspective
Michael Gehler, Guest Editor

Volume 15 (2006)
Sexuality in Austria
Dagmar Herzog, Guest Editor

Volume 16 (2007)
The Changing Austrian Voter

Volume 17 (2008)
New Perspectives on Austrians and World War II
Barbara Stelzl-Marx, Guest Editor

Volume 18 (2009)
The Schüssel Era in Austria

Volume 19 (2010)
From Empire to Republic: Post-World War I Austria

Volume 20 (2011)
Global Austria: Austria's Place in Europe and the World
Alexander Smith, Guest Editor

Volume 21 (2012)
Austrian Lives
Eva Maltschnig, Guest Editor